From sovereign impunity to international accountability

From sovereign impunity to international accountability: The search for justice in a world of states

Edited by Ramesh Thakur and Peter Malcontent

United Nations University Press

TOKYO · NEW YORK · PARIS

© United Nations University, 2004
The views expressed in this publication are those of the authors and do not necessarily reflect the views of the United Nations University.

United Nations University Press
United Nations University, 53-70, Jingumae 5-chome,
Shibuya-ku, Tokyo, 150-8925, Japan
Tel: +81-3-3499-2811   Fax: +81-3-3406-7345
E-mail: sales@hq.unu.edu
General enquiries: press@hq.unu.edu
http://www.unu.edu

United Nations University Office at the United Nations, New York
2 United Nations Plaza, Room DC2-2062, New York, NY 10017, USA
Tel: +1-212-963-6387   Fax: +1-212-371-9454
E-mail: unuona@ony.unu.edu

United Nations University Press is the publishing division of the United Nations University.

Cover design by Joyce C. Weston
Printed in the United States of America

UNUP-1100
ISBN 92-808-1100-2

Library of Congress Cataloging-in-Publication Data

From sovereign impunity to international accountability : the search for justice in a world of states / edited by Ramesh Thakur and Peter Malcontent.
     p.   cm.
Includes bibliographical references and index.
ISBN 9280811002 (pbk.)
1. Crimes against humanity. 2. Criminal liability (International law)
3. Sovereignty, Violation of. 4. International criminal courts. I. Thakur, Ramesh Chandra, 1948– II. Malcontent, Peter.
K5301.F76   2004
345′.0235–dc22   2004007427

Contents

Foreword

The role of law and justice in governance: Regional and global

Richard J. Goldstone

The role of global governance and the sovereignty of nations have been thrown into sharp relief by the events of 11 September 2001. In particular, the role of the rule of law and justice in regional and global governance is being reassessed. In the first half of the twentieth century, national sovereignty reigned supreme. Indeed, it was on the premise of such sovereignty that the League of Nations was established. A number of major consequences arose from that. In the global community, obligations were owed by one nation to another nation or other nations, depending upon the formal treaty obligations they had mutually contracted. The manner in which governments treated their own people was their "internal affair" and was not the business or legitimate concern of other governments or of international organizations. Individuals had no standing in international law – such rights inhered solely in governments. And, apart from piracy, criminal justice was strictly a territorial matter: domestic authorities could prosecute only crimes that were committed within the geographical jurisdiction of their courts.

Since the end of World War II, sovereignty has been in a state of flux. A crucial decision in this context was to grant Nazi leaders a criminal trial rather than have them summarily executed. A new species of criminal offence – crimes against humanity – gave birth to universal jurisdiction. It was a new idea that some crimes were so horrendous that they were crimes not only against the immediate victims or solely the people who lived in the country in which they were committed; they were truly crimes against all of humankind. As such, they could properly be prosecuted before the courts of any country. Jurisdiction in respect of such crimes depended not upon the place where they were committed but rather on the nature of the crime itself. One sees here an important breach of the strict theory of sovereignty. A country could prosecute the citizens of any country for crimes committed in any part of the world.

Another important consequence of the Holocaust was that individual persons became endowed with international human rights. This change is reflected in the Charter of the United Nations and even more explicitly in the Universal Declaration of Human Rights. Those and other rights were spelled out in some detail in the international human rights conventions that were the hallmark of the United Nations during the 1960s.

The first international recognition of universal jurisdiction is to be found in the 1949 Geneva Conventions. A new species of war crimes, called "grave breaches", was established. The courts of all countries ratifying the Conventions are endowed with jurisdiction to prosecute any person suspected of committing a grave breach of the Geneva Conventions. If a country in which such a suspect is found is unwilling or unable to launch such a prosecution, a positive obligation is created under which such a person is to be handed over to another country that is so willing and able.

A similar use of universal jurisdiction is to be found in the 1972 international convention that declared apartheid to be a crime against humanity. Another example is the 1984 Torture Convention. Indeed, it was the universal jurisdiction conferred by the Torture Convention that led the House of Lords in England to confirm the arrest warrant of General Pinochet in 1998. The highest court in England recognized that the Spanish courts were entitled to exercise universal jurisdiction over Pinochet in respect of torture committed in Chile, allegedly on his orders. The Pinochet affair has had important consequences. Present and former oppressive dictators are not as free to travel abroad as they were in years gone by. The former dictator of Ethiopia fled South Africa where he was seeking medical treatment because he feared a warrant for his arrest and extradition to his homeland. A similar fate awaited General Al Duri of Iraq when his arrest was sought in Vienna by a member of that city's municipal council. The prime minister of Israel, Ariel Sharon, will not likely visit Belgium or other European cities after his immunity as prime minister has come to an end. There have been other examples of this signal change in the relationship between countries and their citizens who commit crimes in respect of which there is universal jurisdiction.

Then there is the significant number of truth and reconciliation commissions that have been a feature of some three decades of transitional justice. Such commissions are a means of recording the truth about past serious human rights violations and thereby offer acknowledgement to the victims and facilitate reconciliation between previously warring factions. The use of this instrument in South Africa has been widely admired for the manner in which the evilness of apartheid was laid bare – with the testimony of over 20,000 victims and some 7,000 perpetrators.

Notwithstanding these important developments, these heinous crimes continued to be committed in ever increasing numbers. The number of civilian casualties in international and civil wars continued to mount. It must be recognized that the refinements of international law and especially humanitarian law were not achieving their primary purpose – the protection of innocent civilians in war. At the regional level, there has been a growing readiness to intervene, even militarily, in order to protect democracy and the victims of human rights violations. In southern Africa, the regional organization SADC (the Southern African Development Community) decided to send troops from South Africa and Botswana into Lesotho in 1999 when some military officers arrested the democratically elected civil government in a *coup d'état*. Although they acted at the explicit request of the prime minister of Lesotho, this was none the less a unique occurrence in the region.

Even more dramatic than the Lesotho precedent was the NATO intervention to prevent the continued ethnic cleansing of the Kosovo Albanians by the Serb army and paramilitary forces in 1998. The members of NATO bombed Serbia for 78 days without the consent of the United Nations Security Council and in clear violation of the sovereignty of a member of the international community.

At the global level there has been a significant advance in developing mechanisms for the implementation of international humanitarian law. After World War II there was an expectation at the United Nations that an international criminal court would be established. Indeed, there is a reference to such a court in Article 6 of the Genocide Convention of 1948. However, that expectation was not realized for almost half a century. It was only in light of ethnic cleansing in the former Yugoslavia that the Security Council, to the surprise of most international lawyers, established the ad hoc United Nations International Criminal Tribunal for the former Yugoslavia. That was followed the next year by a similar tribunal for Rwanda.

Following upon significant successes of the United Nations tribunals, the movement for a permanent international criminal court gathered force. In the middle of 1998 a successful diplomatic conference was held in Rome and 120 nations agreed to the terms of a treaty to establish such a court. Since then, 139 nations have signed the treaty. Having received its sixtieth ratification in April 2002, the International Criminal Court (ICC) entered into force in July of that year. At the end of 2003, more than 90 nations had ratified the Rome Treaty. However, it remains disappointing, of course, that the United States has set its face against the ICC, which, in consequence, will be considerably weaker.

I would suggest that it is only because of the functioning of the United Nations tribunals, and the publicity given to the Rome Treaty, that there was a remarkable adherence to the norms and principles of the Geneva Conventions in the 1998 NATO military operations over 78 days in Serbia. There was explicit recognition of the necessity to protect civilian lives and, save for a few well-publicized exceptions, there was substantial compliance with the requirements of the Geneva Conventions. Whether the same can be said of the campaign against the Taliban and al-Qaida forces in Afghanistan is not possible to determine at this stage when little information has been made public by the United States and British governments.

It follows from the foregoing that in recent years there have been substantial advances in the internationalization of criminal law in the area of war crimes. The likely effect of the events of 11 September 2001 in this regard remains to be considered. The first is the international coalition that was set up under the leadership of the United States. I had hoped that it would have been in the interests of that coalition for the ICC to have been recognized as a useful tool in the fight against international terrorism. But that hope has thus far not been realized.

The events of 11 September have also had a significant prejudicial effect on the protection of civil liberties all over the world and no less in democratic nations. In answer to the Security Council call for member states to tighten their relevant laws, human rights protection has not been on the agenda. However, this issue is high on the agenda of the Task Force on International Terrorism, which was established in December 2001 by the International Bar Association, which represents lawyers in 182 countries.

The twentieth century saw the role of law and justice in governance extend beyond the realm of individual nations. Its significance, both regionally and globally, is illustrated by the developments made in international law, especially with regard to the recognition of international human rights, universal jurisdiction and additional international crimes. However, the significant advances with regard to the international recognition of humanitarian law and the ending of impunity for war criminals stand in real danger of being reversed. If the leading democracies turn their back on an international rule of law and if the world's most powerful democracy does not respect its international treaty obligations, there is little hope for support in that direction from the global community.

Preface

Justice and accountability: Local or international?

Martti Ahtisaari

The attempt to develop an effective and just system of international accountability for human rights violations is a striking feature of recent multilateral diplomacy. This development commenced with the establishment of the International Criminal Tribunals for the former Yugoslavia and Rwanda in 1993 and 1994 and peaked with the adoption of the Rome Statute of the International Criminal Court on 17 July 1998. More recently, the UN Security Council has decided to set up a war crimes tribunal in Sierra Leone and an agreement in principle has been concluded between the United Nations and the Cambodian authorities to establish a mixed process to try those accused of genocide in the "killing fields" of the 1970s.

At the same time, efforts to end the impunity enjoyed by heads of state and other high officials have been under way in many national societies and through the use of foreign courts. In 1998 the British House of Lords divested Augusto Pinochet of his immunity relating to his alleged complicity in the torture of thousands of political prisoners in Chile. In February 2000 a case was brought in a Senegalese court against Chad's former dictator Hissene Habre over human rights violations committed during his reign. Two months later, an international arrest warrant was issued in Belgium for the former foreign minister of the Democratic Republic of the Congo, Abdulaye Ndombasi.

Such events constitute an important part of the attempt to bring the rule of law to bear upon international politics. High political office should not constitute an impenetrable shield against legal proceedings. All human beings should be equally accountable, regardless of their position and whether their actions took place in peace or in war. These developments should be widely applauded, even if they are not unproblematic. Although I generally welcome the developments of the past decade, I think some issues still deserve careful consideration and should not be overlooked.

International accountability has sometimes been criticized for selectivity. The Yugoslavia tribunal's resources – over 800 functionaries – are now quite impressive. However, the activity of the Rwanda tribunal and the coming into being of the Sierra Leone tribunal and the Cambodia process are still affected by low political priority and lack of funding. These problems have once again reminded us of the danger of creating two types of justice: one applicable in Europe, one elsewhere. The establishment of the International Criminal Court will improve the situation considerably. Although we still cannot tell what effect the continued opposition of the United States will have, it is important not to allow that opposition to hamper the commencement of the court's activity.

The case for the ICC is further strengthened by the fact that the results of trying foreign political leaders in national courts have remained unimpressive. Pinochet returned to Chile and it is doubtful whether he will ever face trial there. The Senegalese court finally declined jurisdiction over Habre, and the French Court de Cassation upheld the immunity of Libya's Qaddafi in a case concerning the 1989 terrorist attack on a French civilian airplane over Niger. Belgium, too, has found itself in the International Court of Justice as a result of allegedly having violated the immunity of the Congolese minister.

The demand for international accountability is not new. Article 227 of the Versailles Peace Treaty famously indicted William II for a "supreme offence against international morality and the sanctity of treaties". Under Article 228, the German Supreme Court in Leipzig was called upon to try those accused of war crimes. In the end, William found refuge in The Netherlands and the Leipzig trials led to minor sentences for a handful of lesser offenders. Allied efforts to bring the perpetrators of the Armenian genocide of 1915 to justice ended in a fiasco: the British occupation forces had to free the main suspects in exchange for 29 British soldiers captured by Kemal Atatürk's Turkish nationalists.

Bearing these experiences in mind, it was no surprise that at the end of World War II such Allied politicians as Winston Churchill and Henry Morgenthau suggested that the leading Nazis should be summarily executed as soon as they were caught. It may have been Stalin's proposal that as many as 50,000 of them should suffer this fate that made Churchill back down. The Nuremberg trials have sometimes been accused of distributing "victors' justice". Whatever the problems, however, they were crucial in paving the way to national proceedings in a number of states as well as to the war crimes tribunals and the ICC today. The notion of "crimes against humanity" has now been firmly rooted in international law to cover atrocities that until 1945 had no special name. Today, that notion has been extended to include a number of sexual crimes that traditionally involved no criminal responsibility.

Still, after Nuremberg and Tokyo, it was not until the 1990s that any properly *international* accountability for war crimes, let alone for other human rights violations, was established. In the intervening years, some states did convict minor officials for crimes connected with World War II. The Eichmann trial in Israel received much publicity; so did the Barbie, Touvier and Papon trials in France. The trial of Lieutenant Calley over the My Lai massacre involved an effort by American society to deal with excesses committed during the Viet Nam war. The lessons from these experiences are mixed. Hannah Arendt's famous account of the Eichmann trial offers a very detailed view of the problems involved. The didactic or historical purposes of a trial are not always easy to reconcile with its principal objective: the establishment of the guilt or innocence of the accused. None of this makes it any less important to bring those guilty of the most serious violations to justice. This is especially important in order to replace collective guilt with individual responsibility and enable the process of national reconciliation to take place.

In establishing the Yugoslavia, Rwanda and Sierra Leone tribunals, speed was of the essence – hence the involvement of the UN Security Council. However, these situations were quite extraordinary and the institutional solution – establishing judicial bodies with the formal position of subsidiary organs of the Council – was far from optimal. It was no wonder that the tribunals were immediately caught in an inter-institutional quagmire between the Council and the Assembly, the Assembly using its budgetary power to discipline the Council. Some felt that there was a danger that the judicial function would be overshadowed by the Council's primary function of "maintaining international peace and security".

The impressive track record of the Yugoslavia tribunal has effectively tackled the fear that the political processes would override the legal ones. The tribunal's standing and financial position have also improved considerably. The opening of the trial of Slobodan Milosevic might be regarded as the most important development in international criminal law since Nuremberg. I think in general it is important that all political leaders are made aware, through this and similar processes, that they cannot escape justice if they misbehave to the extent that is the case here. Perhaps that is the best form of preventive diplomacy. The task now is to guarantee that Milosevic receives a fair trial – which must include the possibility that he is freed in the end. In the eyes of the general public, the legitimacy of the tribunal will depend much on the process and the outcome of the Milosevic trial.

In an ideal world, the violation of basic rules of humanity would lead automatically to criminal responsibility. After all, international law does make all individuals responsible for certain gross violations. However, lack of a centralized system of accountability has so far prevented this being realized in practice. The aftermath of 11 September 2001 has concentrated international efforts on the fight against terrorism, highlighting the problems connected with the lack of centralized enforcement. Where should Osama bin Laden be put on trial? The difficulties of ensuring a technically satisfactory trial in the United States have often been highlighted, especially by American lawyers. But there is no existing international alternative either. And, whether he is brought to trial in the United States or elsewhere, the doubt must always remain that the political passions involved might overrule the formal exigencies of a regular criminal trial. For such reasons, the creation of the International Criminal Court with overall jurisdiction and through the regular means of a multilateral treaty must be warmly welcomed. In due course, the ICC will certainly become the central organ of a real criminal justice system in the international realm.

I shall conclude with a few words about the limits of criminal law as an instrument for dealing with major international problems. Crime and human rights violations emerge from causes deeply embedded in the structure of societies – poverty, deprivation, social injustice. When courts deal with massive human rights violations arising in connection with civil conflict, they are considering only the visible surface of underlying social problems. Criminal law, however effective, cannot replace the social policies needed to combat deprivation and social injustice. The recent attention to developing a functioning international criminal justice system has to be warmly welcomed, but it should be accompanied by efficient international policies and structures to deal with those root causes. In this area, much remains to be done.

One of the functions of criminal law is to serve as a collective memory of past injustice. A criminal trial brings past suffering into the public arena. It may thus enable a victimized community to deal with trauma and, perhaps, to create the conditions for future social life. But recording past injustice and creating the conditions for national reconciliation are not always best realized through criminal law. The available evidence, even of massive violations, may not always fulfil the formal criteria of criminal accountability. The path from the opening of a mass grave to proving a political leader responsible is long and complex, and success is by no means ensured. In cases such as this, a criminal trial may not always be the best instrument for memory and healing – especially if the leader has to be released because of the lack of formal evidence. On the other hand, if releasing the leader is excluded at the outset, then the legitimacy of the trial may be questioned. All trials must contain an element of risk – namely the risk that the accused is freed. If this aspect is missing, what we have is a show trial: a symbolic process that merely ratifies a conclusion already reached by other considerations. These considerations point to the continued usefulness, in certain cases, of systems such as truth commissions.

Nobody should expect the introduction of the rule of law, including criminal accountability, in international affairs to be an uncomplicated affair. There is no doubt that the objective of ending the culture of impunity is widely shared and that recent developments do offer a glimmer of hope in this regard. However, precisely because the objective is so important, indeed historic, the opportunity should not be spoiled by technical or political mistakes, by rushing ahead when careful deliberation and cool assessment are called for.

Acknowledgements

The origins of this book lie in an international conference, "From a Culture of Impunity to a Culture of Accountability. International Criminal Tribunals, the International Criminal Court, and Human Rights Protection", which was jointly organized by the United Nations University and the Netherlands Institute of Human Rights (SIM) in Utrecht, 26–28 November 2001. During the three-day conference, prominent jurists, political scientists and historians from all over the world presented a range of lectures examining the political, legal and institutional experiences of the ad hoc International Criminal Tribunals for the former Yugoslavia and Rwanda as well as the Rome Statute, which established the permanent International Criminal Court (ICC) that entered into force in 2002. The conference covered a wide field of related issues, ranging from the historical background to the establishment of the tribunals, to their legal basis and jurisdiction, and the rights of both victims and defendants, as well as alternative solutions such as truth and reconciliation commissions. The quintessential "peace diplomat" and former president of Finland, Martti Ahtisaari, opened the conference, and the former prime minister and minister of justice of the Netherlands, Dries van Agt, concluded the event. This volume comprises the best material presented at the conference, thoroughly revised and updated. In addition, there is a specially written foreword by Judge Richard J. Goldstone, Justice of the Constitutional Court of South Africa and former Chief Prosecutor of the Yugoslavia and Rwanda tribunals.

The publication of this book would not have been possible without the assistance and support of many people. In particular, the editors would like to express their gratitude to Hans van Ginkel, Rector of the United Nations University, and Cees Flinterman, Director of the Netherlands Institute of Human Rights, who took the initiative to combine the knowledge and expertise of both organizations in order to accomplish this project. Special thanks go to Edward Newman, academic officer at the Peace and Governance Programme at UNU, who played an important and stimulating role in the organization of the conference as well as the realization of this volume. Furthermore, the editors owe a special debt of gratitude to Peter R. Baehr, Emeritus Professor of Human Rights at Utrecht University, and Adriaan Bos, former legal adviser at the Dutch Ministry of Foreign Affairs and former chairman of the Preparatory Committee for the Establishment of an International Court, who both read the whole manuscript and, based on their own expertise, offered valuable comments on the content. Special thanks are also due to Berber Hettinga and Asja Kalnins, who were of great assistance in the preparation of the final copy. Finally, the editors would like to thank the United Nations University, Utrecht University, the Netherlands Royal Academy of Science (KNAW), and the K. F. Hein Fonds Foundation, whose generous financial support allowed the publication of this book.

Ramesh Thakur
Peter Malcontent

Introduction

Human rights and peace: Two sides of the same coin

Peter Malcontent

Introduction

From the perspective of human rights, the last decade of the twentieth century may be regarded as a turbulent period characterized by positive as well as negative developments.

After the Cold War, the end of the bipolar balance of power created a vacuum in many parts of the world, which allowed religious and ethnic conflicts that had often been smouldering beneath the surface to erupt into instability and conflict. In many cases, these conflicts resulted in gross violations of human rights. In Europe, civil war and ethnic cleansing ravaged the Balkan region. In Africa, countries such as Somalia and Rwanda were confronted with genocide and anarchy.

Ironically, a positive result of these negative developments was the increasing consciousness at the international level that human rights had to be regarded as a precondition for political stability and socio-economic progress. Consequently, human rights started to climb the ladder of international political priorities and became strongly interrelated with the "higher objective" of maintaining international peace and security.

The notion that human rights and peace and security were nothing less than two sides of the same coin was not just an abstract concept. The Security Council of the United Nations, no longer paralysed by political and ideological stalemate between the United States and the Soviet Union, started to mainstream human rights in existing peace and security

instruments such as UN peacekeeping and peace enforcement operations. It also took the initiative to revise an old and almost forgotten
instrument in order to better equip the United Nations to integrate human rights and security. As a result, almost 50 years after the proceedings
of the Nuremberg tribunal ("the mother of all international criminal tribunals"), the Security Council decided to reintroduce the instrument of
international criminal justice by establishing ad hoc tribunals for the
former Yugoslavia and Rwanda in 1993 and 1994, respectively.

In Resolutions 808 and 955, which founded these tribunals, the Security Council showed its determination to put an end to the continuing
violations of international humanitarian law through the prosecution of
individual perpetrators of war crimes, genocide and crimes against humanity in both countries. But this was not the only task ascribed to the
tribunals. Legitimizing the establishment of both tribunals by referring to
Chapter VII of the UN Charter, which empowers the Security Council to
take any necessary action in cases of serious threats against international
peace and security, the Council also hoped that the proceedings of the
two tribunals could contribute to the broader challenge of peace and
stability.

With the establishment of the International Criminal Tribunal for the
former Yugoslavia (ICTY) and the International Criminal Tribunal for
Rwanda (ICTR), a new challenge was launched against the age-old bul-
wark of national sovereignty, which, in spite of an increasing number of
minor cracks since 1945, still functioned as the governing principle on
which inter-state relations have been based since Westphalia. Five decades after Nuremberg, the international community regained its courage
to demand individual accountability for serious violations of human
rights, especially during wartime, even when committed by leading government officials on behalf of the state. National sovereignty no longer
guaranteed immunity and impunity.

How have the two ad hoc tribunals dealt with their difficult tasks of
promoting both human rights and peace and security? And what may be
expected from the new permanent International Criminal Court (ICC),
which entered into force in 2002?[1] These were the central issues discussed during the conference "From a Culture of Impunity to a Culture
of Accountability", organized by the United Nations University (UNU)
and the Netherlands Institute of Human Rights (SIM) in November 2001
in the Netherlands. This volume constitutes an interdisciplinary reflection
of the results of this event and contains 16 chapters written by prominent
lawyers, historians and political scientists.

On the basis of a categorization of the main issues discussed in each
chapter, the book can be divided into three separate although interrelated parts. Part I outlines the historical and political background to the

establishment of the ad hoc tribunals and the ICC, by focusing not only on those factors that contributed to the increasing popularity of these instruments but also on those factors that hampered and still hamper their functioning. The actual functioning of the tribunals and the ICC as judicial mechanisms is dealt with in Part II. What is their record in providing fair trials to victims as well as perpetrators, however heinous their crimes may be? And, more generally, to what extent have they been successful in establishing a culture of accountability without harming other principles and achievements which have proceeded from the same norms and values that initiated the struggle against impunity? The third and last part of this volume concentrates on the effectiveness and limitations of international criminal tribunals in protecting human rights and maintaining peace and security through criminal justice. More specifically, Part III deals with questions and issues such as the effectiveness of international criminal tribunals compared with other, non-judicial instruments such as truth and reconciliation commissions; their competence to deal with actors other than individuals, such as companies; and whether the popularity of international criminal procedures includes the risk of becoming a substitute for earlier meaningful action, creating only an illusion of progress in the field of enhancing human rights and peace and security.

Part I: The historical and political context

This section starts with a historical overview by Paul Lauren, who explains the establishment of the tribunals and the Rome Statute by referring to five "forces of transformations": religious belief; philosophical belief; the ongoing technological revolution, and especially the advances in communications technology; conflicts and revolutions that destroy existing structures of authority and vested interests; and the tragic force of enormous human atrocities, confronting humankind time and time again with the necessity to break through moral thresholds. According to Lauren, these forces were essential to overturning the powerful notion of national sovereignty and the widespread culture of impunity that results from it.

In the following chapters, Michael Biddiss, David Forsythe and George Andreopoulos show that, although there is indeed a changing human rights culture at the international level, major obstacles to accountability still exist. In Chapter 2, Biddiss presents a historical analysis of the limits of international criminal accountability. He shows how, from Nuremberg to the entering into force of the ICC in 2002, the protection shield against accountability – national sovereignty – remained relatively robust in spite of some successful attacks. Even after the atrocities of World War II, progress continued to be hampered by national reservations; the inclusion of the new notion of "crimes against humanity" as Count Four in the indictment of the Allied prosecuting teams against the leaders of the Third Reich before the Nuremberg tribunal is a good illustration of this. By defining crimes against humanity as committed against any population before as well as during wartime, the Allied powers intended to punish not only Nazi crimes committed after the outbreak of the war, but also the extensive persecution of political opponents and Jews within Germany in the 1930s. The devastating effect this new category of international law could have on the principle of national sovereignty during peacetime was clear. The Allied powers realized this all too well and, being afraid that their own invention could turn against them, they restricted the range of Count Four by adding to the definition of crimes against humanity the necessity that there had to be a relationship between Count Four and any of the other crimes within the jurisdiction of the tribunal. In practice, this meant that there had to be a relationship with warfare or its preparation, and, as a result, the judges of the tribunal backed away from crimes inflicted by the Third Reich on its own population in the period 1933–1939.

According to Biddiss, who is more sceptical than Lauren about the post-war move from impunity towards accountability, the tale developing from Nuremberg to a large extent remained a disappointing one. A decisive blow against the conservative exercise of sovereign autonomy was emasculated. Because of their ad hoc character, tribunals such as the ICTY retained the stain of victors' justice; as a result, like the Nuremberg tribunal, they remained sensitive to *tu quoque* rebuttals ("I did it, but you did it too"). Unfortunately, the solution for this problem, the establishment of a *permanent* International Criminal Court, continues to be frustrated by the present dominant world power, the United States.

In Chapter 3, Forsythe offers an in-depth analysis of the widespread aversion in the United States to the ICC. According to him, the insurmountable objections being raised by American politicians as well as academics are remarkable because the ICC operates on the basis of complementarity, meaning that it can transcend national jurisdictional powers only when a state is unwilling or unable to prosecute crimes committed on its territory or by its citizens abroad. Forsythe shows that the US legal objections against the Rome Statute – the fear that it could allow an independent prosecutor to bring indictments against American citizens wherever they are, even when the United States remains a non-ratifying party – are expressions of much deeper political and cultural considerations. First, US aversion to the ICC is determined by what Forsythe defines as "American exceptionalism",[2] a deeply embedded view that real human rights come from the US experience and are then exported to the rest of the world. Because of this longstanding dominant cultural tradition, the United States has manifested persistent difficulty in adjusting to multilateral human rights arrangements that it does not control or heavily influence. Secondly, American exceptionalism is reinforced by the unrivalled power position of the United States in international relations. As a result of this, the United States speaks fondly of international law as long as it does not constrain the exercise of US power. Forsythe specifically refers to the US response to the judgment of the International Court of Justice in the wake of *Nicaragua v. the US (1986)*. Its refusal to abide by the World Court's judgment was possible because there was no countervailing power to compel the United States to implement it.

Like Biddiss and Forsythe, Andreopoulos is sceptical of the evolving international human rights culture as described by Lauren. Andreopoulos places the establishment of the ad hoc tribunals and the ICC into the broader context of linking human rights violations and threats to peace and security in the 1990s, concluding that we are indeed confronted with a rising "global ethos of accountability". At the same time, however, he warns against euphoria by posing the question of whether the rising profile of human rights norms within the security discourse is in fact mere window-dressing or "façade legitimation", providing a gentler face to naked power considerations in pursuit of the national interests of states.

Part II: Functioning in practice

The second part of this volume starts with four contributions centred on the issue of whether international criminal tribunals have been able to bring justice to both victims and perpetrators. Two authors, Christine Chinkin and Michail Wladimiroff, evaluate the tribunals' contribution to the evolution of international criminal and humanitarian law. They explore the extent to which legal thresholds have been lowered to allow for the prosecution of those charged with serious violations, and especially of those whose role is not always easy to establish: alleged perpetrators of gender-related crimes such as rape, and military leaders and civilian superiors suspected of organizing, planning and inciting crimes without actually taking part in atrocities themselves.

In Chapter 5, Wladimiroff describes how the proceedings of the Nuremberg tribunal, the ICTY and the ICTR extended the doctrine of criminal responsibility to include not only factual but also functional responsibility for violations of humanitarian law, whether committed by military commanders or by government officials. Yet Wladimiroff acknowledges that even the provisions of the ICC Statute still make it easier to prosecute military leaders than civilian superiors. Military leaders can already be prosecuted for negligence, whereas civilian superiors can be held functionally responsible for offences only when they are committed with the required intent and knowledge.

In Chapter 6, Chinkin analyses the advances being made by the ICTY and ICTR from a feminist perspective, proceeding from the assertion that the inclusion of sexual offences within the catalogue of international crimes must be accompanied by an understanding of those offences based upon women's experiences of them. Chinkin explains that the ad hoc tribunals have been helpful in this, for example by establishing a less restrictive definition of rape as an international crime. By emphasizing that the offence of rape does not require proof of force and by acknowledging that, in a situation in which an individual may not have protested or fought against sexual activity, such behaviour still can be spoken of as an act of rape, the ICTY and ICTR showed themselves prepared to take into account how women's experiences of offences such as these may differ from those of men.

The question remains, however, how far the ad hoc tribunals and the recently established ICC should go in centralizing the position and perception of the victim. Chinkin applauds the acceptance by the judges of the tribunals of inconsistencies in the evidence when prosecuting sexual offences, because these inconsistencies can be rationally explained by the difficulties of recollecting precise details of traumatic events several years later. Related to this, she also supports the successful inclusion in the Rome Statute of protective measures for witnesses and victims, especially when testifying about the commission of sexual offences.

Contrary to Chinkin, two other authors, Bert Swart and William Schabas, are not convinced that the shift from impunity to individual accountability should be achieved in this way. Schabas argues that the campaign against impunity has resulted in an unacceptable lowering of legal thresholds to increase the opportunities to convict defendants accused of war crimes, genocide and crimes against humanity. However, in Chapter 7 on the provisions on the admissibility of evidence in the Rules of Procedure and Evidence of the international criminal tribunals and the Rome Statute, Swart is positive about the fair trial standards maintained by both ad hoc tribunals. He shows how the legal protection offered to the defendant has been improved as a result of the increasing restraint on accepting hearsay evidence. Both the case law of the ICTY as well as the draft rules of the ICC stress the importance of providing the defence with the opportunity to cross-examine witness statements. Yet Swart also points out a "striking innovation" that could negatively affect the defendants' right to a fair and impartial trial. An important difference between the statute of the ICC and the statutes of the ad hoc tribunals is that the Rome Statute permits victims to take part in the proceedings in their capacity as a witness *and* as a victim. Although from the point of view of the victim this is indeed a welcome innovation, Swart argues that the position of the defendant as a result of this dual role could be seriously undermined. Because the victim could provide information incriminating the accused, the court should not let itself be influenced by information provided by the victim that is not compatible with earlier statements offered in their position as a witness during cross-examination.

Schabas, in Chapter 8, is worried not only about the future but also about the present. He concludes that, in the past, human rights law concerned itself with protecting the accused and was not particularly interested in balancing these rights against the importance of prosecuting offenders. Now, however, it has become torn by another extreme, "one that is oriented towards the victim and that thrives upon conviction". As a result of this, the ICTY, for example, allowed for the use of anonymous witnesses and tended to go along with a more teleological or purposive approach to the interpretation of its statute while moving away from the old rule of giving the benefit of the doubt to the accused.

Other authors have argued that non-governmental organizations (NGOs) contributed to this process. For example, Geoffrey Robertson, in his book *Crimes against Humanity: The Struggle for Global Justice*, refers to the intense lobbying campaigns by more than 800 organizations during the 1998 diplomatic meeting in Rome resulting in the establishment of the ICC Statute. Robertson shows how NGOs such as Amnesty International, in their eagerness to establish an effective court, were prepared to abolish the defence of duress, the defence of necessity and even the defence of self-defence, even though this would result in an ICC that violated the basic human rights of its defendants.[3]

In her contribution on the position of NGOs in gathering evidence and giving witness at international criminal trials (Chapter 9), Helen Durham also argues that "the involvement of NGOs in international criminal proceedings is a complex process fraught as much with danger as with great potential". NGOs have access to networks and grassroots information and are often on-site when atrocities occur. As a result, they have first-hand knowledge of events and the best ability to identify potential witnesses. This puts NGOs in a unique position to gather and present evidence at international criminal trials. Durham, however, also points to the tension between the political nature of many NGOs and the judicial requirement of impartiality. Whereas NGOs can tend to be normative and political, the successful and credible prosecution of those accused of atrocities relies upon due process and an environment free from politics and passion. There is clearly a tension here.

The important question raised by Schabas of whether the tribunals have succeeded in combating impunity without harming other important principles and norms is also dealt with by Madeline Morris in Chapter 10, albeit from a quite different perspective. She questions the democratic legitimacy of the ICC and perceives a tension between the right to freedom from violent abuse and the human right to representative government within the ICC Statute. Morris acknowledges the advantage of the court's complementary authority to investigate crimes committed within the territory of a member state that is unable or unwilling to do so, even when the alleged perpetrator is not a national from one of the states parties to the Rome Statute. Nevertheless, she also emphasizes that, although the court's supranational powers may contribute to the fight against impunity, its superior authority has caused a "democratic deficit" because of the court's organizational structure, which made the Assembly of States Parties its principal governing body. Within this organ, no seats with voting power are reserved for non-member states, in spite of the fact that the court can prosecute their nationals. But if this should happen, what then is the democratic basis for the ICC's power as applied to populations of states that continue to refuse to sign and ratify the ICC Statute?

Part III: Effectiveness and limitations

The last section of this volume deals with the effectiveness of international criminal tribunals in the broader challenge of both protecting human rights and maintaining peace and security. The first two chapters emphasize the positive qualities of international criminal tribunals in comparison with the functioning of national trials and non-judicial instruments such as truth and reconciliation commissions. The next three contributions focus on the limits of the effectiveness of international criminal tribunals in the field of human rights and peace and security.

As Martha Minow states in her book *Between Vengeance and Forgiveness*, the most prominent positive quality of criminal prosecution is that "it transfers the individuals' desires for revenge to the state or official bodies. The transfer cools vengeance into retribution, slows judgment with procedure, and interrupts, with documents, cross-examination, and the presumption of innocence, the vicious cycle of blame and feud."[4] But do these qualifications make international criminal tribunals the superior route towards long-term conflict resolution and reconciliation in fractured societies? According to Kingsley Moghalu, former Special Adviser to the Registrar of the Rwanda tribunal, the answer is positive. In his challenging contribution to this volume (Chapter 11), in which he focuses on the far-reaching judicial precedents established by the ICTR, he defends his position by analysing the functioning of the instrument of criminal prosecution from a comparative perspective. Should we resort to the phenomenon of truth and reconciliation commissions (TRCs) used in many Latin American countries and in South Africa, where they facilitated the transition from repression and apartheid to democracy and majority rule? Although Moghalu acknowledges that this soft law instrument has certain advantages, he regards it as only a secondary or additional option to trials. Because TRCs cannot ensure criminal prosecution of perpetrators of mass crimes, they ultimately fail to address the yearning of the victims for justice. Indeed, a truth and reconciliation commission with the prospect of amnesties for perpetrators who offer full testimonies – as in South Africa – is hardly imaginable in cases of genocide such as the Holocaust or the Rwandese massacre in 1994. It is also questionable in other cases whether truth without justice can heal conflicted societies. In Chile, the truth commission was said to have laid the Pinochet issue to rest, but the polarization within Chilean society after his arrest in London proved otherwise.

Another fundamental benefit of criminal trials is that they differentiate between the main perpetrators, foot-soldiers and bystanders, and thereby alleviate collective guilt, which according to Moghalu and many other transitional justice lawyers can be a significant obstacle to genuine reconciliation within society. Moreover, in spite of the criticism that the ad hoc tribunals were established only as a reaction to the atrocities in the former Yugoslavia and Rwanda, Moghalu believes they serve a deterrent function as well. Although one could argue that the ICTR was not able to preclude new upheavals of ethnic violence in the Great Lakes region, Moghalu points out that, without the precedent of the ICTR and the ICTY, the ICC, which has an important preventive function, would never have been established.

Geoffrey Robertson's contribution in Chapter 12 also emphasizes the positive qualities of international tribunals in protecting human rights and maintaining peace and security. In his search for the best solution to deal with the terrorists responsible for atrocities such as the 11 September attacks, he dissociates himself from national judicial options such as a local jury trial in New York or a trial by a presidentially ordained military commission. The former would result in an emotional event automatically leading to the demand for the death sentence, and the latter would even more fail to conform to a minimum of fair trial guarantees. As a result, any verdict of guilty would be vulnerable to the allegation of subjectivity and certainly would not convince doubters and critics from the Islamic countries. Only an international tribunal or a national trial held in a neutral location, like the Lockerbie trial, could be a solution to this problem. Both options would at least offer the necessary impartiality.

By using one of these options to prosecute Osama bin Laden and his al-Qaida accomplices, not only would the protection of the rights of both victims and perpetrators be guaranteed but, as Robertson emphasizes, international peace and security would also be rendered a good service: "Yet suppose he were to be captured and interrogated, and later sit like Milosevic for some months in a criminal court dock and then, after a reasoned judgment, be locked for the rest of his life in a cell in Finland? Surely this would greatly assist the work of demystifying the man, debunking his cause and de-brainwashing his many thousands of followers."

Instead of underlining the positive qualities of international tribunals, Andrew Clapham focuses in Chapter 13 on their most characteristic weakness; that is, that they have jurisdiction only over natural individual persons and not over states and corporations. One of the negative aspects emanating from the tribunals' incapacity to prosecute judicial persons is that this decreases victims' chances of claiming appropriate reparations for harm done to them by states or companies because only individual representatives can be forced to pay compensation. As a result, processes of reconciliation in societies torn by conflict can be thwarted.

However, Clapham emphasizes that, in spite of the inability of international criminal law to deal with private actors and states, one should not assume that so far it has been concerned solely with the liability of individuals. Returning to the Nuremberg proceedings, he shows how, during the trials against Gustav Krupp and officials of the I.G. Farben Corporation, the prosecutors did everything to put in the spotlight the individual representatives as well as their companies. These efforts did not remain without consequences and directly influenced the recent preparedness of Swiss banks and German industries to conclude reparation settlements with victims of war crimes from which they benefited financially during World War II.

In spite of this positive development, Clapham acknowledges that corporate and state responsibility remained excluded from the ICC Statute. The closest the conference on the Rome Statute came to including corporations was a text suggestion that directors as well as their companies could be prosecuted if the crime committed by the director was committed on behalf of and with the explicit consent of the company and in the course of its activities. Although this proposal was finally rejected, its language found its way into the new texts on terrorism, such as Security Council Resolution 1373 and the new Draft Convention on Terrorism.

In her contribution on the ICC's powers to ban the use of child soldiers in armed conflict (Chapter 14), Julia Maxted also stresses the limitations of the ad hoc tribunals and the ICC in protecting basic human rights and restoring peace and security. By describing the many factors contributing to this problem, she shows that it would be naïve to think that the complex reality can be reckoned with by relying too much on one specific instrument. Maxted points out how the severity of the child soldier problem in part results from the characteristics of conflict in which chaos and suffering have become strategic objectives and armed groups regard the use of children as a cheap and effective means to reach these goals. The child soldier problem is also influenced by the poor economic conditions of many children living in conflict zones. The offer of food and clothing is often sufficient to induce participation in guerrilla armies.

The continuing deterioration in livelihood security, social cohesion and capital is caused not only by conflict but also by recent macroeconomic policies and the HIV pandemic. Therefore, an effective prohibition on involving children in hostilities cannot be reached just by holding particular offenders personally accountable before a tribunal. Broader policy intervention tools should be used too, including increased control on the trade in diamonds and other minerals, the encouragement of small arms moratoriums, the restoration of law and order, the resettlement of former combatants, and, over the long run, provision of the education and employment opportunities that would discourage children and young people from reverting to violence.

Although from a different perspective, Cees Flinterman comes to the same conclusion in Chapter 15. Elaborating on Clapham, he underlines the limited judicial scope of the Rome Statute, which is still focused on grave human rights violations during wartime, in spite of the fact that a growing intersection between international human rights law and international humanitarian law can be observed. The most prominent example is the de-linking of the concept of crimes against humanity from the war nexus requirement in the jurisprudence of the ICTY and the ICC Statute.

Flinterman observes that the scope of the ICC and its jurisdictional powers will remain limited as a result of the continuing refusal of major countries such as the United States and China to ratify the Rome Statute. The road towards a real universal human rights court remains a lengthy one and the ICC may be regarded as only a first important step in that direction. Apart from that, Flinterman warns that an over-reliance on the instruments of international criminal justice increases the risk of a disproportionately large share of the international community's available resources being used for reactive rather than proactive strategies geared towards addressing the structural causes of human rights violations. According to Flinterman, the ICC should be accompanied by measures directed at an increase in the funding of preventive human rights mechanisms such as the UN High Commissioner for Human Rights in Geneva. At the very least, the court's functioning should not result in a decline in other regional and international mechanisms trying to protect universal human rights norms, values and institutions. In fact, existing supervision mechanisms such as the UN Torture Committee could even complement the work of the ICC by investigating and producing evidence.

A vast amount of literature and commentary concerning international criminal justice has preceded the publication of this volume. The contribution of this volume comes with its interdisciplinary approach to the many different aspects of international criminal accountability, within a political as well as a legal context. This book does not pretend to be a definitive or complete account of the contribution that international criminal justice can make to the protection of human rights and peace and security. It would be impossible to offer an in-depth analysis of every aspect of this topic in just one volume; moreover, it is far too early to generate definitive conclusions on the basis of still limited experience. Indeed, despite its high profile, international criminal justice has been implemented in only a very few cases so far.

None the less, on the basis of the experiences already acquired, at least some conclusions can be drawn. As Ramesh Thakur re-emphasizes in the closing chapter, retributive justice is not, by definition, the only road to peace, stability and the protection of human rights. Sometimes, restorative justice through truth and reconciliation commissions may offer a better solution to fractured societies recovering from atrocities. Elaborating on this, an even more important conclusion Thakur draws is that, whatever the choice, it can never be made without consulting the country involved, "not the least because it is that country that paid the price in the past and will have to live with the immediate and long-term consequences of the decisions made".

Notes

1. The ICC was established not on the basis of a Security Council resolution but on the basis of a statute approved during an international diplomatic conference in Rome in 1998.
2. See also David P. Forsythe, *American Exceptionalism and Global Human Rights*, Lincoln: University of Nebraska Distinguished Lecture Series, 1999; Forsythe, "US Foreign Policy and Human Rights: The Price of Principles after the Cold War", in David P. Forsythe, ed., *Human Rights and Comparative Foreign Policy*, Tokyo: United Nations University Press, 2000, pp. 21–48.
3. Geoffrey Robertson, *Crimes against Humanity: The Struggle for Global Justice*, London: Penguin, 1999, pp. 301–302.
4. Martha Minow, *Between Vengeance and Forgiveness: Facing History after Genocide and Mass Violence*, Boston: Beacon Press, 1998, p. 26.

Part I

The historical and political background of international criminal accountability

1

From impunity to accountability: Forces of transformation and the changing international human rights context

Paul G. Lauren

Introduction

The simple but powerful expression "From a culture of impunity to a culture of accountability" implies a transformation nothing short of revolutionary. It should. Within an extremely short period of historical time, the world has experienced a dramatic and radical change in the areas of international human rights, international criminal law and the creation of international tribunals that profoundly affects us today and will affect us in the future. Fully to appreciate the extent of this transformation, the distance travelled and just how far we have come, we need to begin by understanding where the journey started.

The past and its culture of impunity

"The culture of impunity" is an appropriate description for most of the entire experience of human history. In the vast and complex history of the world, the overwhelming majority of those who ever lived and died suffered from some form of human rights abuse. During almost all times and in all places, people found themselves confronting various forms of prejudice and discrimination, with sharp distinctions made on the basis of gender, race, caste or class, religious or political belief, ethnicity, place of origin, or some other form of difference. For this reason, they were not regarded as being fully human, and therefore were never allowed to exercise whatever rights they might claim or that others might claim on their behalf. Instead, traditional societies and imperial regimes from Asia to Africa and from Europe to South America emphasized hierarchical and patriarchal relationships, distinct divisions between the very few rulers and the many ruled, stratification between the powerful and the weak, and obedience to authority rather than personal rights. Common patterns of dominance could be seen in many varieties of privilege and poverty, intolerance and ignorance, despotism and suppression, violence and torture, arrogance and xenophobia, conquest and control, persecution and segregation, and sometimes even genocide. Human bondage and slavery were commonly accepted as the norm.

Of particular importance in understanding this widespread culture of various forms of abuse is one central and overriding fact: virtually all governments regarded how they treated those under their control and the policies they pursued as a matter exclusively within their own jurisdiction. Emperors, pharaohs, caesars, khans, sultans, tsars, kings and eventually prime ministers and presidents all argued that they and the territory they ruled were completely independent and sovereign. How they treated their own people and how they advanced their own interests, including the use of violence and the waging of war as the final arbiter of disputes, were considered their own business and not subject to any outside international standards, scrutiny, criticism or interference.

With the emergence of nation-states, this proposition was not only given more articulate expression, but actually confirmed and codified in international law. During the sixteenth century, for example, the French political philosopher Jean Bodin enunciated the principle of national sovereignty in his book *Les Six Livres de la République*. States, he argued, possessed the unique feature of sovereignty, which he dramatically and defiantly defined as "power absolute and perpetual", "supreme" and "subject to no law". Indeed, claimed Bodin, such sovereign power provided "the distinguishing mark of a state". The state alone possessed the power to decide how it would behave in the world and how it would treat its own people within its own borders and those under its control elsewhere. Bodin described this power as "absolute authority over all the rest without exception" and "without the consent of any superior, equal or inferior being necessary".[1] If the government of a state desired to treat people well and acknowledge that they might have rights, it could. If, instead, it wanted to abuse them, exploit them, persecute them, segregate them, forcibly convert them, torture them or enslave them, it could do that as well. The precise nature of the treatment, however, was considered to be a matter of exclusive domestic jurisdiction.

This doctrine of national sovereignty and its corollary of domestic jurisdiction received reinforcement in many ways. The Treaty of Westphalia signed in 1648 following the Thirty Years War provided recognition, in law as well as in fact, of the power and the authority of sovereign, independent states. Only they could be considered subjects of international law and no international jurisdiction existed to hold individuals criminally responsible for their actions. They recognized no universal authority, such as that of an emperor or a pope or an international organization from above, and no claims from feudal barons or subjects from below. The publication of *Leviathan* only three years later provided even further theoretical justification for the doctrine, particularly when Thomas Hobbes addressed what he described as "the essence of sovereignty". Here he left no doubt about his belief that the sovereign powers of the state and the absolute monarch who acted in its name ruled without challenge, doing "whatsoever he shall think necessary to be done".[2] "In the span of a century", writes one authority on international politics, the doctrine of sovereignty "became unchallengeable either from within the territory or from without. In other words, it had become supreme."[3] Theories are never absolute in practice, but when such a doctrine was both asserted and accepted by governments, victims of human rights abuses were forced to suffer alone and made to understand that they could not look for help or recourse from beyond the borders of their own state. For them, there was nowhere to run and nowhere to hide. Victims therefore remained objects of international pity rather than subjects of international law. As such, government leaders understood for centuries that they could act in the name of their state largely as they wished or were able, in the knowledge that international law applied only to states and shielded them from individual responsibility by the doctrine of national sovereignty, which did so much to create and justify a widespread culture of impunity.[4]

Forces of transformation

Given the formidable power of this culture, both created and maintained by tradition, practice, vested interests and law, it is not surprising that any significant attempts to transform it would require a combination of extraordinary forces. Through time, such forces sufficient to change the political and human rights context did emerge, manifesting themselves in a variety of often unanticipated ways, circumstances and places around the world.[5]

One of these important forces was religious belief. All the world's major religions hold out a vision of the dignity and worth of each person as a member of the same human family. They attempt to teach about the best of possible human relationships rather than the worst, addressing matters of justice, compassion and responsibilities to care for the oppressed or those in need. Although often perverted in historical practice for more secular purposes, these religious beliefs established visions of values, or normative standards, and ideals that proved to be of enormous inspiration and strength for those who campaigned for human rights, even centuries later, especially during times of persecution and suffering. Moreover, by seeking to develop a broad, moral imperative, they also helped establish an ingredient essential for any and all international human rights: a concept of responsibility toward common humanity. Demands or assertions for human rights in one place would have remained forever unanswered, isolated or not localized unless there had been people elsewhere in the world who believed that they had larger responsibilities, or duties, to protect those suffering beyond their own borders.

Philosophical belief contributed another major force of change. Over the course of centuries, philosophers in many diverse times and places wrestled with difficult questions about the worth of each person, social justice, the universality of fundamental principles, duties to others, the responsibilities of governments and the need to protect the individual against the abuse of power by the monarch, the tyrant or the state. The philosophical concept of natural law, for example, eventually included the belief that all humans were endowed with certain natural rights. These existed independently of any political power or authority, and could serve as a standard or measuring rod against which the practices of any regime could be judged. Such natural rights might include life, liberty, the ownership of property, freedom of expression, religious toleration, freedom against torture or cruel and unusual punishment, representative government and free elections, among other civil and political rights. During the nineteenth century, social and economic rights began to be added to this list. In addition, and of particular importance to those who would work so long toward an international criminal court, philosophical belief increasingly argued on behalf of the rule of law and equal protection under the law to limit the power of government leaders and to protect individuals from human rights abuse.

None of these religious or philosophical beliefs, of course, existed in a vacuum; they became manifested in the lives of individual human beings. These were the courageous men and women who refused to accept the prevailing cultures of abuse and impunity of their time, who envisioned a world in which all people enjoyed certain basic rights simply on the basis of being members of the same human family, who believed that they had a responsibility to others, and who refused to be silent in the face of abuse. They resisted falling prey to fear or intimidation by fierce and determined opposition, to scepticism or cynicism generated by the imperfections in humankind and society, or to the notion that they some-how had meekly to accept the world as it was. Instead, they believed that they could make a difference and were willing to make sacrifices and suffer – sometimes at the cost of their lives – for something beyond themselves on behalf of visions of human rights in which they truly believed. Some occupied positions of government leadership; others worked as revolutionaries. Some used their knowledge of the law; others used their skill of the street. Some became famous for their role in dra-matic transformations and led others, whereas most remained largely unknown and served as what Eleanor Roosevelt called "everyday people" who worked on behalf of human rights where they lived and worked in their local neighbourhoods, schools, factories or offices.[6] Without all of these men and women, the advancements in human rights would never have occurred. As anthropologist Margaret Mead once poignantly observed: "Do not make the mistake of thinking that con-cerned people cannot change the world; it is the only thing that ever has."[7]

Still another transforming force was technology. Advances in trans-portation, for example, increasingly began to shrink the world, bringing people closer together and making natural barriers and national borders less important than they had been in the past. Technological develop-ments in weaponry, of course, made killing, oppression and torture even easier; but the resulting horror in turn forced many to commit themselves to defending the sanctity of human life in the face of massive abuses as never before. The technology of communication played a particularly critical role, for it enabled human rights abuses in one part of the world to be known elsewhere. Throughout history, tyrants thrived on darkness, knowing full well that they could largely control or suppress information and that any news about exploitation, conquest, massacre or other abuses could emerge only well after the fact. As one observer noted, "In the old days, news travelled slowly; one scarcely heard what was happening at the other end of the world until the following year. If blood had been spilt, the earth had time to absorb it; if tears had been shed, the sun had time to dry them."[8] This began to change dramatically as the level of awareness of human suffering increased as never before, with mass cir-culation newspapers, print photography, images captured and conveyed by television and, more recently, hand-held video cameras, fax machines, intelligence-gathering satellites and the images and information about human rights violations made instantly available to the world by means of computer technology and the Internet.[9]

Conflict in wars, revolutions and other upheavals provided yet another critical force in transforming the international protection of human rights. All of these events demonstrate the capacity to destroy existing structures of authority, privilege, vested interests and certain claims of national sovereignty. Violence and upheaval tear power away from those unwilling to share it voluntarily, thus opening up new possibilities to make changes previously imagined only in dreams. They may enable, encourage or even force the survivors to re-evaluate the limitations of established ways of thinking and previously accepted values, and to consider new possibilities of what might be and how people ought to treat each other. Upheavals often compel those who lived through them to test their assumptions and seriously consider the legitimacy of existing authority, the purposes of government and claims of national sovereignty, and the degree to which individuals should enjoy certain basic human rights in the future. This is what UN Secretary-General Boutros-Ghali had in mind when he observed: "It is always when the world is undergoing a metamorphosis, when certainties are collapsing, when the lines are becoming blurred, that there is greatest recourse of fundamental reference points, that the quest for ethics becomes more urgent, that the will to achieve self-understanding becomes imperative."[10]

Finally, one of the most important forces of transformation – and perhaps the most tragically ironic – has been gross human atrocities. Tremendous suffering, horrific brutality, massive torture, widespread murder and genocide, and extremely brutal persecution have revealed just how cruel people can be to others in absolutely shocking ways that defy the imagination. These are monstrous, heinous crimes, and the fact that they can be conceived of and committed diminishes us all as human beings. They have demonstrated perhaps as nothing else could the consequences of apathy, of ignoring human rights abuses or of allowing leaders to hide behind a shield of national sovereignty and a culture of impunity. Time and time again, those men and women either eagerly or reluctantly involved with the evolution of international human rights have spoken of this feature and its power to force an individual and collective crossing of a moral threshold sufficient to provoke outrage; hence the often-heard expressions in reaction to overwhelming abuses of "global moral opinion", "the conscience of the international community" and "the conscience of mankind".[11]

All of these forces combined to play profound roles in launching a revolution in international human rights and thereby shifting a culture of impunity toward a culture of accountability. Pioneering efforts in the nineteenth century initiated work to free the enslaved, to assist the exploited, to care for the wounded, to create humanitarian law and to protect those persecuted for their beliefs. With the turn of the twentieth century and then the creation of the League of Nations and the International Labour Organization, those who struggled on behalf of human rights established minority treaties, instituted mechanisms to assist refugees and openly debated the rights of women, children and indigenous peoples. In the wake of World War II and the Holocaust, these were followed by the monumental proclamations of the Charter of the United Nations, the standards established by the Universal Declaration of Human Rights and the International Convention on the Prevention and Punishment of the Crime of Genocide. The momentum continued with a whole series of treaties and treaty-monitoring mechanisms created with the International Convention on the Elimination of All Forms of Racial Discrimination, the International Covenant on Civil and Political Rights, the International Covenant on Economic, Social and Cultural Rights, the International Convention on the Elimination of All Forms of Discrimination Against Women, the International Convention Against Torture, and the International Convention on the Rights of the Child, among others. Each of these important steps indicated a willingness to examine dark places and practices in the world as never before, to confront evils long taken for granted, to explore and expand definitions of human rights, to establish universal standards, to create political precedents, to develop international law and mechanisms for practical enforcement, and to devise special procedures and technical assistance in order to provide international protection to those who suffered from human rights abuses. Throughout this entire process, members of the global community indicated their growing willingness seriously to challenge the traditional boundaries of national sovereignty and domestic jurisdiction. In so doing, they created a context that enabled them to address the difficult issue of international criminal tribunals and human rights protection.

The foundations of international criminal tribunals and human rights protection

The idea of establishing an international court to judge national leaders and others as being individually responsible for gross violations of human rights and international crimes was initiated during the nineteenth century. For example, one of the founders of the International Committee of the Red Cross, Gustav Moynier, who was motivated by his strong Christian convictions, issued a public call for an international tribunal as a means of protecting individuals from the horrors of war.[12] Serious government attention, however, occurred only during World War I. Indeed, shortly after the outbreak of hostilities, people in Allied countries urged that the major enemy soldiers and leaders, especially Kaiser Wilhelm II of Germany, should be brought before an international tribunal and punished as war criminals.[13] As early as October 1914, for example, one writer declared in a thoughtful essay on the evolution of the laws of war:

The thinkers of Europe must combine to find some sanction for the principles of international law; must make it clear that civilization does not ultimately rest upon Might but upon Right ... In particular the dignity and authority of international law must be asserted by the setting up of a judicial tribunal to deal with the men responsible for the invasion of Belgian neutrality. The invasion of Belgium was not an "act of war" but a criminal act, and the nations of the world must devise means to bring the authors of such acts to trial and punishment.[14]

Outrage over the invasion of neutral Belgium and then of neutral Luxembourg was only intensified by subsequent reports of executions of hostages, the sacking of Louvain, U-boat sinkings of passenger ships, Zeppelin bombing attacks against cities with considerable loss of civilian life, and the forced deportation of more than 60,000 Belgian civilians for forced labour in Germany. Added to these atrocities were the many deaths in the twentieth century's first genocide: the massacre of perhaps 1 million Armenians by the Turks.[15] All these acts appeared to break the established bounds of what was called "civilized behaviour", as well as the evolving body of "laws of humanity", and they threatened to destroy initial advances made at the Hague Peace Conferences in the development of international law as a protector of human rights and a deterrent to international violence. Moreover, and very importantly, there began to be a growing awareness of the fact that, just as victims are not abstract entities but real and specific individual people, so too the perpetrators of abuses are not abstract entities of the state but real and specific individuals. Consequently, both public opinion and government authorities began to take serious interest in determining which individuals might have been guilty of causing such slaughter, in bringing them to trial, and in punishing them if necessary.

The British government, for example, appointed its own Committee of Inquiry into the Breaches of the Laws of War, which recommended that "an international tribunal should be established ... for the trial and punishment of the ex-Kaiser as well as other offenders against the laws and customs of war and the laws of humanity".[16] Then, upon the insistence of David Lloyd George of Britain and Georges Clemenceau of France, the issue of war crimes was the first item on the agenda when the Paris Peace Conference convened in January 1919, and this resulted in the creation of the Commission on the Responsibility of the Authors of the War and on Enforcement of Penalties composed of 15 distinguished international lawyers from 10 different countries. It numbered among its members two future judges of the Permanent Court of International Justice, three members of the Institut de Droit International and several editors of the world's three most important journals in international law. Its tasks were to explore allegations of criminal acts in offences against the laws and

customs of war, to consider whether launching a war of aggression constituted an international crime and whether national leaders could be
held personally accountable or culpable, and to draft a constitution and
procedures for an international tribunal appropriate to try the accused.[17]

After weeks of agonizing and often contentious work in struggling
through an attempt to change a culture, the members of the Commission
on Responsibility issued their final report. They provided examples of
the execution of hostages, rape, pillage, use of poison gas, murders and
massacres of civilians and prisoners of war, attacks on hospital ships, and
a long list of similar atrocities "to the eternal shame of those who committed them". Then they explicitly addressed the issue of "the alleged
immunity, and in particular the alleged inviolability, of a sovereign of a
state" from being held accountable for crimes, forcefully declaring their
"desire to state expressly that in the hierarchy of persons in authority,
there is no reason why rank, however exalted, should in any circumstances protect the holder of it from responsibility when that responsibility has been established before a properly constituted tribunal. This
extends even to heads of states ... If the immunity of a sovereign is
claimed ... it would involve laying down the principle that the greatest
outrages against the laws and customs of war and the laws of humanity, if
proved against him, could in no circumstances be punished. Such a conclusion would shock the conscience of civilized mankind."

The Commission therefore concluded: "All persons belonging to enemy
countries, however high their position may have been, without distinction
of rank, including Chiefs of States, who have been guilty of offenses
against the laws and customs of war or the laws of humanity, are liable to
criminal prosecution."[18] To accomplish this objective, the Commission
recommended a more extensive articulation of the laws of humanity and
the creation of an international tribunal.

Such conclusions and recommendations proved to be too radical a departure from the past culture of impunity, however. The United States, in
particular, strongly resisted establishing an international tribunal and
holding individual leaders accountable for their actions, arguing that this
would be a dangerous precedent that would inflict irreparable damage
upon national sovereignty. Secretary of State Robert Lansing, who served
on the Commission, strongly opposed such an unprecedented court "unknown in the practice of nations"; indeed, the views of his country dif-
fered "so fundamentally and so radically" from those of the majority that
he issued a formal dissent from the final report.[19] He argued that the
laws and principles of humanity vary with conscience and circumstance,
and for this reason they should be excluded from consideration in a court
of justice, especially one charged with the administration of criminal law.
Moreover, he believed that international law is based upon the powers of

the sovereign nation-state, which is ultimately bound by no rules except those to which it explicitly consents and is always free to resort to whatever means its leaders judge necessary to protect and advance its welfare. Lansing revealed his thinking about accountability beyond borders most clearly when he tellingly asserted: "The essence of sovereignty [is] the absence of responsibility."[20] This strongly held position at the Paris Peace Conference meant that the Treaty of Versailles did indeed contain a path-breaking provision for the creation of a tribunal to hold war criminals responsible for their actions (Article 227), but that, given the politics and diplomacy of the time, in practice it would never be implemented.[21] The same fate awaited Article 230 of the Treaty of Sèvres with Turkey, which provided the Allies with the right to designate a tribunal for the purpose of trying those persons accused of genocide against the Armenians.[22] As one careful observer notes, "the powerful states were not yet ready to restrict their own sovereignty".[23]

Nevertheless, the idea of developing a culture of accountability and creating some form of international criminal court could not be so easily silenced. Once the passions of vengeance calmed, and once the debate about what came to be called the *Kriegschuldfrage*, or War Guilt Question, raised enough doubts that other leaders might share in the blame for World War I,[24] a number of visionaries began to consider that the establishment of a tribunal might well be able to rise above mere "victors' justice" and actually advance reforms for world order and the protection of human rights. Thus, an Advisory Committee of Jurists met at The Hague in the summer of 1920 to frame the Statute of the Permanent Court of International Justice, as called for in the Covenant of the League of Nations, but further recommended the creation of a High Court of International Justice "to try crimes constituting a breach of international public order or against the universal law of nations".[25] In the following years, a dedicated group of international lawyers and scholars drafted statutes, wrote articles and books, and spoke publicly on behalf of the creation of an international criminal court with jurisdiction over "offences committed contrary to the laws of humanity", including Hugh Bellot of England, Henri Donnedieu de Vabres of France, Vespasian Pella of Romania, Nicolas Politis of Greece, Quintiliano Saldaña of Spain, Elihu Root of the United States and Walter Phillimore of South Africa.[26] In addition, they founded the Association Internationale de Droit Pénale, which became one of the principal forums in which to advance the study of an international court and to confront what Politis described as "the ingrained habit of centuries" – the culture of impunity.[27] Other draft statutes were adopted by non-governmental organizations (NGOs) such as the Inter-Parliamentary Union in 1925 and by scholarly bodies such as the International Law Association in 1926.[28] Similarly, and as a result of the shocking assassination of King Alexander of Yugoslavia and French Foreign Minister Louis Barthou in a terrorist attack, the League of Nations reached a ground-breaking decision in 1937 that an international code was an appropriate means of addressing a crime by adopting a Treaty for the Prevention and Punishment of Terrorism, and that an international tribunal was a suitable mechanism for enforcement by adopting a Convention for the Creation of an International Criminal Court to try terrorist offences.[29] Nevertheless, governments regarded all of these proposals as "very dangerous", too radical and too threatening to the culture of impunity and their claims of national sovereignty.[30] Not one state ratified the Convention for the international criminal court. As one legal expert observed: "The great Powers were thinking only of themselves and of safeguarding their own interests."[31] If any doubt existed about the persistent strength of the culture of impunity, it was answered by Adolf Hitler's statement to his generals in 1939:

I have put my death-head formations in place with the command relentlessly and without compassion to send into death many women and children of Polish origin and language. Only thus we can gain the living space that we need. Who after all is today speaking about the destruction of the Armenians?[32]

With attitudes such as this, it is not difficult to understand why no proposal for an international system of criminal justice was implemented. It would take the disaster of yet another world war and an unimaginable Holocaust to begin to make people and governments change their minds and their policies.

The overwhelming magnitude of the devastation, loss of life and unimaginable violations of human rights that emerged during the course of World War II brought about a revolution in thinking and acting on international human rights as never before in history. The offences were described by leading legal scholars as nothing short of "an orgy of inhuman brutalities"[33] and as "crimes of an enormity unprecedented by reason of the vast numbers of the victims and the capacity for evil of the actors, crimes of a gravity never before equalled because committed by the possessors of the sovereignty of states".[34] Those who lived through the horrifying experience increasingly began to believe that the war and the Holocaust demonstrated an intimate connection between respect for human rights on the one hand and peace and security on the other. That is, those states that grossly abused the rights of their own people were most likely to extend their policies beyond their own borders, using the instrument of war to violate the rights of their neighbours.[35] To address this matter, the members of the victorious coalition agreed not only to incorporate a commitment to promote and encourage respect for human rights and fundamental freedoms prominently within the Charter of the new United Nations, but also to create an International Military Tribunal for the trial of war criminals.[36] This time, the United States actively supported such a policy, particularly Secretary of War Henry Stimson, who argued that America's failure to support any kind of international criminal tribunal after the previous war had contributed to aggression and the unprecedented violation of human rights.[37] Thus, for the first time in history, international courts were established before the eyes of the world in both Nuremberg and Tokyo to try individual persons accused of crimes to commit conspiracy, crimes against the peace, war crimes and, an important new category, "crimes against humanity".[38]

"The wrongs which we seek to condemn and punish", declared Justice Robert Jackson, "have been so calculated, so malignant, and so devastating, that civilization cannot tolerate their being ignored, because it cannot survive their being repeated."[39] The horrifying evidence revealed at these trials simply beggared description and shocked the conscience of humankind. To make it even worse, the defendants claimed that they could not be held responsible. As Adolf Hitler's deputy, Hermann Goering, declared in response to accusations of crimes against humanity: "But that was our right! We were a sovereign state and that was strictly our business."[40] Such claims had worked in the past culture of immunity, but now sounded increasingly hollow and obsolete. They certainly did not persuade the members of the tribunal who passed judgment against the accused individuals. In doing so, however, the judges remained acutely aware of the critical precedents they were setting for the future of international criminal jurisdiction. As Justice Jackson poignantly declared:

We must never forget that the record on which we judge these defendants today is the record on which history will judge us tomorrow. To pass these defendants a poisoned chalice is to put it to our own lips as well. We must summon such detachment and intellectual integrity to our task that this Trial will commend itself to posterity as fulfilling humanity's aspirations to do justice ... [T]he ultimate step ... is to make statesmen responsible to law. And let me make clear that while this law is first applied against German aggressors, the law includes, and if it is to serve a useful purpose it must condemn aggression by any other nations, including those which sit here now in judgment. We are able to do away with domestic tyranny and violence and aggression by those in power against the rights of their own people only when we make all men answerable to the law.[41]

With this objective in mind, the judgments at Nuremberg, and those that followed from the Tokyo trials, made clear that international law applies to all individuals waging war, from the lowest foot-soldier to the highest government official. It places strict limits on the scope of many defences against war crimes punishments, including superior orders, military necessity or acts of sovereign states. It declares aggression, now described as "crimes against peace", to be a violation of international law, for which guilty individual leaders must bear legal responsibility. In addition, it confirms that specific individuals must also be held responsible for any violations of the new category of offences known as "crimes against humanity", which include murder, extermination and enslavement.[42] These judicial decisions, despite their flaws,[43] began to lay the foundation for a new order in international penal law and thereby marked a profound turning point in transforming a culture of impunity into a culture of accountability.

Recent developments concerning international criminal tribunals and human rights protection

An international momentum thus began to build, as demonstrated by the considerable efforts increasingly taking place within the newly created United Nations. The initial principles of international penal law set down at Nuremberg holding individuals personally responsible for their actions, for example, quickly received the unanimous approval of the very first General Assembly. But the members also recognized that, if these war crimes trials were to be more than mere vengeance of the victors, it was "a matter of primary importance" that they lead toward a broader code of international crimes and a system of jurisdiction to deal with similar offences whenever they might occur.[44] To accomplish this objective, the General Assembly appointed a Committee on the Progressive Development of International Law and Its Codification, which recommended that a special International Law Commission develop a criminal code and advised that protection against international crimes required not only a code but also an international judicial authority.[45] The General Assembly did not stop there, and went on in 1948 to approve the ground-breaking and monumental Universal Declaration of Human Rights, establishing what Eleanor Roosevelt described as a common standard valid "for all peoples and all nations"[46] and proclaiming "that human rights should be protected by the rule of law".[47] At the same time, the members of the General Assembly reinforced the idea of an international criminal court to provide protection against violations of human rights by adopting the Convention on the Prevention and Punishment of the Crime of Genocide, providing that persons charged with genocide should be tried either by a tribunal in the state where the act was committed "or by such international penal tribunal as may have jurisdiction with respect to those contracting parties which shall have accepted its jurisdiction".[48] The following year, four Geneva Conventions were adopted, elaborating humanitarian law dealing with the amelioration of the condition of the sick and the wounded, the treatment of prisoners of war and, most innovatively, the protection of civilian populations in time of war.[49] Jean Graven of Switzerland perhaps best summarized the prevailing belief in all of this activity when he concluded:

As long as there is no judicial organ for the trial of international crimes, there will be neither a serious codification of international criminal law nor any serious application of an international sanction. The world will go on living in a judicial anarchy under violence and injustice with the risk of running into destruction.[50]

With this in mind, the United Nations International Law Commission met in hopeful anticipation to formulate the Nuremberg principles, to draft a code of offences and to consider the possibility of establishing an international judicial system for the trial of persons charged with genocide or other crimes. The 15 experts representing the principal legal systems of the world who served on the Commission concluded that the creation of an international criminal court was not only possible and desirable but "necessary".[51] In response, the General Assembly established a Special Committee to prepare concrete proposals for the creation of an international criminal court. Nevertheless, those who worked so hard on these efforts quickly discovered what others both before and since have learned: the advancement of international human rights has always been conditioned by the political climate of the times and by the extent to which governments are willing to submit their own actions to the scrutiny, control or sanction of any independent international authority beyond their own borders.[52] With the emergence of the Cold War and the absolute refusal of its major antagonists to subject themselves to any limitations on their national sovereignty or to outside criticism of their own records on human rights, efforts to create an international criminal court, like all other efforts of the time to establish standards and protect international human rights, came to a grinding halt.

It was only with the emergence of several powerful forces of transformation that this deadlock began to weaken. The vision proclaimed by the Universal Declaration of Human Rights inspired activists within an ever-growing number of NGOs to increase their public pressure on governments and on the United Nations for action rather than simply words. The creation of the European Court of Human Rights in 1959 provided a concrete example that a jurisdictional system transcending national borders and enabling individuals to call governments, including their own, to account for human rights violations could in fact be established.[53] Highly embarrassing television and photographic images, sent around the world, of violence against those who struggled for equality, and then a few actual successes of the civil rights movement, began to change the attitudes of at least some American policy makers toward efforts to enhance international human rights. Of particular importance was the advent of the most powerful and revolutionary developments of the entire twentieth century: the collapse of colonial empires and the emergence of newly independent nations and peoples. Decolonization dramatically transformed the majority within the United Nations, and thereby significantly changed the character, tone, language and much of the agenda of the organization itself. The new majority's passionate concern for the right of self-determination and the right of racial equality made its members determined to mobilize the United Nations in such a way as to break the deadlock that had immobilized the entire process of advancing international human rights.[54]

The results could be seen immediately. The General Assembly adopted the remarkable International Convention on the Elimination of All Forms of Racial Discrimination in 1965, which included the creation of the first international machinery for any UN-sponsored human rights instrument to implement compliance with the treaty itself.[55] This was followed the next year by the historic International Covenant on Civil and Political Rights and the International Covenant on Economic, Social and Cultural Rights.[56] Unwilling to stop there, the General Assembly went on in 1968 to adopt and open for signature the Convention on the Non-Applicability of Statutory Limitations to War Crimes and Crimes Against Humanity.[57] They continued in 1973 with the International Convention on the Suppression and the Punishment of the Crime of Apartheid, dealing with the highly emotional issue of race, declaring that apartheid "is a crime against humanity" and establishing particular mechanisms to implement its provisions and punish those determined to be guilty.[58] This was followed in 1974 by the approval of a Consensus Definition of Aggression and a renewed agreement to consider a permanent international criminal jurisdiction.[59]

Other events and activities occurred outside the meeting rooms of the United Nations. In September 1969, for example, an American Army lieutenant by the name of William Calley, Jr. was charged by the US Army with the murder of over 100 Vietnamese civilians in a little hamlet known as My Lai. Yet the failure to have more meaningful trials was widely condemned abroad as both shallow and hypocritical. When critics loudly proclaimed that the United States had failed to practise in Viet Nam the lessons it had sought to teach the rest of the world during the trials at Nuremberg and Tokyo,[60] the need for an impartial international tribunal to deal with war crimes again became a matter of considerable global attention. This stimulated a number of distinguished legal scholars to create the non-governmental organization Foundation for the Establishment of an International Criminal Court and to lend their expertise to the drafting of a statute for such a court.[61]

All these efforts received unexpected assistance when the Cold War, which had dominated international politics for more than 40 years, finally ended. The fall of the Iron Curtain and the collapse of the Soviet Union dramatically changed both geo-political power structures and attitudes. For example, within just a few weeks of the "Velvet Revolution" and the opening of the Berlin Wall, the General Assembly of the United Nations requested the International Law Commission, when considering a Draft Code of Crimes Against the Peace and Security of Mankind, "to address the question of establishing an international criminal court or other international criminal trial mechanism with jurisdiction over persons alleged to have committed crimes which may be covered under such a code of crimes".[62] The end of the Cold War brought developments in other and often unanticipated ways. For instance, by eliminating those forces that had imposed a particular order upon much of the world, regional conflicts previously held in check now became more likely. The resulting abuses of human rights shocked the world, in particular with the Iraqi invasion of Kuwait and the disintegration of Yugoslavia, and thereby gave even further stimulus to efforts to create an international criminal court.

In August 1990, Iraq under the leadership of Saddam Hussein deliberately launched an armed invasion against unsuspecting Kuwait. The technology of communication quickly revealed horrifying violations of human rights, including hostage-taking, torture, rape, executions and murder of civilians. Widespread revulsion against this aggression and these war crimes was exacerbated by subsequent reports of crimes against humanity, specifically extensive genocide against Iraqi Kurds within Iraq itself. In response, the United Nations Security Council announced that such violations of human rights could no longer be regarded as simply an internal matter by adopting Resolution 688, which directly condemned the Iraqi government for the repression of the civilian population within its own country and explicitly declared that these abuses constituted threats to international peace and security.[63] A number of national leaders began to refer to the precedents of Nuremberg and Tokyo, calling for some kind of a trial of Saddam Hussein.[64] Others were more specific, including the Council of Ministers of the European Communities, which sent a letter to United Nations Secretary-General Pérez de Cuéllar expressing its opinion that "the brutality of the repression and the unprecedented scale of the movement of refugees demand of us that we not content ourselves with mere words in our condemnation of the Iraqi regime". Toward this end, it asked for an examination of "the question of the

personal responsibility of the Iraqi leaders in the tragedy that is unfolding, in particular on the basis of the Convention against Genocide and
the possibility of trying them before an international court".[65] In this regard, the president of the Council of Ministers saw clearly that egregious
cases of human rights abuses, such as these by Saddam Hussein, force the
international community once again to confront the basic conflict of
moving from a culture of impunity to a culture of accountability:

[T]he tragedy that is being acted out at the moment has potential – and this,
unfortunately, is perhaps the only positive aspect – for generating new thinking
that can enhance the quality of international law by making breakthroughs into
areas that have hitherto been barred to it in the name of the sacrosanct principle
of total respect for the territorial integrity of a State.[66]

This vision attracted even greater attention when, at the same time, the
country of Yugoslavia began to disintegrate. With the fall of communist
regimes all around them and the resulting new opportunities for change,
four of the republics declared their independence from the Serbian-
dominated government in 1990–1991. The Yugoslav leader Slobodan
Milosevic called upon ethnic Serbs, especially those living in Croatia and
Bosnia-Herzegovina and including Radovan Karadzic, the self-proclaimed
president of the Serbian Bosnian Republic, to engage aggressively in
armed resistance to this development, to protect themselves and to extend Serbian influence. A civil war ensued that would last for years,
leaving hundreds of thousands of innocent victims in its wake, including
a reported 7,000 Muslim men and boys deliberately exterminated in
Srebrenica, brutalized in an orgy of violence by all sides, unspeakable
atrocities, and genocide described as "ethnic cleansing". Even before the
extensive horrors began, calls rang out for an international criminal tribunal. In a farsighted and courageous essay entitled "Nuremberg Now!"
in the Belgrade newspaper *Borba*, for example, Mirko Klarin wrote that
his own leaders were launching war, calling for mass atrocities and inciting ethnic, religious and racial hatred. Would it not be better, he asked,
"if our big and small leaders were made to sit in the dock instead of at
the negotiating table? And if, with the help of world-famous experts in
international laws of war, we had a Nuremberg Trial of our own, no
matter how small and modest? Not *when* 'this is all over', but *instead of*
whatever might soon befall us. Precisely because of what has already
happened and what is happening now, all of which can quite easily be
shown to be punishable under the terms of the Nuremberg judgment and
other legal documents just as valid here at home as in the rest of the
world."[67]

As widespread media coverage of gross human rights atrocities sent both words and images around the world, and as the terror continued, ever larger numbers of people began to realize the desperate need for an international criminal court. To allow those responsible for these actions to hide behind claims of national sovereignty and avoid prosecution, they reasoned, was the same as condoning their crimes and failing to provide any deterrent to future abuses. As one thoughtful participant explained his thinking:

Confronted by the scope of crimes against humanity and the war crimes being committed ... I was among those who, from the outset, felt that collective conscience could not accept the notion of persons responsible for such crimes in the very heart of Europe half a century after the Second World War going unpunished ... I considered this a real insult to collective conscience and a retreat from the Nuremberg trials.[68]

A number of individuals thus came forward publicly to propose such a court, including the German Foreign Minister, Klaus Kinkel, the French Foreign Minister, Roland Dumas, and human rights advocate Elie Wiesel. Others advocated a criminal court to protect human rights and uphold the rule of law through regional organizations such as the Conference on Security and Co-operation in Europe (CSCE). They based their efforts on the Moscow Declaration, affirming that they "categorically and irrevocably declare that the commitments undertaken in the field of the human dimension of the CSCE are matters of direct and legitimate concern to all participating states and *do not belong exclusively to the internal affairs of the state concerned*".[69] Following a strong recommendation from a special Commission of Experts, the United Nations Security Council unanimously declared in 1993 that it was "*determined to put an end to such crimes and to take effective measures to bring to justice the persons who are responsible for them*" and resolved to establish an international tribunal to prosecute individuals for serious violations of international humanitarian law committed in the territory of the former Yugoslavia.[70] The result was the creation of the first international court since the Nuremberg and Tokyo trials. The path-breaking International Criminal Tribunal for the former Yugoslavia was located in The Hague and given authority to prosecute and try grave breaches of the 1949 Geneva Conventions, violations of the laws or customs of war, genocide and crimes against humanity, including, for the first time, sexual violence and the rape of women.[71]

This action established not only a precedent but also a momentum that made it much easier for members of the international community to respond to other catastrophic human rights crises. Little did they understand, however, just how soon this might occur. Indeed, in the very next year (1994), violence in Rwanda rapidly escalated into genocide and other systematic, widespread and flagrant violations of human rights. Hutu extremists embarked on a killing spree and, within a period of only three months, more than a half million Tutsis and moderate Hutus were killed in a developing country that did not possess technologically sophisticated weapons of "mass destruction". A special rapporteur for Rwanda from the United Nations Commission on Human Rights confirmed the worst media reports, and photographs of the brutality and the loss of innocent lives shocked consciences around the world. The Security Council – already committed to action over Yugoslavia, convinced that violations of human rights threatened international peace and increasingly willing to become more active with the end of the Cold War – lost little time in adopting a resolution to create the International Criminal Tribunal for Rwanda. Tellingly, the language of the resolution reiterated that members of the international community finally were "*determined* to put an end to such crimes and to take effective measures to bring to justice the persons who are responsible for them".[72] The resulting trials produced a number of important precedents and decisions, not the least of which was the official conviction of former Prime Minister Jean Kambanda, marking the first time that any head of government had ever been convicted and punished by an international criminal court for genocide and crimes against humanity.[73] As Secretary-General Kofi Annan said at the time, "There can be no healing without peace; there can be no peace without justice; and there can be no justice without respect for human rights and the rule of law."[74]

With these thoughts and successes in mind, members of the global community, international legal experts and human rights activists increasingly began to believe that the world simply could not continue indefinitely going from one human rights crisis to another, creating ad hoc criminal tribunals for each specific case only if and when unique political forces allowed it. They knew perfectly well that tyrants such as Pol Pot of Cambodia, Idi Amin of Uganda and Augusto Pinochet of Chile had never faced trial for heinous human rights abuses. As British Foreign Secretary Robin Cook observed, the ultimate paradox of criminal behaviour in the past century was that those who murdered one person were "more likely to be brought to justice than those who plot genocide against millions".[75] Consequently, it was argued that genuine respect for human rights, the rule of law and the value of a deterrent against future abuses would occur only if governments established a permanent international criminal court in advance. Thus, the General Assembly acknowledged the considerable interest of the international community in this matter and decided in 1995 to create a Preparatory Commission to carefully study the draft statute for the establishment of an international criminal court, prepared over the course of several years by the International Law Commission.[76] Support was so strong by this stage that governments quickly reached an agreement to convene the extraordinary United Nations Diplomatic Conference of Plenipotentiaries on the Establishment of an International Criminal Court.[77]

In June 1998, the representatives of more than 150 nation-states met in Rome to discuss the proposed independent and permanent international criminal court. Their arduous and often contentious negotiations revealed the continuing clash between those who believed in a culture of impunity and those who believed in the need to establish a new culture of accountability. To create ad hoc tribunals for Yugoslavia and Rwanda was one thing – these tribunals applied only to *others*, whereas this tribunal could apply to *them*. Some governments feared that such a court might be used for political purposes to try their own leaders and soldiers of crimes and therefore were unwilling to take the risk of being held accountable before the eyes of the world. The vast majority, on the other hand, argued that times and attitudes had changed dramatically, that they no longer accepted the unqualified claims of national sovereignty to shield individuals from responsibility, and that an independent, permanent, international criminal court was necessary to protect human rights, to facilitate the rule of law, to deter abuses and to establish international peace and justice. Interestingly enough, they began by reflecting upon the lessons they had learned from the past, noting that they were

Mindful that during this century millions of children, women, and men have been victims of unimaginable atrocities that deeply shock the conscience of humankind,

Recognizing that such grave crimes threaten the peace, security, and well-being of the world,

Affirming that the most serious crimes of concern to the international community as a whole must not go unpunished and that their effective prosecution must be ensured ...

Determined to put an end to impunity for the perpetrators of these crimes and thus to contribute to the prevention of such crimes.[78]

Following intense debate over the course of marathon sessions, the final vote revealed the support of 120 nations, the abstention of 21 and the opposition of 7.[79] Thus, the delegates adopted the landmark Rome Statute of the International Criminal Court, declaring their intention to try specific *individuals* – not states – for war crimes, genocide and crimes against humanity, including newly codified sexual and gender crimes.

They invited all states to ratify the treaty and thereby finally realize the vision of the first permanent international framework to end impunity for crimes.[80]

Visions, reality and historical perspective

The reactions to the signing of the Rome Statute of the International Criminal Court reveal much about the whole process of the evolution of international human rights in terms of visions, reality and historical perspective. Many viewed the statute as moving the world one step closer to a dream come true after decades of effort on behalf of human rights protection. They saw it as a confirmation of the power of visions to inspire, and they responded with an enormous sense of triumphal accomplishment. Some considered the statute with caution, scepticism and/or disappointment, drawing attention to the politicization of the process, the mixed motives of the participants and the flaws that allowed states an "opt out" clause to put themselves beyond the reach of the court, restricted the court's jurisdiction, or otherwise limited state cooperation in ways to produce selective or uneven prosecutions. Still others responded with anger and resentment, viewing the treaty as a threat to their government's national sovereignty and vowing that they would never ratify its terms or be a part of a culture of accountability if the restrictions applied to them. One American senator, for example, expressed the hope "that now the Administration will actively oppose this court to make sure that it shares the same fate as the League of Nations and collapses without US support, for this court truly, I believe, is the monster and it is the monster that we need to slay".[81]

Such reactions have been a part of every international agreement ever negotiated on the subject of human rights, particularly when involving the issue of international criminal courts.[82] Part of the clash between visions of what *might be* and the reality of what *is* has always been the clash between cultures – the culture of impunity and the culture of accountability. Human rights abuses still occur, much remains to be done and many practical problems call for resolution. Indeed, other chapters in this book address precisely some of these matters, including the legal basis and jurisdiction of the international war tribunals and the International Criminal Court, the position of the victim, rules of procedure and evidence, the continuing contest between national sovereignty and international jurisdiction, and possible alternatives.

When considering all these factors, however, it is extremely important to view the accomplishments of the past as well as the tasks ahead from a historical perspective. The evolution of international standards and institutions for human rights has always proceeded in gradual steps, depending upon what was possible at the time. Each step marked a willingness to examine dark places and practices as never before, to confront evils or challenge authority long taken for granted, to expand definitions of human rights, to establish universal standards and norms, and to develop international law and jurisdiction for practical enforcement to provide protection for those who suffer from abuse. As a result of those several powerful forces of transformation – ranging from religious to political belief, courageous individuals, technology, wars and revolutions, and catastrophic human tragedies – a tremendous amount has been accomplished. Never before have human rights been such a part of the political, social, economic, legal or moral landscape or played such an important role in world affairs. Never before have the claims of national sovereignty been so seriously challenged or has there been such open discussion about universal standards and international jurisdiction.[83] Never before has the development of the rule of law and international criminal courts done so much both to protect individual victims against violations of human rights and to punish individual perpetrators responsible for such abuses. As a consequence, and from the perspective of history, this whole process of transformation offers dramatic confirmation of the capacity of humans to change and to move from an entrenched culture of impunity toward a new and evolving culture of accountability for the purpose of providing international protection for human rights.

Notes

1. Jean Bodin, *Les Six Livres de la République* [1576], 6 vols., Paris: Fayard, vol. 1, pp. 179–228 and 295–310.
2. Thomas Hobbes, *Leviathan* [1651], London: Penguin, 1985, pp. 236 and 232.
3. Hans Morgenthau, *Politics among Nations: The Struggle for Power and Peace*, New York: Knopf, 1978, p. 315. See also René Brunet, *La Garantie internationale des droits de l'homme*, Geneva: Grasset, 1947, pp. 29ff.
4. Theory is sometimes modified in practice and exceptions occasionally occur, as in 1474 when an ad hoc criminal tribunal composed of 28 judges from Alsace, Germany, Switzerland and Austria tried and convicted Peter von Hagenbach for rape, murder and other crimes in violation of what they called "the laws of God and man" during his occupation of the town of Breisach.
5. For more discussion about these various forces, see Paul Gordon Lauren, *The Evolution of International Human Rights: Visions Seen*, Philadelphia: University of Pennsylvania Press, 1998, passim.
6. Eleanor Roosevelt, as cited in Blanche Wiesen Cook, "Eleanor Roosevelt and Human Rights", in Edward Crapol, ed., *Women and American Foreign Policy*, Wilmington, Del.: Scholarly Resources Books, 1992, p. 114.
7. Margaret Mead, as cited in Lauren, *The Evolution of International Human Rights*, p. 1.

8. Madame de Gasparin, as cited in Pierre Boissier, *From Solferino to Tsushima*, Geneva: Henry Dunant Institute, 1985, p. 344.

9. See, among others, the websites for Amnesty International (www.amnesty.org); Human Rights Internet (www.hri.ca); and Human Rights Watch (www.hrw.org).

10. Boutros Boutros-Ghali, 14 June 1993, as cited in UN Publication DPI/1394/Rev.1/HR, *World Conference on Human Rights*, p. 6.

11. See, among many examples, William Ewart Gladstone, *Lessons of the Massacre*, London: Murray, 1877, passim; National Archives of New Zealand, EA 2, File 108/11/13/1 (4), memorandum entitled "The Problem of Implementation", 1 December 1949; the Universal Declaration of Human Rights, Preamble; United Nations General Assembly, *Official Records*, Plenary Meetings, 1966, Meeting of 16 December 1966; and H. Gordon Skilling, *Charter 77 and Human Rights in Czechoslovakia*, London: Allen & Unwin, 1981, p. 153.

12. Gustav Moynier, "Note sur la création d'une institution judiciaire internationale", *Bulletin international*, vol. 11, 1872. Other suggestions for an international court began to emerge in the second half of the nineteenth century from writers such as Pasquale Fiore and from conferences such as the Hague Peace Conference of 1899 in an effort to establish some form of jurisdiction over violations of the developing laws and customs of war, but states continued to resist any form of compulsory arbitration or adjudication that might restrict their sovereignty. See Benjamin Ferencz, *An International Criminal Court*, 2 vols., London: Oceana, 1980, vol. 1, pp. 4–20.

13. Other candidates openly discussed for trials before an international tribunal included the leaders of Turkey for alleged genocide against the Armenians and the leaders of Romania for alleged war crimes against German prisoners of war and interned civilians.

14. "Germany and the Laws of War", *Edinburgh Review*, 220, 297, October 1914.

15. See George Andreopoulos, ed., *Genocide: Conceptual and Historical Dimensions*, Philadelphia: University of Pennsylvania Press, 1994, p. 125; and V. N. Dadrian, "Genocide as a Problem of National and International Law: The World War I Armenian Case and Its Contemporary Legal Ramifications", *Yale Journal of International Law*, vol. 14, 1989.

16. "First Interim Report for the Committee of Inquiry into the Breaches of the Laws of War, 13 January 1919", in United Nations War Crimes Commission, *History of the United Nations War Crimes Commission*, London: United Nations War Crimes Commission, 1948, p. 435.

17. See the excellent discussion in James F. Willis, *Prologue to Nuremberg: The Politics and Diplomacy of Punishing War Criminals of the First World War*, Westport, Conn.: Greenwood, 1982.

18. Commission on the Responsibility of the Authors of the War and on Enforcement of Penalties, "Report Presented to the Preliminary Peace Conference", 29 March 1919, as reprinted in the *American Journal of International Law*, vol. 14, 1920, pp. 95–154, especially pp. 116–117.

19. "Memorandum of Reservations Presented by the Representatives of the United States to the Report of the Commission on Responsibilities", 4 April 1919, as reproduced in the *American Journal of International Law*, vol. 14, 1920, pp. 127–151.

20. Robert Lansing, as cited in Willis, *Prologue to Nuremberg*, p. 74.

21. For discussion about Article 227 and related Articles 228–230, see "Treaty of Versailles: Annotations of the Text", in United States, *Foreign Relations of the United States, Paris Peace Conference, 1919*, 13 vols., Washington, D.C.: Government Printing Office, 1942–1947, vol. 13, pp. 371–380. See also James Garner, "Punishment of Offenders against the Laws and Customs of War", *American Journal of International Law*, vol. 14, 1920, pp. 70–94; and, for the non-implementation of these provisions, see A. Mérignhac and E. Lémonon, *Le Droit des gens et la guerre de 1914–1918*, Paris: Tenin, 1921, pp. 580ff.

22. Treaty of Sèvres, Article 230, in Carnegie Endowment for International Peace, *The Treaties of Peace, 1919–1923*, 2 vols., New York: Carnegie Endowment, 1924, vol. 2, p. 863.

23. Ferencz, *An International Criminal Court*, vol. 1, p. 27.

24. See, among others, the monthly periodical edited by Alfred von Wegerer entitled *Die Kriegschuldfrage: Berliner Monatshefte für Internationale Aufklärung*; and Dwight Lee, ed., *The Outbreak of the First World War: Who Was Responsible?*, New York: Heath, 1963.

25. The texts can be found in Lord Phillimore, "An International Criminal Court and the Resolutions of the Committee of Jurists", *British Yearbook of International Law*, vol. 3, 1922–1923, pp. 79–86.

26. See, among many examples, Donnedieu de Vabres, "La Cour permanente de justice internationale et sa vocation en matière criminelle", *Revue internationale de droit pénal*, vol. 1, 1924, pp. 175–201; H. H. Bellot, "La Cour permanente internationale criminelle", *Revue internationale de droit pénal*, vol. 3, 1926, pp. 333–337; and Vespasian Pella, *La Criminalité collective des États et le droit pénal de l'avenir*, Bucharest: Imprimerie de l'État, 1926.

27. Nicolas Politis, as cited in Willis, *Prologue to Nuremberg*, p. 168.

28. See Union Interparlementaire, *Compte rendu de la XXIII conférence*, Paris: Payot, 1926; and International Law Association, *Report of the Thirty-Fourth Conference, "The Permanent International Criminal Court"*, London: Sweet & Maxwell, 1927.

29. Convention for the Creation of an International Criminal Court, in League of Nations, *Monthly Summary of the League of Nations*, vol. XVII, no. 11, November 1937, pp. 289–295.

30. See the position, for example, of Lord Robert Cecil of Britain, in Phillimore, "An International Criminal Court", p. 86.

31. As cited in Benjamin B. Ferencz, "Working Paper on an International Criminal Court", Madrid Conference on the Law of the World, World Peace Through World Law Center, 1979, p. 16.

32. Adolf Hitler to Chief Commanders and Commanding Generals, 22 August 1939, as reproduced in UK Foreign Office, *Documents on British Foreign Policy, 1919–1939*, Third Series, 9 vols., London: His Majesty's Stationery Office, 1949–1955, vol. 7, p. 258.

33. George A. Finch, "Retribution for War Crimes", *American Journal of International Law*, vol. 37, 1943, p. 81.

34. Vespasian Pella, "Towards an International Criminal Court", *American Journal of International Law*, vol. 44, 1950, p. 41.

35. For more on this important connection, see Lauren, *The Evolution of International Human Rights*, pp. 172–198.

36. See United Nations War Crimes Commission, *History of the United Nations War Crimes Commission and the Development of the Laws of War*, London: United Nations War Crimes Commission, 1948.

37. Bradley F. Smith, *The Road to Nuremberg*, New York: Basic Books, 1981, pp. 75–151 and 207–46.

38. See Bradley Smith, *Reaching Judgment at Nuremberg*, New York: New American Library, 1977; and Robert Woetzel, *The Nuremberg Trials in International Law*, London: Stevens, 1962.

39. Robert Jackson, 21 November 1945, in *The Trial of the Major War Criminals before the International Military Tribunal*, 42 vols., Nuremberg: International Military Tribunal, 1947–1949, vol. 2, pp. 98–99.

40. Hermann Goering, as cited in G. M. Gilbert, *Nuremberg Diary*, New York: New American Library, 1961, p. 39.

41. Robert Jackson, 21 November 1945, in *The Trial of the Major War Criminals*, vol. 2, pp. 101 and 154.
42. See *The Trial of the Major War Criminals*, vol. 1, pp. 218ff.; R. John Pritchard and Sonia M. Zaide, eds., *The Tokyo War Crimes Trial: The Complete Transcripts of the Proceedings of the International Military Tribunal for the Far East*, 22 vols. (+ 5 vols. of Index and Guide), New York: Garland, 1981–1987; and Willis, *Prologue to Nuremberg*, p. 175.
43. Among other examples, see the opinion of Justice R. B. Pal from India, in Ferencz, *An International Criminal Court*, vol. 1, pp. 527–538, as well as the excellent chapter in this volume by Michael Biddiss.
44. United Nations General Assembly, Resolution 95 (I), "Affirmation of the Principles of International Law Recognized by the Charter of the Nuremberg Tribunal", 11 December 1946.
45. United Nations General Assembly, Resolution 177 (II), "Formulation of the Principles Recognized in the Charter of the Nuremberg Tribunal", 21 November 1947; and UN Doc. A/332, "Plans for the Formation of the Principles of the Nuremberg Charter and Judgment: Report of the Committee on the Progressive Development of International Law and Its Codification", 21 July 1947.
46. Eleanor Roosevelt, as cited in "Searching Study of Human Rights Declaration", *United Nations Weekly Bulletin*, vol. 5, 1 November 1948, p. 858.
47. United Nations General Assembly, Resolution 217 A (III), "Universal Declaration of Human Rights", 10 December 1948.
48. United Nations General Assembly, Resolution A/RES/260 A (III), "Convention on the Prevention and Punishment of the Crime of Genocide", 9 December 1948.
49. See United Nations Archives/Geneva, SOA, Box 368, File 417/2/01; and Henri Coursier, "L'Evolution de droit international humanitaire", *Recueil des Cours de l'Académie de Droit International*, vol. 99, 1960, pp. 361–465.
50. Jean Graven, as cited in Vespasian Pella, "Towards an International Criminal Court", p. 47.
51. As cited in Ferencz, "Working Paper on an International Criminal Court", p. 29.
52. See Lauren, *The Evolution of International Human Rights*, passim.
53. See www.echr.coe.int.
54. For more discussion, see Lauren, *The Evolution of International Human Rights*, pp. 241–254; and Paul Gordon Lauren, *Power and Prejudice: The Politics and Diplomacy of Racial Discrimination*, San Francisco/Boulder: HarperCollins/Westview, 1996, pp. 197–250.
55. United Nations General Assembly, Resolution A/RES/2106 A (XX), "International Convention on the Elimination of All Forms of Racial Discrimination", 21 December 1965. See also Gerda Weinberger, *Gegen Rassismus und Rassendiskriminierung: Kampfdekade der UNO*, Berlin: Staatsverlag der DDR, 1976; and Marc Bossuyt, *L'Interdiction de la discrimination dans le droit international des droits de l'homme*, Brussels: Bruylant, 1976.
56. United Nations General Assembly, Resolution A/RES/2200 A (XXI), "International Covenant on Civil and Political Rights" and "International Covenant on Economic, Social, and Cultural Rights", 16 December 1966.
57. United Nations General Assembly, Resolution A/RES/2391 (XXIII), "Convention on the Non-Applicability of Statutory Limitations to War Crimes and Crimes Against Humanity", 26 November 1968.
58. United Nations Resolution A/RES/3068 (XXVIII), "International Convention on the Suppression and the Punishment of the Crime of Apartheid", 30 November 1973.
59. United Nations General Assembly, Resolution 3314 (XXIX), "Definition of Aggression", 14 December 1974.

60. See Jay W. Baird, ed., *From Nuremberg to My Lai*, Lexington, Mass.: Heath, 1972; and Joseph Goldstein et al., *The My Lai Massacre and Its Cover-up: Beyond the Reach of Law?*, New York: Free Press, 1976. It is also important to note that only the United States conducted such a war crimes trial against one of its own soldiers.
61. Ferencz, "Working Paper on an International Criminal Court", pp. 32–33.
62. United Nations General Assembly, Resolution 44/39, "International Criminal Responsibility of Individuals and Entities Engaged in Illicit Trafficking", 4 December 1989.
63. United Nations Security Council, Resolution S/RES/0688, 1991, "Resolution on the Situation between Iraq and Kuwait", 5 April 1991.
64. Among others, see George Bush, "Iraqi Atrocities in Kuwait", 15 October 1990, in US Department of State, *Department of State Dispatch*, vol. 1, no. 8, 22 October 1990, p. 205; and Margaret Thatcher, 1 September 1990, in *British Yearbook of International Law*, vol. 61, 1990, p. 602.
65. Letter from Jacques Poos from the Council of Ministers of the European Communities to Secretary-General Pérez de Cuéllar, 16 April 1991, as reproduced in International Criminal Tribunal for the Former Yugoslavia (ICTY), *The Path to the Hague: Selected Documents*, New York: United Nations, 1996, p. 15.
66. Jacques Santer, President-in-Office of the Council of Ministers of the European Communities, 17 April 1991, in ICTY, *The Path to the Hague*, p. 23.
67. Mirko Klarin, "Nuremberg Now!", *Borba*, as reproduced in ICTY, *The Path to the Hague*, p. 35.
68. Letter from Robert Badinter to Antonio Cassese, 24 May 1966, recounting his motives in 1992, as reproduced in ICTY, *The Path to the Hague*, p. 71
69. Conference on Security and Co-operation in Europe, *Document of the Moscow Meeting of the Conference on the Human Dimension of the CSCE*, Moscow: CSCE, 1991, p. 29 (emphasis added). I am very grateful to the staff of the Office of the Organization for Security and Co-operation in Europe in Prague for an appointment as a researcher-in-residence that allowed me to examine the human rights documents on this subject.
70. United Nations Security Council, Resolution S/RES/808, 1993, "Creation of an International Criminal Tribunal for the Former Yugoslavia", 22 February 1993; and United Nations Security Council, Resolution S/RES/827, 1993, "Creation of an International Criminal Tribunal for the Former Yugoslavia", 25 May 1993 (emphasis added).
71. See, among others, www.un.org/icty; Virginia Morris and Michael Scharf, eds., *An Insider's Guide to the International Criminal Tribunal for the Former Yugoslavia: A Documentary History and Analysis*, 2 vols., Ardsley, N.Y.: Transnational Publishers, 1995; the ongoing publication of André Klip and Göran Sluiter, eds., *Annotated Leading Cases of International Criminal Tribunals*, Antwerp: Intersentia, 1999– ; and, on the issue of sexual violence, BBC Report, "Rape: A Crime against Humanity", 22 February 2001.
72. United Nations Security Council, Resolution S/RES/955, 1994, "Establishment of an International Tribunal for Rwanda", 8 November 1994.
73. For more discussion, see Virginia Morris and Michael Scharf, eds., *An Insider's Guide to the International Criminal Tribunal for Rwanda*, 2 vols., Ardsley, N.Y.: Transnational Publishers, 1998; and Kingsley Chiedu Moghalu, "Rwanda Panel's Legacy: They Can Run But Not Hide", *International Herald Tribune*, 31 October–1 November 1998.
74. Kofi Annan, as cited at www.ictr.org, 31 October 2001.
75. BBC Report, "New World Court to Prosecute Tyrants", 20 July 1998.
76. United Nations General Assembly, Resolution 50/46, 1995, "Establishment of a Criminal Court", 11 December 1995.
77. United Nations General Assembly, Resolution 52/160, 1997, "Establishment of a Criminal Court", 15 December 1997.

78. *Rome Statute of the International Criminal Court, Preamble*, UN Doc. A/CONF.183/9, as reproduced at www.un.org/law/icc/statute.
79. Among those that voted "no" were China, Israel, Iraq and the United States.
80. See the homepage of the Rome Statute of the International Criminal Court at www.un. org/law/icc. The Rome Statute entered into force on 1 July 2002, after a minimum of 60 countries had ratified the treaty. See also the homepage of the Coalition for an International Criminal Court at www.iccnow.org.
81. Senator Rod Grams, as cited in John F. Murphy, "The Quivering Gulliver: U.S. Views on a Permanent International Criminal Court", *International Lawyer*, vol. 34, 2000, p. 45. See also Henry Kissinger, "The Pitfalls of Universal Jurisdiction", *Foreign Affairs*, vol. 80, 2001, pp. 86–96.
82. For some broad discussion, see Gary Jonathan Bass, *Stay the Hand of Vengeance: The Politics of War Crimes Tribunals*, Princeton, N.J.: Princeton University Press, 2000; Yves Beigbeder and Theo Van Boven, *Judging War Criminals: The Politics of International Justice*, Basingstoke: Palgrave, 1999; Jerome Ackerman, "The Proposed International Criminal Court", *The Washington Lawyer*, September 2001, pp. 37–40; and David Forsythe, "Politics and the International Tribunal for the Former Yugoslavia", in Roger Clark and Madeleine Sann, eds., *The Prosecution of International Crimes*, New Brunswick, N.J.: Transaction Publishers, 1996, pp. 185–206.
83. See the interesting and suggestive *The Princeton Principles on Universal Jurisdiction*, Princeton: Princeton University Program in Law and Public Affairs, 2001.

2

From the Nuremberg Charter to the Rome Statute: A historical analysis of the limits of international criminal accountability

Michael D. Biddiss

Early in the proceedings of the International Military Tribunal (IMT) at Nuremberg, the British alternate judge, Norman Birkett, wrote as follows: "This is supposed to be, and no doubt is, the greatest trial in history. The historian of the future will look back to it with fascinated eyes."[1] He was, of course, right. Yet the prediction might have been sharper still had he suggested that historians, and indeed lawyers too, would find themselves in the grip of a *haunted* fascination. Even after more than half a century, the Nuremberg trial continues to spook our consciousness. This is undoubtedly owing, in considerable measure, to the sheer horror of the record of Nazi criminality that was detailed in the courtroom. However, for the purpose of present discussions about the creation of a culture of accountability, this chapter will concentrate not so much on the evils of the Third Reich themselves as on the nature and the longer-term influence of the juridical response that these elicited from the principal victor powers of 1945. In essence, it will focus on those parts of Nuremberg's haunting legacy that are derived sometimes from the trial's weaknesses but, perhaps more surprisingly, quite often from its strengths as well. On the one hand, the proceedings contained flaws that, rightly, still trouble us. Yet, on the other, we remain no less disturbed by the painful slowness and incompleteness of the international community's progress towards exploiting the full potentiality of the many merits that also characterized the Nuremberg venture. And let it be added that our anxieties about such wasted opportunities can only have deepened since

11 September 2001, when further spectres were unleashed as much of the world witnessed, in real time through live television, the falling towers of Manhattan.

When we turn our gaze back to the 1940s, it might well seem that, granted the systematically murderous nature of the defeated Nazi regime, a full-scale trial of the surviving German leaders was entirely inevitable at the end of World War II. Yet this would be to misread entirely the much more tortuous history of the path to Nuremberg.[2] By 1942, the Allies were clearer about the need for punishment than about the means, political or judicial, by which it might be arrived at. The Moscow Declaration of November 1943 certainly made plain the determination of Roosevelt, Stalin and Churchill to ensure that, where criminal acts had a specific geographical ambit, the perpetrators would be "sent back to the countries in which their abominable deeds were done in order that they may be judged and punished according to the laws of these liberated countries and of the free governments that will be created therein"; however, where the offences of the major criminals transcended such localization, the processes leading to punishment were left more vaguely dependent on some future "joint decision" by the Allied powers.[3] During 1944, whatever might have been the case inside the more monolithic Kremlin (dominated by a dictator keener on trials than on justice *per se*), there was no agreed on policy within either the American or the British administrations about how to handle this second category of crimes. By the autumn it looked as though both Roosevelt and Churchill were increasingly inclined to support the "Morgenthau Plan", devised by the US Secretary of the Treasury, whose toughness in arguing for a de-industrialized post-war Germany spilled over into his preference for simple summary execution of the Nazi leadership cadre. On that legal front, it was not until early 1945 that the American President began to shift his favour towards the alternative approach embodied in the "Bernays Plan", devised during the previous September within the US Department of War.[4] Once this proposal concerning comprehensive judicial proceedings began to gain the upper hand in Washington, Churchill found himself facing combined American and Soviet pressure to mount a major trial conducted by some specially constituted international tribunal.

In London, there was particularly stout resistance from the head of the judiciary, Lord Chancellor Simon. Early in 1945, he was still standing by the advice he had given to the War Cabinet during the preceding September:

I am strongly of the opinion that the method by trial, conviction, and judicial sentence is quite inappropriate for notorious ringleaders such as Hitler, Himmler,

Goering, Goebbels, and Ribbentrop. Apart from the formidable difficulties of constituting the Court, formulating the charge, and assembling the evidence, the question of their fate *is a political, not a judicial, question*. It could not rest with judges, however eminent or learned, to decide finally a matter like this, which is of the widest and most vital public policy.[5]

This opposition to extensive legal hearings, as distinct from summary process, was almost certainly unwise in general terms. Yet, with reference to particulars, Simon's worries had substance enough to cast shadows over the conduct and legacy of the trial eventually mounted at Nuremberg. How counter-productive might be proceedings that risked becoming, for example, so unduly protracted, so reliant on patchy precedent and retroactive legal invention, or so tarnished by wrangles over defendants' attempts at launching *tu quoque* counter-charges? In essence, how large and indelible might the stain of mere "victors' justice" prove to be? The scale of the problems is suggested, not least, by the fact that – in the era of Andrei Vyshinsky's show trials and of such events as the Katyn massacre – the presence of Soviet judges and prosecutors was only marginally less unthinkable than their absence.[6]

Not until May 1945 – by which time Hitler was dead and victory in Europe had been assured – did the British government reluctantly signal its support for a full-scale trial that would owe much to what Geoffrey Robertson has called "a curious mixture of American idealism and Stalinist opportunism".[7] Under the new Truman presidency, a US delegation, headed by Justice Robert H. Jackson of the Supreme Court, was principally responsible for driving the project forward in such a way that by 8 August (ironically, the same week as the Hiroshima and Nagasaki bombings) a series of ground-rules had been settled through the so-called London Agreement. With France now included among the signatories, the resulting Charter created the four-power International Military Tribunal (IMT).[8] To this each government would appoint one judge plus an alternate, as well as supplying the court with prosecuting staff. The members of the tribunal soon chose the senior British nominee, Lord Justice Geoffrey Lawrence, to preside over hearings at Nuremberg, which eventually stretched from November 1945 to October 1946.[9] During their concluding judgment, he and his colleagues would encapsulate the IMT's claim to jurisdiction in an essentially dualist fashion: "The making of the charter was the exercise of the sovereign legislative power by the countries to which the German Reich unconditionally surrendered; and the undoubted right of these countries to legislate for the occupied territories had been recognized by the civilized world."[10] The latter point was reinforced by the fact that, alongside the "Big Four", 19 other governments had formally expressed adherence to the London

Agreement. The judges went on to claim that the Charter "is not an arbitrary exercise of power on the part of the victorious Nations, but ... the expression of international law at the time of its creation; and to that extent is itself a contribution to international law".[11]

As Simon had anticipated, the precedents for the kind of venture now beginning in Nuremberg were patchy. Granted the stance adopted in Washington during 1945–1946, it is ironical that at Paris in 1919 Robert Lansing, then the US Secretary of State, should have been the principal mouthpiece for the kind of legal conservatism that aimed at restricting the scope of any war-guilt prosecutions. In the event, the "special tribunal" stipulated in Article 227 of the Versailles Treaty to consider the former Kaiser's alleged "supreme offence against international morality and the sanctity of treaties" came to nothing, and other aspects of German war criminality noted in Articles 228–229 were eventually tackled only through the minimalist domestic proceedings conducted by the Reichsgericht at Leipzig. Furthermore, although Article 230 of the Treaty of Sèvres (signed in 1920) did embody the path-breaking stipulation that the Turkish government should hand over to the Allies those responsible for the massacres inflicted on its *own* Armenian population during the war, the agreement was never ratified. Amidst rapidly changing circumstances, it was soon superseded by the less punitive Lausanne Treaty of 1923, negotiated with the new post-Ottoman regime. This contained a "Declaration of Amnesty", which marked a retreat from any demand for prosecution even while seeming to concede through such labelling that crimes had indeed occurred.[12] By 1937, in a situation of rapidly deteriorating inter-state relations, what still remained of the League of Nations was turning its collective mind to the creation of some form of standing International Criminal Court. Although member states approved a Convention for that purpose, not a single government ever got round to ratifying it before the whole project was swamped by the tides of general warfare.[13]

Many of the difficulties subsequently encountered in the Nuremberg undertaking can be most usefully analysed by reference to the categorization of crimes offered in Article 6 of the IMT Charter, and particularly to the four counts of indictment that the Allied prosecuting teams had constructed on that basis by October 1945 against 6 organizations and (at this point) 24 individual defendants.[14] The first such count, evoking a notion of "conspiracy" that had been central to the Bernays scheme and to all subsequent US trial planning, proved problematic from beginning to end. Like the German defence counsel, the Soviet and French prosecutors and judges made heavy weather of a concept more familiar in "Anglo-Saxon" legal approaches to the preparation of group crime. Pervading the proceedings, the conspiracy charge encouraged the accusers to exaggerate the coherence of policy-making within Nazi Germany. Conversely, it spurred the prisoners into stressing the kind of organizational confusion that might assist their claims to have been ignorant of the worst horrors of the regime. In the event, Count One made a significant contribution to the distortion of future writing about the Third Reich. If the prosecutors tended here to prefigure those "intentionalist" historians who have seen the practice of Nazism as the relatively simple unfolding of certain deep-laid ideas, then the defence provided a first sketch for some of the "structuralist" or "functionalist" explanations that have put greater stress on constant improvisations of policy and on confusions of responsibility.[15]

This point is reinforced by the wrangles over Count Two, covering "crimes against peace". Harnessed closely to "conspiracy", it condemned the "planning, preparation, initiation, and waging of wars of aggression, which were also wars in violation of international treaties, agreements, and assurances".[16] Thus, the accusation knotted together many legal and historical complexities. It was easier to show the general aggressiveness of Hitler's foreign policies from 1933 to 1939 than to prove either that these sprang from what Jackson called a "master blueprint"[17] or that they were incontrovertibly criminal in substance. This was an area in which, as Simon had again warned, the law looked weak and the precedents seemed vague. The accusers would have to rely heavily upon effective custom – especially upon evidence that the states beyond Germany had behaved during the 1930s as though they really believed themselves to be confronting a criminal regime. Here the victor powers faced numerous problems. For example, the Nazis' contempt for the League of Nations was doubtless deplorable. Yet the prosecutors' depiction of the organization as a legal linchpin seemed merely hypocritical, granted that the United States had never joined it and that the USSR had even been expelled from it after attacking Finland in 1939. Nor was there anything too convincing about the frequent invocations of the Kellogg–Briand Pact of 1928. Did this not attract such wide formal support for its aim of renouncing war as an instrument of policy precisely because it avoided any definition of "aggression" or any stipulation about mechanisms for practical enforcement against offending powers or persons? Then, again, passages from Hitler's writings and speeches would be quoted in the courtroom so as to berate defendants for their failure to see the criminal intent of his foreign policies, but no prosecutor ever directed the same harsh questions to those Allied "appeasers" who had proved similarly blind.

This was a point that E. L. Woodward, historical adviser to the British Foreign Office, was himself making to trial planners shortly before the signing of the IMT Charter, when he observed: "Up to September 1st

1939, His Majesty's Government was prepared to condone everything Germany had done to secure her position in Europe."[18] Concerning that same pre-war period at least, the defendant Hjalmar Schacht was surely entitled to ask rhetorically in his later memoirs: "How were the German people supposed to realize that they were living under a criminal government when foreign countries treated this same government with such marked respect?"[19] However, even this reluctant complicity by the Allies regarding certain Nazi policies that had been deemed criminal only with convenient hindsight was not the worst of the matter. The cogency of Count Two was even more directly damaged by the Nazi–Soviet Pact that Molotov had signed with defendant Ribbentrop on 23 August 1939, especially as this document prompted the growing (and entirely justified) suspicion that the agreement must have carried some form of secret protocol granting the USSR a free hand in launching its own acts of aggression against eastern Poland, the Baltic states and Finland.[20]

When dealing with the third count, focused on "war crimes" broadly in the conventional senses developed by Hague and Geneva precedents, the accusers did clearly move on to some areas of firmer ground. Yet, even there, *tu quoque* allegations were often lurking to ambush them on issues such as the Katyn massacre, the conduct of submarine warfare or the saturation bombing of German cities.

Finally, in respect of Count Four, based on the newer concept of "crimes against humanity", the way in which both the prosecutors and the judges approached this topic was notably tentative.[21] We might well argue that Nuremberg's proto-historical treatment of what we now call "the Holocaust" was often ill focused (for example, as Donald Bloxham has amply shown, when the proceedings underrated the distinctiveness of the extermination centres within the overall camp system or the extent of the Wehrmacht's direct involvement in the genocide).[22] Nor was the more strictly legal handling of this topic as clear-minded as one might have wished. With regard to the full potential scope of Count Four, the tribunal had its greatest opportunity to register a substantial advance in the cause of promoting human rights protection, particularly by puncturing claims that states should regard themselves as entirely immune from external judgement of their internal affairs. If such deflation of overblown sovereignty had been relevant only to the exceptional circumstances of the surrendered and occupied Germany of 1945, it might not have proved so problematic to the Allies. Instead, it raised among them an unwelcome *future* spectre – that of foreign juridical challenges to the subsequent operation of their own sovereign authority (whether with regard to the operation of Siberian labour camps, or the denial of "Negro" civil rights, or the perpetuation of colonialist racial attitudes within the British and French empires). Ultimately, the judges of the four-power tribunal would back away from condemning as criminal the persecutions that the Third Reich had inflicted on its own citizens or ex-citizens during the peacetime years of the 1930s.[23] In essence, the proceedings managed only to query, rather than comprehensively to repudiate, "statist" doctrines of inviolable sovereignty. Thus, as the subsequent historical record would clearly confirm, the Nuremberg trial in itself registered no truly *decisive* blow against the corruptive exercise of such sovereign autonomy or against the resultant cosy equations between immunity and impunity.

Viewed overall, the legal process that ended early in October 1946 had some measure of success in fulfilling most of its shorter-term objectives. For the first time, an international tribunal had managed not only to adjudicate about matters of individual criminal responsibility but also to reject defence pleas based on "superior orders" or on exemptions supposedly derived from the official position previously held by anyone in the dock.[24] On the basis of largely incontrovertible evidence, the tribunal handed down 12 sentences of death, which were wisely linked more strongly to offences under Counts Three and Four than to the other half of the indictment; 3 defendants were condemned to life imprisonment and 4 to other jail terms; and 3 were acquitted. With the criminality of the Nazi leadership cadre so amply exposed, far fewer fantasies developed inside the defeated nation than had been the case after 1918 – and, surely too, far fewer than would have flourished had the preference of Simon and Churchill for summary execution prevailed. In short, despite its often simplistic intentionalism and its other weaknesses of historical judgement (which themselves testified all too sharply to the tensions that almost inevitably strain the relationship between "truth" and this kind of criminal "justice"),[25] the trial process provided a first chronicling of the origins, course and consequences of Hitlerism in a version that was at least serviceable for the immediate purpose of encouraging democratic stability in the larger portion of post-war divided Germany.

Yet many of those who had mounted the Nuremberg trial were driven by even broader political and legal aims. Not least, there was a hope that the achievements of the IMT would help to lay the foundations for some form of permanent court capable of dealing effectively with violations of international criminal law and of being available to act promptly, irrespective of the specific location of the offences and of the particular national or other loyalties professed by those alleged to have perpetrated them. For those who prioritized the pursuit of such an outcome, the story of the reception of the Nuremberg legacy over the longer term must read largely as a tale of delays and disappointments.

Any initial optimism stemmed partly from the fact that the IMT was only one element in a wider judicial enterprise, for which "Nuremberg" tended to become the generic, even symbolic, label. Its other leading feature was the Tokyo trial (May 1946 to November 1948), following the Allied victory in Asia and the Pacific.[26] There, a further international military tribunal was constituted for the Far East (IMTFE) so as to consider the cases of 28 major Japanese defendants in "Class A", with broadly similar rules to those operative at Nuremberg, but also with provision for the wider participation of 11 Allied powers. Although showing certain parallels with the work of the original IMT, these Far Eastern proceedings also had significant distinctive features of their own. One might cite, for instance, a jurisdictional basis adapted to the direct continuance of a form of Japanese civilian government; the associated problems stemming from the refusal to try, or even simply to depose, Emperor Hirohito as head of state; the prosecution's historically questionable concentration (even more marked than at Nuremberg) on conspiracy and pre-war planning; the *tu quoque* implications of the Hiroshima and Nagasaki bombings; the relatively limited impact of the trial on Japanese public opinion; and the significantly greater range of disagreements that became evident among the IMTFE judges. Here, the comprehensive dissent recorded by Radhabinod Pal of India still stands, despite its defects, as a particularly instructive commentary on the senses in which Japanese expansionism might justly be assessed as only *one* of the imperialisms from which Asia had suffered over recent times.[27]

Contrary to earlier expectations, the first Nuremberg and Tokyo international tribunals were also the last bodies of this kind to adjudicate about alleged offences connected with the global conflict that had ended in 1945. The part of their potential legacy that relied on this specific kind of judicial mechanism was squandered principally because of the onset of the Cold War, but also on account of other competing pressures on time, funding and personnel.[28] However, other forms of trial did continue quite intensively for a few years. In the period down to 1951, nearly all of the Allied states that had been involved in the IMTFE pursued their own separate actions. These involved around 5,700 defendants and were conducted in a way that often rendered better justice than the main Tokyo hearings.[29] The emphasis had now shifted to the conventional war crimes that had been directly committed ("Class B") or planned, ordered and otherwise condoned ("Class C") by Japanese who generally held positions of lesser authority than those brought before the IMTFE. Meanwhile, in Europe, much of the remaining prosecutorial impetus came through cases pursued in their particular zones of occupation both by the British (using the Royal Warrant procedure to focus simply on "war crimes" *stricto sensu*[30]) and by the Americans. The latter showed the greater enthusiasm, and certainly possessed the bigger resources. Such was the context in which the United States arranged, at Nuremberg itself, a series of 12 "subsequent proceedings" running from October 1946 until

April 1949 and covering 185 defendants.[31] This part, at least, of the American trial programme had some claim to be undertaken on behalf of a wider international community, since it was validated by the terms of Control Council Law No. 10, as agreed between the occupying powers. Both the USSR and the new successor regimes established in such countries as Poland and France also conducted trials of alleged offences generally committed at the behest of the Third Reich in their own territories and/or against their own nationals. After the establishment of the Federal Republic of Germany in late 1949, a similar opportunity became available to West German courts as well, albeit in circumstances where even the flawed "denazification" of the previous four years had now lost much of its impetus.

During the immediate post-war phase, the chances of a positive exploitation of the Nuremberg legacy had looked all the more promising, because the work of the IMT and the IMTFE plainly cohered with certain other initiatives aimed at promoting global peace, justice and human rights.[32] Hopes for greater accountability under international criminal law were interwoven with the even broader aspirations (as well as the eventual disappointments) characterizing the new United Nations Organization. The General Assembly's prompt endorsement of the principles embodied in the Nuremberg Charter, and its approval in December 1948 both of the Universal Declaration of Human Rights and of the Genocide Convention, seemed favourable signs. So too did the promulgation of the 1949 Geneva Conventions and of the 1950 European Convention on Human Rights (with unusually promising provisions for effective regional implementation, as gradually achieved by the new European Court of Human Rights).[33] However, encouraging though all this might be, progress was generally more evident at the level of principle than of practice. Possibilities of actual enforcement, on any global scale, were rapidly dwindling. The year 1949 was the one in which the abandonment of a Soviet blockade involving an attempt to starve the civilians of West Berlin coincided with the emergence of the USSR as a rival nuclear power to the United States, and in which the communist take-over of China widened the scope of ideological confrontation. By 1950, with the outbreak of the Korean conflict, Asia and Europe alike were gripped by a Cold War whose intensity left much of the Nuremberg legacy frozen on the agenda of the International Law Commission under conditions of inert glaciation. This was a climate in which avoidance of global warfare between the superpowers would owe much to mutual nuclear deterrence and nothing at all to the achievements of the IMT, and in which it was difficult further to pursue Nazi (or indeed other) accountability on any systematic scale. As Geoffrey Best has observed, "The question became not how to facilitate future Nurembergs but how to prevent them. The solid share in the central workings of the new world organization, which the idea of Nuremberg suggested, was shivered into fragments."[34]

Worse still, over the next four decades or so the principles proclaimed by the IMT with specific regard to Hitlerism were repeatedly violated on behalf of other causes – pursued *ad bellum*, *in bello* and indeed (where human rights protection would become increasingly vital) *extra bellum* too.[35] The instances formed a global catalogue of war crimes and crimes against humanity whose familiar geographical roster – including such places as Hungary, Viet Nam, Cambodia, East Timor, Afghanistan, the Kurdish lands, Uganda, Lebanon or Chile – hardly requires more comprehensive rehearsal here. Such offences were committed largely with impunity. Even where the perpetrators fell from power, they were often likely to find safe havens in the manner that brought Idi Amin from Uganda to Saudi Arabia or Colonel Mengistu from Ethiopia to Zimbabwe. One might well ask, moreover, whether it was only the supposed necessities of *realpolitik* at the beginning of the twenty-first century that explained, for example, why Ariel Sharon (by then premier of Israel) had not yet been compelled to defend himself in court over his contribution to the Sabra and Shatilla massacres undertaken against Palestinian civilians by Lebanese Phalangists when he was Defence Minister back in 1982.[36]

It is tempting to say that, from the early 1950s to the early 1990s, there was a total freeze upon advances towards greater accountability. Although that would not be entirely accurate, we are still unlikely to be euphoric about the very limited progress made during this period in the name of all that "Nuremberg" had once started to symbolize by way of what was needed for the legal protection of a potentially better world order. In the specific context of trials, some former henchmen of the Third Reich did continue to be prosecuted in Europe, but only through a variety of national courts and with rapidly decreasing zeal. When Israel also became involved – most memorably in the 1961 Jerusalem proceedings against Adolf Eichmann – it did so on the basis of an unusual combination of particularistic and universalistic claims. This state could plausibly assert jurisdictional rights, not simply because of the specific anti-Semitic focus of Nazi genocide but also because of the waning prosecutorial enthusiasm of other governments and the continuing absence of any alternative mechanism for the administration of criminal justice on the international plane.[37] As for prosecutions arising from later wars, the example of the United States' domestic handling of the Calley case arising from the My Lai massacre of 1968 proved to be shallow in its moralism and profound in its hypocrisy, serving more to aggravate than to heal the traumas of the Viet Nam conflict.[38]

Such evidence as there was of concerted international efforts to utilize the Nuremberg legacy, with regard not simply to crimes committed during the waging of inter-state warfare but also to offences against international criminal and humanitarian law occurring in circumstances of civil conflict or indeed of "peace" in some sense, now related less directly to trials than to exercises in treaty-making. Even after the initial ferment of such agreements in the later 1940s, the list of relevant compacts continued to grow in a way that looked, at least superficially, quite impressive. It included, for example, The Hague Convention for the Suppression of Unlawful Seizure of Aircraft (1970), the UN Convention on the Suppression and the Punishment of the Crime of Apartheid (1973), the Additional Protocols to the Geneva Conventions (1977) and the UN Convention against Torture (1984). The worth of all such agreements obviously depended on the quality of their drafting. Yet their value also varied according to the number of state signatures and ratifications that they attracted, as well as to the effectiveness of their enforcement mechanisms. The typical situation arising from treaties of this kind was one in which the international community had to rely upon individual governments to act as the agents of any global justice. Not surprisingly, some states that did bother to subscribe proved less willing or less capable than others when it came to fulfilling the obligations that they had theoretically assumed.

The rapidly changing circumstances of the early 1990s clearly prompted thought about a more ambitious reactivation of the Nuremberg legacy. This stemmed less directly from all the post–Cold War rhetoric about the benefits of "a new world order" than from an urgent need to face some of the literally brutal realities (increasingly exposed through the mass medium of television in particular) which that very same order seemed to be perpetuating or even generating. Both in the case of Yugoslavia, where international "protection" would prove especially meaningless to Muslim victims at Srebrenica in 1995, and even more extensively amidst the Hutu massacres of Rwandan Tutsis, the frailties of the United Nations were amply displayed. The Security Council's establishment during 1993–1994 of the ad hoc International Criminal Tribunals for the former Yugoslavia and for Rwanda (ICTY and ICTR) – the first such courts since Nuremberg and Tokyo – originally looked to many like mere tokens of wise action salvaged from the wreckage of growing disaster.

That preliminary view may have turned out to be unduly harsh, in some respects at least.[39] Most particularly, the fall of the Serbian leader Slobodan Milosevic in October 2000 (though it owed more to the intervention of NATO than to the inaction of a United Nations paralysed by threats of a Security Council veto over the Kosovo crisis) eventually led in June 2001 to his transfer into the custody of the ICTY and to the commencement of his trial in February 2002. Despite the fact that at this point Radovan Karadzic and Ratko Mladic (among others indicted) still remained unarrested, the tribunal now had the opportunity of adjudicating upon the accountability of a quondam head of state.[40] When starting to do so, it could doubtless take heart from the points of legal principle recorded by the English and Spanish judges who, from 1998 to 2000, had considered under their separate domestic procedures the case of Augusto Pinochet.[41] Even though the former Chilean dictator and sponsor of state torture soon became destined (in the tradition of Hitler and Hirohito) to escape a substantive trial, the proceedings against Milosevic appeared certain to constitute a notable landmark in the evolution of international criminal and humanitarian law. Their opening phase also indicated how the defendant's strategy would include a version of *tu quoque* rebuttal aimed at maximizing the embarrassment of those NATO powers that, en route to the Dayton Accords of 1995, had once been so keen to court him as a supposed broker of peace.[42]

While noting the efforts of the ad hoc tribunals, we still need to re-emphasize that the truly crowning jewel in the Nuremberg legacy was the hope that it inspired about the future operation of a *permanent* International Criminal Court (ICC). Here, new impetus came when in December 1995 the UN General Assembly authorized an acceleration of the relevant work that hitherto had been grinding so slowly through the mills of the International Law Commission.[43] What might be the salient features of the sort of body now urgently required? It would certainly need to focus on offences, whether committed in peace or in war, of a type covered by the legitimate exercise of a universal jurisdiction in the *erga omnes* mode. Such an ICC would do so, moreover, in a way capable of transcending the limitations – and perhaps especially the taint of "victors' justice" – necessarily associated with implementation through international tribunals constituted merely ad hoc. When necessary, it might aspire to insist on recognition of its own jurisdictional claims wherever national prosecutorial or judicial procedures proved too corrupt or otherwise too ineffective for proper legal action to be pursued. Conversely, if states did possess appropriate mechanisms of criminal jurisdiction and were willing to employ these, such an ICC might then often stand available as a potentially complementary forum, one that could by agreement assume direct responsibility for a limited number of high-profile cases. Similarly, its development could work in symbiosis with some parallel resort, in appropriate circumstances, to the kind of "truth and reconciliation" commissions that were becoming more common from the 1980s onward.[44] Nor would the establishment of such a court relieve the international community of its matching obligation to maintain political and financial support for the kind of preventive efforts – aimed at tackling the *prior* causes of international criminality – that characterized much of the work of the UN High Commission on Human Rights based at Geneva.

Against that background, the most significant recent event is plainly the Rome agreement of July 1998, widely but not universally supported at the point of signature, which focused on the creation of an ICC that would represent a decisive progression beyond the arrangements improvised at Nuremberg and Tokyo, and then again at The Hague and at Arusha for the former Yugoslavia and for Rwanda.[45] Like the IMT itself, this Rome Statute is something from whose weaknesses we have as much to learn as from its strengths. The determination of China to frustrate the ICC's potential has been entirely predictable; yet, as David Forsythe's analysis of American exceptionalism in the next chapter of this present volume serves to suggest, the opposition of the United States has proved to be scarcely less so.[46] Other frailties include the void of definitional and jurisdictional evasion that in Article 5(2) still surrounds the concept of "aggression", which we have already noted as once constituting a doubtful feature of the Nuremberg project too.[47] It is of course arguable that the very existence of the Rome Statute shows how the global community has made, albeit slowly, some progress beyond the achievement registered by the four-power proceedings against the Nazi leadership that were mounted in 1945. However, when we bear particularly in mind the negative stance of the United States and ponder the other grave difficulties that continue to beset the project of actually developing an ICC that would be permanent in its functioning and really effective in its aspirations concerning universality of jurisdiction, we also see just how much the civilized world has yet to do. In April 2002, the statute passed the crucial threshold of 60·ratifications, and thus came into formal effect three months later. Even then, however, it had received a confirmed commitment from only a minority of states within the international system.[48]

Most immediately, let us ponder how much more convincing in moral terms we might have found the new "global campaign against terrorism" had it been launched by a US administration that, in an era when it enjoyed hegemonic status in world affairs, was showing genuine determination to hasten, rather than to subvert by non-ratification, the possible success of an ICC. The potential future value of such a body has indeed been starkly underlined by the events of 11 September 2001 in Manhattan, Washington and Pittsburgh. Yet, over the following year or so, no clear American policy was emerging about judicial treatment of the alleged perpetrators. An Executive Order permitting possible resort to "military commissions" – planned initially in a form barely qualifying as courts at all (though some limited adjustments were later conceded) – had already attracted wide condemnation from beyond the United States, even before George W. Bush got himself into further difficulties over the status and treatment of prisoners held in "Camp X-Ray" at Guantanamo Bay, Cuba. "Whatever the procedures are for military tribunals," the President remarked in December 2001, "our system will be more fair than the system of bin Laden and the *Taliban*."[49] Even so, an acceptance that this is likely to be true hardly amounts to endorsement of his implicit assumption that the United States would be fulfilling its duty *merely* by registering some small measure of improvement upon the brutal habits of al-Qaida.

As Adam Roberts has commented, "The US must be advised by its friends to show more respect for international standards and the decent opinion of mankind."[50] If prosecutions do ensue from the crime against humanity (for it was plainly nothing less than this) perpetrated on "9/11", then the justice that needs to be *seen* to be done on behalf of the global community surely requires the agency of legal mechanisms that are not only superior to such "military commissions" but also capable of transcending the passions bound to dominate any New York jury trial. However, even if the US government suddenly had the sense to reverse its current policies towards the ICC so as to help bring that body into early operation, many signatories of the Rome Statute would still block any attempt to nullify the comforting insurance that they have fixed for themselves, in defiance of the principles of universal jurisdiction, by denying this tribunal any authority to deal with offences allegedly committed before the statute actually entered into force.[51] Sadly, the Bush administration (like Tony Blair's British cabinet) showed no real interest in exploring the kind of compromise project that might involve negotiating within the United Nations to waive some of the United States' jurisdictional entitlement with a view to creating a further ad hoc international tribunal at The Hague in order to deal with the al-Qaida leadership. Nor was the President even demonstrating, alternatively, any willingness to pursue some version of the solution found for the "Lockerbie trial" of alleged aircraft-bombing plotters from Libya, which was adjudicated under Scottish law but extra-territorially in The Netherlands. For the "Manhattan case", this might mean enabling US federal judges to retain responsibility for proceedings that were none the less conducted in the calmer atmosphere of some more "neutral" country.

Bearing in mind the aspirations about a permanent court that were nurtured at Nuremberg and then frustrated for so long thereafter, let us return to Norman Birkett. When he came back to London after the trial, he gave a lecture at the Royal Institute of International Affairs. Not surprisingly, this 1947 address was largely a vindication of what he and his fellow judges had accomplished under the IMT Charter. But there was also a vital note of caution about the kind of law that had been proclaimed from Nuremberg:

As it stands, it applies only to the enemy. One could not, for example, bring before that Court, say, the Soviet Union because of what they did in Finland, or because of what they did in Poland. You could not bring the United States of America, or indeed Britain to judgment for dropping the atomic bomb on Japan. It does not apply. If it continues to apply only to the enemy, then I think that the verdict of history may be against Nuremberg. What is really needed is that, after this start – if I may say it with great respect and modesty, this very fine start – the United Nations should build upon it a code that is applied not merely to the enemy but to all. And if that is done, then I believe that Nuremberg will stand the test of history and may indeed be the corner stone in that House of Peace to which every loyal and true citizen aspires.[52]

Whatever the nature of the jury that delivers such "verdicts of history", it seems destined to remain locked in argument for a very long time ahead. Meanwhile, particularly under the conditions now prevailing or emerging in our contemporary world, much of the text of the Rome Statute reflects only feebly what would really be needed to actualize the full positive potential of the Nuremberg bequest as a contribution to the construction of the House of Peace, and indeed of the Temple of Human Rights as well.

Taking an overall historical perspective, perhaps the best we can say is that, even prior to any test of its actual enforcement, the Rome agreement of 1998 enters into our story as an episode containing some elements of a renewed beginning. If so, we also need to acknowledge that the international community is still a very long way from any happy ending – that is, from the effective completion of the kind of edifice towards which Birkett rightly aspired. In the meantime, we will continue – and indeed *must* properly continue – to feel haunted by the history of the years since 1945–1946, during which there has been such global squandering of so much that might have been more beneficially constructed from the legacy bequeathed to us by the Nuremberg tribunal.

Notes

1. Entry in Birkett's diary, 21 January 1946, quoted in H. Montgomery Hyde, *Norman Birkett: The Life of Lord Birkett of Ulverston*, London: Hamish Hamilton, 1964, p. 504.
2. See, particularly, Bradley F. Smith's contributions, *The Road to Nuremberg*, London: André Deutsch, 1981; and *The American Road to Nuremberg: The Documentary Record, 1944–1945*, Stanford, Calif.: Hoover Institution Press, 1982. Also, Arieh J. Kochavi, *Prelude to Nuremberg: Allied War Crimes Policy and the Question of Punishment*, Chapel Hill: University of North Carolina Press, 1998; and Kirsty Buckthorp, "The Politics of Justice: Allied War Crimes Policy during the Second World War", unpublished Ph.D. thesis, University of Birmingham, 1999.
3. For the text of the Moscow Declaration, 1 November 1943, see Smith, *The American Road to Nuremberg*, pp. 13–14.

4. For the text, dated 15 September 1944, see Smith, *The American Road to Nuremberg*, pp. 33–37.
5. For the text, dated 4 September 1944, see Smith, *The American Road to Nuremberg*, pp. 31–33. Note also Simon's paper to Cabinet of 16 April 1945, ibid., pp. 155–157.
6. See George Ginsburgs, *Moscow's Road to Nuremberg: The Soviet Background to the Trial*, The Hague: Nijhoff, 1996. For the general Stalinist position, expressed in a volume issued under Vyshinsky's editorial authority, see also A. N. Trianin, *Hitlerite Responsibility under International Law*, London: Hutchinson, 1946.
7. Geoffrey Robertson, *Crimes against Humanity: The Struggle for Global Justice*, London: Penguin, 2000, p. 211.
8. For the text of the Charter, see *The Trial of the Major War Criminals before the International Military Tribunal* (cited hereafter as "*IMT*"), 42 vols., Nuremberg: International Military Tribunal, 1947–1949, vol. 1, pp. 8–10. Note also *Report of Robert H. Jackson, US Representative to the International Conference on Military Trials, London 1945*, Washington, D.C.: US Department of State, 1949.
9. The general historical literature includes Michael Biddiss, *The Nuremberg Trial and the Third Reich*, London: Longman, 1992; Michael Marrus, *The Nuremberg War Crimes Trial, 1945–46: A Documentary History*, Boston, Mass.: Bedford, 1997; Bradley F. Smith, *Reaching Judgment at Nuremberg*, London: André Deutsch, 1977; Telford Taylor, *Anatomy of the Nuremberg Trials: A Personal Memoir*, Boston, Mass.: Little Brown, 1992; and Ann and John Tusa, *The Nuremberg Trial*, London: Macmillan, 1983. Note also Norman E. Tutorow, ed., *War Crimes, War Criminals, and War Crimes Trials: An Annotated Bibliography and Source Book*, Westport, Conn.: Greenwood, 1986. For a major effort at wider contextualization, see Gary J. Bass, *Stay the Hand of Vengeance: The Politics of War Crimes Tribunals*, 2nd edn., Princeton, N.J.: Princeton University Press, 2002.
10. *IMT*, vol. 1, p. 218. See also William B. Simons, "The Jurisdictional Bases of the International Military Tribunal at Nuremberg", in George Ginsburgs and V. N. Kudriavtsev, eds., *The Nuremberg Trial and International Law*, Dordrecht: Nijhoff, 1990, pp. 39–59.
11. *IMT*, vol. 1, p. 218.
12. For an overview of issues relevant to the period immediately after 1918, see James F. Willis, *Prologue to Nuremberg: The Politics and Diplomacy of Punishing War Criminals of the First World War*, Westport, Conn.: Greenwood, 1982; and Bass, *Stay the Hand of Vengeance*, pp. 58–146.
13. See "Convention for the Creation of an International Criminal Court", *Monthly Summary of the League of Nations*, vol. 17, no. 11, November 1937, pp. 289–295.
14. For the full text of the indictment, see *IMT*, vol. 1, pp. 27–92. A recent and most valuable contribution to the literature on preparations for the trial is Richard Overy, *Interrogations: The Nazi Elite in Allied Hands, 1945*, London: Allen Lane, 2001. Only 22 defendants (including Martin Bormann in absentia) were eventually tried. A grid of the pattern of accusations and of the final verdicts and sentences is provided in Biddiss, *The Nuremberg Trial and the Third Reich*, p. 93.
15. For an excellent survey of the nature and significance of these historiographical disputes, see Ian Kershaw, *The Nazi Dictatorship: Problems and Perspectives of Interpretation*, 4th edn., London: Arnold, 2000.
16. *IMT*, vol. 1, p. 42.
17. *IMT*, vol. 19, p. 418, on 26 July 1946.
18. Public Record Office, Kew, London: FO 371/50985/6534, 2 August 1945.
19. Hjalmar Schacht, *Account Settled*, London: Weidenfeld & Nicolson, 1949, p. 185.
20. For the text of the Pact and Secret Protocol, see Jeremy Noakes and Geoffrey Pridham, eds., *Nazism, 1919–1945: A Documentary Reader, Vol. 3: Foreign Policy, War, and Racial Extermination*, new edn., Exeter: Exeter University Press, 2001, pp. 135–137. An

example of milder, British, embarrassment is considered by Patrick Salmon, "Crimes against Peace: The Case of the Invasion of Norway at the Nuremberg Trials", in Richard Langhorne, ed., *Diplomacy and Intelligence during the Second World War*, Cambridge: Cambridge University Press, 1985, pp. 245–269, 315–320.

21. For my more detailed consideration of this issue, see Michael Biddiss, "Human Rights and 'Crimes against Humanity': The Development of a Supranational Concept at the Nuremberg Trials", in Carole Fink and Antoine Fleury, eds., *Human Rights in Europe since 1945*, Bern: Lang, 2003, pp. 22–43. Note also Egon Schwelb, "Crimes against Humanity", *British Yearbook of International Law*, vol. 23, 1946, pp. 178–226; M. Cherif Bassiouni, *Crimes against Humanity in International Criminal Law*, Dordrecht: Nijhoff, 1992; Robertson, *Crimes against Humanity*, especially chap. 6; and Roger S. Clark, "'Crimes against Humanity' at Nuremberg", in Ginsburgs and Kudriavtsev, eds., *The Nuremberg Trial and International Law*, pp. 177–212.

22. See Donald Bloxham, *Genocide on Trial: War Crimes Trials and the Formation of Holocaust History and Memory*, Oxford: Oxford University Press, 2001, especially parts II and III.

23. See *IMT*, vol. 1, pp. 254–255.

24. Article 7 of the Charter denied immunity even to heads of state. With Hitler dead, this was more relevant in theory than in practice to the case against Admiral Doenitz, who had very briefly succeeded him during the final week of the Reich.

25. See, generally, Bloxham, *Genocide on Trial*; also Michael Biddiss, "The Nuremberg Trial: Two Exercises in Judgment", *Journal of Contemporary History*, vol. 16, 1981, pp. 597–615; Lawrence Douglas, *The Memory of Judgment: Making Law and History in the Trials of the Holocaust*, New Haven, Conn.: Yale University Press, 2001; and Richard J. Evans, *Telling Lies about Hitler: The Holocaust, History, and the David Irving Trial*, London: Verso, 2002.

26. See, generally, R. John Pritchard and Sonia M. Zaide, eds., *The Tokyo War Crimes Trial: The Complete Transcripts of the Proceedings of the International Military Tribunal for the Far East*, 22 vols. (+ 5 vols. of Index and Guide), New York: Garland, 1981; and Richard H. Minear, *Victors' Justice: The Tokyo War Crimes Trial*, Princeton, N.J.: Princeton University Press, 1971. Note also Roger S. Clark, "Nuremberg and Tokyo in Contemporary Perspective", in Timothy L. H. McCormack and Gerry J. Simpson, eds., *The Law of War Crimes: National and International Approaches*, The Hague: Kluwer, 1997, pp. 171–187.

27. See Radhabinod Pal, *International Military Tribunal for the Far East: Dissentient Judgment*, Calcutta: Sanyal, 1953. Note also Elizabeth S. Kopelman, "Ideology and International Law: The Dissent of the Indian Justice at the Tokyo War Crimes Trial", *International Law and Politics*, vol. 23, no. 373, 1991, pp. 373–444; and, for the retrospective observations of another IMTFE judge, see B. V. A. Röling and A. Cassese, eds., *The Tokyo Trial and Beyond: Reflections of a Peacemonger*, Cambridge: Polity, 1993.

28. See, for example, Donald Bloxham, "'The Trial That Never Was': Why There Was No Second International Trial of Major War Criminals at Nuremberg", *History*, vol. 87, no. 285, 2002, pp. 41–60.

29. For this wider picture, see Philip R. Piccigallo, *The Japanese on Trial: Allied War Crimes Operations in the East, 1945–1951*, Austin, Tex.: University of Texas Press, 1979.

30. See A. P. V. Rogers, "War Crimes Trials under the Royal Warrant: British Practice, 1945–1949", *International and Comparative Law Quarterly*, vol. 39, 1990, pp. 780–800.

31. See *Trials of War Criminals before the Nuremberg Military Tribunals under Control Council Law No. 10*, 12 vols., Washington, D.C.: US Government, 1949; also, Telford Taylor, *Final Report to the Secretary of the Army on the Nuremberg War Crimes Trials under Control Council Law No. 10*, Washington, D.C.: US Government, 1949.

32. For a general survey, see Robertson, *Crimes against Humanity*, chap. 2; note also the

separate sections by Roger S. Clark and by I. A. Lediakh jointly headed "The Influence of the Nuremberg Trial on the Development of International Law", in Ginsburgs and Kudriavtsev, eds., *The Nuremberg Trial and International Law*, pp. 249–283.

33. For relevant texts, see generally Ian Brownlie, ed., *Basic Documents on Human Rights*, 3rd edn., Oxford: Clarendon, 1992.

34. Geoffrey Best, *Nuremberg and After: The Continuing History of War Crimes and Crimes against Humanity*, Reading: University of Reading (Stenton Lecture), 1984, p. 6.

35. See Geoffrey Best, *War and Law since 1945*, Oxford: Clarendon, 1994, for a fine survey that highlights the increasing overlap between the laws of war and the developing corpus of international humanitarian law.

36. An Israeli commission of inquiry itself found Sharon "personally responsible", but no prosecution followed. More recently, attempts have been made through the Belgian courts to register an indictment against him. In January 2002, Elie Hobeika, who might well have been a crucial prosecution witness, became the victim of an unknown assassin. On 12 February 2003, the Belgian Supreme Court ruled that, although Sharon was entitled to enjoy immunity so long as he remained prime minister of Israel, thereafter it would indeed proceed to hear the war crimes lawsuit brought against him by survivors from the Sabra and Shatilla massacres. Belgium's relevant parliamentary legislation was subsequently weakened in a way that made any such trial unlikely.

37. See Hannah Arendt, *Eichmann in Jerusalem: A Report on the Banality of Evil*, revised edn., Harmondsworth: Penguin, 1977; also, Douglas, *The Memory of Judgment*, pp. 97–182; and Henry J. Steiner and Philip Alston, *International Human Rights in Context: Law, Politics, and Morals*, 2nd edn., Oxford: Oxford University Press, 2000, pp. 1138–1142.

38. See Telford Taylor, *Nuremberg and Vietnam: An American Tragedy*, Chicago: Quadrangle, 1970; Jay W. Baird, ed., *From Nuremberg to My Lai*, Lexington, Mass.: Heath, 1972; and Joseph Goldstein et al., *The My Lai Massacre and Its Cover-up: Beyond the Reach of Law?*, New York: Free Press, 1976.

39. For the achievements of the ICTY and ICTR so far, see the ongoing series André Klip and Göran Sluiter, eds., *Annotated Leading Cases of International Criminal Tribunals*, 3 vols. to date, Schoten: Intersentia, 1999– ; Steiner and Alston, *International Human Rights in Context*, pp. 1143–1192; and Bass, *Stay the Hand of Vengeance*, pp. 206–275.

40. By the time that the Milosevic trial had begun, the ICTR had already convicted if not a head of state then at least a former head of the Rwandan government, Jean Kambanda, on charges that included the crime of genocide.

41. On the British side, the most crucial feature was the final majority ruling made on 24 March 1999 by seven law lords in the House of Lords, *Ex Parte Pinochet* (No. 3), for which, see Steiner and Alston, *International Human Rights in Context*, pp. 1198–1216.

42. For analysis of some of the issues available to be raised in this manner, see Brendan Simms, *Unfinest Hour: Britain and the Destruction of Bosnia*, London: Allen Lane, 2001.

43. UN General Assembly Resolution 50/46, "Establishment of a Criminal Court", 11 December 1995. For much of the earlier story, see Benjamin Ferencz, *An International Criminal Court: A Step Towards World Peace – A Documentary History and Analysis*, 2 vols., London: Oceana, 1980.

44. For further comment on such bodies, see Steiner and Alston, *International Human Rights in Context*, pp. 1216–1247.

45. Essential documentation on the Rome agreement is conveniently provided, and regularly updated, on the official ICC website at www.un.org/law/icc/; note, additionally, the material provided from the NGOs supporting the "Coalition for the ICC" at www.igc. org/icc/. See also Roy S. Lee, ed., *The International Criminal Court: The Making of the Rome Statute – Issues, Negotiations, Results*, The Hague: Kluwer, 1999; and Timothy L. H. McCormack and Gerry J. Simpson, "Achieving the Promise of Nuremberg: A

New International Criminal Law Regime?", in McCormack and Simpson, eds., *The Law of War Crimes*, pp. 229–254.

46. For a summary of the official US comment on the conclusion of the Rome negotiations, and particularly for American disquiet about the implications of Article 12 (covering circumstances of potential liability for nationals of non-ratifying states), see Lee, *The International Criminal Court*, pp. 632–635. Early in 2003, besides the United States and China, other particularly significant non-ratifying states included India, Pakistan, Iran, Iraq and Israel.

47. Article 5(1) gives jurisdiction over genocide, crimes against humanity, war crimes and "the crime of aggression"; but, concerning the last of these, Article 5(2) defers any implementation until there is agreement about "defining the crime and setting out the conditions under which the Court shall exercise jurisdiction with respect to this crime". The offence is missing from the Statute of the ICTY, and (perhaps more understandably) from that of the ICTR as well.

48. On 1 July 2003 (the first anniversary of the ICC's formal existence), the number of ratifications stood at 90, and the broader tally of state signatories at 139.

49. As reported in *The Independent*, 29 December 2001.

50. Adam Roberts, "Even Our Enemies Have Rights", *The Independent on Sunday*, 20 January 2002.

51. See *Rome Statute of the International Criminal Court*, 17 July 1998, UN Doc. A/CONF.183/9, Articles 11 and 24.

52. Sir Norman Birkett, "International Legal Theories Evolved at Nuremberg" (Lecture at Chatham House, 27 March 1947), *International Affairs*, vol. 23, no. 3, 1947, p. 325.

3

International criminal justice and the United States: Law, culture, power

David P. Forsythe

Introduction

George Kennan and others have made much of an alleged legal strain in American thinking about foreign policy.[1] In contemporary times, the United States has carefully dissected the Rome Statute, which would create an International Criminal Court (ICC), and vigorously objected to various parts of it.[2] These US legal arguments about international criminal justice, however, are embedded in cultural and power considerations far deeper than the particular legal arguments against the ICC that have been subjected to so much analysis by lawyers. The twin reality of American exceptionalism and US commitment to power politics remains essential to the US orientation to the ICC and other forms of international criminal justice. Precise legal arguments are but the superstructure of this enduring fundamental reality.

American exceptionalism

American exceptionalism is alive and well at the start of the twenty-first century, comprising one of the two deep reasons informing US opposition to the ICC.[3] That the United States saw itself as a city on a hill, a beacon to others, was well known prior to the Ronald Reagan era, which epitomized this cultural trait.[4] From the founding of the republic, the dominant self-image was of a good and great people, divinely inspired to lead the world – by example at home or activism abroad – to greater respect for personal freedom.[5] The US Constitution and its Bill of Rights symbolized this superior commitment. As such, US law was not to be trumped by international law to the contrary. In the words of contemporary constructivist theorists of international relations, the identity of the United States was constructed "from below" on the basis of domestic factors. It was not constructed "from above" on the basis of international law negotiated from many national experiences.[6] Whereas some states – for example, Hungary – manifest a constitution that gives clear primacy to international law, the United States does not. Hungary, fearful of the lessons of its own past, wanted to bind itself firmly to the human rights guarantees of international law.[7] The United States, supremely confident of its past as selectively remembered, has recently accentuated its commitment to the supremacy of national over international law.[8] Some prominent recent practitioners of US foreign policy, with an eye on the growing emphasis on international human rights and criminal justice, even state that treaties are not legally binding, not really law.[9]

American exceptionalism as a cultural phenomenon is broadly and especially evident in US approaches to internationally recognized human rights. The United States preaches universalism, but it practises national particularity and cultural relativism.[10] The dominant view in Washington is that real human rights come from US experience and are then exported to the rest of the world.[11] The United States almost never intentionally accepts internationally recognized human rights that cause the United States to change its domestic laws and policies on human rights.[12]

This was true in the 1940s when human rights became part of routinized international relations, and it remains true today. The United States wanted human rights language in the UN Charter but, especially aware of its legally sanctioned racial discrimination, resisted efforts to make that language more precise and judicially enforceable. The same view explains US leadership for the 1948 Universal Declaration of Human Rights as a statement of aspirations rather than binding norms. It is well known that the United States either does not accept human rights treaties that do not fit with American culture – for example, the International Covenant on Economic, Social and Cultural Rights – or attaches reservations by whatever name to those treaties it does accept so as to ensure that no domestic changes will be made, and no litigation endured, under those treaties.[13] From 1945 until today, the United States has never been keen on accepting international standards on human rights that lead to meaningful restrictions on its own policies.

American exceptionalism manifests itself not only in law but also in policy. If one is superior to the rest, then one has reason to chart a separate course. American exceptionalism thus underlies unilateral and sometimes isolationist policies, in diplomatic history as well as contemporary foreign policy. The United States might choose to help the League of Nations in the Manchurian crisis or in efforts to do something about slavery in Liberia, but Washington would not commit to League membership and its daily obligations. The early George W. Bush administration also favoured systematic unilateralism over institutionalized multilateralism – at least until 11 September 2001. During its first six months, the administration refused to negotiate flexibly on such subjects as global warming (the Kyoto Protocol), regulation of small arms in armed conflicts and complex emergencies, treaty improvements to control biological weapons, and mutually acceptable missile defence systems.

Unilateralism allowed neo-isolationism to resurface. Washington wanted to pick and choose where to engage, and to walk away from situations – such as nation-building – demanding engagement but whose engagement offered little prospect of national advantage. This course of action, based on narrow and short-term nationalism, was openly advocated by Bush's National Security Advisor, Condoleezza Rice, and by another of his trusted foreign policy advisers, Richard N. Haass.[14] Engaging on a quotidian basis to manage problems of world order collectively, regardless of a self-appointed special American role, was not the preferred course of action. This orientation was at times very close to American isolationism as practised in the 1920s and 1930s.[15]

Because of American exceptionalism, a view deeply embedded in American culture, the United States has manifested persistent difficulty in adjusting to almost all contemporary multilateral arrangements it does not control or heavily influence.[16] Even if the United States gets what it wants from these arrangements, as in the United Nations 95 per cent of the time, important American circles manifest general hostility because of things disliked 5 per cent of the time.[17] The parallels between US attitudes toward the United Nations and toward the ICC are thus striking. One should understand the history of US failure to pay its assessed dues to the United Nations as primarily a symbolic or ideological matter, because the amount of money is inconsequential in Washington. The primary issue is really the "audacity" of the United Nations in trying to do things opposed by important political circles in the United States, whether regarding UN acceptance of the Palestine Liberation Organization before Washington was ready, or UN willingness to promote economic development in Cuba. The United States simply refuses to accept the need for compromise.[18] (There are always situations in which standing firm in opposition to the majority is the right policy, such as the US opposition to the 1975 UN General Assembly Resolution equating Zionism with racism, later rescinded in 1991, but then introduced in the UN World Conference against Racism at Durban, South Africa, in 2001.)

There remains a lack of American proportion and understanding about a world of 190 "sovereign states" reflecting various cultures and interests. It is against this background that one should evaluate the George W. Bush administration on matters discussed here, which William Pfaff has accurately done: "The motivation of the new decision-makers in Washington is quite simple. They want the United States to have its way. They do not want to rule the world ... They believe that the United States is the best of all countries, with the right ideas; that it deserves to prevail in international disputes because it is right."[19] Contemporary US foreign policy is characterized by a pronounced tendency toward arrogance,[20] a hubris deeply rooted in American exceptionalism.[21]

American exceptionalism is not entirely exceptional, however. Some other nations, such as France, the Netherlands and Canada, have their own version of exceptionalism. Most other nations see themselves in a positive light, with beneficial radiation to other parts of the world. American exceptionalism is different in two ways, both of which relate to international criminal justice. Many other versions of national exceptionalism relate well to multilateralism and limits on the national role. The French, among other points, pride themselves on leadership in the European Union. The Dutch pride themselves on meeting, or coming close to meeting, targets set at the United Nations for development assistance to the poorer states. The Canadians pride themselves on contributions to UN peacekeeping. American exceptionalism is much more unilateralist by comparison, accepting fewer restrictions on national policy-making.[22] And, secondly, there is much more power put at the service of American exceptionalism.

American power

American exceptionalism is reinforced by the "unipolar moment" characterizing international relations after the Cold War. US power is unrivalled in many dimensions: the hard power of military coercion; the economic power that stems from the world's largest national economy; the soft power that comes from being associated with human rights, with its subset of democratic rights, and with notions of personal freedom. The application of power to secure political objectives is almost always more difficult than an inventory of putative power would suggest, whether in Yugoslavia in 1999 or Afghanistan in 2001. Still, American power is unrivalled by other states since the end of the Cold War, and perhaps unrivalled by any actor or probable combination of actors since the peak of the British Empire or maybe the Roman Empire.

Hegemonic stability theory posits that hegemonic powers create international institutions to try to stabilize international relations in ways to their liking. The United States did so after World War II, for example, by leading in the creation of the United Nations, the World Bank, the International Monetary Fund and the North Atlantic Treaty Organization (NATO). The point to be stressed here is that this form of multilateralism reflected few constraints on US independence. True, for example, the United States agreed to relatively independent secretariats in all these intergovernmental organizations, but these manifested weak authority and power compared with state members. True, after about 1970 the United States had to tolerate a UN General Assembly not to its liking, but its resolutions were easy enough to disregard. It is well known that the United States has the veto in the UN Security Council, dominates NATO, does not draw loans from the World Bank or IMF and thus does not have to meet the standards imposed through their conditionality. American power has been only marginally restricted by the international institution-building since 1945.

The exception that proves the general rule concerns the World Trade Organization (WTO) and its dispute resolution panels. Here the United States has recently accepted meaningful international procedures that restricted national independence, and the United States has had several national standards disallowed by WTO panels. In general, the United States agreed to WTO restrictive rules, and has not withdrawn from the WTO system despite losing several "cases", because the United States needs trade with others. There is some countervailing power in trade relations, and so the principle of reciprocity applies. Faced with countervailing power, and wanting to be associated with trade liberalization under the principle of regulated economic liberalism, the United States so far has stayed the course under the current WTO system of adjudicating trade disputes. It is the only major and persistent limitation on national decision-making that the United States has accepted in contemporary international relations.

But one should not confuse the general pattern with the exception. One needs to see the debate over the ICC in this broad perspective. In general, the United States speaks fondly of international law via affectionate generalities while striving mightily to oppose an effective rule of law in international relations. An effective international law would constrain the exercise of US power. One might recall Manley Hudson's erudite but skewering commentary that the United States "seldom loses an opportunity to profess its loyalty to international arbitration in the abstract ... [T]he expression of this sentiment has become so conventional that a popular impression prevails that it accords with the actual policy of the United States."[23] One might also recall US unbridled criticisms of the International Court of Justice (ICJ) in the wake of *Nicaragua v. the US (1986)*, its refusal to abide by that judgment and its subsequent withdrawal from the compulsory jurisdiction of the ICJ. There was no countervailing power to compel the United States to implement the court's judgment. The United States clearly has not followed the advice of President Dwight Eisenhower when he said, "It is better to lose a point now and then in an international tribunal and gain a world in which everyone lives at peace under the rule of law."[24] As a result, the United States may find from time to time that it is a defendant before an international tribunal such as the ICJ, as with regard to the Vienna Convention on Consular Relations and the rule that alien defendants facing capital punishment are entitled to consultation with their state representatives. The record of US compliance with the law is less than meritorious.[25]

There is thus ample reason to observe that, contrary to a rigorous or expansive understanding of hegemonic stability theory, great powers do not make great multilateralists.[26] If multilateralism does not just reflect hegemonic power but actually seriously restricts that power, then the evidence is very clear during the American unipolar moment. The WTO aside, the United States opposes international norms that bind itself. The United States, as is well known, favoured the creation of the two ad hoc criminal tribunals created by the UN Security Council in 1993 and 1994 to further international criminal justice in the former Yugoslavia and in Rwanda. As is also well known, however, the United States vigorously objects to the ICC, which might assert jurisdiction over Americans. The two ad hoc courts were intended to restrict others, not the United States. When commencing armed action in Yugoslavia in 1999, the United States found that it had to accept the jurisdiction of the ICTY. Having led in fashioning the ICTY and its statute, the United States could hardly argue that its writ did not apply to armed conflict in the territory of the former Yugoslavia. One can only imagine the controversy that would have transpired had the independent Prosecutor responded to allegations of war crimes by NATO states by proceeding to investigate those allegations seriously, with a view to possible indictments of US personnel. The United States, of course, was spared that dilemma by the decision of the Prosecutor not to proceed beyond a preliminary staff report.

The basic point remains. The United States generally opposes the creation of international law and organizations that might seriously restrain the independent or unilateral exercise of US power. Washington desires to have both the international rule of law and extensive national independence in international relations. It has yet fully to comprehend that the two objectives are in fundamental conflict much of the time. In Afghanistan as elsewhere, the last thing the United States wants is for international legal authorities to be looking over its collective shoulder regarding the selection of bombing targets or the choice of weapons. Other states, especially in the Council of Europe and the European Union, have come to understand that the serious restriction of national independence is the price that one must pay for the rule of law in behalf of improved protection of human rights (and prosperity and peace). But, as the Republican Representative Beureuter stated after chairing hearings on the ICC in the House of Representatives of the US Congress, "They [officials of the EU states] are willing to give up elements of their sovereignty – it's quite clear – and we are not and should not be."[27]

American legal arguments and politics

US objections to various aspects of the Rome Statute are by now well known to those who follow the debate. The fact that these criticisms are not persuasive to most scholars and legal experts turns out to be of little importance in US politics, reflecting the continuing pull of the deep reasons for American exceptionalism and power politics. There is, however, one problem for Washington that has not drawn adequate attention – the likelihood that a conscientious Prosecutor would find fault with some US policies in armed conflicts.

Most Democratic officials as well as virtually all Republican ones manifest firm opposition to the ICC, with the Democrats disagreeing with Republicans regarding only process, not present legal substance. Given that the overall commentary on the ICC in American political circles – even beyond sitting officials – is decidedly negative, with the only support coming from certain academics and non-governmental organizations (NGOs), it is clear that the United States will not ratify the ICC Statute in the foreseeable future. US experiences in Yugoslavia and Afghanistan confirm the official wisdom about the inadvisability of ratification, as discussed below.

The issues

There are two major US concerns about the Rome Statute, and a third one will surface in the near future. Then there are several minor ones. One of the major concerns, although probably off the mark itself, should lead to a serious discussion. All the other concerns remain minor in terms of legal logic. What counts in the last analysis, however, is not legal logic but political orientations.

A first US concern focuses on Article 12 of the Rome Statute, which allows personnel of non-states parties to fall under the jurisdiction of the ICC if the acts in question were committed in the territory of a state party to the statute. The United States objects that treaties are binding only on those that consent to be bound. Thus the United States argues that its failure to ratify should shield American nationals from prosecution. Yet other treaties, on terrorism for example, contain similar provisions entailing legal exposure for individuals from states that have not ratified. The Nuremberg tribunal went forward without the consent of any German government. Modern international law clearly allows certain law-making treaties, covering crimes of major importance, to provide a basis for prosecution of individuals from non-ratifying states.[28]

US insistence on its position on this point meant that the United States was prepared to gut the entire ICC project in order to exempt itself. Had the treaty been in existence at the time Iraq invaded Kuwait, and had Iraq not ratified, Saddam Hussein and his policy makers would have been beyond the reach of the ICC. It is no wonder that most other states and their supporters in the NGO community reject the US position on Article 12.

Concerted US attempts to get an explicit and special exemption for itself failed. This was the quest for political exceptionalism and is somewhat different from, but consistent with, the cultural phenomenon of American exceptionalism discussed above. The United States claims a special role, based on its pre-eminent power position, in enforcing international peace and security. Since the United States supposedly takes the lead in peace enforcement operations, it argues it should not have to respond to frivolous complaints through the ICC. But other states also consistently deploy their troops abroad in various peace operations. For example, the United Kingdom and France, which accept the ICC, supplied the most troops to the UN Protection Force (UNPROFOR) in the Balkans, and took the most casualties in that nasty situation between 1992 and 1995. Sometimes UNPROFOR was given an enforcement mandate under UN Charter Chapter VII, and not just a peacekeeping mandate under Charter Chapter VI. Moreover, the United States avoided direct military involvement on the ground in Bosnia up until 1995, as it did when Australia led a peace mission in East Timor and when the Japanese led a peace mission in Cambodia. Still further, the British have engaged in combat with the United States in places such as the Persian Gulf and Afghanistan. So, although the United States did lead the coalition to liberate Kuwait and to punish the Taliban government for its support of the al-Qaida terrorist network, among other enforcement operations (as in Haiti and Somalia), the United States is hardly alone in placing its military personnel in harm's way in the name of international peace and security. Again, it is not surprising that US arguments on this point failed to carry the day at Rome in 1998.

In a second and related major concern, the United States also objects to the possibility that an independent Prosecutor, with the approval of a chamber of three judges, could bring indictments against US personnel. The United States preferred a court controlled by the Security Council, where the United States possesses the veto. Even given the principle of complementarity on which the ICC is based, which acknowledges the primary responsibility of states to investigate and, if warranted, prosecute for international crimes, one cannot be sure that US personnel would always be – or should always be – shielded from ICC inquiry. Various actors have stated that the United States has nothing to fear from existing ICC provisions, that the ICC was constructed to deal with brutal authoritarians and not with the personnel of liberal democracies such as the United States. But independent prosecutors and courts do not always act as predicted. It is certainly possible that a *responsible* Prosecutor and judicial panel might authorize proceedings over the objections of the United States.

The projected problem is not so much a rogue Prosecutor, because of the well-known constraints on that role (for example, only complementary authority, subject to pre-indictment review by a judicial chamber, and with possible delay imposed by the UN Security Council). True, the US experience with national independent prosecutors such as Kenneth Starr, who carried on a prolonged and expensive investigation of possible wrong-doing by President Clinton, has been – to put it kindly – not entirely positive. This experience did affect the approach of the Clinton administration to the ICC.[29] Some observers have not had an entirely favourable attitude toward assertive European legal authorities that pressed for criminal proceedings against the former President of Chile, Augusto Pinochet.[30] One cannot completely discount what Washington would see as a rogue Prosecutor, but – as widely recognized – that worst-case scenario is not highly probable.

The more probable crisis in the functioning of the court, however, would most likely come from a *conscientious* Prosecutor who found questionable US policies in armed conflict involving choices of targets and/or weapons. He (or she) might find – as is normally the case in such situations – that no authority in the United States wanted to carry out a serious investigation of executive choices. When national passions run high, as in armed conflict when US military personnel are put in harm's way, US domestic authorities are not likely to deviate from the "rally round the flag" syndrome that works to the advantage of the imperial presidency. Even in calmer times, courts in the United States do not like to challenge the "political" branches on controversial foreign policy questions. And the Congress has shown repeatedly in recent decades that, despite its pretensions to be equal with the executive in foreign policy matters, it will usually defer to presidential decisions involving the use of military force rather than take a critical stand. Only if the US military operation, as directed by the executive, turns sour over time is the Congress likely to raise penetrating questions about the conduct of military force.

Even if one assumes that we will not again see US behaviour similar to that which occurred after the 1968 My Lai massacre in Viet Nam, when the military first attempted to cover up rather than investigate events,[31] American legal exposure under the ICC cannot be ruled out. Historically speaking, US choice of targets and weapons in military operations is not beyond reasoned critique. There are former judges of the ICTY who believe Carla del Ponte was in error in not pursuing an investigation of NATO bombing policies in Yugoslavia in 1999.[32] No US authority has taken up the question of US military attacks on a pharmaceutical plant in the Sudan in 1998. There has been no public inquiry into civilian deaths during the US invasion of Panama in 1989. No domestic authority in the United States would relish undertaking an objective review of the US choice of targets and weapons in Afghanistan during 2001.[33] Serious questions by independent legal scholars have been raised regarding NATO bombing of TV stations, electrical grids important to the civilian population, and dual-use installations such as bridges in Yugoslavia in 1999.[34] Yet there has been no independent domestic investigation.

Much rhetoric in Washington focuses on theoretical trials of lower-ranking US military personnel in the ICC. The real probability – given the ICC principle of complementarity, US military justice and US politics – is the bringing of charges against a high official such as a Secretary of Defense for a pattern of targeting or the systematic choice of weapons that result in what a prosecutor would consider war crimes or crimes against humanity.

There is a third concern that is being formulated at the time of writing and no doubt will be adopted eventually by US spokespersons.[35] That is the objection based on a "democratic deficit". This argument stresses that the ICC, unlike say the US Supreme Court, is not embedded in a broader system of democratic policy-making. So the argument runs, the ICC will make a number of very broad judgments, not just narrow and technical ones.[36] Since the ICC will in effect "legislate" on a variety of weighty issues, and since its Prosecutor and judges will have the opportunity to overturn policy established by national democracies, the court should be opposed. There is no political check on the ICC; the court does not answer to any political body.

This argument has a certain ring of truth to it, similar to arguments about a democratic deficit in the WTO and European Union. There are at least three counter-arguments. One is that the United States has not been a champion of democracy in international relations, whether at the United Nations itself or in related forums such as the WTO. Thus its arguments about a democratic deficit in the ICC should not be given great weight until Washington shows a broader concern for majority rule in international policy-making. The second counter-argument is that legitimacy can come from other than majority rule. This argument is based in part on the observation that all liberal democracies restrain majority rule by independent courts with appointed judges, precisely to protect human rights from the tyranny of the majority. The third counter-argument is that the Prosecutor and judges of the ICC do answer to the Assembly of States Parties, which elected them.

Other US legal concerns are minor in terms of legal importance, although some of them get much play in Congress. Some in the United States object to foreign states being able to delegate prosecution of Americans to the ICC. But there is no international rule against such a process. The US Constitution does not travel with Americans, and the United States already allows foreign states to try Americans according to foreign procedure. Indeed, the Rules of Procedure of the ICC may be an improvement over certain states' judicial proceedings where Americans can already be tried. Nevertheless, the United States is making efforts to amend its Status of Forces Agreements with many countries to prevent such a delegation.

The ICC's obligations are layered upon more general obligations in international law. Since genocide, crimes against humanity and grave breaches of the 1949 Geneva Conventions entail universal jurisdiction, states can already try US personnel under those general provisions, regardless of the new regime constructed via the ICC. The only change is that, whereas individual states might be unwilling to prosecute Americans given the power of the United States and its ability to retaliate, an ICC Prosecutor with the responsibility to oversee particular crimes might feel no such restraint.

Some in the United States object to lack of trial by jury in the ICC. Although the subject is complex, in general one can say that US military courts do not always use trial by jury in court martial proceedings.

The political process

There is broad and deep bipartisan opposition to the ICC.[37] In the fall of 2001, the Congress, on the basis of considerable bipartisan agreement, attached the Craig Amendment to the funding bill for several federal departments. This measure, duly signed by President George W. Bush, albeit with qualifying statements, prohibited the use of these funds for cooperation with, or assistance or other support to, the ICC and its Preparatory Committee. At roughly the same time, the Senate followed the lead of the House in adopting its version of the American Servicemembers Protection Act, which more broadly prohibits US cooperation with the ICC. Again the votes reflected bipartisan opposition. After adjustments in the conference committee, the Congress produced a bill that President George W. Bush signed into law in August 2002. This law, sometimes referred to as "the Hague invasion act", authorizes the President to use force to free any US citizen detained in connection with the ICC, among its other provisions.[38]

The more cosmopolitan and less vitriolic of the Republican critics of the court, such as Secretary of State Colin Powell, no doubt aware of the lobbying for the ICC by US allies in Europe, downplayed the controversy and simply said that the United States did not need the elaborate ICC.[39] There were numerous less restrained attacks on the ICC by Republicans, such as that by Senator Rod Grams, who wanted "to make sure that it shares the same fate as the League of Nations and collapses without US support, for this court truly, I believe, is the monster and it is the monster that we need to slay".[40] There are no important cracks in the official Republican consensus against the ICC. They do not intend to submit the Rome Statute to the Senate for advice and consent. In fact, President Bush "unsigned" President Clinton's signature on the Rome Treaty, thus signifying no intention to act in keeping with the treaty's terms.

The Bush administration sought to pressure many states into signing bilateral agreements stipulating that no American citizen would be turned over to the ICC. The administration also blocked further UN peacekeeping deployments until the UN Security Council voted a one-year immunity measure for all US personnel serving in military deployments authorized by the Council. These steps by Washington created much friction with particularly its European allies, but in the last analysis many of them caved in to US power.

Although one can locate a few Democrats who openly support the ICC in its current form,[41] this is rare. The more prevalent Democratic position is that the current ICC is unacceptable, but that the United States should stay engaged and explore the opportunities for negotiated change.[42] This was essentially the position of President Clinton at the very end of his term, when he belatedly signed the Rome Statute, although indicating he would not send it to the Senate for advice and consent. The mainstream Democratic position as of 2003 allows them to attack the Republicans for being unilateralists or isolationists, without exposing themselves to what they fear is the domestically damaging charge that they favour American personnel being tried in the ICC. But, given that reservations cannot be submitted to the Rome Statute and that as of early 2003 it does not appear that ratifying states will agree to any amendments desired by the United States, Democrats actually offer no alternative to the Republican rejection of the ICC. They stress process, but have no specific alternative to the substantive gridlock. The Democratic Senator Joseph Biden, having replaced Jesse Helms as Chair of the Senate Foreign Relations Committee for a time, took essentially the same line as Senator Helms: "Nothing trumps our Constitution, no international court, unless we voluntarily, under our constitutional process, agree to submit to that court."[43] When the Republican Richard Lugar replaced Senator Biden as Chair of the Senate Foreign Relations Committee, there was no change in attitude toward the ICC.

The American Bar Association, prominent human rights organizations and many academics support the ICC, but this has had not the slightest effect on official Washington opinion. A number of prominent Americans such as Henry Kissinger went public against the ICC.[44] This is understandable, given their past involvement in such things as the brutal war in Viet Nam and their support for, even possible active involvement in, such things as systematic repression in places like Chile. They fear that US officials would not have the same freedom in choosing whatever policies seem necessary in a dangerous world. What they are demanding – for example, control of the ICC by the UN Security Council – is irrelevant to the rest of the international community. Despite the irrelevance of their arguments internationally, they lend prestige to the attacks on the ICC domestically.[45]

In the final analysis, much emotionalism holds sway, especially in Congress. Members of Congress from both political parties will not accept any possibility, no matter how justified or limited, that American personnel might be defendants in the ICC. They are not prepared to face the question that some US decisions about targets and weapons might be on the wrong side of international law. Washington officials in both political branches are less interested in an effective international criminal justice system, and more interested in preserving full US independence of policy-making – with the lack of legal accountability that that posture entails. Realists, who stress the primacy of power politics, understand why the US military does not want to be second-guessed about military strategy and tactics. There are controversies from Yugoslavia in 1999 and Afghanistan from 2001 that might merit international criminal inquiry. The Pentagon, in particular, does not want to have to defend its decisions to international jurists in the ICC.

Conclusions

Given the anticipated reality in the near future of legal exposure of US personnel under the ICC, the issue comes down to a costs–benefits analysis of ratification versus non-ratification. The ICC has come into being, with most US allies ratifying. That being clear, should the United States continue its opposition to an independent Prosecutor, or should the United States ratify and then have a role in the selection of the Prosecutor and judges, as well as a role in helping to prosecute brutal authoritarians? If, as was apparently the case in both Yugoslavia and Afghanistan, the United States can show a clear effort by military lawyers and high officials to minimize civilian damage in the selection of targets and weapons, does the United States really have much to fear from the ICC? Should the fears of a worst-case scenario about a "rogue" Prosecutor be offset by the good that could be done by a functioning ICC with US support?[46] After all, non-ratification by the United States damages its position in international relations, creating conflict with allies and causing disassociation from notions of human rights and international law. The United States is not well positioned to help with the prosecution of future Saddam Husseins. So there is a real cost to current US policy, undertaken in the name of preventing a projected cost. However much this damage might be discounted by current thinking in official Washington, the damage remains real.

This type of costs–benefits calculation is far from being the dominant discourse in Washington regarding the ICC. Much emotional nationalism prevails, especially in Congress, based on American exceptionalism. The discourse emphasizes national constitutional protection for military individuals. But the cited constitutional provisions pertain neither to military courts nor to Americans abroad. The discourse is primarily emotive or sentimental, based on the *a priori* rejection of the ICC passing legal judgment on American citizens.[47] There is virtually no discussion of the probability of justified indictments of high policy makers for their systematic and broad decisions about targets and weapons in armed conflict. This absence is particularly pronounced in the Pentagon, which of course is not surprising. In the last analysis, official Washington is not prepared to accept muscular international legal limits on national military decisions.

Whereas the Clinton administration was sandwiched between the exceptionalists in Congress and the Realists in the Pentagon, the George W. Bush administration faced no such dilemma, as it seemed to endorse both the exceptionalist and the Realist reasons for opposing the ICC.

It may turn out to be the case that, like the acerbic debate in Washington over US payments to the puny assessed budgets of the United Nations, the debate about the ICC is mostly about symbols and ideology.

The ICC may not be very central to international relations in the future. First, the principle of complementarity means that, when a state properly investigates and perhaps prosecutes any of the three crimes covered by the Rome Statute, the ICC remains inactive. Second, the ICC will probably need to give due deference, or a margin of appreciation, to democratic governments giving priority to truth commissions and other forms of post-conflict social justice in the quest for national reconciliation.[48] International criminal justice may not be the preferred path to improved world order; it has not been in places such as South Africa and El Salvador. Third, a wise Prosecutor will also realize that there is not much long-term gain for the ICC in alienating the most powerful state in the world, whose cooperation will probably prove necessary for the arrest of some suspects and for the financial and diplomatic well-being of the court. Thus, the ICC may not be so active as its champions assume.

Be that as it may in the future, the present reality swirling around the ICC is of clear and persistent conflict between two views. Most states and international NGOs desire more "legalization" regarding genocide, crimes against humanity and war crimes, and therefore want that law to be better specified and adjudicated.[49] On the other hand, the United States seems determined to exempt its national decisions touching upon these issues from authoritative international review, whether for exceptionalist or Realist reasons. The larger question, therefore, is whether the United States can be entangled in international arrangements to such an extent that it is required to rethink its self-image and redefine its national interests. Some observers believe that a large part of contemporary world affairs concerns the orderly transfer of state sovereignty to international authorities.[50] But it is not at all clear that the United States is prepared to engage in this process as regards the ICC.[51]

Notes

1. George Kennan, *American Diplomacy 1900–1950*, Chicago: University of Chicago Press, 1951.
2. David Scheffer, point man on this subject for the Clinton administration, has given his views in "The United States and the International Criminal Court", *American Journal of International Law*, vol. 93, no. 1, 1999, pp. 12–22. For excellent overviews, see Sarah B. Sewall and Carl Kaysen, eds., *The United States and the International Criminal Court: National Security and International Law*, Lanham, Md.: Rowman & Littlefield for the American Academy of Arts and Sciences, 2000; a special issue of *Law and Contemporary Problems*, vol. 64, no. 1, 2001; Council on Foreign Relations, "Toward an International Criminal Court?: Three Options Presented as Presidential Speeches", New York, 1999. For background, see Yves Beigbeder, *Judging War Criminals: The Politics of International Justice*, London: Macmillan, 1999.

3. The George W. Bush inaugural address is permeated by the theme of American exceptionalism.

4. For the importance of American exceptionalism in the United States, see Samuel P. Huntington, "American Ideals versus American Institutions", in John Ikenberry, ed., *American Foreign Policy: Theoretical Essays*, 3rd edn., New York: Longman, 1999, pp. 221–253.

5. For a stimulating treatment, see Michael Hunt, *Ideology and US Foreign Policy*, New Haven, Conn.: Yale University Press, 1987.

6. Alexander Wendt, *The Social Theory of International Politics*, Cambridge: Cambridge University Press, 1999.

7. Gabor Kardos, "Human Rights and Foreign Policy in Central Europe", in David P. Forsythe, ed., *Human Rights and Comparative Foreign Policy*, Tokyo: United Nations University Press, 2000, pp. 224–249. Similarly, Andrew Moravcsik believes it was not the larger but rather the smaller European states that were primarily responsible for the European human rights regime. "The Origins of Human Rights Regimes: Democracy Delegation in Post War Europe", *International Organization*, vol. 54, no. 2, 2000, pp. 217–252. See below regarding why great powers tend not to be great multilateralists in some ways.

8. Detlev F. Vagts, "The United States and Its Treaties: Observance and Breach", *American Journal of International Law*, vol. 95, no. 2, 2001, pp. 277–312. US courts have developed several lines of reasoning, such as the last in time rule, in order to find that international law is sometimes not in legal force in the US jurisdiction.

9. John Bolton, "The Global Prosecutors: Hunting War Criminals in the Name of Utopia", *Foreign Affairs*, vol. 78, no. 1, 1999, especially pp. 158–159. In constructing his argument, Bolton simply ignores considerable contradictory evidence, such as US jurists holding that international law is indeed US law and that certain cases will be decided on the basis of international law.

10. It is with the United States in mind that one can say that a universalist is a relativist with power.

11. See, further, Stephanie Grant, "The United States and the International Human Rights Treaty System: For Export Only?", in Philip Alston and James Crawford, *The Future of UN Human Rights Treaty Monitoring*, Cambridge: Cambridge University Press, 2000.

12. Even under the International Covenant on Civil and Political Rights, ratified in 1992, the United States has never accepted the first optional protocol on private petitions, and the submission of its first report to the UN Human Rights Committee led to controversy in the Senate as to whether that Committee had the authority to make general comments on the US report. Several Senators adopted the restrictive view – which ironically was the Soviet position during the Cold War. On the other hand, the United States did accept a protocol related to the Convention on the Rights of the Child prohibiting the use of soldiers in combat position who were under the age of 18. This provision required a slight change in the policies of the US Defense Department. This latter matter tends to be the exception that confirms the general rule to the contrary.

13. William Schabas, "Spare the RUD or Spoil the Treaty: The United States Challenges the Human Rights Committee on Reservations", in David P. Forsythe, ed., *The United States and Human Rights: Looking Inward and Outward*, Lincoln, Nebr.: University of Nebraska Press, 2000, pp. 110–130.

14. Condoleezza Rice, "Promoting the National Interest", *Foreign Affairs*, vol. 79, no. 1, 2000, pp. 45–62. Richard N. Haass, *Intervention: The Use of American Military Forces in the Post–Cold War World*, Washington, D.C.: Brookings, 1999.

15. The George W. Bush administration specifically, and Republicans in general, have no monopoly on this orientation. The Clinton administration manifested similar traits, es-

pecially early in that administration. All states tend to match ends and means, desires and resources. No state can right all the wrongs of the world, but there is a difference between ignoring foreign problems because they interfere with self-preoccupation and trying to arrive at a division of labour that would allow the problems to be managed. Multilateralism contributes precisely to the latter approach.

16. See Edward C. Luck, *Mixed Messages: American Politics and International Organization 1919–1999*, Washington, D.C.: Brookings, 1999. "From a US perspective, the purpose of the UN is to augment national policy options, not to limit them" (p. 294).

17. Thomas Friedman, "American Snubbing of the United Nations is Silly", *International Herald Tribune*, 30 May 2001, p. 8.

18. The Helms–Biden legislation that led to US agreement to pay UN arrears was in essence a unilateral diktat: the United States listed a number of demands that the United Nations would have to meet before payments would be made.

19. *International Herald Tribune*, 27 May 2001, p. 10.

20. See further, for example, Chalmers Johnson, *Blowback: The Costs and Consequences of American Empire*, New York: Henry Holt [Owl Books], 2000; William Pfaff, *Barbarian Sentiments: America in the New Century*, New York: Hill & Wang, 2000.

21. For passing references to US arrogance in relation to the ICC, see the chapters by Weschler and Nash in Sewall and Kaysen, eds., *The United States and the International Criminal Court*.

22. American exceptionalism is similar to Swiss exceptionalism in its unilateralist orientation. On Swiss exceptionalism, see further Elizabeth Olson, "Sky Falls in on the Swiss: Tranquillity Is a Victim", *New York Times*, 21 November 2001, p. A-4. A Swiss is quoted: "we believe we are very special, and that makes it very difficult to change."

23. Quoted in David P. Forsythe, *The Politics of International Law*, Boulder, Colo.: Lynne Rienner, 1990, p. 3.

24. Ibid., p. 55.

25. See, further, *Germany v. United States*, summer 2001, in which the World Court held that the United States had violated the Vienna Convention on Consular Relations when it allowed a capital case to go forward in Arizona against two German nationals despite the fact that they were not afforded contact with German officials. The convicted Germans were executed shortly after the ICJ ruling. There had been a previous matter of US capital punishment of a Paraguayan national in Virginia that similarly violated the procedural requirements of the Vienna Convention. At the time of writing, a scheduled execution in Oklahoma raising similar issues had been delayed. Also, in early 2003 the World Court ordered a stay of execution for three Mexicans facing capital punishment in the United States; once again, the issue for the ICJ was proper notification to consular officials under the Vienna Convention on Consular Relations.

26. Steven Holloway, "US Unilateralism at the UN: Why Great Powers Do Not make Great Multilateralists", *Global Governance*, vol. 6, no. 3, 2000, pp. 361–382.

27. Hearing before the Committee on International Relations, House of Representatives, 25–26 July 2000, "The International Criminal Court", www.amicc.org/usinfo/congress_hearings.html.

28. Michael P. Scharf, "The ICC's Jurisdiction over the Nations of Non-Party States", in Sewall and Kaysen, eds., *The United States and the International Criminal Court*, pp. 213–236.

29. See, further, the chapter by Lawrence Weschler in Sewall and Kaysen, eds., *The United States and the International Criminal Court*, pp. 85–114.

30. The distinguished commentator Ramesh Thakur, Vice Rector of the United Nations University, believes that national officials should not have to answer to disparate national proceedings regarding criminal justice as compared with a centralized procedure in the ICC.

31. Among many sources, see Joseph Goldstein, et al., *The My Lai Massacre and Its Cover-up: Beyond the Reach of Law?*, New York: The Free Press, 1976.
32. Confidential interviews, 2000.
33. Human Rights Watch raised questions about the US use of cluster bombs in Afghanistan; 18 December 2002, www.hrw.org/reports/2002/us-afghanistan.
34. See, for example, the statement by Ruth Wedgwood, Professor of Law at Yale University, Hearing before the Committee on Foreign Relations, United States Senate, 14 June 2000, "The International Criminal Court: Protecting American Servicemen and Officials from the Threat of International Prosecution", www.amicc.org/usinfo/congress_hearings.html. Professor Wedgwood believes that certain US military policies might run afoul of international legal review, and that an international court has no business reviewing such matters as US bombing of electrical grids and TV stations in Yugoslavia in 1999.
35. Interviews, fall 2001.
36. Note that the crime of aggression will be included in the subject matter jurisdiction of the court, when that concept is adequately defined.
37. See, further, Robert W. Tucker, "The International Criminal Court Controversy", *World Policy Journal*, vol. 18, 2001, pp. 71–82.
38. The bill was intentionally misnamed to produce broad support in the name of American military personnel abroad. But eventually it became known that the intent of the bill was to protect high officials from any ICC review of their decisions. See Elizabeth Becker, "On World Court [*sic*], US Focus Shifts to Shielding Officials", *New York Times*, 7 November 2002, p. A-4.
39. See the exchange between Senator Dodd (Dem., Conn.) and Secretary Powell in Hearing before the Committee on Foreign Relations, United States Senate, 20 June 2001, "US Security Interests in Europe", www.amicc.org/usinfo/congress_hearings.html.
40. Quoted in John F. Murphy, "The Quivering Gulliver: US Views on a Permanent International Criminal Court", *International Lawyer*, vol. 34, 2000, p. 45.
41. See Press Release, 13 November 2000, by Congressman Patrick J. Kennedy (Dem., R.I.), "Why the International Criminal Court Is Important to the US and the International Community", www.house.gov/patrickkennedy/oped001113-criminal-court.htm.
42. Bill Richardson, "America's Interest in an International Court", *New York Times*, 21 August 2001. Richardson was a former Democratic Member of Congress, Representative to the United Nations and Secretary of Energy. See also the statement by Christopher Dodd (Dem., Conn.), *Congressional Record*, p. S9859, 26 September 2001, http://thomas.loc.gov/home/r108query.html; and the remarks by Senate majority leader Tom Daschle (Dem., So. Dakota), Speech, "A New Century of American Leadership", Woodrow Wilson Center, 9 August 2001, www.senate.gov/~daschle/pressroom/speeches/2001A09615.html.
43. Press Conference with Senator Joseph Biden (Dem., Del.), 28 June 2001.
44. Henry Kissinger, "The Pitfalls of Universal Jurisdiction", *Foreign Affairs*, vol. 80, no. 4, 2001, pp. 86–96. Henry Kissinger, *Does America Need a Foreign Policy: Toward a Diplomacy for the 21st Century*, New York: Simon & Schuster, 2001, chapter 7. In the latter, Kissinger rhetorically asks (at p. 31): "What, for our survival, must we seek to prevent no matter how painful the means?" Although he never explicitly answers this question, the raising of it indicates his pessimistic realism that is not sympathetic to legal review of the exercise of power.
45. See, further, Ralph G. Carter and Donald W. Jackson, "The International Criminal Court: Present at the Creation?", in Ralph G. Carter, ed., *Contemporary Cases in US Foreign Policy: From Terrorism to Trade*, Washington, D.C.: Congressional Quarterly Press, 2002, pp. 364–386.

46. See, further, the chapter by Nash in Sewall and Kaysen, eds., *The United States and the International Criminal Court*, pp. 153–164.

47. One wonders just how far American society has evolved since 1919 when a Senator from Missouri said in the debate on the Permanent Court of International Justice, attached to the League of Nations Covenant: "Think of submitting questions involving the very life of the United States to a tribunal on which a nigger from Liberia, a nigger from Honduras, a nigger from India ... each have votes equal to that of the great United States." Quoted in Paul Gordon Lauren, *Power and Prejudice: The Politics and Diplomacy of Racial Discrimination*, Boulder, Colo.: Westview, 1988, p. 113.

48. See chapter 11 by Scharf in Sewall and Kaysen, eds., *The United States and the International Criminal Court*.

49. On the "legalization" of world politics, see the special issue of *International Organization*, vol. 54, no. 3, 2000. For an analysis of international criminal justice consistent with this type of theoretical approach, see Christopher Rudolph, "Constructing an Atrocities Regime: The Politics of War Crimes Tribunals", *International Organization*, vol. 55, no. 3, 2001, pp. 655–691. For a less theoretical analysis of the movement in contemporary international relations toward supranational courts, see Mary L. Volcansek, ed., *Law above Nations: Supranational Courts and the Legalization of Politics*, Gainesville, Fl.: University Presses of Florida, 1997.

50. Robert Wright, "America's Sovereignty in a New World", *New York Times*, 24 September 2001, p. A-31. Peter Sutherland, "Europeans Lead in the Trek to Global Governance", *International Herald Tribune*, 8 November 2001.

51. See, further, the exchange between Marc Thiessen, spokesperson for Senator Jesse Helms, and Mark Leonard, linked to Tony Blair, in "When Worlds Collide", *Foreign Policy*, no. 123, 2001, pp. 64–74.

4

Violations of human rights and humanitarian law and threats to international peace and security

George J. Andreopoulos

Introduction

In recent years there has been a plethora of writings on the growing trend of identifying human rights and humanitarian crises as threats to international peace and security. Some analysts have welcomed this development as reflecting the rising profile of human rights and humanitarian norms within the security discourse. Others have criticized it as a series of ad hoc responses with not much of an afterthought on the implications of such linkages, or as mere window dressing, or "façade legitimation".[1] In the latter case, norms provide the kinder, gentler face of naked power considerations in pursuit of state interests.

This chapter will analyse and assess certain critical features of this trend and the concomitant debate on the mainstreaming of human rights and humanitarian norms. In attempting to answer this question, issues pertaining to key aspects of collective security, the role of norms in international politics and the specific characteristics of the accountability discourse, as this has unfolded in the post–Cold War era, will be addressed. Although these issues involve the dynamic interplay of international, regional and domestic actors and processes, the emphasis in this chapter is on the United Nations system.[2]

Revisiting collective security

Collective security offers a useful entry point for discussion of this issue because the debate primarily centres on the United Nations Security

Council's new-found activism.[3] According to a recent study, between 1946 and 1989 the UN Security Council (UNSC) adopted 646 resolutions (on average fewer than 15 per year). Out of these resolutions, six recognized the existence of a threat to international peace and security.[4] During the 1990–1999 period, the UNSC adopted 638 resolutions (on average close to 64 per year). Out of these, 19 explicitly referred to threats to international peace and security.[5] The decisional context for such activism relates to early post–Cold War euphoria and the "collective response" in the Gulf conflict in 1991. This interest has been manifested in exuberant US Presidential remarks on a "New World Order" relating to the enhanced normative status of the rule of law and of cooperative conduct, and in the UN Secretary-General's comments on the immediate aftermath of Iraq's defeat. President Bush Sr.'s reference to "the shared responsibility for freedom and justice"[6] and Pérez de Cuéllar's claim that public attitudes are shifting "towards the belief that the defense of the oppressed ... should prevail over frontiers and legal documents"[7] attempted to delineate the contours of a revitalized collective security mechanism. Such a mechanism would ensure responsive action not only in situations of breaches of inter-state peace but also in situations of humanitarian breaches resulting from the lack of governmental respect for human dignity[8] and of governmental accountability in cases of serious and systematic violations of such dignity.

This emphasis on the potentially beneficial impact of a revitalized United Nations, and in particular of a Security Council that would function as the UN Charter framers intended it, has brought a new scrutiny of collective security and its key assumptions.[9] Despite their opposition to the balance of power mentality that characterizes the Realist School, collective security proponents share a key assumption with the Realists: states are rational, unitary actors that operate in an anarchic environment which shapes their conduct (anarchy is an independent variable).[10] The main difference between collective security and the self-help world of Realism is the belief that stability can emerge through cooperation, rather than through competition,[11] and thus the effects of anarchy can be mitigated. Institutions (such as the United Nations) can play a role in transforming state conduct in ways consistent with the dictates of collective security.

This transformational image rests on three key notions: the indivisibility of peace, the commitment of all states to join in an effort to contain the aggressor (all for one, and one for all) and the moral negation of neutrality. Although the notion of the indivisibility of peace can in certain circumstances be consistent with calculations of self-interest (after all, if states believe that the threat to or breach of peace in one part of the world will eventually adversely affect their interests, it is imperative that they do something about it), its ramifications do place a heavy burden on member states. In general terms, a commitment to the indivisibility of peace can be fulfilled only on the basis of a prior undertaking to defend "the anonymous victim of an attack" from "the anonymous aggressor".[12]

There is little doubt that, theoretically, collective security demands a lot from member states and there is an inherent tension between the requirements of collective security and its basic assumption that states are rational actors.[13] Moreover, as Realists have pointed out, despite its belief in the stabilizing effects of cooperative conduct, collective security does not adequately explain how states overcome their fears and build trust, since the theory recognizes that one or more states may harbour aggressive intent. Given the fact that, theoretically, any state can be a potential aggressor, "collective security admits that no state can ever be completely certain about another state's intentions, which brings us back to a realist world where states have little choice but to fear each other".[14]

Moving from theory to practice, the record of collective security systems has given us little to cheer about. The dismal record of the League of Nations and the performance of the United Nations during the Cold War era have raised serious doubts about the prospects for an effective collective security mechanism.[15] This scepticism has been primarily – but not exclusively – expressed by Realists.[16] Even collective security proponents admit that collective security "requires an extraordinary act of political faith for states to repose confidence in the system".[17] To attribute, as some analysts do, the failure of the League and of the United Nations to "military, economic, and political conditions at the national level, not collective security itself"[18] does not really address the main criticism of collective security's relevance. This becomes more obvious when the very same analysts conclude that "the histories of the League and the UN demonstrate only that collective security does not always work, not that it cannot work";[19] yet the pertinent question here is, when does collective security work?[20]

The post–Cold War period, if anything, has exacerbated many of these misgivings. The allied military operation Desert Shield/Desert Storm against Iraq in 1991, which launched the discussion on UN activism, has generated a lot of debate not only on the legal basis for the use of force[21] but also on the contextual factors that shaped the humanitarian protection provided to the Kurds in the immediate aftermath of the conflict.[22] Whereas proponents have seen in these actions the makings of a "new humanitarian order",[23] critics have seen policies and outcomes consistent with hegemonic/balance of power considerations.

To be sure, a Realist perspective is helpful in explaining the lack of specificity in Resolution 678, which authorized the use of force against Iraq for its illegal invasion and occupation of Kuwait: was the legal basis for action Article 42 (Security Council-authorized action) or Article 51 (individual or collective self-defence) of the UN Charter, or did the whole operation come under the UNSC's general competence in the area of international peace and security? Why was it consistent with the interests of the United States and of its key allies to leave the legal basis unclear (with only a general reference to Chapter VII of the UN Charter)? Moreover, a Realist perspective can provide useful insights into the delicate balancing act reflected in Resolution 688, which was subsequently used by the United States, the United Kingdom and France to legitimize their military intervention in northern Iraq in order to establish "safe havens" for the suppressed Kurdish population. The resolution is instructive in what it includes as well as in what it leaves out. Despite the fact that it was drafted in the context of the Kurdish repression, there is no reference to the Kurds in the key operative provisions (the relevant passage "expresses the hope ... that an open dialogue will take place to ensure that the human and political rights of all Iraqi citizens are respected").[24] Moreover, there is no reference to self-determination, let alone Kurdish self-determination. On the contrary, the resolution reaffirmed the international community's commitment to – among others – "the sovereignty, territorial integrity and political independence of Iraq".

A plausible Realist reading would be as follows. For obvious geopolitical reasons, Iraq had to withdraw from Kuwait. Given the uncertainty of the international community's collective response, the United States and the United Kingdom felt that, in order to ensure Iraqi's withdrawal, there had to be a reference to individual/collective self-defence. Such a reference, which appeared in the second resolution relating to the crisis,[25] would ensure that, if a UN-authorized collective response failed to materialize, action could still be taken under Article 51. This option was left open throughout the crisis, including Resolution 678, in which the UNSC – acting under Chapter VII of the UN Charter – authorized member states to "use all necessary means" to implement the initial and all subsequent resolutions. By reaffirming all previous resolutions (including the preambular references to individual or collective self-defence) and by leaving the legal basis unclear, the enabling resolution provided the US-dominated alliance with maximum legal flexibility in the pursuit of its desired objectives.

Likewise, in the aftermath of the war and in response to the concern expressed over the plight of the persecuted Kurds, Resolution 688 sought to achieve a delicate balance: on the one hand to add a humanitarian layer to the intrusive mechanisms established under Resolution 687 (which provided for the cease-fire terms with Iraq), while on the other hand to temper any centrifugal tendencies within Iraq that could both benefit other "troublemakers" in the region (Iran) and create serious domestic problems for supportive regional allies (Turkey, Syria).[26]

This analysis questions some of the basic premises of the argument for a "new humanitarian order" and points to some of the problems associated with collective security. Resolution 688 cannot be understood outside the context of the international community's response to a very traditional breach of the peace. Although humanitarian considerations underscored the passage of Resolution 688, the linkages to international peace and security have been legitimized owing to the overall context of measures for the restoration of inter-state peace. Intra-state peace drew its relevance from its relation to the hierarchically superior norm of the prohibition of inter-state aggression.

Turning to collective security, the operational flexibility allowed by the uncertain legal basis indicated that collective action is not a rule-governed but a power-driven activity. This brings into the picture the earlier concern about the lack of trust, so central to Realist critiques of collective security. Issues relating to the intentions of other states necessitated the constant reference to individual or collective self-defence. For the United States and its allies, rational and responsible conduct, in such a context, is consistent not with the deferment of immediate self-interest (individual or collective self-defence) but with the assertion of its primacy over the uncertainty of UN-authorized action.

This thesis raises serious questions regarding key collective security assumptions, but it does not convey the full story.[27] Whereas these UNSC actions signalled contested analyses and assessments of the collective security framework and the positioning of humanitarian crises within it, it was a series of subsequent UNSC actions that truly opened the Pandora's box on these issues. In the process, they rekindled the debate concerning the relevance of norms and their causative impact in international relations.

Human rights and humanitarian norms and the security discourse

If the Gulf War experience and the humanitarian dimensions of Operation Provide Comfort could be accommodated within the Realist framework, subsequent cases of UNSC engagement, especially those in response to internal armed conflict and/or humanitarian crises proved to be more resistant to Realism's embrace. In several of these cases, it was the enormity of the unfolding humanitarian crisis *per se* that seemed to elicit Council action, with at times no more than a tenuous reference to the transboundary impact of key "New World Order" indicators such as refugee flows.

The examples of Somalia and Angola are instructive in this regard. In Somalia, it was the very "extortion, blackmail and robbery to which the international relief effort was subjected and the repeated attacks on the personnel and equipment of the United Nations" that led to the adoption of Security Council Resolution 794 authorizing the use of "all necessary means to establish as soon as possible a secure environment for humanitarian relief operations in Somalia".[28] The UNSC's determination of a threat to international peace and security was based on "the magnitude of the human tragedy caused by the conflict ... further exacerbated by the obstacles being created to the distribution of humanitarian assistance".[29] Boutros Boutros-Ghali later claimed that the Somali case had set a United Nations precedent: "It decided for the first time to intervene militarily for strictly humanitarian purposes."[30]

In Angola, the failure of UNITA to accept the results of the 1992 elections and the continuing military activities that contributed to "the further deterioration of an already grave humanitarian situation" led to the adoption of Security Council Resolution 864. The resolution reflected the Council's determination that the situation constituted a threat to international peace and security, "as a result of UNITA's military actions".[31] With the very same resolution, the Council imposed sanctions against UNITA.

There are three key considerations here. First, in both situations, the increased suffering of the civilian population as a result of the action of one or more actors (UNITA in Angola, various factions in Somalia), compounded by the obstacles created (by them) in the delivery of humanitarian assistance, contributed to the marked deterioration of the humanitarian situation. The internal humanitarian situation (manifested in often massive and systematic violations of international humanitarian law), variously (and often tenuously) linked to transboundary indicators, emerges as a common theme in post–Cold War UNSC activism.

Second, in both situations, there are expressed references to violations of international humanitarian law and direct condemnations of such violations. Here, both cases follow the precedent set by the relevant resolutions in the Gulf conflict.[32] In the case of Angola, the resolution condemned "the repeated attacks ... by UNITA against United Nations personnel" and reaffirmed "that such attacks are clear violations of international humanitarian law".[33] In the case of Somalia, the resolution demanded "that all parties, movements and factions ... cease and desist from all breaches of international humanitarian law".[34]

Third, and related to the second, there is increasing emphasis on the accountability of non-state actors (individuals and groups), and in particular of non-state armed groups. In the Angolan case, the targeting of UNITA via a Chapter VII resolution (imposition of sanctions) created an interesting precedent for the international accountability of such actors. In a similar vein, in the Somali case, the relevant resolution condemned these violations and affirmed "that those who commit or order the commission of such acts will be held individually responsible in respect of such acts".[35] It has been argued that the subsequent, unsuccessful and – for many analysts – ill-conceived hunting down of Mohammed Farah Aideed was but an attempt at accountability in the midst of the brewing confrontation between the second UN Operation in Somalia (UNOSOM II) and Aideed's military faction.[36]

Do references to internal humanitarian crises coupled with invocations of norms of international humanitarian law and the emphasis on the consequences of non-adherence matter? In particular, do they modify in any meaningful way the security discourse? Recently, there has been a lot of discussion on the role of ideas and norms in international relations.[37] Going beyond the Realist focus on material factors as determinants of political outcomes, several studies have challenged Realist assumptions in several key issue areas, including that of security policy in both its domestic and international variants.[38] Although material considerations remain relevant, this body of literature has been critical of the view that ideas and norms should be considered as mere epiphenomena, nothing more than vehicles for the legitimization of pre-existing interests, with no causal role in policy outcomes.[39] However, the growing relevance of the ideational perspective is bounded in some of these analyses – especially those written from a neoliberal perspective – by the shared (with Realists and neo-Realists) premises of the rational actor model, premises that relate to the aforementioned stable and exogenous nature of these interests. Thus, although acknowledging the potential impact of normative considerations, they do not envisage a constitutive relationship among identities, interests and norms.[40]

Going a step further, critical theorists have brought forward the notion that reality is socially constructed and that the international system is not a given that forces states to behave as rational egoists. Rather, identities and interests are shaped and reshaped in a discursive process of shared meanings. The goal here is, according to one analyst, to define national interest in terms of the international community;[41] or, to put it otherwise, national interest has no separate and distinct meaning from that of the international community. In this view, norms, perceived as inter-subjective ideas on proper conduct, cannot be easily manipulated to crudely reflect power considerations, but have a generative power that, though affected by strategic and material factors, can also shape these factors.[42]

In the human rights/humanitarian context, an ideational perspective would emphasize (at a minimum) the staying power of human rights and humanitarian norms and their impact on policy outcomes in situations where national interests would dictate a different course of action.[43] Any credible argument along those lines should exhibit an awareness of the complexities of the decisional context in question, and in particular of the varied and uneven ways in which norms could affect decision-making processes and institutions. In the United Nations system, for example, this has been repeatedly demonstrated by the permeability of the General Assembly's discourse to human rights and humanitarian norms, in contrast to the relative impermeability (until recently) of its counterpart in the Security Council.[44]

In a similar vein, any examination of the Somalia operation should draw a distinction between the decision to intervene in the first place and the decisions pertaining to the military's mission and to the designation of the appropriate force package in support of the mission.[45] A Realist perspective is clearly relevant in analysing and assessing the behaviour of the Unified Task Force on the ground in Somalia (in particular its reluctance to pursue a comprehensive disarmament programme),[46] but less so in the context of the initial decision to intervene. It must be borne in mind that, despite all the scenarios about "mission creep", the Bush Sr. administration was well aware of the fact that humanitarian assistance in Somalia was not the equivalent of setting up "soup kitchens".[47] Thus, the notion as perpetrated by the mass media (particularly in the early phases of Operation Restore Hope) that this would be an anodyne operation, and hence could be explained as a low- to zero-risk goodwill gesture, is simply belied by the facts.

So what could account for the decision to intervene in the first place, bearing in mind the administration's awareness of the risks involved? A plausible Realist analysis would argue that the policy most consistent with the country's interests at that juncture would favour either abstention or an attempt to improve the delivery of supplies to local airfields, which had originated under the auspices of Operation Provide Relief.[48] Yet neither of these options was chosen. Any attempt to provide an answer has to take into consideration the rising profile of broader human rights and humanitarian concerns within the peace maintenance discourse, as evidenced in the Secretary-General's *Agenda for Peace*, the unfortunate experience of UNOSOM I, the plight of Somali civilians[49] and the targeting of relief agencies by armed gangs on the ground. The often-quoted statement by Boutros-Ghali comparing and contrasting international action in the case of Yugoslavia with inaction during the disintegration of Somalia should be assessed within the broader framework of a discourse increasingly sensitive to negative or inequitable responses in the face of humanitarian catastrophes – catastrophes characterized by massive and systematic violations of international human rights and international humanitarian law. In such a context, one of the most important legacies of the Somalia case was the tension between the normative considerations that underpinned the decision to intervene and the Realist considerations that shaped the conceptual and operational contours of the military's mission.

However, the potential contribution of a normative approach lies beyond an exposure of the lack of correspondence between exogenously defined interests and particular courses of action. Rather, as constructivists have sought to argue, the infusion of the normative dimension constitutes the starting point for deliberative undertakings on the very nature and boundaries of the international security arena. Thus, any issue relating to the post–Cold War tendency to link unfolding humanitarian crises to threats to international peace and security, a linkage premised on the causative impact of an internal crisis on the security of other states, could not be adequately addressed without a reconsideration of the very concept of the (international) community itself[50] – a reconsideration that would set the decisional context for the identification of its security needs.

To be sure, there are no easy answers here. But the importance of such an enquiry lies elsewhere. By raising these questions and by pointing to the inadequate explanations offered by conventional readings of security-related developments, a human rights/humanitarian-based perspective acquires a vital entry point into the critical deliberations occurring at the high table of security politics. A key catalyst in this process is the recent prominence of the quest for accountability.

The quest for accountability

Probably the most dramatic transformation in the nature of contemporary international affairs has been the general acceptance of the proposition that certain universal principles are deemed enforceable, either by the United Nations or, in extreme situations, by a group of states ... Moreover, such international conventions as those condemning genocide, torture, or war crimes, are said to be enforceable by national judges ... In addition, an International Criminal Court ... will invest a prosecutor with the power to start investigations of alleged violations of international law at the request of any signatory state ... *These innovations reflect the new conventional wisdom, according to which traditional principles of sovereignty and non-interference in the domestic affairs of other countries are the principal obstacles to the universal rule of peace and justice.*[51]

With a few minor changes, this passage could have been written by an ideational theorist, and probably one on the fringes for that matter. After all, it does take quite a leap of faith to characterize recent developments as reflective of a consensus in the international community (general acceptance), and to link the enforcement of the relevant norms to peace maintenance and justice. Nevertheless, this passage is cited from Henry Kissinger's recent book *Does America Need a Foreign Policy?* Has Henry Kissinger, one of the most hard-nosed Realists, suddenly realized the impact of the enforcement of human rights and humanitarian norms, and thus the demise of one of the canons of Realist thought, namely the epiphenomenal nature of normative considerations?[52] Although there is an obvious "Realist" answer to Kissinger's concerns – namely, the adverse impact of his future travel plans on his personal security and well-being – his remarks point to a series of potentially important developments.

At the more general level, the past decade has witnessed a series of events suggesting the emergence of what could be termed "a global ethos of accountability", manifested through the dynamic interplay of international, regional and domestic justice options.[53] These justice options have involved judicial proceedings (Pinochet in the United Kingdom, the "Rwanda four" in Brussels) as well as non-judicial mechanisms, in particular truth and reconciliation commissions, which are a product of, and a contribution to, rising societal expectations of critical confrontations with their abusive past.[54]

An important indicator of this trend is the growing intersection between international human rights law and international humanitarian law. This intersection has been primarily manifested in the Statutes of the two ad hoc International Criminal Tribunals for the former Yugoslavia and Rwanda (ICTY and ICTR) and in their evolving jurisprudence, which has contributed to the clarification and refinement of key concepts in these two bodies of law. Among the most prominent examples are the de-linking of the concept of crimes against humanity from the war nexus requirement[55] and the changing parameters of the status of protected persons in accordance with the Geneva Conventions.

Concerning crimes against humanity, the Appeals Chamber of the ICTY ruled in the *Tadic* case that "it is by now a settled rule of customary international law that crimes against humanity do not require a connection to international armed conflict. Indeed, as the prosecutor points out, customary international law may not require a connection between crimes against humanity and any conflict at all."[56] On protected persons, the Appeals Chamber of the ICTY upheld the Trial Chamber's finding that Article 4 of Geneva Convention IV was applicable in the context of the conflict in Bosnia-Herzegovina. Hence, the Bosnian Serbs detained in the Celebici camp should be regarded as "having been in the hands of a party to the conflict ... of which they were not nationals" and, therefore, as protected persons.[57] In this context, the Appeals Chamber concurred with the prosecution that "depriving victims, who arguably are of the same nationality under domestic law as their captors, of the Protection of the Geneva Conventions solely based on that national law would not be consistent with the object and purpose of the Conventions".[58] Thus, the Appeals Chamber relied on a broad and purposive interpretation of the Geneva Conventions consistent with the tenor of the comment by the International Committee of the Red Cross that "the Conventions have been drawn up first and foremost to protect individuals, and not to serve State interests".[59]

Another important and related indicator is the increasing emphasis on the humanitarian aspects of civilian protection. This can be seen in the plethora of UNSC resolutions that cite the suffering of civilians and the obstacles created to the delivery of humanitarian assistance, including the targeting of humanitarian personnel, as threats to international peace and security and thus necessitating some type of responsive action.[60] In addition, the UN Secretary-General's first two reports on the protection of civilians in armed conflict placed the debate on the "imposition of appropriate enforcement action" squarely on the international community's agenda.[61] Among the relevant factors for such a course of action, the Secretary-General pointed to "[t]he scope of the breaches of human rights and international humanitarian law, including the numbers of people affected and the nature of the violations".[62] The controversy generated by the Secretary-General's remarks at the 1999 annual session of the UN General Assembly, as well as the ensuing debate, were powerful reminders that – irrespective of short-term outcomes – security's imperviousness to humanitarian considerations was eroding.

Although violations of human rights and/or humanitarian norms could constitute legitimate triggers for action, the quest for accountability has another critical dimension. According to the UN Secretary-General's second report on the protection of civilians in armed conflict, criminal justice can have an impact on confidence-building and reconciliation in post-conflict societies and "can deter crimes in current and future conflicts".[63] To be sure, this is quite a tall order for an "emerging paradigm of international criminal justice"[64] and, despite certain optimistic early assessments, the jury is still out on the conflict prevention role of judicial mechanisms.[65] Having said that, however, the importance of such linkages between conflict prevention and accountability mechanisms lies in the extent to which they generate interesting questions and hypotheses, and thus provide entry points in the security discourse (in this context, its conflict prevention dimension). Would the continuing and effective functioning of already existing accountability mechanisms enhance the global appeal of human rights and humanitarian norms and in the process contribute to their internalization in the political culture and domestic practices of the societies in question? What are the critical variables that can facilitate/obstruct this process? The jury may still be out, but the terms of the debate may also be shifting.

On the mainstreaming of norms: Words of caution

Although the exact nature, extent and impact of all these developments constitute legitimate subjects for debate, their outright dismissal as mere sideshows is becoming increasingly untenable. As the deliberative process unfolds, two words of caution are in order. The first relates to the impact of these developments on the prospects for a viable collective security system. If this trend continues, international security's diminishing imperviousness to humanitarian considerations will exacerbate the tension between the requisite confidence in the collective security system, in particular the system's emphasis on restraining military action, and the imperative for the system's response to a growing array of threats to and breaches of the peace.[66] Moreover, the proliferation of potential humanitarian triggers for enforcement action will test member states' commitment to an already questionable UN record on issues of effectiveness and impartiality. If there is any doubt on this, one has to look no further than the debate that took place in the 1999 annual session of the General Assembly. Although the debate was indicative of the rising profile of humanitarian considerations, it also reconfirmed the deepening North/South divide on the merits of enforcement action to halt or prevent violations of humanitarian or human rights law, even when such action is to be viewed as a last resort option.[67]

The second word of caution relates to the particular direction in which the emphasis on human rights and humanitarian issues seems to be moving. The increasing relevance of the accountability discourse is a positive development, but its legal dimension seems to be prevailing over non-legal approaches for the promotion of accountability-sensitive outcomes. Up to a certain point, this is a reflection of the continuing preoccupation with standard-setting and legal enforcement within the human rights paradigm. However, the recent over-reliance on the international criminal justice model poses certain risks. The most serious risk is that a disproportionately large share of the international community's available resources will be drawn into reactive rather than proactive strategies, thus enabling states to refrain from more complex, costly and time-consuming protective initiatives geared towards addressing the structural causes of human rights violations.[68]

A good example of this worrisome trend can be found in none other than the United Nations system itself.[69] The two ad hoc tribunals for the former Yugoslavia and Rwanda have grown exponentially within the span of less than a decade. As of May 2002, the International Criminal Tribunal for the former Yugoslavia has 1,248 staff members from 82 countries, and its budget has grown from the original US$276,000 in 1993 to US$223,169,800 for the biennium 2002–2003 (which averages approximately US$111,000,000 per year).[70] The International Criminal Tribunal for Rwanda has 872 staff members from 80 countries, and its budget for the biennium 2002–2003 stands at US$177,739,400 (which averages approximately US$88,000,000 per year).[71] Currently, the combined budget of the two ad hoc tribunals stands at approximately US$200,000,000 per year. By contrast, the activities of the Office of the High Commissioner for Human Rights (OHCHR), as indicated in its 2002 Annual Appeal, will require US$78,233,896 for the year; out of this figure, US$22,455,150 will come from the UN regular budget, and the rest is expected from voluntary contributions.[72] What is noteworthy in this context is that the United Nations provides to the OHCHR – a department of the UN Secretariat created the same year as the ICTY and with a global mandate for the promotion and protection of human rights – a little over one-tenth of the money that it appropriates for two international criminal justice mechanisms with limited subject matter, temporal and geographic jurisdiction. The argument here is not that the budget of the two ad hoc tribunals should be cut; few would question the valuable work performed by these tribunals. What is argued, instead, is the need for a long-overdue reorientation towards proactive protective initiatives.

Concluding remarks

Given the (at best) uneven record of progress, it is tempting to revert to old clichés of the "half-empty versus half-full glass" variety. This static image would do injustice to what is essentially a dialogic process that is – slowly but steadily – transforming human rights and humanitarian issues from peripheral into more high-profile items on the security agenda. Going beyond what often seems to be a series of ad hoc responses, this process may lead to a more serious rethinking of the meaning of the international community, of common security and of the causative impact of human rights and humanitarian norms. If the quest for humane outcomes is to be taken seriously, such rethinking is imperative.

Notes

1. Expression used by Martti Koskenniemi, "The Place of Law in Collective Security", *Michigan Journal of International Law*, vol. 17, p. 471. The belief in the use of norms as façade legitimation is associated with the Realist school of thought in international relations.
2. Two prominent examples of such interplay are the situations in Kosovo and in Liberia. In the former, an argument has been made that the initial Security Council resolutions characterizing the situation in the Federal Republic of Yugoslavia as a threat to inter-

national peace and security provided at least partial legal cover for the subsequent NATO action (Operation Allied Force). In addition, several analysts have pointed out that Resolution 1244 might have granted *ex post facto* legitimacy to NATO action; see "Editorial Comments: Nato's Kosovo Intervention", *American Journal of International Law*, vol. 93, pp. 831–869 (the comments by Ruth Wedgwood and Louis Henkin). In particular, Louis Henkin wrote: "For Kosovo, Council ratification after the fact in Resolution 1244 – formal ratification by an affirmative vote of the Council – effectively ratified what earlier might have constituted unilateral action questionable as a matter of law" (ibid., p. 834). Concerning the latter, the Security Council's *ex post facto* support of intervention in Liberia by the Economic Community of West African States, as indicated in Resolution 788 (1992), as well as its endorsement of the regional organization's request for sanctions, are indicative of the "systematic and effective cooperation between the United Nations and regional organizations" (*Further Report of the Secretary-General*, UN Doc. S/26200, 1993; quoted in Sean D. Murphy, *Humanitarian Intervention: The United Nations in an Evolving World Order*, Philadelphia: University of Pennsylvania Press, 1996, p. 164).

3. Although, according to the UN Charter, the General Assembly does have a role in the maintenance of peace and security, and it has tried to act in situations of Council inaction (most prominently with the Uniting for Peace Resolution, a resolution whose legality is a matter of debate), the primary responsibility for the maintenance of peace and security rests with the UNSC. Moreover, according to Article 25 of the UN Charter, all members agree to accept and carry out the Council's decisions, in contrast to the General Assembly's resolutions, which are recommendatory.

4. These were the cases of Palestine, Resolution 54 (1948); Congo, Resolution 161 (1961); Southern Rhodesia, Resolution 217 (1965); Pakistan, Resolution 307 (1971); Cyprus, Resolution 353 (1974); and South Africa, Resolution 418 (1977) – Simon Chesterman, *Just War or Just Peace? Humanitarian Intervention and International Law*, Oxford: Oxford University Press, 2001, p. 115. During the same period, the Council made three determinations as to breaches of the peace (ibid., p. 114). Finally, the actions of two states were labelled "aggression" (South Africa and Israel) – Koskenniemi, "The Place of Law in Collective Security", p. 458.

5. Chesterman, *Just War or Just Peace?*, Appendix 3, pp. 238–240. During the same period, the Council made one determination as to breach of the peace: Resolution 660 relating to Iraq's invasion and occupation of Kuwait.

6. *Address before a Joint Session of the Congress on the Persian Gulf Crisis and the Federal Budget Deficit*, 11 September 1990; http://bushlibrary.tamu.edu/papers/1990/90091101.html.

7. UN Press Release SG/SM/4560, *Secretary-General's Address at the University of Bordeaux*, 1991.

8. I use the term "human dignity" despite certain reservations. Although it is used in fundamental human rights documents (the preamble of the Universal Declaration of Human Rights begins with a recognition "of the inherent dignity ... of all members of the human family"), it is a rather problematic term. Although all societies have notions of human dignity, not all societies have well-developed conceptions of human rights. I will not get into the debate here, but for more information on the distinction between human dignity and human rights, see Rhoda E. Howard and Jack Donnelly, "Human Dignity, Human Rights and Political Regimes", in Jack Donnelly, *Universal Human Rights in Theory and Practice*, Ithaca, N.Y.: Cornell University Press, 1989, pp. 66–87.

9. For classic treatments of collective security, see Inis Claude, *Power and International Relations*, New York: Random House, 1962, pp. 94–204, and his *Swords into Plowshares: The Problems and Progress of International Organization*, 4th edn., New York: McGraw-Hill, 1984, pp. 245–285. On the relevance of collective security in the post–

Cold War European context, see Charles A. Kupchan and Clifford A. Kupchan, "Concerts, Collective Security, and the Future of Europe", *International Security*, vol. 16, no. 1, Summer 1991, pp. 114–161. For a critique of collective security, see Richard K. Betts, "Systems of Peace or Causes of War? Collective Security, Arms Control, and the New Europe", *International Security*, vol. 17, no. 1, Summer 1992, pp. 5–43.

10. "[C]ollective security ... may also be described as a rationalistic approach to peace ... the stock in trade of collective security is diplomatic, economic, and military sanctions-equipment for inducing rational decision to avoid threatened damage to the national self-interest" (Claude, *Swords into Plowshares*, pp. 249–250).

11. Kupchan and Kupchan, "Concerts, Collective Security, and the Future of Europe", p. 118.

12. Claude, *Swords into Plowshares*, p. 254.

13. The best discussion of the requirements of collective security is in Claude, *Swords into Plowshares*, pp. 249–261.

14. John J. Mearsheimer, "The False Promise of International Institutions", *International Security*, vol. 19, no. 3, 1994–1995, p. 31.

15. Even those who are prepared to acknowledge certain UN accomplishments usually confine their praise to the organization's work in the area of human rights and humanitarian issues. For example, Richard Falk has noted that the United Nations "has made a more lasting contribution to the quality of world order and the human condition in this domain [human rights] than in relation to either peace and security or economic development, the two issue areas to which the UN is most associated" ("The Challenges of Humane Governance", in George Andreopoulos, ed., *Concepts and Strategies in International Human Rights*, New York: Peter Lang Publishing, 2002, p. 21).

16. Betts writes that "the main theoretical argument against collective security is that its normative rules have been discredited by the empirically validated rules of balance of power" ("Systems of Peace or Causes of War?", p. 12). For a more detailed discussion of collective security's shortcomings, see ibid., pp. 17–22. This of course does not mean that there are no problems associated with the correspondence between the theory of balance of power systems and historical reality (as Betts himself acknowledges), but such a concern is beyond the focus of this chapter.

17. Claude, *Swords into Plowshares*, p. 256.

18. Kupchan and Kupchan, "Concerts, Collective Security, and the Future of Europe", p. 128.

19. Ibid., p. 129. The authors attempt to argue that, given the problems of ideal collective security, a concert-based structure whose precursor is the Concert of Europe – formed in the immediate aftermath of the Napoleonic wars (1815) – may be the solution. They consider concerts to be "an attenuated form of collective security". It is beyond the scope of this chapter to address the merits of their analogy between post-Napoleonic and post–Cold War Europe. However, the designation of the Concert of Europe as a form of collective security system is incorrect. As several analysts have pointed out, what was at the heart of the Concert of Europe was the maintenance of the balance of power, a goal clearly antithetical to collective security (see Mearsheimer, "The False Promise of International Institutions", p. 36; Betts, "Systems of Peace or Causes of War?", p. 27); Claude calls it "a system of de facto great power hegemony ... sitting around a conference table does not transform selfish nationalists and arrogant power politicians into a collegium of ... justice-oriented statesmen of humanity" (*Swords into Plowshares*, p. 28).

20. In the concluding section of his critique of collective security, Claude observes that "collective security is not unrealistic about *power*; it is unrealistic about *policy*" (*Power and International Relations*, p. 204).

21. Oscar Schachter, "United Nations Law in the Gulf Conflict", *American Journal of International Law*, vol. 85, pp. 452–473; and Burns Weston, "Security Council Resolution 678 and Persian Gulf Decisionmaking: Precarious Legitimacy", *American Journal of International Law*, vol. 85, pp. 516–535.

22. The basis for this protection was Security Council Resolution 688 (UN SCOR, 46th Sess., 2082 mtg, UN Doc. S/RES/688, 1991).

23. Francis Deng and Larry Minear wrote: "By overriding Iraqi sovereignty to provide humanitarian assistance and protection to the Kurds, the UN Security Council has paved the way for the current discussion of a new humanitarian order in which governments are held – by force, if necessary – to higher standards of respect for human life" (*The Challenges of Famine Relief: Emergency Operations in the Sudan*, Washington, D.C.: Brookings Institution, 1992, p. 8). For a critical assessment of the "New World Order", see Richard Falk, "Reflections on the Gulf War Experience: Force and War in the United Nations System", unpublished paper (on file with the author).

24. Although, in the preamble, there is a reference to the Kurdish plight, this is presented as part of the wider abuse to which the Iraqi civilian population was being subjected – "Gravely concerned by the repression of the Iraqi civilian population in many parts of Iraq, including most recently in Kurdish-populated areas". Similar language is found in the operative section of Resolution 688.

25. "Affirming the inherent right of individual or collective self-defense, in response to the armed attack by Iraq against Kuwait" (from the preamble of Resolution 661).

26. Especially Turkey, which made airbases available for the air campaign against Iraq, shut down the Iraqi oil pipeline that led to the port of Ceyhan, and had to contend with its own "Kurdish problem". In addition, as a result of an agreement between Turkey and the United States, the United Kingdom and France, a multinational rapid-reaction brigade was to be stationed there to protect the Kurds. The Operation, ominously codenamed Poised Hammer, was to ensure – among other things – that "Iraq complies with the UN Security Council resolution that has to do with refugees" (Lawrence Freedman and David Boren, "'Safe Havens' for Kurds in Post-war Iraq", in Nigel S. Rodley, ed., *To Loose the Bands of Wickedness: International Intervention in Defence of Human Rights*, London: Brassey's, 1992, p. 73). For different legal arguments on Resolution 688 and its relation to Operation Provide Comfort, as well as to the intervention in defence of the Iraqi Shiites, see Murphy, *Humanitarian Intervention*, pp. 182–198; and Chesterman, *Just War or Just Peace?*, pp. 196–206.

27. Although reference to the protection of the Kurds was excluded from Resolution 687, the resolution itself provided sufficient grounds for monitoring Iraqi activities without the added complication arising from the protection of the Kurds and of the Shiites. Here, US domestic policy considerations may have played a role, particularly in relation to President Bush Sr.'s decision to deploy US troops in support of the "safe havens" policy. That decision was announced five days after the US Senate passed a resolution referring to a "moral obligation" to provide humanitarian assistance for Iraqi refugees (see Murphy, *Humanitarian Intervention*, p. 172, n123).

28. Security Council Resolution 794, 3 December 1992; United Nations Department of Public Information, *The United Nations and the Situation in Somalia*, New York, DPI/1321/Rev. 3, June 1994, p. 41.

29. Ibid.

30. *Yearbook of the United Nations*, 1993; quoted in Chesterman, *Just War or Just Peace?*, p. 142. Once the operation was launched, the conduct of the Unified Task Force (Somalia) and, in particular, its reluctance to disarm the different factions cast a long shadow on the long-term prospects of the operation; for a discussion along these lines, see below. For a good discussion of the overall importance of the disarmament, de-

mobilization and reintegration (DDR) process, see Dirk Salomons, "The Moment of Truth: Disarmament, Demobilization and Reintegration of Former Combatants as Indicators of a Successful Peace Process", paper presented at the workshop on "Humanitarian Operations and Civil Conflicts", John Jay College of Criminal Justice, CUNY, 1– 2 December 2000 (on file with the author).

31. Security Council Resolution 864, 15 September 1993; United Nations Department of Public Information, *The United Nations and the Situation in Angola*, New York, DPI/ 1552/PKO/Rev. 1, February 1995, pp. 43 and 45.

32. For example, in the preamble to Resolution 666, the UNSC reaffirmed Iraq's full responsibility under international humanitarian law "in respect of the safety and well-being of third State nationals" (United Nations Department of Public Information, *Resolutions of the United Nations Security Council and Statements by Its President Concerning the Situation between Iraq and Kuwait (2 August 1990–16 November 1994)*, New York, DPI/1104/Rev.5, December 1994, p. 11).

33. *The United Nations and the Situation in Angola*, p. 44.

34. Security Council Resolution 794.

35. Ibid.

36. For a discussion of the background leading to the showdown between Aideed's clan militia and UNOSOM II, see Tom Farer, "Rescuing Human Rights: The Prospect for Humanitarian Interventions", in George Andreopoulos, ed., *Concepts and Strategies in International Human Rights*, pp. 89–90.

37. Judith Goldstein and Robert Keohane, "Ideas and Foreign Policy: An Analytical Framework", in Judith Goldstein and Robert Keohane, eds., *Ideas and Foreign Policy: Beliefs, Institutions and Political Change*, Ithaca, N.Y.: Cornell University Press, 1993, pp. 3–30. Studies on particular issue areas include Audie Klotz, *Norms in International Relations*, Ithaca, N.Y.: Cornell University Press, 1995; and Ward Thomas, *The Ethics of Destruction: Norms and Force in International Relations*, Ithaca, N.Y.: Cornell University Press, 2001. Klotz's study focuses on the emergence of the global norm of racial equality, and Thomas's study on the norms governing the use of force.

38. Peter J. Katzenstein, "Coping with Terrorism: Norms and Internal Security in Germany and Japan", in Goldstein and Keohane, eds., *Ideas and Foreign Policy*, pp. 265–295; and Matthew Evangelista, *Unarmed Forces: The Transnational Movement to End the Cold War*, Ithaca, N.Y.: Cornell University Press, 1999.

39. In the context of this discussion, "ideas" refer to individually held beliefs about right and wrong, whereas "norms" relate to collective expectations of appropriate conduct. For more on this, see Ronald Jepperson, Alexander Wendt and Peter J. Katzenstein, "Norms, Identity, and Culture in National Security", in Peter J. Katzenstein, ed., *The Culture of National Security: Norms and Identity in World Politics*, New York: Columbia University Press, 1996, pp. 33–75.

40. See also the relevant comments by Klotz, *Norms in International Relations*, pp. 21–27; and Thomas, *The Ethics of Destruction*, pp. 8–26.

41. Alexander Wendt, "Anarchy Is What States Make of It: The Social Construction of Power Politics", *International Organization*, vol. 46, no. 2, 1992, p. 400.

42. Needless to say, in each of the aforementioned schools of thought there are variations and disagreements, which are beyond the scope of this chapter.

43. See also the discussion in Goldstein and Keohane, "Ideas and Foreign Policy". For a discussion of the role of moral considerations in the decision to go to war, see David A. Welch, *Justice and the Genesis of War*, Cambridge: Cambridge University Press, 1993.

44. For a study of this contrast in the context of the norm of racial equality, see Klotz, *Norms in International Relations*, pp. 39–54.

45. For a discussion of the military's decision to back the "large option" for intervention

and its reluctance to seek – in the process – significant cooperation with civilian agencies involved in relief work, see John M. George, "The Politics of Peace: The Challenge of Civil–Military Cooperation in Somalia", paper presented at the Conference on "Security and Humanitarian Action: Who is Winning? A US–Europe Dialogue in the Wake of September 11, 2001", Columbia University, 24–25 May 2002.

46. I have discussed this at greater length in George Andreopoulos, "On the Prevention of Genocide: Humanitarian Intervention and the Role of the United Nations", in Andreopoulos, *Concepts and Strategies in International Human Rights*, pp. 104–105.

47. In announcing the decision to send US troops to Somalia, President Bush Sr. made the following statement: "Our mission is humanitarian, *but we will not tolerate armed gangs ripping off their own people, condemning them to death by starvation ... [T]he outlaw elements in Somalia must understand this is serious business*" (George Bush, "Humanitarian Mission to Somalia: Address to the Nation, Washington, D.C., 4 December 1992", *U.S. Department of State Dispatch*, vol. 3, no. 49, 7 December 1992; quoted in Walter Clarke and Jeffrey Herbst, "Somalia and the Future of Humanitarian Intervention", *Foreign Affairs*, vol. 75, no. 2, 1996, pp. 74–75; my emphasis).

48. For a brief discussion of Operation Provide Relief, see George, "The Politics of Peace".

49. According to the Office of Foreign Disaster Assistance of the United States Agency for International Development, in the month of September 1992 only 40 per cent of the airlifted food was reaching the needy civilian population (Susan Rosegrant and Michael D. Watkins, "A 'Seamless' Transition: United States and United Nations Operations in Somalia – 1992–1993 (A)", Kennedy School of Government Case Program, 1996; quoted in George, "The Politics of Peace").

50. Koskenniemi, "The Place of Law in Collective Security", p. 472.

51. Henry Kissinger, *Does America Need a Foreign Policy? Toward a Diplomacy for the 21st Century*, New York: Simon & Schuster, 2001, p. 234; my emphasis.

52. In his discussion of the principle of universal jurisdiction, Kissinger attributes its spread partly "to the intimidating passion of its advocates" (ibid., p. 273). Bearing in mind that the campaign for universal jurisdiction, although supported by certain states, has been primarily orchestrated by non-governmental organizations, we are witnessing another spectre haunting Realist thought – key aspects of the international agenda being increasingly shaped by the transnational mobilization of human rights and humanitarian activists. For a good overview of universal jurisdiction, and of the legal, ethical and practical problems associated with its application, see International Council on Human Rights Policy, *Hard Cases: Bringing Human Rights Violators to Justice Abroad. A Guide to Universal Jurisdiction*, Geneva: International Council on Human Rights Policy, 1999.

53. Here I follow some of the remarks in George Andreopoulos, "On the Accountability of Non-state Armed Groups", paper presented at the Columbia University Seminar on Human Rights, 15 April 2002.

54. On truth commissions, see Priscilla Hayner, *Unspeakable Truths: Confronting State Terror and Atrocity*, New York: Routledge, 2001. For a discussion of the complexities shaping the work of truth commissions, see Audrey Chapman and Patrick Ball, "The Truth of Truth Commissions: Comparative Lessons from Haiti, South Africa, and Guatemala", *Human Rights Quarterly*, vol. 23, no. 1, 2001, pp. 1–43.

55. This linkage, which had confined crimes against humanity to wartime atrocities, was a legacy of the Nuremberg Charter. Other examples would include refinements in the command responsibility doctrine and the characterization of rape as a crime against humanity.

56. *Prosecutor v. Tadic*, Case No. IT-94-1, Appeals Chamber. Decision on the Defense Motion for Interlocutory Appeal on Jurisdiction, 2 October 1995, para. 141, www.un.org/icty/ind-e.htm.

57. *Prosecutor v. Zejnil Delalic, Zdravko Mucic, Hajim Delic, and Esad Landzo* (Celebici Case), Case No. IT-96-21-A, Appeals Chamber Judgment, 20 February 2001, para. 106, www.un.org/icty.

58. Ibid., para. 81.

59. Ibid., quoted in para. 96; see also the remarks by Theodore Meron, "The Humanization of Humanitarian Law", *American Journal of International Law*, vol. 94, 2000, http://web.lexis-nexis.com/universe/.

60. Some of these cases (Angola, Somalia) have already been referred to in the previous section.

61. Report of the Secretary-General to the Security Council on the protection of civilians in armed conflict, S/1999/957, 8 September 1999 (first report); and Report of the Secretary-General on the protection of civilians in armed conflict, S/2001/331, 30 March 2001 (second report). The quoted sentence is from the first report.

62. S/1999/957.

63. S/2001/331.

64. Expression used by the Secretary-General in the second report, S/2001/331.

65. Among recent studies that address this issue, see Richard Goldstone, *For Humanity: Reflections of a War Crimes Investigator*, New Haven, Conn.: Yale University Press, 2000; and Gary Jonathan Bass, *Stay the Hand of Vengeance: The Politics of War Crimes Tribunals*, Princeton, N.J.: Princeton University Press, 2000. Some have argued that the two ad hoc tribunals (ICTY and ICTR), and in particular the former, are already having a deterrent effect and are contributing to post-conflict peace-building; see Payam Akhavan, "Beyond Impunity: Can International Criminal Justice Prevent Future Atrocities?", *American Journal of International Law*, vol. 95, pp. 7–31. This is clearly premature on at least two grounds: (1) the sample is statistically insignificant; and (2) some of the key outcomes cited (for example, the conciliatory behaviour of local political parties influenced by the elimination of indicted leaders) are both over-determined and by no means settled. However, the hypothesis merits further investigation, as current situations evolve and new cases emerge.

66. As Inis Claude notes in his discussion of the objective requirements of collective security, "it [collective security] can expect to retain their [participating states'] loyal support only if it succeeds in reducing, rather than increasing, their exposure to the perils of military involvement" (*Swords into Plowshares*, p. 258).

67. See, for example, the statements made by the representatives of India and Indonesia. For the Indian statement, see "Agenda item 9: General Debate", *Statement by Mr. Jaswant Singh, Minister for External Affairs*, 22 September 1999, www.un.int/india/ind39htm. The Indonesian foreign minister was very critical of the "spectacle of a UN Security Council ... venturing out to take over the work of other UN organs in such fields as human rights, democracy and humanitarian aid" (*Statement by H.E. Mr. Ali Alatas, Minister for Foreign Affairs, Republic of Indonesia, at the 54th Session of the UN General Assembly, New York*, 23 September 1999, www.un.int/indonesia/speeches/ga/plenary/ga-092399.html).

68. As former Finnish President Martti Ahtisaari at the start of the conference "From a Culture of Impunity to a Culture of Accountability", Utrecht, 26–28 November 2001, noted in his keynote address: "Crime and human rights violations emerge from causes deeply embedded in the structure of societies: poverty, deprivation, social injustice ... The recent attention to developing a functioning international criminal justice system has to be warmly welcomed – but we should not forget that it should be accompanied by efficient international policies and structures that are intended to deal with those root causes. In this area, much remains to be done."

69. This paragraph echoes a similar argument made by James Silk, "International Criminal

Justice and the Protection of Human Rights: The Rule of Law or the Hubris of Law?" (on file with the author).

70. www.un.org/icty/glance/keyfig-e.htm, accessed 20 September 2002.

71. www.ictr.org/wwwroot/ENGLISH/geninfo/ictrlaw.htm, accessed 20 September 2002.

72. Office of the United Nations High Commissioner for Human Rights, *Annual Appeal 2002: Overview of Activities and Financial Requirements*, www.unhchr.ch/pdf/annual3.pdf.

Part II

The functioning of ad hoc tribunals and the ICC

5

The individual within international law

Michail Wladimiroff

Introduction

For a very long time states were considered to be responsible for the *faits et gestes* of individuals during armed conflicts. Legal instruments that dealt with the protection of non-combatants and civilians originally addressed themselves to states, not to individuals. The concept that individuals are just agents of a state changed over time into the understanding that individuals are responsible for their own behaviour during an armed conflict. Now, persons who participate in the planning, preparation or execution, or otherwise contribute to the commission, of crimes during an armed conflict are held individually responsible. An interesting element of this international recognition of individual criminal responsibility is its functional interpretation. This initially led to command responsibility; later it included any persons acting in an official capacity, such as government officials and even heads of state. The doctrine of functional interpretation of responsibility was initially directed at military commanders, because such persons have a personal obligation to ensure the maintenance of discipline among troops under their command. There is substantial case law in which the doctrine of command responsibility has been considered. Most cases deal with the military or paramilitary accused. Other persons acting in an official capacity, such as political leaders, not being commander-in-chief, and public officials, have been held liable only in recent decades.

In this chapter I examine the development of the criminal responsibility of individuals for violations of humanitarian law.

Historical background

Issues involving the individual responsibility of officials during an armed conflict are not new. More than 2,000 years ago, in 500 BC, a Chinese philosopher, Sun-Tzu, writing about the art of war observed that commanders are responsible for the actions of their men.[1] The Indian Code of Manu,[2] relating to the practice of war on land, dates back to 200 BC. In the Western world, comparable rudimentary rules are to be found in ancient Greek and Roman law.[3] Later, Islamic Sharia law[4] reflected such rules as well. Regulations on the lawful use of force during armed conflict are also found in diverse military codes dating back to the Middle Ages. Classic natural law theory supposes a close connection between the individual and international rights and obligations.

The first recorded trial of a commander held criminally responsible for the murders and plunder by his troops was in 1474.[5] An early academic comment on command responsibility was made by the great Dutch scholar Grotius,[6] who asserted that rulers might be held responsible for the crime of a subject if they knew it and did not prevent it when they could and should have. During the same period, King Gustav of Sweden promulgated his Articles of Military Laws to Be Observed in the Wars,[7] which, in Article 46, provided that no colonel or captain shall command his soldiers to do any unlawful thing, and whoever does so shall be punished. More such documents were issued in Europe in the eighteenth century. In the United States, the Articles of War were enacted in 1775, pinpointing military commanders' duties during an armed conflict, to be followed in the nineteenth century by the famous Lieber Code of 1863.[8] In Europe, the Brussels Declaration of 1874,[9] the German Army Regulations of 1902[10] and the British Manual of Military Law of 1929[11] were accompanied, at the turn of the century, by the first and rudimentary Hague Conferences on the Laws and Customs of War.[12]

In the twentieth century, the 1907 Hague Convention Respecting the Laws and Customs of War and annexed Regulations[13] provided more clearly the conditions that a combatant must fulfil to be accorded the rights of a lawful belligerent. That condition requires the forces of the parties to the Convention to be commanded by a person responsible for his subordinates. The responsibility of individuals, though limited to the military, was affirmed after World War I, for example in the Treaty of

Versailles[14] with regard to Germany, calling for the trial of the Kaiser, the Supreme German Commander. That treaty provided, more generally, for the right of the Allied and Associated Powers to bring before military tribunals persons accused of having committed acts in violation of the laws and customs of war. However, no such military tribunals were formed and no accused individuals were prosecuted. I should also mention the Treaty of Sèvres of 1920,[15] which, *inter alia*, dealt with the responsibility of the "Young Turks" for the Armenian genocide. Again, no trials were instituted.

After World War II, the provisions of the 1907 Hague Convention on the Laws and Customs of War and annexed Regulations were complemented and supplemented by a number of agreements, including the 1949 Geneva Conventions[16] and, in more detail, Articles 86 and 87 of the 1977 Geneva Protocol I,[17] as reaffirmed in Article II of the 1968 Convention on the Non-Applicability of Statutory Limitations to War Crimes and Crimes Against Humanity.[18] The issues of functional responsibility, including that of civilians, were plentiful in the post–World War II prosecutions before the International Military Tribunals of Nuremberg and Tokyo. Articles 6 and 7 of the Nuremberg Charter[19] made it utterly clear that the official position of an accused, be it a military commander or public official, would not be sufficient to free him from responsibility for crimes committed under the Charter. The Nuremberg Charter included heads of state; for opportunistic reasons, so that Emperor Hirohito would be left alone, the Tokyo Charter[20] did not.

Since these post-war trials, command or superior responsibility has become a recognized principle in international law, well founded by the case law of both military tribunals. These principles were then formulated into the Nuremberg Principles, prepared by the International Law Commission and submitted and affirmed by the General Assembly of the United Nations in 1950.[21] The same principles were, in part, the inspiration for Article 7 of the Statute of the International Criminal Tribunal for the former Yugoslavia (ICTY) in 1993,[22] for Article 6 of the Statute of its sister tribunal for Rwanda (ICTR) in 1994[23] and, since 1998, for the statutory provisions in the framework of the International Criminal Court (ICC).[24] The principles also played a role in national prosecutions, as for example in the United States in the 1970s over the My Lai killings during the Viet Nam war;[25] in the 1980s in Israel through the findings of the Kahan Commission,[26] which investigated the invasion of Lebanon that led to the massacre in the Palestinian refugee camps of Sabra and Shatilla; in the 1990s in Germany regarding the former East German President, Erich Honecker,[27] and his successor, Egon Krenz;[28] and, more recently, in the Pinochet case.[29]

Functional individual responsibility

In classic international law, the general thrust of state responsibility is based on the establishment of the imputability to the state of certain wrongs committed by its agents or organs. The first codifications of customary international law maintain the principle that the state, rather than the individual, is responsible under international law for breaches of law and customs of war. Once this mechanism came to be questioned, the focus of responsibilities for offences during an armed conflict shifted step by step to individuals and their role with respect to the offences. It resulted in the norm that all individuals are accountable for violations of humanitarian law, committed or otherwise instituted or permitted by themselves or by others for whom they are responsible.

The common notion of individual responsibility takes as a starting point the idea that a person is responsible for his or her own actions. Once individual responsibility played a role in international law, the same notion was applied: a person who participates in the planning, preparation or execution or otherwise contributes to the commission of serious violations of international humanitarian law should be held criminally responsible. And indeed the Nuremberg and Tokyo rulings[30] imposed responsibility upon the individual in a personal capacity for involvement in the commission of human rights violations. Where individual responsibility for common offences came to include accountability for functional responsibilities, the concept of criminal responsibility in international law expanded in the same way. Commanders and superiors are treated as perpetrators and accomplices when they have incited or allowed or failed to prevent crimes committed in the line of duty under their command. Modern individual criminal responsibility in international law includes both factual and functional responsibility.

The scope of individuality

The ICC, like its earlier models at Nuremberg, Tokyo, The Hague and Arusha, is targeted at the major criminals responsible for large-scale atrocities. Most of the persons accused before the ICC will not be the actual perpetrators of the crimes; they have not sullied their hands with flesh and blood. Rather, they will be accomplices, those who organized, planned and incited genocide, crimes against humanity and war crimes. The ICC Statute represents the present international consensus on the criminal responsibility of individuals. The system of criminal responsibility under the ICC Statute is an improvement on previous international instruments. Article 25(3) of the ICC Statute provides for *individual*

criminal responsibility for crimes within the jurisdiction of the court if
that person:

(a) Commits such a crime, whether as an individual, jointly with another
    or through another person, regardless of whether that other person is
    criminally responsible;

(b) Orders, solicits or induces the commission of such a crime which in
    fact occurs or is attempted;

(c) For the purpose of facilitating the commission of such a crime, aids,
    abets or otherwise assists in its commission or its attempted commis-
    sion, including providing the means for its commission;

(d) In any other way contributes to the commission or attempted com-
    mission of such a crime by a group of persons acting with a common
    purpose. Such contribution shall be intentional and shall either:

    (i) Be made with the aim of furthering the criminal activity or crim-
         inal purpose of the group, where such activity or purpose in-
         volves the commission of a crime within the jurisdiction of the
         Court; or

    (ii) Be made in the knowledge of the intention of the group to com-
         mit the crime.

In addition, Articles 28 provides for a *functional* criminal responsibility of
military commanders and (civilian) superiors. While paragraph (a) states
that:

a military commander or person effectively acting as a military commander shall
be criminally responsible for crimes within the jurisdiction of the Court committed by forces under his or her effective command and control, or effective authority and control as the case may be, as a result of his or her failure to exercise
control properly over such forces

paragraph (b) states:

With respect to superior and subordinate relationships not described in paragraph (a), a superior shall be criminally responsible for crimes within the jurisdiction of the Court committed by subordinates under his or her effective authority and control, as a result of his or her failure to exercise control properly
over such subordinates.

Under the ICC Statute, individual responsibility can be approached in
two different ways. The first is to consider the planners and organizers as
principal offenders, as, for example, the Jerusalem Court[31] did when it
held Eichmann to be a principal offender, in the same way that two or
more persons who collaborate in forging a document are all principal offenders. The alternative is to try planners and organizers as accomplices,
who aid or abet, if directly and substantially, the principal offenders.

Another improvement is the issue of conspiracy, which has vexed international criminal law since Nuremberg. Under the common law system, a conspiracy is committed once two or more persons agree to commit a crime, whether or not the crime itself is committed, whereas in systems inspired by the Napoleonic tradition[32] conspiracy is generally viewed as a form of complicity or participation in an actual crime or an attempted crime. However, a few systems on the continent of Europe[33] developed a midway position by penalizing the overt planning to commit crimes (hence the requirement of plurality of intended crimes) whether or not the intended crimes are committed. Whereas neither the ICTY Statute nor the ICTR Statute deals with the issue, the ICC Statute strikes a compromise by adopting a midway position: conspiracy requires the commission of some overt act, without imposing the requirement that the crime itself is actually committed. This compromise, however, does not fully reflect the provision of conspiracy of the Genocide Convention.[34]

Mental element

Criminal responsibility is concerned with intentional and knowing behaviour, often described by the Latin expression *mens rea*, or guilty mind. Where there are different degrees of intention, ranging from mere negligence to recklessness and full-blown intent with premeditation, the general standard set for the mental element of violations of humanitarian law is intent and knowledge. The general requirement includes *dolus eventualis*, where someone means to cause the consequences of his or her behaviour and is aware that such consequences will occur in the ordinary course of events. It should be observed, however, that most crimes in international humanitarian law have their own built-in *mens rea*: genocide requires an intent to destroy the protected group; and crimes against humanity involve a deliberate widespread or systematic attack against a civilian population. Many war crimes include the adjectives "wilfully",[35] "intentionally"[36] or "treacherously".[37]

Military responsibility

Since the precept of individual criminal responsibility for one's own actions became recognized in international law, much of the literature and opinions of courts, especially since World War II, has concentrated on the other aspect of the doctrine: culpability for failure to prevent the unlawful acts of subordinates. The issue here is the applicable test for that culpability. National courts have established a number of tests ranging from a failure to act to prevent the unlawful activity when the military commander "could have known" to "having actual knowledge". As an exception to the general standard discussed before, the international doctrine has accepted functional responsibility of military commanders by drawing the line where the commander "should have known"[38] of the unlawful activity. This is clearly a responsibility based on negligence and not on *culpa in causa*. Not only does the military commander have a duty to take all necessary and reasonable measures within his power to prevent the commission of an unlawful act by subordinates under his command, but he also has an obligation to take all necessary and reasonable steps to keep himself sufficiently informed in order to be reasonably able to prevent the unlawful acts of his subordinates. The Germans call this the principle of functional caution (*Garantenstellung*) of a superior: a superior has to vouch for his men and should therefore do everything reasonable to make that possible. The statutes of the ICTY, ICTR and ICC take the matter further by including culpability when failing to take necessary and reasonable measures to punish perpetrators or to submit the matter to the competent authorities for investigation and prosecution.[39] Here, the same test deriving from the *Garantenstellung* applies: the commander must take all necessary and reasonable measures within his power to repress the commission of unlawful acts. In both cases – prevention and repression – a military commander is therefore under an obligation to exercise effective control over his subordinates.

Mixed situations

Military standards are perhaps higher than their civilian counterparts for two reasons. There is a need to preserve a higher standard of discipline in a military structure, whose concomitant is the superior's responsibility, and there are differences in the effectiveness of deterrence in military and civilian life. The issue of the superior responsibility of non-military personnel does not rely on whether they are themselves part of the military. The proper inquiry is whether they exercised command and control as effective military commanders. Thus, a distinction has to be made between the commander-in-chief, who may be a civilian, and other civilians who may be in the military chain of command and who have effective command and control responsibilities. Being *amicus curiae* in the *Milosevic* case,[40] I should perhaps not elaborate much further on the matter. I shall limit myself to the observation that a commander-in-chief, despite the title, may fail to exercise the full powers of his office. Conversely, a civilian who occupies a position of military command and control may actually make decisions on strategic or tactical matters or both. It is essentially an evidentiary issue. I mention this, because evidentiary problems are more acute in this area of command responsibility when civilians do not have a pre-established function in a well-defined hierarchy in which command and control responsibilities are commensurate to rank. Civilians who are placed in such roles may drift in and out of the decision-making process, raising questions about the permanence of their roles. In principle, however, command responsibility with military and paramilitary activity is the same for all persons in command, whether or not they are part of the military hierarchy. The difference concerns the legal and factual assumptions that apply to military personnel who are part of a chain of command.

Civilian superior responsibility

Civilians can be held responsible for the behaviour of others when they are in a superior position to, and are able to control the behaviour of, subordinates. Such superiors may work in a state hierarchical structure or be politicians or leaders of commercial enterprises. Those who are not a part of the military or subject to its control do not fall under the command responsibility norms and standards as just discussed. In this respect, acceleration of the development of international law through both ad hoc tribunals has affected the functional (criminal) responsibility doctrine regarding civilians as well. After the Nuremberg trials, the Statutes of the ICTY and ICTR clearly established the criminal responsibility of civilian superiors[41] on a comparable footing to the earlier established military command responsibility. The common test is to apply the criteria of knowledge or awareness, power or authority, and acceptance or negligence. The case law derived therefrom refined that accountability further into a mature system of criminal responsibility, as reflected in the present Statute of the ICC. In the decision on the Rule 61 hearing in the *Karadzic* and *Mladic* cases,[42] the Trial Chamber applied the functional approach, observing that those who have the ability to influence events through their positions of superior authority should be brought to justice. In the decision on the Rule 61 hearing in the *Nikolic* case,[43] the Trial Chamber applied the principle of criminal responsibility by omission as well, noting that Nikolic held the position of camp commander and that his responsibility also arose by virtue of his position of authority when failing to prevent such crimes.

During the drafting process of the ICC Statute, the point was raised whether civilian superiors would incur the same degree of responsibility as military commanders and whether civilian superiors would be in the same position as military commanders to prevent or repress the commission of crimes by their subordinates and to punish perpetrators.[44] Article 28 of the ICC Statute regulated the issue by separating the two responsibilities into two different paragraphs. The military paragraph provides for an extra test of "should have known" whereas the civilian paragraph does not.

Miscellaneous

The prosecution of individuals accused of having committed crimes is classically a matter within the sovereign competence of the national state, derived from the usual criteria such as the nationality of the perpetrator or the *locus delicti*. The character of violations of humanitarian law, however, makes such crimes a universal matter regardless of nationality and location. Consequently, individual responsibility for violations of humanitarian law has become a global issue and the shift of focus from state responsibility to individual responsibility would become meaningless if individuals could hide behind the sovereignty of their state. The trend in international law is to rule out all barriers that would allow any form of impunity for violations of humanitarian law.

Immunity of government leaders, ministers of foreign affairs and heads of state is well established in international law[45] – immunity *ratione personae*. The same applies to former functionaries – immunity *ratione materiae*. Under international law, national courts for common crimes should respect both immunities. However, the present international instruments, such as the Vienna Treaty,[46] dealing with such immunities do not specifically address the responsibility of the protected persons for violations of humanitarian law. The trend in national law is to deny immunity *ratione materiae* to former officials, as the English law lords did in the *Pinochet* case,[47] and to respect the immunity *ratione personae* of acting dignitaries. On an international level, such immunities are denied in the Nuremberg Charter,[48] the statutes of both ad hoc tribunals[49] and the ICC Statute.[50] The scope for criminal responsibility for violations of humanitarian law in international prosecutions is therefore almost absolute. The only exception to this responsibility may be the age of the accused, as I will discuss below.

The principle is that heinous crimes ought not to go unpunished. Yet that principle may clash with the principle of non-retroactivity, which is based on the idea that individuals should not be liable for acts that they could not know to be criminal.[51] At the Nuremberg trials this collision of principles was an issue, but nowadays it applies rarely, if at all. That the violations of international law listed in the ICTY and ICTR Statutes deal retroactively with events in the former Yugoslavia and Rwanda has not been a serious matter of discussion. If debated, the issue concerns the description of the elements that constitute a violation of humanitarian law under the statute. The Rome Statute has dealt with this problem[52] and, moreover, the International Criminal Court has competence only over crimes committed after its official implementation.[53]

Let me conclude with the matter of child soldiers in armed conflicts and criminal responsibility. This was an issue during the drafting process of the Rome Conference. Some wanted a single, specific age, which varied from 7 to 21; others preferred to have a low age under which no criminal responsibility would exist, a high age with full responsibility, and a span in between the two where consideration could be given to the person's maturity or insight into the wrongfulness of the conduct. Under Article 26 of the ICC Statute, the balance was struck at the age of 18.

Conclusion

The trend to individual responsibility for offences during an armed conflict has been one of several steps over time, which only recently developed into a mature system of responsibility. The first step was to acknowledge the responsibility of military commanders for their personal actions and functional contributions to violations of the law and the customs of war, or for their failures to prevent such violations. The next step was to include such responsibilities in national and later in international instruments. The following step was to oblige states parties to declarations and treaties to institute national proceedings against suspected offenders. The final step was the universal acceptance of the norm that all individuals are accountable for violations of humanitarian law, committed or otherwise instituted or permitted by themselves or by others for whom they are responsible. Modern individual criminal responsibility for violations of humanitarian law includes a functional accountability and is, except in the case of minors, of an absolute character.

This concept of functional responsibility became a recognized principle in international law at the Nuremberg trials, was further developed in the legal framework of both the ICTY and the ICTR, and is now codified in the statutory provisions of the Statute of the International Criminal Court. Yet the individual responsibility of civil superiors differs from military command responsibility. The military commander has the *Garantenstellung* of a superior who is also functionally (criminally) responsible for negligence: he has to vouch for his men and he should therefore do everything reasonable to make that possible. Civilian superiors are functionally (criminally) responsible only when they have the required intent and knowledge.

The trend, however, is to tighten the standard of criminal responsibility of civilian superiors. Therefore, I would not be surprised if future case law were to apply the test of negligence of functional duties to civilian superiors as well. This would be consistent with the present culture of the accountability of all, including heads of state.

Notes

1. Sun-Tzu, *The Art of War*, trans. S. Griffith, Oxford: Clarendon Press, 1963, p. 125.
2. Niagendra Singh, "Armed Conflicts and Humanitarian Laws of Ancient India", in C. Swinarski, ed., *Studies and Essays on International Humanitarian Law and Red Cross Principles*, The Hague: Nijhoff, 1984, p. 531.
3. M. C. Bassiouni and P. Manikas, *The Law of the International Criminal Tribunal for the Former Yugoslavia*, Irvington-on-Hudson, N.Y.: Transnational, 1996, p. 482.
4. Ibid., p. 482, n4.
5. The trial of Peter von Hagenbach before a tribunal of 28 judges of the Holy Roman Empire in Breisach, reported in Georg Schwarzenberger, *International Law as Applied by International Courts and Tribunals*, London: Stevens, 1968, p. 462.
6. Hugo Grotius, *De Jure Belli ac Pacis Libri* [1625], trans. F. Kelesy, Oxford: Clarendon Press, 1925, p. 523.
7. William Hays Parks, "Command Responsibility for War Crimes", *Military Law Review*, vol. 62, no. 1, 1973, p. 5.
8. Francis Lieber, *Instructions for the Government of the Armies of the United States in the Field*, promulgated as General Orders No. 100, Adjutant General's Office, 24 April 1863; reprinted in Dietrich Schindler and Jiri Toman, eds., *The Laws of Armed Conflicts*, 3rd rev. edn., Dordrecht: Nijhoff, 1988.
9. Project of an International Declaration Concerning the Laws and Customs of War, signed in Brussels, 27 August 1874, mentioned in Bassiouni and Manikas, *The Law of the International Criminal Tribunal for the Former Yugoslavia*, p. 484.
10. *Kriegsbrauch im Landkriege*, mentioned in Bassiouni and Manikas, *The Law of the International Criminal Tribunal for the Former Yugoslavia*, p. 486.
11. See M. C. Bassiouni, *International Crimes: Digest/Index of International Instruments*, New York: Oceana, 1986, p. 143.
12. See Adam Roberts and Richard Guelff, *Documents of the Laws of War*, 3rd edn., Oxford: Oxford University Press, 2000, pp. 59–66.
13. The Hague Convention IV Respecting the Laws and Customs of War on Land, signed at The Hague, 18 October 1907; see Roberts and Guelff, *Documents of the Laws of War*, p. 67.
14. Treaty of Peace between Germany and the Allied and Associate Powers, signed at Versailles, 28 June 1919; see M. C. Bassiouni, *Crimes against Humanity in International Criminal Law*, Dordrecht: Nijhoff, 1992, p. 373.
15. Treaty of Sèvres, signed on 10 August 1920 but never ratified.
16. Geneva Conventions III and IV, signed at Geneva, 12 August 1949; see Roberts and Guelff, *Documents of the Laws of War*, pp. 243 and 299.
17. Protocol I to the Geneva Conventions of 12 August 1949, signed in Geneva, 6 June 1977; see Roberts and Guelff, *Documents of the Laws of War*, p. 419.
18. Convention on the Non-Applicability of Statutory Limitations to War Crimes and Crimes Against Humanity, General Assembly Resolution 2391 (XXIII), Annex, 26 November 1968, 754 UNTS 73.

19. London Agreement and Charter of the International Military Tribunal, signed in London, 8 August 1946; see "Substantive and Procedural Aspects of International Criminal Law", in Gabrielle Kirk McDonald and Olivia Swaak-Goldman, eds., *The Experience of International and National Courts, Volume II, Part 1, Documents and Cases*, The Hague: Kluwer Law International, 2000, p. 59.
20. Charter of the International Military Tribunal for the Far East, signed in Tokyo, 19 January 1946; see Kirk McDonald and Swaak-Goldman, *The Experience of International and National Courts*, p. 73.
21. "Principles of International Law Recognized in the Charter of the Nuremberg Tribunal and in the Judgment of the Tribunal, adopted by the International Law Commission and submitted to the General Assembly", *Yearbook of the International Law Commission, 1950*, vol. 2, New York: United Nations, 1957, p. 374; see Kirk McDonald and Swaak-Goldman, *The Experience of International and National Courts*, p. 191.
22. *Statute of the International Tribunal for the Prosecution of Persons Responsible for Serious Violations of International Humanitarian Law Committed in the Territory of the former Yugoslavia since 1991*, Resolution 827, 25 May 1993 (amended 13 May 1998 by Resolution 1166 and 30 November 2000 by Resolution 1329); see Basic Documents ICTY, *Yearbook 2001*, GV.E/F01.III.P.1.
23. *Statute of the International Criminal Tribunal for Rwanda*, Resolution 955, 8 November 1994; see Roberts and Guelff, *Documents of the Laws of War*, p. 615.
24. *Statute of the International Criminal Court*, signed in Rome, 17 July 1998; see Roy S. Lee, ed., *The International Criminal Court*, The Hague: Kluwer Law International, 1999, p. 479.
25. Doug Linder, "An Introduction to the My Lai Courts-Martial", www.law.umkc.edu/faculty/projects/ftrials/mylai/mylai.htm.
26. Linda A. Malone, "The Kahan Report, Ariel Sharon and the Sabra–Shatilla Massacres in Lebanon: Responsibility under International Law for Massacres of Civilian Populations", *Utah Law Review*, 1985, p. 374.
27. The trial of Honecker before the court of Moabit was stayed in 1992 because of his unfitness to stand trial; Honecker died in Chile in 1994.
28. Judgment of the Bundesgerichtshof of 9 November 1999 (confirmed by the Bundesverfassungsgericht on 11 January 2000).
29. Ex parte Pinochet 1998 (1), *All England Reports*, vol. 4, p. 897; Ex parte Pinochet 1999 (2), *All England Reports*, vol. 1, p. 577; Ex parte Pinochet 1999 (3), *All England Reports*, vol. 2, p. 97.
30. Robert Woetzel, *The Nuremberg Trials in International Law: With a Postlude on the Eichmann Case*, London: Stevens, 1962.
31. *Attorney General of Israel v. Eichmann*, I.L.R., vol. 36, p. 5, Judgment (First Instance).
32. Those of France, Belgium, the Netherlands, Spain and Portugal. Compare also Italy and Germany, Austria and Switzerland.
33. As, for example, in the Netherlands.
34. The UN Convention on the Prevention and Punishment of the Crime of Genocide, signed in New York, 11 December 1948; Roberts and Guelff, *Documents of the Laws of War*, p. 179.
35. See, for example, Article 8(2)(a)(i), (iii) and (vi) of the ICC Statute.
36. See, for example, Article 8(2)(e) (i–iv), (ix) and (xxiv–xxv) of the ICC Statute.
37. See, for example, Article 8(2)(b)(xi) of the ICC Statute.
38. See, for a discussion of policy issues, Bassiouni and Manikas, *The Law of the International Criminal Tribunal for the Former Yugoslavia*, p. 345.
39. Article 7(3) of the ICTY Statute, Article 6(3) of the ICTR Statute and Article 28(a)(ii) and (b)(iii) of the ICC Statute.
40. My appointment as *amicus curiae* was terminated on 10 October 2002.

41. Report of the Secretary-General, UN Doc. S/25704 (annex to Resolution 808, 1993), paras. 53–59.
42. *Karadzic* and *Mladic* cases, IT-95-5-R61 and IT-95-18-R61, 11 July 1996, paras. 41, 65, 74, 79 and 81–83.
43. *Nikolic* case, IT-94-2-R61, 20 October 1995, para. 24.
44. See W. A. Schabas, *An Introduction to the International Criminal Court*, Cambridge: Cambridge University Press, 2001, pp. 83–92.
45. Compare the judgment of 14 February 2002 of the International Court of Justice in the Arrest Warrant Case (*Congo v. Belgium*), www.icj.cij.org, paras. 53–55.
46. Vienna Convention on Diplomatic Relations, signed 16 April 1961, UN Doc. A/Conf. 20/13.
47. See note 29 and *European Journal of International Law*, vol. 10, 1999, pp. 237 and 653.
48. Article 7 of the Nuremberg Charter.
49. Article 7(2) of the ICTY Statute and Article 6(2) of the ICTR Statute.
50. Article 27 of the ICC Statute.
51. Compare Articles 32 and 33 of the ICC Statute.
52. See Article 9 of the ICC Statute (*Report of the Preparatory Commission for the International Criminal Court, 13–31 March and 12–30 June 2000*, PCNICC/2000/1/Add.2).
53. Article 11(1) of the ICC Statute.

6

Gender-related crimes:
A feminist perspective

Christine Chinkin

Introduction

Gender-related crimes are committed most frequently, although not exclusively, against members of one sex, or they have different consequences for women and men.[1] These crimes include rape, sexual slavery, sterilization and forced impregnation. Although most sexual offences can be, and are, perpetrated against men as well as women (the exception being forced impregnation), they still remain primarily directed at women, because they are women and may have gender-specific consequences such as pregnancy, HIV/AIDS, which may be transmitted to children,[2] and specific bodily harm caused by forced sterilization. It is important to recognize crimes of sexual violence against women and their gender-specific consequences, but exclusive concentration on them depicts women primarily as victims of armed conflict rather than as agents for change or as autonomous actors in the international arena. The emphasis on women as victims of sexual crimes, which define them through their sexuality and reproductive capacity rather than as holistic beings, must not be allowed to obscure the many other ways in which women are affected by the commission of international crimes.[3] Exclusive focus on women as victims of such crimes is also a disservice to men. There is a significant silence about sexual offences committed against men, and identifying sexual offences as crimes that are committed solely against women facilitates the stereotyping of men who suffer such violence as in some sense feminized and shamed.

116

Legal excavation has shown that the laws and customs of war had long prohibited crimes of sexual violence, indeed that they had become "core crimes".[4] Patricia Sellers asserts that "rape and other forms of sexual violence are core crimes within humanitarian law, and, as such, inductively shape the very interpretation of the procedural doctrines and the breadth of substantive crimes within humanitarian law".[5] Nevertheless, they have remained largely hidden, as evidenced by the comparatively few provisions explicitly directed towards their prohibition in the international legal instruments, the lack of definition of key concepts and the paucity of direct reference and application at earlier war crimes trials such as those at Nuremberg and the International Military Tribunal for the Far East (Tokyo).[6] However, the high media profile given to reporting of rapes on a "massive, organized and systematic scale"[7] in the conflicts surrounding the break-up of the former Yugoslavia, the enslavement of women in rape camps and the use of rape and sexual violence as an instrument of war and genocide in Bosnia and Rwanda[8] led to demands, especially from women's international and local non-governmental organizations (NGOs), that crimes against women be taken seriously and be included in the jurisdiction of the ad hoc international tribunals that were established by the Security Council for the prosecution of crimes in former Yugoslavia (ICTY)[9] and Rwanda (ICTR).[10] In the statutes of both tribunals, rape was explicitly included as a crime against humanity,[11] although following the Geneva Conventions it was not spelled out as a grave breach of those Conventions[12] or as a violation of the laws and customs of war.[13] Nevertheless, through bold prosecutorial policy, there have been a number of convictions in the ad hoc criminal tribunals for the commission of sexual offences, against both women[14] and men.[15]

Similar demands for the inclusion of sexual offences within its jurisdiction were subsequently made in the negotiations for the Statute for a Permanent International Criminal Court. The agreed text of the statute adopted by the Rome Conference in 1998[16] goes beyond that for the ad hoc tribunals by explicitly including as crimes against humanity rape, sexual slavery, enforced prostitution, forced sterilization, forced pregnancy and sexual violence, as well as persecution on grounds of gender.[17] Rape, sexual slavery, enforced prostitution, enforced sterilization, forced pregnancy and outrages on personal dignity are war crimes because they violate the laws and customs of war.[18] They are the same as offences committed in internal armed conflicts – the equivalent of common Article 3 of the Geneva Conventions.[19] Each of these offences has been defined in the finalized draft text of the Elements of Crimes.[20] In addition, associated issues, such as protection for witnesses and victims, especially when testifying about the commission of sexual offences,[21] and the gender composition of the court,[22] were successfully included in the statute. Thus there is now a significant body of treaty law providing for the prosecution of these various offences before international criminal tribunals.

In addition, the linkages and differences between emerging international criminal law relating to sexual offences and to violations of human rights, especially those of women, are explored in the detailed reports of Special Rapporteurs of the UN Commission on Human Rights[23] and in judgments of the regional human rights courts. The latter have analysed sexual abuse as violating human rights within the terms of their respective conventions; for example, rape as amounting to torture contrary to Article 3 of the European Convention for the Protection of Human Rights and Fundamental Freedoms[24] and Article 5 of the Inter-American Convention on Human Rights.[25] This jurisprudence supplements that of the international criminal tribunals, but their different orientation (state responsibility for violation of the relevant convention as opposed to individual criminal responsibility) means that the human rights institutions and international criminal tribunals do not always conceptualize offences in the same way.[26]

Together, all these developments make gender-related crimes a striking example of the move from impunity to accountability under international criminal law that took place throughout the 1990s. Indeed, the ICTY Appeals Chamber asserted that: "The general question of bringing justice to the perpetrators of crimes such as rape, was one of the reasons that the Security Council established the tribunal."[27]

However, the movement for the recognition of crimes of violence under international law has not been consistently forward. The inclusion of some of these crimes, notably forced pregnancy, became highly controversial at Rome, with alliances between the Holy See and Islamic states seeking to undermine the developments associated with the jurisprudence of the ICTY and ICTR. Another point of contention at Rome was what understanding should be given to the concept of gender, resulting in its limitation to biological differences rather than providing for a fuller understanding of the socially constructed roles of women and men.[28]

This chapter looks at some aspects of gender-related offences in international criminal law from a feminist perspective.[29] It first discusses what is meant by a feminist perspective and then assesses some aspects of the jurisprudence of the ad hoc tribunals from this standpoint.

Gender-related crimes: Feminist perspectives

Violent sexual crimes can be analysed from a number of different perspectives, for example through comparison with domestic criminal laws, jurisprudence and procedures, or from a historical standpoint. This chapter takes a feminist perspective. There is, of course, no single feminist perspective, but rather many different viewpoints – some of which may be in conflict with each other – of diverse women across the globe. Nevertheless, a common starting point is that feminist analysis takes "gender as its primary category, places women at the center of its inquiry, and strives to create a progressive praxis to end the oppression of and discrimination against women".[30] A feminist analysis proceeds from the assertion that the inclusion of sexual offences within the catalogue of international crimes must be accompanied by an understanding of those offences based upon women's experiences of them.

Taking account of women's experiences of crime requires listening and responding to the women's own stories about what has occurred to them. The explicit inclusion of gender-related offences in the jurisdiction of international tribunals is one important inroad into the long silence about crimes against women, particularly in armed conflict, that made these the forgotten crimes of international law.[31] Feminist analysis requires asking where there is still silence today.

An important aspect of the prosecutions of such offences before the ICTY and ICTR is that they have provided a respectful[32] and authoritative space for some (but comparatively few) women to speak out about what happened to them, albeit mediated by legal personnel and Rules of Procedure and Evidence. Indeed, it was through female witnesses, who spontaneously told of rape and sexual assault as integral to attacks upon them and their children in the Rwanda genocide, that the rulings on genocidal rape became possible. In *Prosecutor v. Jean-Paul Akayesu*, witness J, a Tutsi woman, told how her six-year-old daughter had been raped by three Interahamwe who killed her father, and that she had heard that young girls were raped at the Taba *bureau communal* (communal administrative building). Another Tutsi woman, witness H, said that she had been raped in a sorghum field and that she had seen other Tutsi women being raped.[33] This evidence caused the proceedings to be adjourned and the indictments to be amended to include charges of multiple rapes, testified to by many witnesses, which had earlier not been taken into account.[34] This episode shows both how gender-specific crimes can still remain invisible and the importance of the inclusion of female judges in international tribunals. It was only the intervention of Judge Navanethem Pillay that ensured the continuation of this unsought evidence.

Other factors are also important in ensuring that women are able to speak of what has occurred to them. Such factors include, for example, male and female investigators who have received training in gender sensitivity and in dealing with survivors of sexual violence, the provision of an understanding, non-judgemental forum for the taking of evidence, and the assurance of confidentiality and effective protective measures for those who are prepared to testify and for their families.[35]

Legal proceedings are not the only place where women's accounts can be collected and preserved as part of the historical record. Other arenas have been created within the UN system, such as in the personal stories included in the reports of the Special Rapporteur on violence against women.[36] Formal avenues have been supplemented by the activities of NGOs, for example, through the testimony given by female victims of violence in armed conflict at the Vienna World Conference on Human Rights in 1993 and the Fourth World Conference on Women in Beijing in 1995. One of the most striking NGO initiatives was the Women's International War Crimes Tribunal held in Tokyo in December 2000.[37] At this "People's Tribunal", elderly Asian women broke their silence about their fate over 50 years previously as "comfort women" to the Japanese military during Japan's military activities throughout Asia and the Pacific before and during World War II.[38] The tribunal condemned these acts as sexual slavery and asserted the individual criminal responsibility of accused individuals and the state responsibility of Japan for violations of international criminal law.[39] A people's tribunal lacks the formal imprimatur of international law and thus cannot impose legal accountability. Nevertheless, such initiatives ensure that women's voices may eventually be heard and provide an informed and legal analysis of the violations of international criminal law. As such, they are additional instruments in the fight against impunity. The gap in international accountability that was to some extent filled by the Women's Tribunal evidences that the voices of women are still significantly absent from many crucial decision-making arenas, including national judicial proceedings,[40] national decision-making to use force, national and international peace processes,[41] and on-the-ground negotiations about the delivery of food and other humanitarian supplies during conflict.

The Women's International War Crimes Tribunal was concerned with historical events that occurred over half a century ago in a very different form of warfare from that most often encountered today. Today's conflicts, described as "new wars",[42] are most frequently fought within states. Direct fighting between identified sides is rare; rather there are long-term campaigns of terror and attacks on towns and villages, typically with small arms and low-technology weapons.[43] Violence and the very goals of fighting are directed at the civilian population, predominantly women, children and elderly men. Ethnic cleansing is pursued through the commission of gross violations of human rights and the spread of terror. There is a high level of population displacement, causing disruption to the provision of essential services. Criminalization and war have become inextricably entwined, for example through looting of humani-

tarian and military supplies, drug trafficking and illegal sales of the resources that maintain the conflict, such as diamonds and timber in African conflicts. For many protagonists there is little incentive to seek
peaceful settlements. Just as the international law on the commission of
crimes against women is being rewritten, the inadequacies of international humanitarian law in the face of the changes wrought by new
wars are being exposed.

Gender-related crimes

The purposes of sexual violence

"Violence against women during times of armed conflict has been a
widespread and persistent practice over the centuries. There has been an
unwritten legacy that violence against women during war is an accepted
practice of conquering armies."[44] Feminist analysis requires asking why
this is so and why sexual offences are deemed to be in some sense inevitable in armed conflict. The Special Rapporteur on violence against
women has discussed some of the reasons, such as the inherent misogyny
of military establishments; the fact that sexual violence against women is
seen as a means of humiliating the opposition by demonstrating victory
over the men of the other group who have failed to protect their women;
to gain support for the use of force by men to protect their women; to
terrorize populations and induce civilians to flee their homes and villages;
and as a "perk" for soldiers and an inducement to display courage on the
battlefield.[45]

The cases before the ad hoc tribunals present a number of these reasons for sexual violence. They confirm that rape and sexual abuse of the
civilian population are public crimes of violence inherent in the aims of
the warring parties.[46] They are not the private or personal acts of individual fighters that can somehow be distanced from the broader picture.
A number of examples can be given. In *Akayesu*, sexual violence and
mutilation were recognized as an "integral part of the process of destruction specifically targeting Tutsi women and specifically contributing
to their destruction and to the destruction of the Tutsi group as a
whole".[47] Such targeting had had a long incidence that went back well
before the events of April 1994. Similarly in *Kayishema*, in describing the
massacre of children and the rape of women, it was said that "[n]o Tutsi
was spared".[48] Their ethnicity and sex together determined the fate of
Tutsi women who were subjected to sexual violence because of their
gender.[49] Tutsi men were killed; Tutsi women were subjected to sexual
violence and mutilation by being kept alive for a short time for these

purposes before they were killed. This element of sex discrimination, that women are raped because they are women, was made more explicit by the ICTY in the *Celebici* case, where Trial Chamber II concluded that "[v]iolence suffered by Cecez in the form of rape was inflicted upon her by Delic because she is a woman ... this represents a form of discrimination which constitutes a prohibited purpose for the offense of torture".[50]

A particular manifestation – and purpose – of rape is forced pregnancy. Forced pregnancy comprises two separate acts: the forcible impregnation, that is rape,[51] and then the forced carrying of the foetus through to birth, through denial of access to abortion and detention. Forced pregnancy, where a woman of one group is deliberately forced to bear the child of another group with the intent to have her give birth to a child of the father's and not the mother's group, has been held to constitute genocide within Article II(d) of the Genocide Convention.[52]

The recognition of genocidal rape is important, but it has had an unfortunate consequence in the Statute of the International Criminal Court, where forced pregnancy as a crime against humanity is limited to the "intent of affecting the ethnic composition of any population".[53] The reasons for this restrictive understanding of forced pregnancy relate to religious objections to abortion, as clarified by the writer that the definition "shall not in any way be interpreted as affecting national laws relating to pregnancy". However, in no other instance is there a requirement for an additional intent or motive for the offence to constitute a crime against humanity. Forced pregnancy is the only sexual offence that is committed exclusively against women, and yet gender identity is subjugated to that of ethnicity.

Sexual violence is used in armed conflict as an instrument of terror, intended to displace citizens and to humiliate and shame the community.[54] Indeed, the deliberately induced trauma of rape may be genocidal in precisely the opposite way from forced impregnation, that is "as a measure intended to prevent births" because of a subsequent refusal to procreate.[55] In *Kunarac*, the terror of ethnic cleansing (which was totally successful) was described as taking on a very personal dimension with respect to women because it became an instrument of the Bosnian Serb forces to apply whenever and against whomsoever they wished. Such sexual terrorism – epitomized by the finding against Kunarac that he "expressed with verbal and physical aggression his view that the rapes against the Muslim women were one of the many ways in which the Serbs could assert their superiority and victory over the Muslims"[56] – constitutes an assertion of power and humiliation. Sexual terror is also used to distort the concepts of protector and protected. In *Kunarac*, Trial Chamber II found the evidence to show that the authorities who were meant to protect the victims ignored their suffering and instead helped guard the women in detention and, when asked for help, joined in their abuse. Thus the head of police, Dragan Gagovic, was personally identified as attending the detention centres, taking women and raping them.[57]

Understandings of gender-related offences

Prosecution for sexual violence by the ad hoc tribunals has had to be fitted into the crimes over which they have jurisdiction. Accordingly, forms of sexual violence have been considered as war crimes;[58] as "cruel treatment"[59] and "outrages on personal dignity"[60] constituting breaches of Geneva Conventions common Article 3; as a violation of the laws and customs of war; as a crime against humanity; as constituting torture[61] and enslavement;[62] and as genocide. In each case, the other elements of the particular crime must be present. Thus, for sexual violence to constitute a crime against humanity, it must have been committed as part of a widespread or systematic attack against a civilian population;[63] for rape to be genocidal, the prosecution must show that it was committed with the intent to destroy in whole or in part a group characterized on defined grounds;[64] and to constitute torture, rape must display the elements of torture. For rape to constitute a breach of common Article 3 of the Geneva Conventions, the violation must be an infringement of international humanitarian law, either customary or within the terms of a treaty; it must constitute a breach of a rule protecting important values and have grave consequences for the victim; it must entail individual criminal responsibility; there must be a close nexus between the violations and the armed conflict; and it must be committed against a person taking no active part in the conflict.[65]

As well as fitting within the appropriate category of crime, the tribunals have had to consider definitions of individual crimes. Although rape was explicitly included within international instruments,[66] there was no international law definition for the act of rape and no applicable general principles. How the law constructs rape determines who has in fact been raped, so that, where there is dissonance between survivors' perceptions of the offence that has been committed against them and the law's verdict on this point, the impunity granted means that the law ceases to have relevance for them. It must be remembered that this is precisely what happens in rape trials in many national jurisdictions where there are higher rates of acquittal than for other offences.[67] Such impunity is often based upon the myths and stereotypes about rape, for example that, since "nice" women do not get raped, the victim must have consented, that sexually experienced women always consent to sex or that, if rape had really occurred, it would have been immediately reported and that not doing so suggests that rape is being subsequently alleged to cover the woman's sexual misconduct. Such myths ignore the realities of the trauma of rape, the practical and security reasons against reporting rape, especially in conflict, and the fear and shame experienced by the survivors. If impunity for sexual violence is to cease in international criminal law, it is essential that such myths are confronted and dispelled. It is therefore important that the definitions, understandings and procedures for the prosecution of such crimes reflect the perspectives of women and that prevailing myths about sexual offences in domestic arenas are not perpetuated in international ones. The tribunals have shown themselves generally to be sensitive to the realities of sexual violence and have taken a less restrictive view of rape than is prevalent within some national jurisdictions.

The tribunals had to evolve their own definitions of rape and other sexual offences and there are divergent views between the different trial chambers. The lack of any internationally agreed on definition has led judges to examine the rape laws of the major legal systems of the world to determine commonalities and to deconstruct the elements of the crime. One definition is that in *Prosecutor v. Anto Furundzija*[68] where rape is defined through mechanical description of body parts. ICTY Trial Chamber II held that the *actus reus* of rape constitutes:

(i) the sexual penetration, however slight:
   (a) of the vagina or anus of the victim by the penis of the perpetrator or any other object used by the perpetrator; or
   (b) of the mouth of the victim by the penis of the perpetrator
(ii) by coercion or force or threat of force against the victim or a third person.[69]

This definition has the advantage of ensuring the inclusion of male rape and of non-penile rape,[70] but is also controversial for its appearing to require coercion or force and its failure to refer to other factors that would make an act of sexual penetration non-consensual or non-voluntary.[71] Further, a mechanical description of objects and body parts fails to capture the aggression of rape. In *Akayesu*, the ICTR Trial Chamber I pointed out that the definition of torture within the Convention against Torture and Other Cruel, Inhuman and Degrading Treatment[72] does not list specific prohibited acts, but rather attempts to get to the essence of state-sanctioned violence.[73] The chamber recognized rape as an act of aggression and "as a physical invasion of a sexual nature, committed on a person under circumstances which are coercive. Sexual violence, which includes rape is considered to be any act of a sexual nature which is committed on a person under circumstances which are coercive."[74] This definition not only avoids the mechanical description of acts, but also goes to the heart of the contested issues of consent and coercion.[75] Consent is an especially controversial issue, as it raises many of the myths and prejudices of rape. Consent may be implied from the victim's silence and failure to fight her aggressor. The issue of consent has been raised in various ways before the tribunals. In *Akayesu*, a number of women from the Taba commune were not killed at once, but returned and sought refuge at the *bureau communal*. They stayed there, as they had nowhere else to go and "death would be waiting for them anywhere else". The Interahamwe and police raped many at the *bureau communal* and in other places around the area, such as the cultural centre, sorghum fields and forests. It was subsequently argued that they had implicitly consented to sexual intercourse because they had stayed in their place of refuge and had not fled. In *Kunarac*, the defendant claimed that one of the women had voluntarily sought him out for sexual intercourse and she had taken an active role in it and that, accordingly, there had been no rape. These arguments demonstrate the advantage of the emphasis on "coercive circumstances" in the *Akayesu* definition of rape rather than on coercion as in *Furundzija*. Coercive circumstances address the situation where an individual may not have actually protested or fought against sexual activity, but only because of fear and the desperate nature of the situation. Although such a victim may not have been directly forced, coercion is inherent in armed conflict and in the presence of military personnel and those responsible for ethnic cleansing and mass killings. The definition of rape in international criminal law is, in the context of the particular crimes within the tribunals' jurisdiction, a war crime, a crime against humanity and genocide – with all the elements of force, terror and helplessness that are integral to situations where such offences are committed. The domestic law context of rape is quite different and the definition in international law might therefore be expected to be less restrictive than under national jurisdictions. The expression "coercive circumstances" is broad enough for an assessment of the precise situation that confronted the particular victims.

In *Kunarac*, Trial Chamber II emphasized issues of coercion, consent and implied consent. It concluded that what appears to be common to legal systems around the world is "the basic underlying principle ... that sexual penetration will constitute rape if it is not truly voluntary or consensual on the part of the victim".[76] It emphasized the victim's sexual autonomy and personal integrity, thereby rejecting the concept of implied consent and delay in reporting as relevant.[77] The chamber identified three elements as especially applicable to understandings of rape: sexual activity accompanied by force or threat of force; sexual activity accompanied by force or a variety of other specified circumstances that "made the victim particularly vulnerable or negated her ability to make an informed refusal"; and sexual activity that occurs without consent.[78] It adopted the *Furundzija* definition, but addressed the issue of consent by adding a final sentence derived from *Akayesu*: "Consent for this purpose must be consent given voluntarily, as a result of the victim's free will, assessed in the context of the surrounding circumstances."[79] Consistently with this approach, the Trial Chamber did not accept that international law requires "proof of force, threat of force or coercion".[80]

The tribunal applied its understanding of rape and focused on the experience of the female victims, not that of the male perpetrator. It accepted the evidence of the witness who, Kunarac alleged, had consented to, and even initiated, sex that another soldier had threatened her with death unless she satisfied his commander, Kunarac. The chamber was unmoved by Kunarac's claim that he did not know she was acting out of fear. In the general context of war and the position of Muslim women and girls detained at that time, it was not credible that he was "confused by her motives".

As is apparent, there are currently varying perspectives on the definition of rape within the ad hoc tribunals, and a decision from the Appeals Chamber is awaited. The International Criminal Court will not have to determine its own definition, which was agreed to in the finalized draft text of the Elements of Crimes.[81] This text is regressive in that it again itemizes body parts and emphasizes coercion and force rather than the victim's autonomy, sexual integrity and lack of consent.

The ad hoc tribunals have also given short shrift to dishonest attempts to discredit witnesses, especially female ones. In *Akayesu*, for example, the defence had scorned a pregnant woman's act of climbing a tree to hide there for a week, coming down for food only at night. The Trial Chamber responded that "[w]hat the defense characterized as the 'fantasy' of this witness, which may be 'of interest to psychologists and not justice,' the witness characterized as desperation, answering his challenge with the suggestion, 'If somebody was chasing you, you would be able to climb a tree.'"[82] The judges have been understanding about inconsistencies in evidence, implicitly rejecting stereotypes of women as unreliable and hysterical witnesses. They have accepted that inconsistencies can be rationally explained by the difficulties of recollecting precise details several years later, trauma,[83] the difficulties of translation, and illiteracy.[84] In *Kunarac*, the Trial Chamber accepted that the very nature of the ordeal might inhibit precise details of the detention, such as the sequence of events, exact times and dates. While needing to ensure the reliability of witnesses, the tribunals have shown themselves sensitive to the realities of sexual violence and have rejected the distorted pictures presented by defendants.

Sexual violence is perpetrated in many forms other than rape. The ICTR has noted that it "could include forced nudity, forced sterilization or experimentation, sexual mutilation, sexual threats, rape and so forth".[85] It need not include sexual penetration or even physical contact. The recognition of humiliating and degrading acts as well as sexual mutilations and threats as constituting forms of sexual violence is another significant advance in international criminal law. The reports are replete with accounts of women being forced into behaviours that cause male ridicule while being deeply distressing and frightening for the female victims. Humiliation is clearly gendered by, for example, forced nakedness, women being required to do gymnastics naked, to perform public exercises displaying naked thighs in front of large numbers of people,[86] or to dance naked on the table.[87] Outrages on personal dignity[88] are similarly gendered. In *Kunarac*, for example, witnesses told how the sexual exploitation and sale of women were accompanied by laughter at the small payments and the inclusion of a truckload of washing powder.[89] Allocating insufficient food and leftover scraps to the detained victims also underlines their unimportance, the control of their captors and their humiliation.[90] The Trial Chamber in *Kunarac* stressed the inherent objective of preserving human dignity. It held that the loss of dignity need not cause "lasting suffering" to constitute a violation of international criminal law and that it is irrelevant that the victim recovers or overcomes the effect of the outrage.[91] The victim and the perpetrator may view humiliation differently, and an objective test of what constitutes an outrage might fail to take account of the victim's personal experience of suffering. In *Kunarac*, neither an objective nor a subjective test was definitively preferred, and an outrage on personal dignity was held to be "any act or omission which would be generally considered to cause serious humiliation, degradation or otherwise be a serious attack on human dignity".[92] This is appropriate, provided that, in determining what is "generally considered" to be humiliating, the gender of both victims and perpetrators, as well as other factors such as age, status and cultural understandings, are taken into account.

Just as *Akayesu* was crucial to the understanding of genocidal rape, *Kunarac* elucidated the concept of enslavement as a crime against humanity (also previously undefined in international humanitarian law) and emphasized its gendered aspects. Muslim women in Bosnia were detained at the Foca camp and were found to be physically and psychologically unable to leave the places to which they had been taken. Enslavement is not restricted to the characteristics of the African slave trade, but is present when there is the exercise of any or all of the powers attaching to the right of ownership over a person.[93] Such powers of ownership present themselves through the refusal of sexual autonomy and denial of choice for the detained women. These women had to provide sexual services on demand. When a woman has no right to refuse any man, where such matters as abortion, contraception and personal hygiene are totally under the control of her abusers and she has "[n]ow-here to go and no place to hide",[94] then her captors exercise ownership over her and she is subject to enslavement. Other manifestations of the exercise of ownership were the designation of some women as the personal property of particular men.

An important aspect of enslavement as defined in *Kunarac* is that the detained women were required to perform tasks that are typically assigned to women and are seen as "women's roles", such as cooking and cleaning, with demands for sexual access. Performance of domestic tasks can be perceived as "natural" and too mundane to constitute forced labour or to be an aspect of enslavement. However, at Nuremberg it was recognized that forcing women to perform domestic tasks can constitute slave labour; in that case, it was the sending of 500,000 female domestic labourers to Germany to relieve German housewives and the wives of German farmers.[95] Most importantly, once the women's condition is understood as enslavement, since no one can consent to slavery, the issue of consent to sexual activity becomes irrelevant.

Conclusion

It is apparent that there have been considerable advances in moving away from the invisibility of, and impunity for, the commission of gender-related offences under international criminal law. The ad hoc tribunals have led the way by commencing prosecutions for sexual offences and in exploring the gendered aspects of a range of offences. In so doing, they have reconsidered such offences as genocide, enslavement and torture to take account of how women's experiences of them differ from those of men. As has been indicated, not all judges are ready to take this approach, and the importance of including women in all roles throughout the processes cannot be overstated.[96]

The opportunities for the international prosecution of gender-related crimes are no longer limited to the ICTY and ICTR.[97] After receiving its sixtieth ratification on 11 April 2002, the International Criminal Court, in accordance with Article 126 of the Rome Statute, came into effect on 1 July 2002. The statute contains more complete provisions with respect to the prosecution of gender-related crimes than have ever previously existed and these provide the court with the framework for their prosecution. However, the inclusion of these offences in the statute and the subsequent negotiation of the relevant elements of crimes and rules of procedure and evidence have been controversial. In some instances, the jurisprudence of the ad hoc tribunals has been rejected[98] and more restrictive terms have been agreed on. Further, the International Criminal

Court has jurisdiction only over the "most serious crimes of international concern" and is complementary to national jurisdictions.[99] In light of the bad domestic record in many states on prosecuting rape and sexual offences, it is important that the Prosecutor keeps a watchful brief to ensure that these offences do not slip into the national domain and become ignored both there and in the International Criminal Court.

However, even if the International Criminal Court proves to be able and willing to promote international accountability for crimes of sexual violence, attention should not be limited to criminal prosecution. Criminal law is reactive and limited to punishment of the convicted. The Statute of the International Criminal Court makes some inroads through a broad provision for victims within the criminal process and for reparations.[100] Such steps are untried at the international level, but must themselves be accompanied by attention to other long-term financial and practical remedies, such as medical care, support, shelters and refuges, resettlement and retraining. True accountability for the commission of crimes against women requires a holistic approach in which criminal prosecution constitutes just one strand.

Notes

1. This definition is taken from the Committee on the Elimination of All Forms of Discrimination against Women, General Recommendation No. 19, *Violence against Women*, 29 January 1992, UN Doc. A/47/38: "The definition of discrimination includes gender-based violence, that is, violence that is directed against a woman because she is a woman or that affects women disproportionately."

2. For example, Georges Nzongola-Ntalaja, *The Congo from Leopold to Kabila*, London: Zed Books, 2002, p. 242, describes the high rate of HIV/AIDS among Congolese women raped by fighting forces in the Congo.

3. Judith Gardam and Hilary Charlesworth, "Protection of Women in Armed Conflict", *Human Rights Quarterly*, vol. 22, 2000, p. 148; Hilary Charlesworth and Christine Chinkin, *The Boundaries of International Law: A Feminist Analysis*, Manchester: Manchester University Press, 2000, chapter 8.

4. Patricia Viseur Sellers, "The Context of Sexual Violence: Sexual Violence as Violations of International Humanitarian Law", in Gabrielle Kirk McDonald and Olivia Swaak-Goldman, eds., *Substantive and Procedural Aspects of International Criminal Law: The Experience of International and National Courts*, The Hague: Kluwer Law International, 2000, vol. I, p. 263.

5. Ibid., p. 264.

6. For the presentation of legal argument and evidence about the commission of these crimes at the Nuremberg tribunal and the International Military Tribunal for the Far East, see ibid., pp. 277–293.

7. Security Council Resolution 820, 17 April 1993.

8. *Shattered Lives: Sexual Violence during the Rwandan Genocide and Its Aftermath*, New York: Human Rights Watch, 1996.

9. Security Council Resolution 827, 25 May 1993.

10. Security Council Resolution 955, 8 November 1994.

11. *Statute of the ICTY*, Article 5(g); *Statute of the ICTR*, Article 3(g).

12. Convention for the Amelioration of the Condition of the Wounded and Sick in Armed Forces in the Field, 12 August 1949, 75 UNTS 31, Article 50; Convention for the Amelioration of the Condition of the Wounded, Sick and Shipwrecked Members of Armed Forces at Sea, 12 August 1949, 75 UNTS 85, Article 51; Convention Relative to the Treatment of Prisoners of War, 12 August 1949, 75 UNTS 135, Article 130; Convention Relative to the Protection of Civilian Persons in Time of War, 12 August 1949, 75 UNTS 287, Article 147; Protocol Additional to the Geneva Conventions of 12 August 1949 and Relating to the Protection of Victims of International Armed Conflicts (Protocol I), 8 June 1977, 1125 UNTS 3, Article 85.

13. Christine Chinkin, "Rape and Sexual Abuse of Women in International Law", *European Journal of International Law*, vol. 5, 1994, p. 326.

14. The importance of prosecutions in *Prosecutor v. Anto Furundzija* (hereafter *Furundzija*), Case No. IT-95-17, 10 December 1998, *Appeal* (hereafter *Furundzija, Appeal*), Case No. IT-95-17/1-A, 21 July 2000 (prosecution of a single incident of rape) and in *Prosecutor v. Dragoljub Kunarac, Radomir Kovac and Zoran Vukovic*, Case Nos. IT-96-23, 22 February 2001, and IT-96-23/1 "Foca" (hereafter *Kunarac*) (first prosecution based solely on sexual violence against women and sexual enslavement in rape camps) cannot be overstated.

15. See, for example, *Prosecutor v. Dusko Tadic* (hereafter *Tadic*), Case No. IT-94-17, May 1997, para. 45 (male sexual mutilation); *Prosecutor v. Zejnil Delalic Zdravko Mucic aka "Pavo", Hazim Delic Esad Landzo aka "Zenga"* (hereafter *Celebici*), Case No. IT-96-21, 16 November 1998, para. 1039 (male sexual abuse).

16. *Rome Statute of the International Criminal Court*, 17 July 1998, UN Doc. A/CONF.183/9.

17. Ibid., Article 7(1)(g)(h) and 7(2)(f)(g).

18. Ibid., Article 8(2)(b)(xii).

19. Ibid., Article 8(2)(e)(vi).

20. *Report of the Preparatory Commission for the International Criminal Court*, PCNICC/2000/1/Add 2, November 2000.

21. *Rome Statute of the International Criminal Court*, Article 68.

22. *Rome Statute of the International Criminal Court*, Article 36(8)(a)(iii), requires "[a] fair representation of female and male judges". Article 36(8)(b) requires states parties to take into account "the need to include judges with legal expertise on specific issues, including, but not limited to, violence against women or children".

23. See, for example, *Report of the Special Rapporteur on Violence against Women, Its Causes and Consequences: Ms. Radhika Coomaraswamy*, E/CN.4/1998/54, 26 January 1998; *Report of the Special Rapporteur on Violence against Women, Its Causes and Consequences: Report of the Mission to Rwanda on the Issues of Violence against Women in Situations of Armed Conflict*, E/CN.4/1998/54/Add.1, 4 February 1998 (hereafter *Report of the Mission to Rwanda*); *Special Rapporteur on Systematic Rape, Sexual Slavery and Slavery-like Practices: Gay McDougall*, E/CN.4/Sub.2/1998/13.

24. See, for example, *Aydin v. Turkey* (Case 57/1996/676/866) 3 Butterworths Human Rights Cases, p. 300.

25. See, for example, *Mejia Egocheaga v. Peru* (Case 10.970; Report 5/96, 1996) 1 Butterworths Human Rights Cases, p. 229.

26. For example, ICTY Trial Chamber II has determined that torture under international humanitarian law need not be committed by, or at the instigation or acquiescence of, a public official as required under international human rights law (*Kunarac*, para. 497).

27. *Furundzija, Appeal*, para. 201.
28. Gender is understood as referring to "the two sexes, male and female, within the context of society. The term 'gender' does not indicate any meaning different from the above" (*Rome Statute of the International Criminal Court*, Article 7(3)).
29. There are many fuller accounts; see, especially, Kelly Dawn Askin, *War Crimes against Women: Prosecution in International War Crimes Tribunals*, The Hague: Nijhoff, 1997; Judith Gardam and Michelle Jarvis, *Women, Armed Conflict, and International Law*, Boston, Mass.: Kluwer, 2001.
30. Shefali Desai, "Hearing Afghan Women's Voices: Feminist Theory's Reconceptualization of Women's Human Rights", *Arizona Journal of International and Comparative Law*, vol. 16, 1999, pp. 805 and 806.
31. Judith Gardam, "Women and the Law of Armed Conflict: Why the Silence?", *International and Comparative Law Quarterly*, vol. 46, 1997, p. 55.
32. This may not always be the case. It has been reported that three judges in the ICTR laughed during a woman's lengthy testimony of how she was raped. They later asserted that the laughter was directed at defence counsel's questioning, but such an incident must have a detrimental impact on how the tribunal is regarded by potential witnesses; Chris McGreal, "Second Class Justice", *Guardian*, Analysis and Comment, 10 April 2002, p. 15.
33. *Prosecutor v. Jean-Paul Akayesu, Judgment* (hereafter *Akayesu*), Case No. ICTR-96-4, 2 September 1998, paras. 416–417.
34. The Special Rapporteur on violence against women has reported she was "absolutely appalled that the first indictment on the grounds of sexual violence at the ICTR was issued only in August 1997, and then only after heavy international pressure from women's groups" (*Report of the Mission to Rwanda*, Part III, para. 1).
35. Christine Chinkin, "The Protection of Victims and Witnesses", in Kirk McDonald and Swaak-Goldman, eds., *Substantive and Procedural Aspects of International Criminal Law*, p. 451.
36. *Report of the Mission to Rwanda*, Part II, gives the stories of Bernadette, Monique, Denise, Jeanne, Donatilla and Marcelinne. Such accounts are both personalized and representative of how women suffered genocide in Rwanda.
37. Christine Chinkin, "Women's International Tribunal on Japanese Military Sexual Slavery", *American Journal of International Law*, vol. 95, 2001, p. 335.
38. Maita Gomez, *From the Depths of Silence: Voices of Women Survivors of War*, Quezon City, the Philippines: Asia Centre for Women's Human Rights, 2000.
39. The Women's International War Crimes Tribunal for the Trial of Japan's Military Sexual Slavery, *The Prosecutors and the Peoples of the Asia-Pacific Region v. Hirohito Emperor Showa and Others and the Government of Japan*, Case No. PT-2000-1-T, 4 December 2001, corrected 31 January 2002.
40. *Report of the Mission to Rwanda*, Part III, para. 1, condemns the lack of prosecutions of sexual offences in the courts of Rwanda.
41. In Security Council Resolution 1325, 31 October 2000, the Council calls for the broader participation of women in peace-making, peace-building and post-conflict reconstruction.
42. Mary Kaldor, *New and Old Wars: Organized Violence in a Global Era*, Cambridge: Polity Press, 1999.
43. Julie Mertus, *War's Offensive on Women: The Humanitarian Challenge in Bosnia, Kosovo and Afghanistan*, Bloomfield, Conn.: Kumarian Press, 2000, pp. 21–25.
44. *Report of the Special Rapporteur on Violence against Women, Its Causes and Consequences, Ms. Radhika Coomaraswamy*, submitted in accordance with Commission Resolution 1997/44, E/CN.4/1998/54, 26 January 1998, Part I, para. 1.

45. Ibid., paras. 2–6.
46. "Like torture, rape is used for such purposes as intimidation, degradation, humiliation, discrimination, punishment" (*Akayesu*, paras. 597–598).
47. *Akayesu*, para. 731. See also *Prosecutor v. Musema* (hereafter *Musema*), Case No. ICTR-96-13, 27 January 2000, paras. 933–934.
48. *Prosecutor v. Kayishema* (hereafter *Kayishema*), Case No. ICTR-95-1, 21 May 1999, para. 532.
49. "This sexualized representation of ethnic identity graphically illustrates that Tutsi women were subjected to sexual violence because they were Tutsi. Sexual violence was a step in the process of destruction of the Tutsi group – destruction of the spirit, of the will to live, and of life itself" (*Akayesu*, para. 732).
50. *Celebici*, para. 941. In *Kunarac*, the interaction between religion and sex was emphasized: "Radomir Kovac and Zoran Vukovic mistreated Muslim girls and women, and only Muslim girls and women, because they were Muslims" (*Kunarac*, para. 592).
51. *Karadzic and Mladic* (hereafter *Karadzic and Mladic*), Case No. IT-95-5, Rule 61 Hearing, para. 64: "The aim of many of the rapes was enforced impregnation."
52. *Akayesu*, para. 507: "In patriarchal societies ... an example of a measure intended to prevent births within a group is the case where, during rape, a woman ... is deliberately impregnated by a man of another group, with the intent to have her give birth to a child who will consequently not belong to its mother's group." See also *Karadzic and Mladic*, Rule 61 Hearing, para. 64.
53. *Rome Statute of the International Criminal Court*, Article 7(2)(f).
54. *Karadzic and Mladic*, Rule 61 Hearing, para. 64.
55. *Akayesu*, para. 507; *Kayishema*, para. 117.
56. *Kunarac*, para. 583.
57. *Kunarac*, para. 576.
58. *Furundzija, Appeal*, para. 210.
59. *Tadic*, paras. 724–726; *Celebici*, para. 1066; *Prosecutor v. Tihomir Blaskic*, IT-95-14, 3 March 2000, paras. 692, 695, 700.
60. *Kunarac*, para. 436.
61. *Celebici*, paras. 475 and 495; *Furundzija, Appeal*, para. 114.
62. *Kunarac*, paras. 515–543.
63. *Statute of the ICTY*, Article 5; *Statute of the ICTR*, Article 3; *Rome Statute of the International Criminal Court*, Article 7.
64. Rape and sexual violence constitute genocide "in the same way as any other act as long as they were committed with the specific intent to destroy, in whole or in part, a particular group, targeted as such" (*Akayesu*, para. 731). See also *Furundzija*, para. 172.
65. *Kunarac*, para. 407.
66. See, for example, Convention Relative to the Protection of Civilian Persons in Time of War, Article 27; Protocol I, Article 76(1); Protocol Additional to the Geneva Conventions of 12 August 1949, and Relating to the Protection of Victims of Non-International Armed Conflicts (Protocol II), 8 June 1977, 1125 UNTS 609, Article 4(2)(e).
67. A United Kingdom report has shown that only 1 in 13 reported rapes results in a conviction: "At each stage of the legal process, stereotypes and prejudices play a part in decision-making" (Vera Baird, "You've Been Raped. Why Bother Reporting It?" *Guardian*, 10 April 2002, G2, p. 16).
68. *Furundzija*, para. 185. This definition was not part of the appeal.
69. The Trial Chamber held oral rape to be "a most humiliating and degrading attack upon human dignity" and "that such an extremely serious sexual outrage as forced oral penetration should be classified as rape" (*Furundzija*, para. 183).

70. For example, witness KK testified that the Interahamwe inserted wood into the sexual organs of a dying woman (*Akayesu*, para. 686).
71. *Kunarac*, para. 438.
72. Convention against Torture and Other Cruel, Inhuman and Degrading Treatment, 10 December 1984, 1465 UNTS 85.
73. *Akayesu*, para. 597.
74. *Akayesu*, para. 598. This definition was accepted by the Trial Chambers in *Celebici*, para. 479, and *Musema*, para. 965.
75. There is also the complex question of whether consent is a defence to rape (as implied by ICTY/ICTR Rules of Procedure and Evidence, Rule 96) or whether its presence denies the very existence of the crime; see *Kunarac*, paras. 462–464.
76. *Kunarac*, para. 440.
77. Ibid., para. 441. "Sexual autonomy is violated wherever the person subjected to the act has not freely agreed to it or is otherwise not a voluntary participant" (ibid., para. 457).
78. Ibid., paras. 439–456.
79. Ibid., para. 460.
80. Ibid., fn 1119.
81. *Report of the Preparatory Commission for the International Criminal Court, Addendum, Part II, Finalized Draft Text of the Elements of Crimes*, PCNICC/2000/1/Add 2, 2 November 2000, Article 7(1)(g): "1. The perpetrator invaded the body of a person by conduct resulting in penetration, however slight, of any part of the body of the victim or of the perpetrator with a sexual organ, or of the anal or genital opening of the victim with any object or any other part of the body. 2. The invasion was committed by force, or by threat of force or coercion, such as that caused by fear of violence, duress, detention, psychological oppression or abuse of power, against such person or another person, or by taking advantage of a coercive environment, or the invasion was committed against a person incapable of giving genuine consent."
82. *Akayesu*, para. 455.
83. In *Furundzija*, the impact upon memory and reliability of treatment for post-traumatic stress disorder (PTSD) was argued. The Trial Chamber concluded that "[t]here is no reason why a person with PTSD cannot be a perfectly reliable witness". The Appeals Chamber upheld this decision (*Furundzija, Appeal*, para. 122).
84. *Akayesu*, para. 455.
85. Ibid., para. 688.
86. Ibid.
87. Other elements may add to the humiliation, for example age (*Kunarac*, para. 767).
88. Geneva Conventions, common Article 3(1)(c).
89. *Kunarac*, paras. 756 and 775.
90. Ibid., para. 752.
91. Ibid., paras. 501 and 503. Trial Chamber I in *Prosecutor v. Zlatko Aleksovski*, Case No. IT-95-14/1, 25 June 1999, paras. 54–56, had required the humiliation to be "real and lasting".
92. *Kunarac*, para. 507.
93. Ibid., para. 539.
94. Ibid., para. 740.
95. Ibid., para. 523.
96. The appointment of Patricia Viseur Sellers as Legal Adviser for Gender-related Crimes in the Office of the Prosecutor of the ICTY and ICTR has been essential for the developments described in this chapter.
97. An "independent special court" has been established for Sierra Leone (Security Council Resolution 1315, 14 August 2000).

98. For example, the rejection of the possibility of anonymity as a protective measure for witnesses (*Prosecutor v. Tadic, Decision on the Prosecutor's Motion Requesting Protective Measures for Victims and Witnesses*, 10 August 1995, paras. 53–86). The *Rome Statute of the International Criminal Court*, Article 68, is more restricted.
99. *Rome Statute of the International Criminal Court*, Article 1.
100. *Rome Statute of the International Criminal Court*, Article 75.

7

International criminal courts and the admissibility of evidence

Bert Swart

Admissibility of evidence: A comparative perspective

It is the main duty and responsibility of international criminal courts, as of national criminal courts, to decide on the guilt of individual persons accused of having committed criminal offences. We all know how difficult these decisions can be in national systems of justice, and how insufficient diligence or lack of respect for the rights of the accused may lead to miscarriages of justice. In this respect, the situation of international criminal courts is certainly not easier than that of national courts; perhaps it is even more difficult. A vivid and impressive example of the difficulties and dangers involved in deciding on the criminal responsibility of individual persons is provided by the decisions of the Trial Chamber and the Appeals Chamber of the International Criminal Tribunal for the former Yugoslavia (ICTY) in the case of *Zoran Kupreskic and Others*. Although, in its judgment of 14 January 2000, the Trial Chamber held five of the six accused guilty of having committed one or more international crimes, in its judgment of 23 October 2001 the Appeals Chamber arrived at the conclusion that three other accused should also have been acquitted. In the case of two of the accused, the reversal of the Trial Chamber's judgment by the Appeals Chamber rests on an exceptionally methodical and thorough analysis of the available evidence, in particular an eyewitness's identification of the accused. The Appeals Chamber concluded that the Trial Chamber had erred in accepting the evidence of the witness.[1]

It is the purpose of the law of evidence to guide juries and judges alike in their endeavour to arrive at the truth and to prevent them from effecting miscarriages of justice. Part of that law consists of rules determining whether or not information may be admitted as evidence; in other words, whether or not that information may be used by the trier of facts to decide on the charges. Now what do we mean when we say that information that has become available is, or is not, "admissible" as evidence in a criminal trial? The first thing to note here is that the word "admissible" may well refer to different matters in different criminal justice systems.

When lawyers coming from civil law justice systems say that evidence is inadmissible, they normally refer to the fact that it may not be used because it has been obtained improperly, in violation of some rule or principle. For instance, a private home may have been searched without a warrant, a suspect may have made a statement to the police without having been informed of his right to remain silent, a blood or DNA sample may have been analysed in violation of the applicable rules.

For lawyers coming from common law systems of justice, the concept of inadmissibility has a much broader meaning. In these systems, there may be many situations in which evidence has to be excluded for reasons that have nothing to do with the propriety of the way it has been obtained. Such reasons may be related to the relevance and probative value of the information available or to the adverse impact it may have on the quality of the decision-making process. Evidence must, for instance, be excluded if it has no relevance to the case at hand or if it is, on its face, too unreliable to be used. Traditional prohibitions on the use of hearsay evidence come to mind here. Evidence may also be excluded, despite the fact that it might have some probative value, if to admit it would be unduly prejudicial to the accused. Information about an accused's previous convictions is an example. On the other hand, in civil law systems, rules requiring that evidence be excluded because of its inherent unreliability have become very rare indeed.[2]

Related to this conceptual variation between civil and common law justice systems is another difference, which largely explains the disparity in concepts. The archetype of a criminal trial in common law systems is the trial by jury. In that type of trial, in which a jury decides on the facts, it is the role of the trial judge to "determine the range of evidence upon which the jury is called to return a verdict".[3] The judge filters the available information that may be offered to a jury, by deciding on its admissibility. Ideally, the jury will not know what information the judge has excluded as evidence and the reasons for the decision. In these trials, the judge makes a first selection of the evidence, after which the jury will decide the case on the basis of the evidence that has been declared admissible. We are thus confronted with two distinct stages in the process leading to a final decision on the charges against the accused. In trials in which there is no jury but where a judge determines both facts and law (the so-called bench trial), these distinct stages are preserved. The judge will first decide on questions of admissibility and at a later stage decide on the charges. On the other hand, the archetype of a criminal trial in civil law systems of justice is a trial in which professional judges try the facts. Here, traditionally no need is felt to divide the decision-making process into two different stages. All questions regarding the probative value and weight of evidence will normally be decided after the trial has come to an end and a decision must be made on the charges. More often than not this is even true for certain types of cases in which some civil law systems make use of juries or lay judges. The judgment of a court in a civil law system of justice will (have to) explain what evidence has been used in the case of a conviction and why a court thought it proper to make use of it. This contrasts with juries in common law systems, which are not required to explain their decisions.

Finally, I offer a few remarks on corroboration. In order to prevent miscarriages of justice, absolute rules with regard to corroboration are sometimes adopted. These rules include forbidding, for instance, that an accused is convicted solely on the basis of the testimony of a single witness, or solely on the basis of his or her confession. For obvious reasons, such rules are not popular and they have disappeared or tend to disappear both in civil law and in common law systems. At present, by far the most important rule of corroboration is one that has been developed by the European Court of Human Rights during recent decades. This is the rule forbidding national courts to convict an accused if his or her conviction would be based solely, or to a decisive extent, on the testimony of a witness whom the accused has not been given an adequate and proper opportunity to question.[4] In common law systems of justice, the testimony of that witness would normally already have been ruled inadmissible at an earlier stage of the proceedings.

The ad hoc tribunals for the former Yugoslavia and Rwanda

The statutes

As far as evidence is concerned, the following three characteristics of the two statutes are especially relevant:
1. There are no juries and all the accused will be tried by professional judges. In this respect the statutes follow the precedents of the Nuremberg and Tokyo tribunals.

2. Neither statute contains specific provisions on evidence. For instance, there is nothing in the statutes with regard to admissibility of evidence or corroboration. It is entirely left to the tribunals themselves to adopt such rules in their Rules of Procedure and Evidence. In this respect, the tribunals have been accorded even more freedom than the Nuremberg and Tokyo tribunals in their charters.[5]

3. Both statutes require that the judgments of the tribunals be accompanied by "a reasoned opinion in writing". In the practice of the tribunals, this requirement has been understood as entailing an obligation to explain in detail the reasons for attaching weight to the available evidence as well as to make clear why that evidence enabled a Trial Chamber, or did not enable it, to establish the guilt of the accused beyond reasonable doubt. This makes it possible for an Appeals Chamber to assess whether or not any "reasonable tribunal of fact could be satisfied beyond reasonable doubt that the accused had participated in the criminal conduct".[6]

The Rules of Procedure and Evidence

Both tribunals have adopted Rules of Procedure and Evidence. The provisions on evidence in the rules of the ICTY were thoroughly revised and expanded in December 2000; the same is not the case for the rules of the International Criminal Tribunal for Rwanda (ICTR). In this chapter, I will mainly concentrate on the rules of the ICTY.

Rules 89–98 of the Rules of Procedure and Evidence of the tribunals are concerned with evidentiary matters. Rule 89 contains a number of "General Provisions". The first two of these, Sub-rules (A) and (B), both stress the *sui generis* character of the law of evidence of the tribunals. First, pursuant to Sub-rule (A), a chamber shall apply the rules of evidence set forth in Rules 89–98 and "shall not be bound by national rules of evidence". One may presume that the words "national rules of evidence" refer to the rules of evidence of the state on whose territory the evidence has been collected. Thus, in principle, it is not decisive whether or not the evidence has been collected in conformity with the laws of that state or whether or not the evidence would be relevant or admissible according to its laws.[7] Secondly, Sub-rule (B) provides that, in cases not otherwise provided for in Rules 89–98, a chamber "shall apply rules of evidence which will best favour a fair determination of the matter before it and are consonant with the spirit of the statute and the general principles of law". The words "general principles of law" refer to the "general principles of law recognized by civilized nations" in Article 38 of the Statute of the International Court of Justice.[8] Among other things, Sub-rule (B) makes clear that the tribunals are not bound by the law of evidence of a particular group of states such as common law or civil law countries.[9] They must shape their own law of evidence in harmony with their own standards of fairness and particular needs, taking into account the object and purpose of their statutes. The practical consequences of this fundamental starting point will become clear in the discussion of the various admissibility requirements in the rules.

Meanwhile, in the rules of both tribunals a fundamental choice has been made in favour of distinguishing between admissibility of evidence on the one hand and its weight on the other. This division of the decision-making process, together with the provisions in the rules on the presentation of evidence, entails that a trial before the tribunals resembles much more a criminal trial in a common law justice system than that in a civil law system. It is the bench trial of common law systems that has provided the model for the rules of both tribunals, rather than the trial by professional judges in civil law systems.[10] Lawyers coming from civil law systems may wonder how necessary and desirable it is to have a separate stage in the proceedings in which decisions are made on the admissibility of evidence. After all, unlike the members of a jury, the judges are professionals with considerable experience.[11] Moreover, the judges who decide on questions of admissibility are the same ones who, at a later stage, decide on the charges. At that later stage, they will still be aware of the existence of evidence that has been excluded, and this might, in some way or another, influence their thoughts. Finally, lawyers from civil law systems would ask whether it would not be easier and better to determine the reliability of a particular item of evidence in the context of all the evidence that has become available rather than in isolation.[12] In my opinion, however, the system adopted by the rules may well have its advantages. It enables the parties to the proceedings to discuss, and the judges to decide, a range of preliminary questions first and to concentrate on issues of a rather different nature later. This may well be conducive to the transparency of a criminal trial and the decision-making process.

The revised rules of the ICTY contain four general requirements, which apply to all types of evidence and must be fulfilled before such evidence may be admitted. First, according to Rule 89(C), any relevant evidence that is deemed to have probative value may be admitted. This, of course, implies that evidence that is not relevant or has no probative value should be excluded. Moreover, pursuant to Rule 89(D), a chamber may exclude evidence if its "probative value is substantially outweighed by the need to ensure a fair trial". Finally, Rule 95 states that "no evidence shall be admissible if obtained by methods which cast substantial doubt on its reliability or if its admission is antithetical to, and would seriously damage, the integrity of the proceedings". Other provisions deal in detail with specific matters, such as the admissibility of witness testimony, a confession by the accused, evidence of a witness in the form of a written statement, the testimony of expert witnesses, and a victim's prior sexual conduct.

A study of the rules with regard to the proceedings before the Trial Chamber, including the Rules of Evidence, makes clear that the parties to the proceedings – the prosecution and the defence – have been accorded the same procedural rights and responsibilities. One of the consequences is that the prosecution and the defence have to comply with the same standards as regards the admissibility of evidence presented by them. To the extent that the rules secure that the defence enjoys procedural equality with the prosecution and is not put at any disadvantage, the rules observe the principle of "equality of arms" enshrined in human rights conventions. Meanwhile, in *Prosecutor v. Zlatko Aleksovski*, the Appeals Chamber of the ICTY adopted the point of view that the concept of equality of arms also forbids the reverse, putting the prosecution at procedural disadvantages in comparison with the defence. In this approach, as a party to the proceedings "acting on behalf and in the interests of the community, including the interests of the victims of the offence charged", the prosecution is also entitled to a fair trial. Consequently, for instance, standards cannot be more lenient for the defence than for the prosecution where the admissibility of hearsay evidence is concerned.[13] The point of view that human rights conventions grant the prosecution the right to a fair trial seems dubious to me.[14] Yet without a doubt the rules express what probably is the most fundamental characteristic of a criminal trial in common law systems of justice: the trial is a contest between two parties, an "engagement between two adversaries".[15] In this adversarial process, equal procedural weapons and equal chances of victory to the contestants are essential conditions for the legitimacy of the outcome.[16] On the other hand, in criminal proceedings in civil law systems, being predominantly structured as an "official inquiry" as regards the admission of evidence, there seems to be less resistance to procedural inequalities favouring the accused.

With the limited exception of Sub-rule 90(B), dealing with the testimony of young children, there are no provisions in the rules requiring corroboration of evidence. On the contrary, Rule 96 explicitly provides that, in cases of sexual assault, no corroboration of the victim's testimony shall be required. More generally, over the years both tribunals have repeatedly and consistently refused to adopt the *unus testis nullus testis* rule, which requires that the testimony of a single witness may never be accepted without the need for corroboration. In the words of the Appeals Chamber in the case of *Zoran Kupreskic and Others*, the "Trial Chamber is at liberty, in appropriate circumstances, to rely on the evidence of a single witness".[17] This indicates that the need for corroboration entirely depends on the degree of credibility of the statement of a witness in the case at hand.[18]

Relevance

Pursuant to Sub-rule 89(C), evidence must be relevant to the case in order to be admitted. The rules and the case law of the ICTY offer a few examples of evidence that should be considered irrelevant. Rule 96 provides that prior sexual conduct of the victim shall not be admitted into evidence. According to a Trial Chamber, one of the purposes of this provision is to "prevent situations where the admission of certain evidence may lead to a confusion of the issues, therefore offending the fairness of proceedings".[19] In another decision, a different Trial Chamber held that "evidence of prior good, or bad, conduct on the part of the accused before the armed conflict began is rarely of any probative value before the International Tribunal" and that, "as a general principle of criminal law, evidence as to the character of an accused is generally inadmissible to show the accused's propensity to act in conformity therewith".[20] In the same decision, this Trial Chamber also refused generally to admit evidence of crimes committed by other parties to the armed conflict in Bosnia, on the ground that international humanitarian law imposes obligations on parties to an armed conflict that must be complied with regardless of the conduct of the other party or parties.[21]

Probative value and hearsay

More controversial is the requirement of Sub-rule 89(C) that evidence must have probative value in order to be admitted. The controversies mainly relate to the admissibility of hearsay evidence. From the beginning, the various Trial Chambers of the ICTY and the ICTR have always consistently refused to decide in favour of generally excluding hearsay evidence, to adopt all traditional restrictions with regard to the admissibility of hearsay evidence that are usual in common law systems of justice, or to establish exhaustive rules pre-determining the admissibility of hearsay evidence.[22] Appeals Chambers have followed their example. A good example of the general approach adopted by the tribunals is provided by a decision of the Appeals Chamber in *Prosecutor v. Aleksovski*, which is concerned with the question of whether transcripts of evidence given by a witness in one trial may be admitted as evidence in another trial.[23] The Appeals Chamber starts by remarking that it is the well-settled practice of the ICTY that hearsay evidence is admissible and that, therefore, relevant out-of-court statements that a Trial Chamber considers probative are admissible under Sub-rule 89(C). It then goes on to say that:

> Since such evidence is admitted to prove the truth of its contents, a Trial Chamber must be satisfied that it is reliable for that purpose, in the sense of being voluntary, truthful and trustworthy, as appropriate; and for this purpose may consider both the content of the hearsay statements and the circumstances under which the evidence arose ... The absence of the opportunity to cross-examine the person who made the statements, and whether the hearsay is "first-hand" or more removed, are also relevant to the probative value of the evidence. The fact that the evidence is hearsay does not necessarily deprive it of probative value, but it is acknowledged that the weight or probative value to be afforded to that evidence will usually be less than that given to the testimony of a witness who has given it under a form of oath and who has been cross-examined, although even this will depend on the infinitely variable circumstances which surround hearsay evidence.

A variety of motives seem to be behind the relatively liberal attitude of the tribunals in admitting hearsay evidence. The first is that international tribunals should not be unduly restricted by "the sometimes elaborate rules" in national jurisdictions with regard to hearsay evidence, especially rules in common law systems that are of a predominantly technical nature.[24] International tribunals are not national courts. In *Prosecutor v. Aleksovski*, the Appeals Chamber remarked that it is the purpose of the rules to promote a fair and expeditious trial and that in this respect Trial Chambers must have "the flexibility to achieve this goal".[25] One may note in passing that there seems to be a certain trend within a number of common law systems towards relaxing traditional rules with regard to the admissibility of hearsay evidence. The second consideration relates to the absence of juries. Since professional judges try cases, there is "no jury to be shielded from prejudicial material".[26] Finally, since trials before the international tribunals consume an extraordinary amount of time, there is a strong interest in expediting them as much as possible.[27] This need to expedite trial proceedings also led to amendments of the Rules of Evidence of the ICTY in 1998 and 2000.

Nevertheless, the discretion to admit hearsay evidence is not absolute. It is, therefore, not difficult to find decisions excluding evidence in the absence of sufficient indicia of its reliability or because to admit it would be unduly prejudicial to the accused. Three decisions may be mentioned here. The first is a decision of the Appeals Chamber of the ICTY in *Prosecutor v. Kordic and Cerkez* with regard to the admissibility of an out-of-court statement of a deceased witness constituting the only evidence with regard to the presence of an accused in a particular place at a particular time. In that decision, the Appeals Chamber stated that the reliability of a statement is relevant to its admissibility and not just to its weight. In its view, "a piece of evidence may be so lacking in terms of the indicia of reliability that it is not 'probative' and is therefore inadmissible". After reviewing all the circumstances in which the statement was made and recorded, and noting that the witness had never been subjected to cross-examination, the chamber then ruled that the statement was so lacking in reliability that it should have been excluded by the Trial Chamber as being without probative value under Sub-rule 89(C).[28] A year earlier, the Trial Chamber in the same case refused to admit written statements of seven eyewitnesses with regard to the attack on a Bosnian village. The Trial Chamber held that, "while it could admit the witness statements under Rule 89(C), this is not an appropriate case for the exercise of its discretion under that provision, as it would amount to the wholesale admission of evidence untested by cross examination ... and would be of no probative value".[29] Finally, in a later decision in the case, the same chamber refused to admit into evidence documentary material based on anonymous sources or hearsay statements submitted by the prosecution at a very late stage of the proceedings. Noting that the defence would no longer have an opportunity of cross-examining any witness about the reports, the Trial Chamber concluded that the probative value of the evidence was so reduced that it was substantially outweighed by the need to ensure a fair trial. Therefore, pursuant to Sub-rule 89(D), it excluded the evidence.[30]

The case law of the ICTY suggests that the admissibility of hearsay evidence mainly depends on two factors. The first is whether the evidence provides information about the acts and conduct of the accused and may, thereby, incriminate him or her directly. The second is whether the witness has been cross-examined or whether there will still be an opportunity to do so. This is confirmed by the revision of the rules of December 2000. On that occasion, a new Sub-rule (F) was included in Rule 89, providing that a chamber "may receive the evidence of a witness orally or, where the interests of justice allow, in written form". Oral evidence is the rule, written evidence the exception. Moreover, a new and rather detailed Rule 92 *bis* now regards proof of facts other than by oral evidence.[31] It applies to the evidence of witnesses in the form of written statements, including transcripts of evidence given by a witness in proceedings before the tribunal and written statements of witnesses who are unavailable because they have died, cannot be traced or are physically or mentally unable to testify orally. It has been rightly said that the new rule systematizes and clarifies the existing jurisprudence of the admission of written statements.[32]

Pursuant to Sub-rule (A), Rule 92 *bis* applies to the evidence of a witness in the form of a written statement "which goes to the proof of a matter other than the acts and conduct of the accused as charged in the indictment". Sub-rule (A) lists a number of factors militating in favour of or against the admission of evidence in the form of written statements, which a Trial Chamber must take into account in deciding whether or not it will admit the evidence. One of the factors militating against admitting a statement is that it appears to be unreliable or that its prejudicial effect outweighs its probative value. Another is that, in the given circumstances, it is appropriate for the witness to attend cross-examination.[33]

Among other things, Sub-rule (B) of Rule 92 *bis* requires that a statement be accompanied by a written declaration of the witness that his or her statement is true and correct to the best of his or her knowledge and belief. Moreover, the statement must have been made before a competent national authority or a presiding officer appointed by the tribunal, who must also verify certain matters. Sub-rule (C) provides that statements not satisfying the requirements of Sub-rule (B) may nevertheless be admitted if the witness appears to be unavailable and there are satisfactory indicia of the reliability of his or her testimony. Sub-rule (D) is concerned with transcripts of evidence given by a witness in other proceedings before the tribunal. Finally, it is worth mentioning that Rule 91, on the false testimony of witnesses, has been revised to include false statements of a person in a written statement taken in accordance with Rule 92 *bis*, which the person knows or has reason to know may be used as evidence in proceedings before the tribunal.

It is tempting to draw from Sub-rule 89(F) and Rule 92 *bis* the *a contrario* conclusion that evidence of a witness in the form of a written statement that goes to proof of "the acts and conduct of the accused as charged in the indictment" may never be admitted. If that interpretation is correct, the revision of the rules of 2000 would have effected a rather dramatic restriction on the admissibility of this category of hearsay evidence, especially as regards written statements of witnesses who are unavailable because they have died, can no longer be traced or are physically or mentally unable to testify orally. One wonders whether an absolute prohibition to admit evidence in the form of written statements of unavailable witnesses does not go too far. Meanwhile, a different interpretation of the rules also seems possible if one assumes that the admissibility of hearsay evidence in the form of written statements with regard to the acts and conduct of the accused is governed not by Rule 92 *bis* but only by Rule 89. If that interpretation is correct, it is reasonable to expect that hearsay evidence that goes toward the proof of the acts and conduct of the accused will at any rate not be admitted by the tribunal under conditions that are less strict than those applicable where other matters are concerned.[34]

The need to ensure a fair trial

Pursuant to Sub-rule 89(D), evidence may be excluded if its probative value is substantially outweighed by the need to ensure a fair trial. The case law of the ICTY provides a few examples of decisions with regard to the application of the sub-rule. All cases concern situations in which the evidence a party seeks to introduce has apparently been obtained properly. The discussion rather is whether that evidence should nevertheless be excluded because to admit it might be unfair to the other party. For instance, a reason not to admit the evidence may be that the other party has not been given an opportunity to examine it beforehand and thereby to prepare a proper defence.[35] Evidence of documents may be excluded on the basis of the sub-rule if "the material is based on anonymous sources or hearsay statements that are incapable of now being tested by cross-examination".[36] On the other hand, the sub-rule does not generally forbid the admission of documents "simply on the ground that their purported author has not been called to testify in the proceedings".[37] Finally, Sub-rule (D) protects not only the legitimate interests of the defence but those of the prosecution as well.[38]

Illegally obtained evidence

The fourth and last general requirement for evidence to be admissible is laid down in Rule 95. Evidence must be excluded if it has been obtained by methods that cast substantial doubt on its reliability. It is also inadmissible if its admission is antithetical to, and would seriously damage, the integrity of the proceedings. There seems to be an overlap here with Rule 89(D). Rule 95 is, moreover, supplemented by Rule 5, which is concerned with the consequences of non-compliance with the rules themselves. Rule 95 is regarded as a "residual exclusionary provision" in relation to other rules.[39] Here, I will concentrate on illegally obtained evidence.

One area where Rule 95 may lead to the exclusion of evidence is the questioning of an accused or a suspect. Rules 42, 43 and 63 of the Rules of Procedure and Evidence of the ICTY contain strict and exacting provisions with regard to the rights of an accused and a suspect during questioning by the Prosecutor, as well as to the recording of the questioning on tape or videotape, provisions that are considerably stricter and more exacting than those in most national systems of criminal justice. Finally, Rule 92 provides that a confession by the accused given during questioning by the Prosecutor shall, provided the requirements of Rule 63 were strictly complied with, be presumed to have been free and voluntary unless the contrary is proved. The logical implication of Rule 92 is that non-observance of these requirements should lead to the confession being excluded as evidence. The same may well be the case for non-observance of the requirements of the rules during the questioning of an accused who did not confess or during the questioning of a suspect. As a Trial Chamber has remarked: "It seems to us extremely difficult for a statement taken in violation of Rule 42 to fall within Rule 95, which protects the integrity of the proceedings by the non-admissibility of evidence obtained by methods which cast substantial doubt on its reliability."[40]

In recent years, several of the accused have complained that the Prosecutor did not observe the applicable provisions when questioning them. These complaints relate to the validity of a waiver by suspects of their right to be assisted by counsel of their choice, to the length of time of the questioning, which made it oppressive in the given circumstances, and to the recording of the questioning. All complaints have been rejected by the Trial Chambers.[41] One of these decisions also dealt with the important question of whether, for a statement to be admissible, national authorities must have observed the requirements of the rules where national standards with regard to interviewing suspects and the accused are less exacting than those adopted by the tribunal. In that case, the Austrian police initially questioned the accused under Austrian law, which prevents counsel from being present during the questioning. The Trial Chamber held that, even if "it is conceded that the Austrian provision restricting the right to counsel" was not irreconcilable with Article 6 of the European Convention of Human Rights, "there is no doubt that it is inconsistent with the unfettered right to counsel" under the statute and Rule 42. However, it further held that, though the Austrian rules relating to silence and confession "are contradictory to the relevant rules in Rule 42, they do not fall below fundamental fairness and such as to render admission antithetical to or to seriously damage the integrity of the proceedings". It nevertheless excluded the statements before the Austrian police, not on the basis of Rule 95 but on that of Rule 5.[42]

Decisions of the tribunal on the propriety of the evidence-collecting process in other situations are rare indeed. One example is provided by a decision of a Trial Chamber with regard to the legality of the seizure of documents in the home of an accused by Austrian police officers acting pursuant to a search warrant issued by an Austrian investigating magistrate. During the execution of the search warrant, the procedural laws of Austria were not fully complied with. The Trial Chamber held that there was no reason to exclude the documents "merely because of a minor breach of procedural rules which the trial chamber is not bound to apply".[43] Another decision concerns the legality of the seizure of documents in a municipal building by the Prosecutor, with the assistance of the

NATO Stabilisation Force (SFOR), pursuant to a search warrant issued by the tribunal itself.[44] The Trial Chamber held that there was no need for the Prosecutor to seek the consent of Bosnia and Herzegovina in carrying out the investigation since the search and the seizure of the documents were perfectly within the powers of the Prosecutor provided for in the statute. Some students of the law of international cooperation in criminal matters may well be surprised by the fact that the Trial Chamber allowed the defence to raise the issue of violation of state sovereignty at all. However, the Trial Chamber here followed the important precedent created by the Appeals Chamber in the case of *Prosecutor v. Tadic*, where the point of view that an accused individual may not raise defences based on violations of state sovereignty was rejected in the strongest terms.[45]

The International Criminal Court

General characteristics

A comparison of the Statute of the International Criminal Court (ICC) with those of the two ad hoc tribunals in the field of evidence reveals common characteristics as well as differences.[46] A trial before the ICC has in common with a trial before the tribunals that it is a trial not by jury but by professional judges, who are obliged to explain their judgments. In this respect, Article 74, paragraph 5, provides that the decision of the Trial Chamber shall contain a full and reasoned statement of its findings on the evidence and conclusions. On the other hand, a major difference from the statutes of the tribunals is that the Rome Statute contains a provision on evidence. Article 69 of the statute lays down a number of basic principles concerning the taking and the use of evidence. It also provides that the Rules of Procedure and Evidence shall regulate certain matters in more detail. Pursuant to Article 51 of the statute, however, the Assembly of States Parties will adopt these rules, not the court itself. Thus, the role of the judges in shaping the law of evidence has been radically reduced when compared with their role under the statutes of the tribunals. Provisions with regard to evidence are included in Rules 63–75 of the finalized draft text of the Rules of Procedure and Evidence prepared by the Preparatory Committee for the Establishment of an International Court in 2000.

It is clear from Article 69 of the statute and other articles, as well as from the draft rules, that proceedings before the court resemble those observed in a bench trial in common law jurisdictions rather than procedures before a court in a civil law jurisdiction. Pursuant to paragraph 3 of

Article 69, it is the primary responsibility of the parties themselves to submit evidence, while paragraph 4 empowers the court to rule on the relevance or admissibility of any evidence. In this respect, Sub-rule 1 of Rule 64 provides that issues relating to relevance and admissibility must, as a rule, be raised at the time when the evidence is submitted to a chamber. Thus, in matters of evidence, one is again confronted with two distinct stages in the proceedings leading to a decision on the charges against the accused.[47]

Another characteristic the law of evidence of the ICC shares with that of the ad hoc tribunals is that there are no provisions in the statute or the rules requiring corroboration of evidence in certain cases. On the contrary, Sub-rule 4 of Rule 63 explicitly provides that "a Chamber shall not impose a legal requirement that corroboration is required in order to prove any crime within the jurisdiction of the court, in particular, crimes of sexual violence".

Relevance and admissibility of evidence

Although in the Rules of Procedure and Evidence of the ad hoc tribunals relevance is a requirement for evidence to be admitted, Article 69 of the statute distinguishes relevance and admissibility and this seems to have no procedural or other consequences. Both in wording and in content, the provisions in the statute on relevance and admissibility of evidence are strongly reminiscent of the corresponding provisions in the rules of the ad hoc tribunals. The similarities in approach are striking and far outweigh the differences.

Pursuant to Article 69, paragraph 4, of the statute, a Trial Chamber may refuse to accept evidence because it has no relevance to the case. An application of that principle can be found in Rule 71 of the draft rules. It provides that, as a rule, a chamber shall not admit evidence of the prior or subsequent sexual conduct of a victim or a witness. Moreover, principle (d) of Rule 70 forbids a chamber to infer, in cases of sexual violence, credibility, character or predisposition to sexual availability of a victim or witness by reason of the sexual nature of the prior or subsequent conduct of a victim or witness.

According to Article 69, paragraph 4, the court may also refuse to admit evidence for lack of sufficient probative value or because the evidence may cause prejudice to a fair trial. Unlike the corresponding provisions in the rules of the ad hoc tribunals, paragraph 4 also explicitly permits a chamber to exclude the evidence for the reason that its admission may cause prejudice to "a fair evaluation of the testimony of a witness". Here, Rules 70 and 71 of the draft rules, which are concerned with sexual violence and sexual conduct, again come to mind. As far as the probative value of evidence is concerned, it is, of course, important to note that the first two paragraphs of Article 69 express a clear preference for oral testimony over other types of evidence. As far as testimony recorded by means of video or audio technology and documents and written transcripts are concerned, paragraph 2 permits their introduction as a matter of principle. Significantly, however, the paragraph adds that "these measures shall not be prejudicial to or inconsistent with the rights of the accused". Rule 68 of the draft rules draws a number of consequences from that restriction. Pursuant to the rule, previously recorded testimony of a witness as well as transcripts or other documented evidence of such testimony may be admitted only if both the Prosecutor and the defence had an opportunity to examine the witness during the recording or will have the opportunity to do so during the proceedings before a Trial Chamber. Hearsay evidence is thus largely ruled out, although perhaps to a lesser extent than is the case in the rules of the ICTY as revised in 2000.

Paragraph 7 of Article 69 regards evidence improperly obtained. It is strongly reminiscent of Rule 95 of the two ad hoc tribunals. Evidence obtained by means of a violation of the statute or of internationally recognized human rights shall not be admitted provided that one of the two following conditions is met: first, that the violation casts substantial doubt on the reliability of the evidence, and, second, that to admit the evidence would be antithetical to, and would seriously damage, the integrity of the proceedings. In this respect, it is important to note that the provision in the statute and the draft rules with regard to the rights of suspects and the accused during questioning, as well as those on the recording of the questioning, are basically similar to the corresponding provisions in the rules of the ad hoc tribunals.[48]

Finally, paragraph 8 of Article 69 provides that, when deciding on the relevance or admissibility of evidence collected by a state, the court shall not rule on the application of the state's national law. This provision more or less corresponds with Sub-rule 89(A) in the rules of the ad hoc tribunals.

Participation of victims in the proceedings

One striking innovation of the Statute of the International Criminal Court, when compared with the statutes of the ad hoc tribunals, is that Article 68, paragraph 3, of the statute permits victims to take part in the proceedings in their capacity as victims. Pursuant to paragraph 3, the court may permit them to present their views and concerns where their personal interests are affected. The question that merits to be mentioned here is how the expression by a victim of his or her views and concerns relates to the law of evidence. Paragraph 3 provides the beginning of an answer: it must be done in a manner that is not prejudicial to or inconsistent with the rights of the accused and a fair and impartial trial. It is certainly not inconceivable, and is even likely, that, in expressing his or her feelings, the victim will want to provide information that incriminates the accused, or is prejudicial to him or her in other ways. It would seem that the court may not use that information in reaching its decision on the charges or on a sentence to be imposed, unless the victim has been cross-examined as a witness at an earlier moment during the proceedings and provided there are no differences between what the person declared in his or her role as a witness and expressed in his or her role as a victim. Another solution would be to apply to the victim the rules with regard to the examination of witnesses, as seems to be the practice before the ad hoc tribunals. At any rate, a confusion of roles should be avoided, and the court will have to consider carefully how this can be achieved.

Concluding remarks

It is my personal belief that, on the whole, the two ad hoc tribunals have adopted high standards of fairness in evidential matters and have succeeded in maintaining them in the (few) trials that have come to an end, even if not everyone, especially not lawyers coming from common law jurisdictions, will be satisfied in all respects. It is to be hoped that the International Criminal Court as well as other tribunals, such as the Special Court for Sierra Leone and the panels for East Timor, will be able to meet the same standards of fairness in adjudicating international crimes. This is, of course, important in itself. Yet it is the more so because, to a greater or lesser degree, these international bodies provide role models for national criminal justice systems all over the world.

Notes

1. *Prosecutor v. Zoran Kupreskic and Others, Judgment*, Case No. IT-95-16-A, 23 October 2001, paras. 77–246.
2. An isolated example is provided by Article 341, paragraph 3, of the Dutch Code of Criminal Procedure, which excludes the use of statements made by an accused during his or her trial as evidence against a co-accused in the same trial.
3. A. A. S. Zuckerman, *The Principles of Criminal Evidence*, Oxford: Clarendon Press, 1989, p. 40.
4. The court's first decision here is that of 24 November 1986 in the case of *Unterpertinger v. Austria*, Series A-110. Many other decisions have followed.
5. Articles 17–21 of the Charter of the Nuremberg tribunal and Article 13 of the Charter of the Tokyo tribunal. See also Gideon Boas, "Admissibility of Evidence under the

Rules of Procedure and Evidence of the ICTY: Development of the 'Flexibility Principle' ", in Richard May et al., eds., *Essays on ICTY Procedure and Evidence: In Honour of Gabrielle Kirk McDonald*, The Hague: Kluwer Law International, 2001, p. 264.

6. *Prosecutor v. Zoran Kupreskic and Others, Judgment*, para. 41.

7. Although the sub-rule does not absolutely forbid a chamber to take the laws of that state into account in reaching a decision. See *Prosecutor v. Zejnil Delalic and Others, Decision on Mucic's Motion for the Exclusion of Evidence*, Case No. IT-96-21-T, 2 September 1997, paras. 49–53, and *Prosecutor v. Zejnil Delalic and Others, Decision on the Tendering of Prosecution Exhibits 104–108*, Case No. IT-96-21-T, 9 February 1998, para. 14.

8. For a discussion see Boas, "Admissibility of Evidence under the Rules of Procedure and Evidence of the ICTY", pp. 266–269.

9. *Prosecutor v. Tihomir Blaskic, Decision on Standing Objection of the Defence to the Admission of Hearsay with No Inquiry as to Its Reliability*, Case No. IT-95-14-T, 21 January 1998, para. 5. See also *Prosecutor v. Dario Kordic and Mario Cerkez, Decision on the Prosecution Application to Admit the Tulica Report and Dossier into Evidence*, Case No. IT-95-14/2-T, 29 July 1999, para. 12, and *Prosecutor v. Zlatko Aleksovski, Decision on Prosecutor's Appeal on Admissibility of Evidence*, Case No. IT-95-14/1-A, 16 February 1999, para. 19.

10. R. May, "Proof-Taking before International Tribunals", in C. M. Breur et al., eds., *New Trends in Criminal Investigation and Evidence*, Antwerp: Intersentia, 2000, pp. 457–458.

11. See Fabricio Guariglia, "The Admission of Documentary Evidence and of Alternative Means to Witness Testimony in Proceedings before the International Criminal Tribunal for the former Yugoslavia", in Horst Fischer et al., eds., *International and National Prosecution of Crimes under International Law: Current Developments*, Berlin: Berlin Verlag, 2001, p. 670.

12. A perfect expression of this philosophy can be found in the remark of the Trial Chamber in *Prosecutor v. Tihomir Blaskic* that "the proceedings were conducted by professional Judges with the necessary ability for first hearing a given piece of evidence and then evaluating it so as to determine its due weight with regard to the circumstances in which it was obtained, its actual contents and its credibility in light of all the evidence tendered". See *Prosecutor v. Tihomir Blaskic, Judgment*, Case No. IT-95-14-T, 3 March 2000, para. 35. For a more thorough discussion of common law and civil law approaches, see Almiro Rodrigues and Cécile Tournaye, "Hearsay Evidence", in May et al., eds., *Essays on ICTY Procedure and Evidence*, pp. 292–293.

13. See *Prosecutor v. Zlatko Aleksovski, Decision on Prosecutor's Appeal on Admissibility of Evidence*, paras. 22–28, with regard to Sub-rule 89(D). The same opinion was already held in *Prosecutor v. Dusko Tadic, Decision on the Prosecutor's Motion Requesting Protective Measures for Victims and Witnesses*, Case No. IT-94-1-T, 10 August 1995, para. 55.

14. The cases cited by the Appeals Chamber deal either with situations in which the defence did not enjoy equal opportunities or with procedural inequalities in civil cases. No international human rights instrument enables supervisory bodies to receive petitions of the prosecution claiming to be the victim of a violation of its right to a fair trial.

15. Mirjan R. Damaska, *The Faces of Justice and State Authority: A Comparative Approach to the Legal Process*, New Haven, Conn.: Yale University Press, 1986, p. 3.

16. Ibid., pp. 103 and 106. It is, of course, consonant with the adversarial process to dispense with specific procedural requirements on the basis of an agreement between the parties. An example is provided by *Prosecutor v. Miroslav Kvocka and Others, Decision to Proceed by Way of Deposition Pursuant to Rule 71*, Case No. IT-98-30-PT, 15 November 1999.

17. *Prosecutor v. Zoran Kupreskic and Others, Judgment*, para. 33, referring to earlier case law. See also Richard May and Marieke Wierda, "Evidence before the ICTY", in May et al., eds., *Essays on ICTY Procedure and Evidence*, pp. 254–255, and Patricia Viseur Sellers, "Rule 89(C) and (D): At Odds or Overlapping with Rule 96 and Rule 95?" in May et al., eds., *Essays on ICTY Procedure and Evidence*, pp. 280–281.

18. In its decision of 9 November 1999 in the case of *L.N. v. The Netherlands* (Application No. 39024/97), the European Court of Human Rights considered it unnecessary to decide on the question of whether "the *unus testis nullus testis* rule is among the guarantees vouchsafed by Article 6 of the Convention". In *Prosecutor v. Dusko Tadic, Judgment*, Case No. IT-94-1-T, 7 May 1997, paras. 535–539, the Trial Chamber arrived at the conclusion that the requirement of corroboration is not part of customary international law.

19. *Prosecutor v. Zejnil Delalic and Others, Decision on the Prosecutor's Motion for the Redaction of the Public Record*, Case No. IT-96-21-T, 5 June 1997, para. 48.

20. *Prosecutor v. Zoran Kupreskic and Others, Decision on Evidence of the Good Character of the Accused and the Defence of tu quoque*, Case No. IT-95-16-T, 17 February 1999.

21. Ibid. See also *Prosecutor v. Zoran Kupreskic and Others, Judgment*, paras. 210–211.

22. See, for instance, *Prosecutor v. Dusko Tadic, Decision on Defence Motion on Hearsay*, Case No. IT-94-1-T, 19 January 1998; *Prosecutor v. Zejnil Delalic and Others, Decision on the Motion of the Prosecutor for the Admissibility of Evidence*, Case No. IT-96-21-T, 19 January 1998; *Prosecutor v. Théoneste Bagosora, Decision on the Defence Motion for Pre-Determination of Rules of Evidence*, Case No. ICTR-96-7-T, 8 July 1998.

23. *Prosecutor v. Zlatko Aleksovski, Decision on Prosecutor's Appeal on Admissibility of Evidence*, para. 15.

24. Ibid., para. 19. See also May and Wierda, "Evidence before the ICTY", p. 251.

25. *Prosecutor v. Zlatko Aleksovski, Decision on Prosecutor's Appeal on Admissibility of Evidence*, para. 19.

26. *Prosecutor v. Zejnil Delalic and Others, Decision on the Motion of the Prosecution for the Admissibility of Evidence*, para. 20. See also May, "Proof-Taking before International Tribunals", p. 460.

27. May and Wierda, "Evidence before the ICTY", pp. 256–257.

28. *Prosecutor v. Dario Kordic and Mario Cerkez, Decision on Appeal Regarding Statement of a Deceased Witness*, Case No. IT-95-14/2-T, 1 December 2000.

29. *Prosecutor v. Dario Kordic and Mario Cerkez, Decision on the Prosecution Application to Admit the Tulica Report and Dossier into Evidence*, para. 23.

30. *Prosecutor v. Dario Kordic and Mario Cerkez, Decision on Prosecutor's Submissions Concerning "Zagreb Exhibits" and Presidential Transcripts*, Case No. IT-95-14/2-T, 11 December 2000.

31. Replacing former Rule 94 *ter*, introduced in 1998.

32. Guariglia, "The Admission of Documentary Evidence and of Alternative Means to Witness Testimony in Proceedings before the International Criminal Tribunal for the former Yugoslavia", p. 680.

33. An important decision on the interpretation of Rule 92 *bis* is *Prosecutor v. Slobodan Milosevic, Decision on Prosecution's Request to Have Written Statements Admitted under Rule 92bis*, Case No. IT-02-54-T, 21 March 2002. The decision has regard to written statements of witnesses concerning the acts and conduct of alleged co-perpetrators and/ or alleged subordinates of the accused. The Trial Chamber ruled that the phrase "acts and conduct of the accused" does not cover acts and conduct of other persons than the accused, be they alleged co-perpetrators, subordinates or still other persons. Secondly, in exercising its discretion under Rule 92 *bis*, the Trial Chamber attached decisive weight to the fact that the written statements related to events (a campaign aimed at expelling the Kosovo Albanians) that constituted an important issue between the par-

ties. It therefore decided to admit the statements as evidence provided that the accused would have the opportunity to cross-examine the witnesses in court.

34. For earlier discussions on how to interpret the Rules of Evidence, see *Prosecutor v. Zlatko Aleksovsi, Decision on Prosecutor's Appeal on Admissibility of Evidence*, para. 17, and *Prosecutor v. Dario Kordic and Mario Cerkez, Decision on Appeal Regarding Statement of a Deceased Witness*, paras. 26–28. See also Guariglia, "The Admission of Documentary Evidence and of Alternative Means to Witness Testimony in Proceedings before the International Criminal Tribunal for the former Yugoslavia", p. 680.

35. *Prosecutor v. Zejnil Delalic and Others, Decision on Motion by the Defendants on the Production of Evidence by the Prosecutor*, Case No. IT-96-21-T, 8 September 1997.

36. *Prosecutor v. Dario Kordic and Mario Cerkez, Decision on Prosecutor's Submissions Concerning "Zagreb Exhibits" and Presidential Transcripts*, paras. 39–40.

37. *Prosecutor v. Zejnil Delalic and Others, Decision on the Motion of the Prosecutor for the Admissibility of Evidence*, para. 22.

38. See *Prosecutor v. Zlatko Aleksovski, Decision on Prosecutor's Appeal on Admissibility of Evidence*, para. 27.

39. *Prosecutor v. Zejnil Delalic and Others, Decision on Mucic's Motion for the Exclusion of Evidence*, para. 44.

40. Ibid., para. 43.

41. *Prosecutor v. Zejnil Delalic and Others, Decision on the Motion on the Exclusion and Restitution of Evidence and Other Material Seized from the Accused Zejnil Delalic*, Case No IT-96-21-T, 9 October 1996; *Prosecutor v. Zejnil Delalic and Others, Decision on Mucic's Motion for the Exclusion of Evidence*; *Prosecutor v. Zejnil Delalic and Others, Decision on the Motions for the Exclusion of Evidence by the Accused, Zejnil Delalic*, 25 September 1997. See also the judgment of the Appeals Chamber in *Prosecutor v. Zejnil Delalic and Others*, Case No. IT-96-21-A, paras. 528–564.

42. *Prosecutor v. Zejnil Delalic and Others, Decision on Mucic's Motion for the Exclusion of Evidence*, paras. 51 and 55.

43. *Prosecutor v. Zejnil Delalic and Others, Decision on the Tendering of Prosecution Exhibits 104–108*, para. 20. The decision does not make clear which provisions of Austrian law were not complied with.

44. *Prosecutor v. Dario Kordic and Mario Cerkez, Decision Stating Reasons for Trial Chamber's Ruling of 1 June 1999 Rejecting Defence Motion to Suppress Evidence*, Case No. IT-95-14/2-T, 25 June 1999.

45. *Prosecutor v. Dusko Tadic, Decision on the Defence Motion for Interlocutory Appeal on Jurisdiction*, Case No. IT-94-1-AR72, 2 October 1995, para. 55.

46. For analyses of the system of evidence in the statute, see Hans-Jörg Behrens and Donald K. Piragoff, "Article 69: Evidence", in Otto Triffterer, ed., *Commentary on the Rome Statute of the International Criminal Court*, Baden-Baden: Nomos Verlagsgesellschaft, 1999, pp. 889–916, and Helen Brady, "The System of Evidence in the Statute of the International Criminal Court", in Flavia Lattanzi and William A. Schabas, eds., *Essays on the Rome Statute of the International Criminal Court, Volume 1, Ripa Fagnano Alto*: Il Sirente, 1999, pp. 279–302.

47. Although neither paragraph 9 of Article 64 nor paragraph 4 of Article 69 seems to make this obligatory. Both paragraphs provide only that the court "may" rule on relevance and admissibility. But see also Sub-rule 3 of Rule 63.

48. See Article 55 of the statute and Rule 112 of the draft rules.

8

Balancing the rights of the accused with the imperatives of accountability

William A. Schabas

Introduction

Although there have been a few acquittals by the ad hoc International Criminal Tribunals for the former Yugoslavia (ICTY) and for Rwanda (ICTR),[1] these have been relatively rare when set alongside the pattern of conviction. One straightforward explanation may be that the Office of the Prosecutor has carefully investigated the facts, presenting cases for indictment and trial only after sober, professional and impartial assessment of the likelihood of a conviction. Nevertheless, some writers have attributed the low score of the defence to inadequate, and sometimes even incompetent, counsel, to the poor resources available to the defendant, and to a playing field that seems to tilt in one direction.

Developments over the past decade or so aimed at moving "from a culture of impunity to a culture of accountability" have been driven principally by human rights concerns. It is now generally accepted that human rights treaties impose upon states certain obligations not only in a vertical sense, that is, as regards acts for which they themselves are responsible towards those subject to their jurisdiction, but also in a horizontal sense, that is, a kind of duty of "due diligence" to prevent individuals from committing serious violations of the rights of others, and to investigate and punish such violations when they do take place. This approach is now well recognized in the case law of the principal human rights bodies.[2] Traditionally, however, international human rights advocates have been

154

essentially wary and suspicious of criminal law, which is usually at the cutting edge of repression and closely bound up with many serious human rights violations. It is a body of law focused, at least historically, upon the rights of the detained and of the accused.

To some extent, human rights law has been transformed in its shift from a defence-based to a prosecution-based perspective. This has resulted in significant tension and even incoherence. It has proved challenging to retain loyalty to those confronted with the criminal justice system when the new goal, in the name of combating impunity, is to ensure that those once held out as the victims of human rights violations are now put away in jail, and preferably for a very long time. In the past, human rights law concerned itself with protecting the accused and the detained, and was not particularly interested in balancing these rights against the importance of prosecuting offenders. The exercise is now considerably more complicated. Some of the difficulties resulting from the contradictions that characterize human rights law as it moves from impunity to accountability are examined in this chapter.

Anonymous witnesses

A not uncommon feature of unfair trials in repressive societies is the use of anonymous witnesses. For what must be obvious reasons, an accused who does not know the identity of those who testify against him or her is at a great disadvantage. The International Criminal Tribunal for the former Yugoslavia was only a few months into the preliminaries of its first accused, Dusko Tadic, when the Prosecutor filed a motion requesting a number of protective measures for witnesses, including, in some cases, anonymity.[3] The measures sought were a rather severe encroachment upon the rights of the defence. Moreover, the debate itself on the motion in some sense was not a fair fight because the Trial Chamber welcomed, as *amici curiae*, several non-governmental organizations and independent academics who had intervened to bolster the arguments of the Prosecutor. The Prosecutor argued that such protective measures were necessary in order to allay fears of the victims and witnesses that they, or members of their family, would suffer retribution, including death or physical injury. Absent such measures, it was contended that they might refuse to testify. Impunity would be the consequence.

The defence argued that, although it was not unthinkable that the identity of witnesses be withheld in criminal proceedings, such cases were limited to situations where the witness was not a victim but rather a fortuitous bystander, and where, as a result, the identity of the witness would be irrelevant. The defence pointed to an important precedent of the European Court of Human Rights that held the use of anonymous witnesses to be contrary to the fair trial guarantees set out in Article 6 of the European Convention of Human Rights.[4]

The judges had allowed for anonymous witnesses when they adopted the Rules of Procedure and Evidence in early 1994.[5] In ruling on the motion, the Trial Chamber noted that, in enacting the rules, "every attempt was made to comply with the internationally recognized standards of fundamental human rights".[6] But it said that the judicial interpretation given by other judicial bodies to Article 6 of the European Convention, as well as to Article 14 of the International Covenant on Civil and Political Rights,[7] which was the model for the fair trial provision in its own statute, was of only "limited relevance".[8] The three judges pointed to the special circumstances of the Yugoslavia tribunal, saying it was, "in certain respects, comparable to a military tribunal, which often has limited rights of due process and more lenient rules of evidence".[9] These remarks seem particularly shocking in the aftermath of 11 September 2001. To make matters worse, the Trial Chamber observed that the fair trial guarantees in the tribunal's statute were already more generous than those allowed to prisoners of war under the third Geneva Convention of 1949,[10] which is probably the lowest due process threshold to be found in either humanitarian or human rights law. The Trial Chamber concluded:

As such, the Trial Chamber agrees with the Prosecutor that the International Tribunal must interpret its provisions within its own context and determine where the balance lies between the accused's right to a fair and public trial and the protection of victims and witnesses within its unique legal framework. While the jurisprudence of other international judicial bodies is relevant when examining the meaning of concepts such as "fair trial", whether or not the proper balance is met depends on the context of the legal system in which the concepts are being applied.[11]

The Trial Chamber added that most major international human rights instruments allow some derogation from recognized procedural guarantees in situations of war, such as that prevailing in Bosnia and Herzegovina at the time.[12]

A much different approach was taken by the dissenting judge, Sir Ninian Stephen, who considered the case law of the European Court to be rather decisive with respect to applying the fair trial provisions of the ICTY Statute as well as the rules enacted pursuant to them. "[T]he general principle enunciated by the EH of HR in those cases and in particular in *Kostovski* I regard as providing clear guidance as to what are internationally recognized standards regarding the rights of an accused," he wrote.[13] Judge Stephen's dissent served only to highlight the very different philosophies at work and a judicial quarrel over whether the tribunal would be "defence friendly" or "prosecution friendly". Certainly, the tone of the majority was hardly very deferential to the rich jurisprudence on fair trial guarantees that has been developed in international human rights law since the adoption, on 10 December 1948, of the Universal Declaration of Human Rights.

This was not a particularly auspicious beginning for the tribunal, at least as far as the rights of the accused were concerned. References to military tribunals, derogation and "special circumstances" making established fair trial jurisprudence of marginal relevance hinted at a frightening encroachment on fundamental rights. At any rate, it was a sign of the difficulties being faced by international justice as it effected its own transition "from a culture of impunity to a culture of accountability". Since then, the Prosecutor of the Yugoslavia tribunal has shown little interest in applying for anonymity orders in order to protect witnesses and victims, although they seem still to be rather common at the companion Rwanda tribunal.

Rules of interpretation

One of the techniques that has been used to establish an appropriate balance between the prosecution and the accused is the use of principles of interpretation in the application of criminal law. Under the common law, defence-friendly rules of interpretation were often used to attenuate harsh statutes that imposed capital punishment for even the most minor of offences. The classic rule of strict construction, sometimes expressed as giving the benefit of a doubt to the accused (*in dubio pro reo*), is of ancient origin, as the Latin expression suggests. Contemporary international human rights law says nothing as such about rules of interpretation. Yet some norms that are well recognized within the catalogue of international human rights, such as *nullum crimen sine lege*, are not unrelated.[14] Nevertheless, once the view is taken that international human rights norms protect the victim as much as the accused, any justification for a rule of strict construction evaporates. The law must then balance two competing interests, and this suggests a purposive or teleological approach to interpretation.

The first *Yearbook of the International Criminal Tribunal for the Former Yugoslavia*, published in 1994, states that "[i]n drafting the rules, the judges of the Tribunal tried ... to strike a balance between the strictly constructionist and the teleological approaches in the interpretation of its statute".[15] However, in their case law both ad hoc tribunals have given only marginal attention to the canon of strict construction of penal law.

In an early interlocutory ruling in *Prosecutor v. Tadic* on jurisdiction, the ICTY Appeals Chamber held that "any doubt should be resolved in favour of the Defence in accordance with the principle *in dubio pro reo*".[16] In *Prosecutor v. Kayishema*, Trial Chamber II of the ICTR wrote: "The Trial Chamber agrees that if a doubt exists, for a matter of statutory interpretation, that doubt must be interpreted in favour of the accused."[17] In *Prosecutor v. Akayesu*, Trial Chamber I of the ICTR said that "the general principles of law stipulate that, in criminal matters, the version favourable to the accused should be selected".[18] Later in the same judgment, it said: "Given the presumption of innocence of the accused, and pursuant to the general principles of criminal law, the Chamber holds that the version more favourable to the accused should be upheld."[19]

The only detailed discussion of the principle of strict construction of penal statutes is that of Trial Chamber II *quater* in the *Celebici* case:

It is for the legislature and not the court or judge to define a crime and prescribe its punishment. It is the well-recognized paramount duty of the judicial interpreter, or judge, to read into the language of the legislature, honestly and faithfully, its plain and rational meaning and to promote its object. The rule of strict construction requires that the language of a particular provision shall be construed such that no cases shall be held to fall within it which do not fall both within the reasonable meaning of its terms and within the spirit and scope of the enactment. The accepted view is that if the legislature has not used words sufficiently comprehensive to include within its prohibition all the cases which should naturally fall within the mischief intended to be prevented, the interpreter is not competent to extend them. A strict construction requires that no case shall fall within a penal statute which does not comprise all the elements which, whether morally material or not, are in fact made to constitute the offence as defined by the statute. It has always been the practice of courts not to fill omissions in legislation when this can be said to have been deliberate. It would seem, however, that where the omission was accidental, it is usual to supply the missing words to give the legislation the meaning intended. The paramount object in the construction of a criminal provision, or any other statute, is to ascertain the legislative intent. The rule of strict construction is not violated by giving the expression its full meaning or the alternative meaning which is more consonant with the legislative intent and best effectuates such intent. The effect of strict construction of the provisions of a criminal statute is that where an equivocal word or ambiguous sentence leaves a reasonable doubt of its meaning which the canons of construction fail to solve, the benefit of the doubt should be given to the subject and against the legislature which has failed to explain itself. This is why ambiguous criminal statutes are to be construed *contra proferentem*.[20]

By and large, these are isolated remarks. Far more popular has been the teleological or purposive approach to construction, which the tribunals have derived from Article 31 of the Vienna Convention on the Law of

Treaties. Very early in the evolving jurisprudence of the ad hoc tribunals, two judges sitting in the Trial Chambers, McDonald and Vohrah, recognized that, although the Statute of the ICTY was not technically a treaty, nevertheless "the rules of treaty interpretation contained in the Vienna Convention on the Law of Treaties appear relevant".[21] In an interlocutory decision in *Prosecutor v. Bagosora*, the ICTR Appeals Chamber declared that Article 31 of the Vienna Convention applied *mutatis mutandis* to the Statute of the International Criminal Tribunal for Rwanda.[22] In the *Celebici* case, Trial Chamber II *quater* of the ICTY stated: "It is well settled that an interpretation of the Articles of the Statute and provisions of the Rules should begin with a resort to the general principles of interpretation as codified in Article 31 of the Vienna Convention on the Law of Treaties."[23]

In other important decisions concerning interpretation of the provisions of the statutes, judges have applied the interpretative scheme set out in the Vienna Convention but without citing it. In the *Tadic* jurisdictional decision, for example, there was no explicit reference to the Vienna Convention, yet, in substance, the majority of the Appeals Chamber applied the principles set out in that instrument.[24] In the *Tadic* appeal on the merits, a differently constituted Appeals Chamber referred to an advisory opinion of the International Court of Justice rather than to the Vienna Convention as authority for what amounts to a jurisprudential gloss of Article 31(1): "The first duty of a tribunal which is called upon to interpret and apply the provisions of a treaty is to endeavour to give effect to them in their natural and ordinary meaning in the context in which they occur."[25]

Explanations of the rationale for reference to the Vienna Convention have been rare. In one decision, Judges McDonald and Vohrah, after noting that the Trial Chambers of both tribunals, as well as the Appeals Chamber, have constantly resorted to the Vienna Convention for the purpose of interpreting the statutes, described the statutes as *sui generis* international legal instruments that resemble treaties. Because the Vienna Convention codifies logical and practical norms that are consistent with domestic law, continued the two members of the Appeals Chamber, customary international law dictates the application of its principles to international instruments that are not treaties.[26] In his dissenting views in the same case, Judge Shahabuddeen took a comparable approach, determining that the tribunal was entitled to refer to general principles of interpretation pursuant to the Vienna Convention on the Law of Treaties because these are norms generally accepted in domestic jurisdictions.[27] However, if the basis for teleological interpretation is to be found in comparative criminal law, or in the "general principles of law", then strict construction ought to play a more important role.

The large and liberal construction given to the ICTY Statute has had serious consequences for the defence. There are many examples where a strict construction would have resulted in a far better result for the accused. To take one of the most well-known examples, in the *Tadic* jurisdictional decision of 2 October 1995, the Appeals Chamber held that the definitions of war crimes in the subject matter jurisdiction of the tribunal, as set out in Articles 2 and 3, covered a broad range of un-enumerated offences committed in internal as well as non-international armed conflict.[28] Had the Appeals Chamber held that the benefit of the doubt should go to the accused, it would surely have opted for a more narrow approach.

The interpretative approach of the Appeals Chamber, although hardly good news for the defence, was also somewhat unnerving for states in the process of creating the permanent International Criminal Court (ICC). Concerned with their own self-interest, and with a judiciary that might depart too readily from the terms of a treaty, they included a provision within the Statute calling for strict construction. Article 22(2) reads as follows:

The definition of a crime shall be strictly construed and shall not be extended by analogy. In case of ambiguity, the definition shall be interpreted in favour of the person being investigated, prosecuted or convicted.[29]

Had there been anything similar in the statutes of the ICTY, it is at any rate arguable that the approach to the jurisdiction taken by the Appeals Chamber in *Tadic* might well have been quite different.

Penalties

International human rights law has much to say on the subject of criminal penalties. It is, of course, hostile to capital punishment, but it also proscribes in a general way all forms of cruel, inhuman or degrading punishment. In the most specific general provision dealing with punishment, Article 10, paragraph 3, of the International Covenant on Civil and Political Rights declares that "[t]he penitentiary system shall comprise treatment of prisoners, the essential aim of which shall be their reformation and social rehabilitation".[30] The United Nations Human Rights Committee, in its second general comment on Article 7 of the International Covenant on Civil and Political Rights, has stated that "[n]o penitentiary system should be only retributory; it should essentially seek the reformation and social rehabilitation of the prisoner".[31] Rehabilitation's importance in criminal sentencing is also recognized in the Standard Minimum

Rules for the Treatment of Prisoners as approved by the UN Economic and Social Council (ECOSOC).[32] The American Convention on Human Rights states: "Punishments consisting of deprivation of liberty shall have as an essential aim the reform and social re-adaptation of the prisoners."[33] In the Document of the Moscow Meeting of the Conference on the Human Dimension of the Conference on Security and Co-operation in Europe (CSCE), the participating states undertake to "pay particular attention to the question of alternatives to imprisonment".[34]

This type of approach to criminal sentencing is oriented largely towards the interests of the offender, even if it can also be argued that rehabilitation favours society as a whole. Yet, from the moment the concerns of victims are factored into the equation, the approach changes dramatically. Suddenly the two classic purposes of criminal sentences (from the standpoint of criminal law and criminology rather than that of human rights) – retribution and deterrence – rear their heads. Punishment is no longer focused on reforming the perpetrator. Instead, it becomes a technique to "satisfy" the victim, to provide "justice" and to protect society by preventing recurrence. Human rights law suddenly becomes more concerned with keeping people in prison rather than getting them out. Nor should detention be too comfortable, because it might soften its retributive impact and thereby "offend the feelings of the victims".

Getting the balance right among these competing values has not proved a simple matter for international criminal justice. The statutes of the ad hoc tribunals are silent on the subject of the objectives to be served by criminal punishment, as is the Rome Statute of the ICC, aside from an obscure reference to deterrence in the Preamble – "Determined to put an end to impunity for the perpetrators of these crimes and thus to contribute to the prevention of such crimes." In sending Dusko Tadic to prison for 20 years, Judge Gabrielle McDonald and her two colleagues said that "retribution and deterrence serve as a primary purpose of sentence".[35] The ICTR, in *Prosecutor v. Rutaganda*, has expressed similar views: "It is clear that the penalties imposed on accused persons found guilty by the tribunal must be directed, on the one hand, at retribution of the said accused, who must see their crimes punished, and above that, on the other hand, at deterrence, namely to dissuade for good, others who may be tempted in the future to perpetrate such atrocities by showing them that the international community shall not tolerate the serious violations of international humanitarian law and human rights."[36] Similar formulations occur again and again in the judgments, including those of the Appeals Chamber.[37] In *Prosecutor v. Kunarac* in 2002, the Appeals Chamber confirmed once again the significance of retribution as an objective of punishment by the ad hoc tribunals.[38]

The ad hoc tribunals have sent their harsh messages of retribution and deterrence in deeds as well as in words. Some of the sentences are stunning in their length, the most severe being that of 46 years imposed on General Krstic for his responsibility in the Srebrenica massacre.[39] Other examples of long sentences include 45 years for General Tihomir Blaskic[40] and 40 years for Goran Jelisic.[41] The ICTY Statute does not rule out the possibility of conditional release or parole for Krstic, Blaskic or Jelisic, but neither does it provide any assurances that this will be offered them.[42] Yugoslavia itself, prior to the war, confined custodial sentences to a maximum of 20 years, anything longer being considered cruel, inhuman and degrading. Even the Rome Statute of the International Criminal Court limits terms of imprisonment to 30 years, although it also allows for a sentence of life imprisonment "when justified by the extreme gravity of the crime and the individual circumstances of the convicted person".[43] In the case of a life sentence, though, the Rome Statute provides for a mandatory consideration of parole after 25 years.[44]

The traditional orientation of human rights law in the area of sentencing has always been towards the rehabilitation of the offender. Obviously, harsh and lengthy terms of imprisonment with uncertain parole provisions do little to promote this value. There have been only isolated references to rehabilitation in the jurisprudence of the ad hoc tribunals.[45] In the *Celebici* case, the Trial Chamber noted that retribution was "an inheritance of the primitive theory of revenge", pointing to its incompatibility with the policy of the Security Council in establishing the tribunal, which was directed towards reconciliation of the parties. "A consideration of retribution as the only factor in sentencing is likely to be counter-productive and disruptive of the entire purpose of the Security Council, which is the restoration and maintenance of peace in the territory of the former Yugoslavia. Retributive punishment by itself does not bring justice," the Trial Chamber warned.[46] Such remarks are, however, exceedingly rare in the sentencing judgments of the ad hoc tribunals.

Defences and criminal participation

International human rights law addresses the procedural issues involved in criminal trial, but has very little specifically to say about the substantive offences. Of course, there is authority for the view that a state cannot criminalize certain types of conduct without running afoul of other fundamental norms. For example, human rights bodies have condemned using criminal law to restrict homosexual activity.[47] Nevertheless, it might also be argued that a human rights approach to criminal law means it should be reserved for intentional offences. One of the rare relevant references here is Article 6(2) of the International Covenant on Civil and

Political Rights, which declares that the death penalty must be limited to only the "most serious crimes". In an authoritative interpretation of this provision, the ECOSOC has held that this should mean only intentional crimes.[48]

It does not seem to be an unreasonable extrapolation of these norms to claim that international criminal prosecution of crimes with the stigma of genocide, crimes against humanity and war crimes – or, to take the words used in the Preamble of the Rome Statute, "the most serious crimes of concern to the international community as a whole" – should be crimes in the true sense, in that they require proof of intention to commit the crime (*mens rea*). Perhaps the proof of this assertion can be found in the observation that an intent requirement creeps into the very definitions of such crimes. For example, genocide must be an act committed "with the intent to destroy" specific protected groups.

Surprisingly, however, the campaign against impunity seems to dictate rather low thresholds for the mental elements of crimes, the better to convict, one might say. This is particularly apparent in a widespread suspicion of the role that defences play in the criminal trial. An early manifestation was the provision in the first version of the Rules of Procedure and Evidence of the ICTY, adopted in February 1994, dealing with gender crimes that bluntly excluded the defence of consent to a charge of rape.[49] The judges quickly realized the absurdity of the provision. Rape may be defined somewhat simplistically as sexual relations without consent. If there is no defence of consent, then sexual relations – whether voluntary or involuntary – become serious crimes of which, logically, both participants should be guilty. Within a few months, the judges amended the rules so as to codify ways in which consent might be invalid, for example when obtained by threats.[50] Yet this seemed more face-saving than anything else, because consent obtained by threats is no consent at all, and lawyers hardly need a rule to make such an uncontroversial and self-evident point.

The same sort of problem arose with the defence of duress. In *Prosecutor v. Erdemovic*, a majority of the Appeals Chamber ruled the defence to be simply inadmissible in cases of crimes against humanity.[51] This means that a perpetrator whose intent has been completely neutralized or destroyed by compulsion may still be found guilty of one of the most heinous crimes. Accordingly, genocide and crimes against humanity become punishable for those who lack intent, and thereby become what are essentially strict liability offences.

We see the same thing in the prohibition of the defence of superior orders. The scope of the defence at customary law was established by the Leipzig trials, held pursuant to Articles 228–230 of the Treaty of Versailles.[52] The defence, which is generally allowed in national criminal law systems, was available to the extent that the order was not manifestly unlawful. The Charter of the International Military Tribunal at Nuremberg opted to prohibit the defence altogether, an example that was followed in the statutes of the ad hoc tribunals.[53] The Rome Statute attempted to return to the customary law principles, but only partially, because the defence is restricted by a new limitation: "For the purposes of this article, orders to commit genocide or crimes against humanity are manifestly unlawful."[54] Even this was not enough for many human rights non-governmental organizations, which condemned Article 33 of the Rome Statute as a tragic concession to impunity, as they had done with the defences of duress and of self-defence. The same unease with defences can be found in the academic literature.[55]

The same enlargement of the scope of criminal responsibility appears in the area of participation in crimes. Here, the law is constantly being broadened in order to facilitate the conviction of those whose role in the crimes is difficult to establish under ordinary principles. In *Tadic*, the Appeals Chamber advanced a broad theory of collective criminal liability by which those who participate in a "joint criminal enterprise" may be found guilty of the natural and foreseeable acts of those who share their common purpose.[56] The advantages to the Prosecutor were immediately evident, and the indictment of Slobodan Milosevic for crimes against humanity committed in Kosovo in early 1999 was subsequently amended so as to incorporate this new theory of criminal responsibility.[57] Although different in nature, the concept of command responsibility, which is codified in the ad hoc statutes as well as in Article 28 of the Rome Statute, has many of the same practical consequences. It facilitates the conviction of a commander for crimes committed by subordinates. The commander is guilty if he or she "should have known" the crimes would be committed, words that flag an offence of negligence rather than a true crime of intent.

Those whose principal concern is with the danger of convicting the innocent are aroused when they hear of limitations on defences or of legal techniques to expand criminal responsibility into areas of collective guilt or negligence. The fear is of ensnaring individuals who, although far from angelic, lack the levels of moral culpability that make their offences the most highly stigmatized known to the criminal law – genocide, crimes against humanity and war crimes. Those whose principal concern is with the fear of acquitting the guilty, of course, view such measures as helpful tools for more effective prosecution.

Concluding remarks

Establishing an appropriate balance in both the procedural and substantive rules of criminal law that recognizes the rights of the defence and yet does not impose insurmountable obstacles to the prosecution is a considerable challenge. All systems of criminal justice wrestle with these issues.

Human rights law has developed a complex catalogue of norms applicable to the criminal justice system. These begin with the premise that a person confronting prosecution requires protection from what is one of the state's most repressive organs. Fair trial norms of international human rights law are, at least as originally conceived, fundamentally indifferent to whether or not the criminal justice system actually functions effectively in its social mission of identifying offenders and seeing to their conviction and punishment. For example, the major provisions in the human rights treaties dealing with due process rights do not contain limitations clauses that attempt to balance individual rights (for example, freedom of expression, of religion, of association and of the right to privacy) with the collective rights of society as a whole.

In contrast with the human rights lawyer, who, at least historically, seeks a fair trial that respects the rights of the defence irrespective of guilt, the criminal lawyer is more anxious that the system works effectively and accurately not only in sorting out the offenders from those who are truly innocent, but also in establishing appropriate degrees of responsibility among those who have committed serious crimes. In this context, rather than being an end in itself, fairness is more a means to an end resting on the assumption that truth will emerge from the judicial duel if the rules are not skewed in favour of one side or the other.

The transition in human rights "from a culture of impunity to a culture of accountability" has shifted the focus. None the less, whereas in the past human rights law sought to protect the rights of the accused without real regard to guilt or innocence, it is now torn by another extreme, one that is oriented towards the victim and that thrives upon conviction. This is driving rules of procedure and evidence, and other aspects of criminal law, into a more repressive mode, as the examples discussed in this chapter demonstrate.

Aside from what are, in a sense, abstract issues about fairness, we may ask whether such approaches will increase the likelihood of the innocent being convicted. The answer can only be affirmative, although some human rights advocates obsessed with accountability may feel this is a reasonable price to pay. The great English jurist Sir William Blackstone said it was better for 10 guilty men to go free than for an innocent person to suffer.[58] Blackstone understood that this was all about striking a fine balance. Whether international criminal law has found the right equilibrium between the rights of the defence and the interests of prosecution is something that will need to be constantly revisited, just as it is done in national justice systems that function fairly and effectively. There is, however, a clear danger that, in rejecting impunity and struggling to

ensure accountability, the imperatives of conviction are given dispropor-
tionate priority.

Notes

1. For a recent example, see *Prosecutor v. Kupreskic et al., Appeal Judgment*, Case No. IT-95-16-A, 23 October 2001.
2. The Inter-American Court of Human Rights authored the leading case in this area: *Velasquez Rodriguez v. Honduras*, 29 July 1988, Series C, No. 4. From the Human Rights Committee, see *Bautista de Arellana v. Colombia* (No. 563/1993), UN Doc. CCPR/C/55/D/563/1993, paras. 8.3.10; *Laureano v. Peru* (No. 540/1993), UN Doc. CCPR/C/56/D/540/1993, para. 10. From the European Court of Human Rights, see *Streletz, Kessler and Krenz v. Germany*, European Court of Human Rights, 22 March 2001, para. 86; *Akkoç v. Turkey*, European Court of Human Rights, 10 October 2000, para. 77.
3. *Prosecutor v. Tadic, Decision on the Prosecutor's Motion Requesting Protective Measures for Victims and Witnesses*, Case No. IT-94-1-T, 10 August 1995.
4. *Kostovski v. The Netherlands*, Series A, Vol. 166, 23 May 1989, para. 42.
5. Rules of Procedure and Evidence, IT/14, Sub-rules 75 (A) and (B)(iii).
6. *Prosecutor v. Tadic*, para. 17.
7. International Covenant on Civil and Political Rights, (1976) 999 UNTS 171.
8. *Prosecutor v. Tadic*, para. 27.
9. Ibid., para. 28. Along the same lines, see the remarks of Judge Shahabuddeen in *Prosecutor v. Kovacevic, Individual Opinion of Judge Shahabuddeen*, Case No. IT-97-24-AR73, 2 July 1998, p. 4.
10. *Prosecutor v. Tadic*, para. 29.
11. Ibid., para. 30.
12. Ibid., para. 61.
13. *Prosecutor v. Tadic, Separate Opinion of Judge Stephen on the Prosecutor's Motion Requesting Protective Measures for Victims and Witnesses*, Case No. IT-94-1-T, 10 August 1995, p. 19.
14. Indeed, under common law, the principle of non-retroactivity of criminal offences is a rule of interpretation rather than a fundamental norm as such.
15. *Yearbook of the International Criminal Tribunal for the Former Yugoslavia*, New York: United Nations, 1994, para. 53.
16. *Prosecutor v. Tadic, Decision on Appellant's Motion for the Extension of the Time-Limit and Admission of Additional Evidence*, Case No. IT-94-1-A, 15 October 1998, para. 73. See also *Prosecutor v. Erdemovic, Separate and Dissenting Opinion of Judge Cassese*, Case No. IT-96-22-A, 7 October 1997, para. 49.
17. *Prosecutor v. Kayishema and Ruzindana, Judgment*, Case No. ICTR-95-1-T, 21 May 1999, para. 103.
18. *Prosecutor v. Akayesu, Judgment*, Case No. ICTR-96-4-T, 2 September 1998, para. 319; cited by the Appeals Chamber in *Prosecutor v. Akayesu, Judgment*, Case No. ICTR-96-4-A, 1 June 2001, fn. 329. See also *Prosecutor v. Rutaganda, Judgment*, Case No. ICTR-96-3, 6 June 1999, para. 51; *Prosecutor v. Musema, Judgment*, Case No. ICTR-96-13, 27 January 2000, para. 155; *Prosecutor v. Bagilishema, Judgment*, Case No. ICTR-95-1A-T, 7 June 2001, Ch. III, para. 2.1.1s.
19. *Prosecutor v. Akayesu*, para. 501.
20. *Prosecutor v. Delalic et al., Judgment*, Case No. IT-96-21-T, 16 November 1998, paras. 408–413. On *contra proferentem*, see also *Prosecutor v. Tadic, Opinion and Judgment*, Case No. IT-94-1-T, 7 May 1997, para. 713.

21. *Prosecutor v. Tadic, Decision on the Defence Motion for Interlocutory Appeal on Jurisdiction*, Case No. IT-94-1-AR72, 10 August 1995, para. 18. See also *Prosecutor v. Erdemovic, Joint Separate Opinion of Judge McDonald and Judge Vohrah*, Case No. IT-96-22-A, 7 October 1997, para. 3.

22. *Prosecutor v. Bagosora et al., Decision on the Admissibility of the Prosecutor's Appeal from the Decision of a Confirming Judge Dismissing an Indictment against Théoneste Bagosora and 28 Others*, Case No. ICTR 98-37-A, 8 June 1998, paras. 28–29.

23. *Prosecutor v. Delalic et al.*, para. 1161.

24. *Prosecutor v. Tadic, Decision on the Defence Motion for Interlocutory Appeal on Jurisdiction*, Case No. IT-94-1-AR72, 2 October 1995, paras. 71–142.

25. *Prosecutor v. Tadic, Judgment*, Case No. IT-94-1-A, 15 July 1999, para. 282.

26. *Kanyabashi v. Prosecutor, Joint and Separate Opinion of Judge McDonald and Judge Vohrah*, Case No. ICTR-96-15-A, 3 June 1999, para. 15. See also *Kanyabashi v. Prosecutor, Dissenting Opinion of Judge Shahabuddeen*, Case No. ICTR-96-15-A, 3 June 1999, p. 21; *Kanyabashi v. Prosecutor, Joint Separate and Concurring Opinion of Judge Wang and Judge Nieto-Navia*, Case No. ICTR-96-15-A, 3 June 1999, paras. 10–13; *Nsengiyumva v. Prosecutor, Joint and Separate Opinion of Judge McDonald and Judge Vohrah*, Case No. ICTR-96-12-A, 3 June 1999, para. 14.

27. *Kanyabashi v. Prosecutor, Dissenting Opinion of Judge Shahabuddeen*, pp. 21–22. Also *Nsengiyumva v. Prosecutor*, Case No. ICTR-96-12-A, Dissenting Opinion of Judge Shahabuddeen, 3 June 1999.

28. *Prosecutor v. Tadic, Decision on the Defence Motion for Interlocutory Appeal on Jurisdiction*, Case No. IT-94-1-AR72, 2 October 1995, paras. 71–142.

29. *Rome Statute of the International Criminal Court*, 17 July 1998, UN Doc. A/CONF.183/9.

30. International Covenant on Civil and Political Rights, (1976) 999 UNTS 171.

31. "General Comment 20/44", UN Doc. CCPR/C/21/Rev.1/Add.3, para. 10.

32. ECOSOC Res. 663C(XXIV); as amended, ECOSOC Res. 2076(LXII), §56–59.

33. *American Convention on Human Rights*, (1978) 1144 UNTS 123, OASTS 36, Art. 5(6).

34. Document of the Moscow Meeting of the Conference on the Human Dimension of the Conference on Security and Co-operation in Europe, Art. 23.2(ii).

35. *Prosecutor v. Tadic, Sentencing Judgment*, Case No. IT-94-1-T, 14 July 1997. See also *Prosecutor v. Delalic et al., Judgment*, Case No. IT-96-21-T, 16 November 1998, para. 1235; *Prosecutor v. Erdemovic, Sentencing Judgment*, Case No. IT-96-22-T, 29 November 1996, para. 64; *Prosecutor v. Kupreskic et al., Judgment*, Case No. IT-96-16-T, 14 January 2000, para. 838; *Prosecutor v. Todorovic, Sentencing Judgment*, Case No. IT-95-9/1-S, 31 July 2001, §28.

36. *Prosecutor v. Rutaganda, Judgment and Sentence*, Case No. ICTR-96-3-T, 6 December 1999, para. 456. See also *Prosecutor v. Serushago, Sentence*, Case No. ICTR-98-39-S, 2 February 1999, para. 20; *Prosecutor v. Musema, Judgment*, Case No. ICTR-96-13-T, 27 January 2000, para. 986.

37. *Prosecutor v. Aleksovski*, Case No. IT-95-14/1-A, 24 March 2000, para. 185; *Prosecutor v. Delalic et al., Judgment*, Case No. IT-96-21-A, 20 February 2001, para. 806.

38. *Prosecutor v. Kunarac et al., Judgment*, Case No. IT-96-23-A, 12 June 2002, para. 385.

39. *Prosecutor v. Krstic, Judgment*, Case No. IT-98-33-T, 2 August 2001, para. 727.

40. *Prosecutor v. Blaskic, Judgment*, Case No. IT-95-14-T, 3 March 2000.

41. *Prosecutor v. Jelisic, Judgment*, Case No. IT-95-10-T, 14 December 1999.

42. M. Cherif Bassiouni and Peter Manikas, *The Law of the International Tribunal for the Former Yugoslavia*, Ardsley, NY: Transnational Publishers, 1996, p. 710.

43. *Rome Statute of the International Criminal Court*, Art. 77.

44. See William A. Schabas, "Life, Death and the Crime of Crimes: Supreme Penalties and the ICC Statute", *Punishment & Society*, vol. 2, 2000, p. 263.

45. *Prosecutor v. Serushago*, para. 39; *Prosecutor v. Furundzija, Judgment*, Case No. IT-95-

17/1-T-10, 10 December 1998, para. 291; *Prosecutor v. Erdemovic, Sentencing Judgment*, Case No. IT-96-22-S, 5 March 1998, para. 16(i); *Prosecutor v. Tadic, Sentencing Judgment*, para. 61; *Prosecutor v. Kayishema and Ruzindana, Judgment*, paras. 12 and 26; *Prosecutor v. Kupreskic et al., Judgment*, para. 839.

46. *Prosecutor v. Delalic et al., Judgment*, para. 1231.

47. *Dudgeon v. United Kingdom*, Series A, No. 45, 22 October 1981; *Norris v. Ireland*, Series A, No. 142, 26 October 1988; *Toonen v. Australia* (No. 488/92), UN Doc. CCPR/C/50/D/488/1992.

48. Safeguards Guaranteeing the Rights of Those Facing the Death Penalty, ECOSOC Res. 1984/50.

49. Rules of Procedure and Evidence, IT/32, Rule 96(ii).

50. Rules of Procedure and Evidence, IT/32/Rev.1, Rules 6(ii)(a–b).

51. *Prosecutor v. Erdemovic, Joint Separate Opinion of Judge McDonald and Judge Vohrah*.

52. *Empire v. Dithmar and Boldt* (Hospital Ship "Llandovery Castle"), I.L.R., vol. 2, 1921, p. 437, 16 *American Journal of International Law*, p. 708; *German War Trials, Report of Proceedings before the Supreme Court in Leipzig*, Cmd. 1450, London: HMSO, 1921, pp. 56–57.

53. *Charter of the International Military Tribunal*, 82 UNTS 279, 1951, Annex, Art. 8; *Statute of the International Criminal Tribunal for the former Yugoslavia*, UN Doc. S/RES/827, 1993, Annex, Art. 7(4); *Statute of the International Criminal Tribunal for Rwanda*, UN Doc. S/RES/955, 1994, Annex, Art. 6(4).

54. *Rome Statute of the International Criminal Court*, Art. 33.

55. Eric David, *Principes de droit des conflits armés*, 2nd edn., Brussels: Bruylant, 1999, p. 694.

56. *Prosecutor v. Tadic, Judgment*, Case No. IT-94-1-A, 15 July 1999, para. 204.

57. *Prosecutor v. Milosevic et al., Second Amended Indictment*, Case No. IT-99-37-PT, 29 October 2001, paras. 16–18.

58. William Blackstone, *Commentaries on the Laws of England*, 1765, Book IV, Chapter 27.

9

We the people: The position of NGOs in gathering evidence and giving witness at international criminal trials

Helen Durham

Introduction

The enforcement of international criminal law has undergone spectacular advances in the past few years. Significant progress in this area includes the creation and workings of the ad hoc International Criminal Tribunals for the former Yugoslavia (ICTY)[1] and Rwanda (ICTR)[2] and the development and entry into force of the Rome Statute for the International Criminal Court (ICC).[3] Furthermore, the implementation[4] and use of international criminal law[5] all over the world to strengthen the capacity for domestic courts to prosecute those accused of atrocities add "bite" to the "bark" of universal jurisdiction. These developments indicate that the international community is finally getting serious about establishing a culture of accountability.

Concurrently, the turbulent pluralism of civil society has demonstrated its crucial role in international criminal proceedings. Traditionally, states are the exclusive subjects of international regulation. However, international criminal law is unique in that it represents a departure from the traditional approach and also imposes criminal responsibility upon individuals.[6] It takes the political and makes it personal. It puts names and faces to horrible and complex historical events. It dissects activities often sanctioned by states and lays blame upon individual citizens.

Members of civil society and non-state actors, in particular non-governmental organizations (NGOs), also create synergies between the political and personal. They connect the global with the local, often translating complex international issues into activities to be undertaken by concerned citizens in their own community – be this fundraising, letter writing, lobbying or general education. NGOs are currently the most basic form of popular participation and representation in the modern world. Thus, the relationship between NGOs and international criminal law, philosophically, should be a close one. Furthermore, NGOs have a unique capacity to assist in providing international trials with evidence, and thus the relationship is solid in practical terms as well.

It is in this context that this chapter aims to explore the sense of human agency involved in international criminal law. As expressed by Harold Koh:

International human rights law is enforced ... not just by nation-states, not just by government officials, not just by world historical figures, but by people with the courage and commitment to bring international human rights law home through a transnational legal process of interaction, interpretation and internalization.[7]

This chapter will focus upon civil society in the broadest terms, which includes a range of non-state actors, and will in particular consider NGOs. It is important to attempt to give some definition to the term "NGO". This is not an easy task because of the very nature of non-governmental organizations – NGOs vary in size, structure, focus, membership, formality and subject matter. To generalize about them is to obscure their most salient feature – diversity. Since the 1945 San Francisco Conference which created the United Nations, NGOs have been a driving force behind the development and implementation of policies relating to human rights.[8] The United Nations immediately recognized the potential for a role for "non-governmental organizations" and coined the term in the UN Charter.[9] The term itself is broad and its definition is based on the negative. The crucial point is that these groups are not states. There are specific prerequisites that must be satisfied before a group may apply for consultative status as an NGO within the UN system. However, this chapter will not limit itself to this technical definition. One commentator has come up with the following definition of NGOs after reviewing a large range of such actors:

An NGO is any non-profit-making, non-violent, organized group of people who are not seeking government office. An international NGO is a non-violent, organized group of individuals who are not seeking government. The members of an international NGO will usually be NGOs from different countries, but they can also have any mixture of individuals, companies, political parties, NGOs or other international NGOs as members.[10]

This is not an ideal interpretation, because it is very broad. However, it does highlight the number of organizations that could fit the general definition of an NGO.

There has been a dramatic increase in the number and activities of NGOs working directly with the United Nations,[11] and in recent times they have become a significant force in global politics. State sovereignty, although the basis of international law, is being challenged by technology, religion, ecological concerns, "universal" human rights, trade and finance, security and the development of common agendas not linked to territory.[12] Technological developments in the area of communications, such as e-mail and the Internet, are independent of territory and in many countries are easily accessible. Some observers perceive such changes as signs of growing pluralism and global democratization.[13] Classical power structures are no longer able to claim complete control of information. In such a changing environment, the NGO has become an increasingly powerful "voicepiece for multi-layered transnational identities that are barely audible in the current state-dominated systems".[14]

Yet, the rise of "people power" in the international legal arena is viewed by some commentators as not at all positive. It is responsible for the creation of the "global idiot",[15] and any individual or group with a fax machine and a modem has the potential to distort public debate. There is no guarantee that passion and commitment will always come equally packaged with awareness and intelligence. NGOs have been criticized for their lack of independence from states, difficulties with accountability, mismanagement and internal politics.[16]

In relation to the area of international criminal prosecutions, it is important to acknowledge that there can be problems associated with NGOs playing a strong role. The successful and credible prosecution of those accused of atrocities relies upon due process and an environment isolated from politics and passion. In Justice Bates' closing remarks at a war crimes trial after World War II he stated that:

The surest safeguard against totalitarian disregard for human life and liberty is uncompromising adherence to the principles of the administration of justice, which does not humour heat and revenge, but rather, protects man therefrom.[17]

NGOs are organizations very often full of "heat" and politics. Individuals involved in a group attempting to influence world politics are bound to feel passionate about particular issues of concern. As one commentator writes about NGOs:

We should not deceive ourselves and say that these organizations are not political. They are perhaps not partisan, but they are political in several fundamental respects: they look for political space in society, adapt to new circumstances, try to be effective, and seek a significant measure of public credibility.[18]

Thus the challenge is to identify those areas in international criminal prosecutions where NGOs can contribute and those areas where caution should be noted. In what follows, I shall examine the various issues involved in NGOs gathering evidence. Using the experience of the ICTY, I suggest some practical methods that may assist the ICC and future criminal trials in utilizing the specific skills of NGOs.

NGOs gathering and presenting evidence

NGOs are in a unique position to gather and present evidence at international criminal trials. This capacity is reflected in the statutes of the ad hoc tribunals and the ICC. Article 18 of the ICTY Statute states:

The Prosecutor shall initiate investigations *ex-officio* or on the basis of information obtained from any source, particularly from Governments, United Nations organs, intergovernmental and non-governmental organizations.

Article 15(2) of the ICC Statute allows the Prosecutor to investigate *proprio motu* on the basis of information provided from "reliable sources", as well as to receive written and oral testimony at the seat of the court. In this article, specific mention is made of NGOs. There is also the capacity for international criminal institutions to receive *amicus curiae* briefs from organizations,[19] and thus NGOs can contribute in a more formal way to the quest for international justice.

However, as stated previously, the involvement of NGOs in international criminal proceedings is a complex process fraught as much with danger as with great potential. To start with, the term "NGO" and the broader concept of civil society do not encompass a homogeneous group of organizations – many non-state actors, in particular humanitarian agencies, wish for protection against having to "bear witness" at legal proceedings, whereas others enthusiastically embrace the concept. The former want to continue to fulfil their mandate of relieving the suffering of victims on the ground and delivering services during periods of crisis. Organizations such as the International Committee of the Red Cross (ICRC),[20] which has a mandate to assist victims during times of armed conflict, often require cooperation from those in power that necessitates that these actors remain separate from any penal system. Denouncing offenders could allow such organizations to be accused of taking a partial approach and thus limit access to relieve the suffering of victims.[21] In the case of the ICRC, the issue of the organization's right not to be compelled to give evidence or information relating to its own activities at international criminal trials was confirmed by the *Simic* judgment at the ICTY.[22] Furthermore, the ICC's Draft Rules of Procedure and Evidence have a general clause, to be found in Rule 73, that protects the confidentiality of certain information collected in the course of the ICRC's activities.[23]

Human rights actors, on the other hand, tend to be less visible undertaking practical operations and providing direct aid to the victims in the field. Instead, many human rights organizations focus upon advocacy issues and the "mobilization of shame". Thus, the giving of evidence at international trials can involve less threat to their daily work. As Graham Blewitt, Deputy Prosecutor at the ICTY, noted:

NGOs, which focus on human rights, by their very nature, are well equipped to assist the Tribunals in their investigation work. I say this because human rights organizations focus on the monitoring and reporting of human rights violations and seek to prevent future violations. This function is not inconsistent with that of the Tribunal.[24]

Compared with humanitarian organizations, human rights actors are generally less reliant upon trust and detailed negotiations with potential perpetrators. For example, large and respected human rights actors such as Amnesty International and Human Rights Watch often gather their data in the countries where human rights abuses occur and then design the major campaigns of denunciation aimed at educating the international community in cities such as London and New York. In this sense, human rights organizations often have to be extremely discrete about the initial source of their information and have strict verification processes. With less direct and daily access to the victims, human rights actors, compared with humanitarian actors, may occasionally encounter difficulty in obtaining evidence. However, there are fewer restrictions on the use of this information once it is in the possession of human rights organizations.

Several large human rights actors have substantial technical expertise in international criminal law. As a group, respected human rights organizations also have the support of the academic community and the media. This, combined with the willingness and the commitment to give evidence, can result in human rights actors playing a crucial role in international criminal prosecutions. It is important to note that civil society cannot be neatly divided into these two groups – humanitarian and human rights actors. Obviously, these two categories do not fit every organization and a number of actors will fall into both groups at different times during their various activities. For example, organizations such as Médecins Sans Frontières have a humanitarian mandate and are also involved in advocacy work such as providing evidence at international trials. There is also a practical need to acknowledge the integral inter-relationship between human rights activities and humanitarian relief.[25] However, for the purposes of this chapter, these categories demonstrate the need to understand the diversity and complexity of the various mandates of non-state actors and NGOs.[26]

Apart from the lack of willingness of some non-state actors, particularly humanitarian organizations, to provide evidence at international criminal prosecutions, perhaps the most serious danger in the relationship between NGOs and the ICTY, ICTR and ICC is the tension between the political nature of many such organizations and the judicial requirement of impartiality. As noted previously, NGOs have the potential to move beyond the bias often found in state-centric political systems. However, it is important for non-state actors providing evidence or information to do so not for their specific political purposes but through their expertise and unique capacities. Furthermore, the gathering of evidence can actually create problems if the task is performed by NGOs incorrectly and with a lack of professionalism. Rather than assisting, the involvement of some NGOs with little understanding of the legal process may be detrimental to those involved in prosecution. However, these concerns need to be carefully considered and addressed and do not detract from the enormous benefits that NGOs bring to the international criminal process.

On the positive side, NGOs have access to networks and "grass-roots" information in a way that officials of the tribunal do not and cannot have. Very often, survivors and witnesses are suspicious and fearful of formal bodies. In many instances it is servants of the state, such as the military or civil servants, who have caused the harm. Thus, witnesses often prefer to talk to non-state actors, in the form of either local community groups or established and well-known international NGOs. This is particularly so in the area of sexual assault and gender-related crimes, and the role of many women's organizations and networks has proven to be essential in creating trust and confidence for women to provide evidence to the ICTY and ICTR.[27]

NGOs, particularly humanitarian organizations, are likely to be on the site or nearby when atrocities occur, to have first-hand knowledge of events and to be best able to identify potential witnesses. As discussed previously, whereas some humanitarian actors have grave concerns in relation to becoming involved in international criminal litigation, others, such as Médecins Sans Frontières, do not. These groups and a large number of human rights organizations are able to get direct and indirect access to important information. This is particularly true of human rights actors who were involved in a country well before the particular events occurred and thus have credibility in the eyes of the local population.

The ICTY and ICTR have provided some relief for NGOs concerned about confidentiality when providing information. Rule 70 of the tribunals' Rules of Procedure and Evidence states:

If the Prosecutor is in possession of information which has been provided to the Prosecutor on a confidential basis and which has been used solely for the purpose of generating new evidence, that initial information and its origin shall not be disclosed by the Prosecutor without the consent of the person or entity providing the initial information and shall in any event not be given in evidence without prior disclosure to the accused.

However, this rule is specific to a limited type of situation; thus NGOs cannot assume that in providing evidence they will always be "protected".

NGOs and civil society have much to offer to international criminal trials. Beyond the provision of evidence, it must be remembered that NGOs contributed significantly to the establishment of the ad hoc tribunals by bringing to the attention of the world's media the breaches of international humanitarian law – in particular in the Balkans in the early 1990s. The reports of mass rapes of women in the former Yugoslavia "had an electrifying effect and became a significant factor in the demand for the creation of the International tribunal".[28] In disseminating the horrors of the conflict, a large number of NGOs suggested solutions in the form of the prosecution of those responsible. NGOs also greatly assisted the Commission of Experts[29] in the gathering of initial details for the United Nations before it decided to create the ICTY. The role played by NGOs in the creation of the ICC Statute was crucial,[30] and civil society continues to educate the press, disseminate information about proceedings, provide technical expertise, lobby for adequate funds and support witnesses throughout prosecutions in existing proceedings. These activities are not without complexity. However, to overestimate the capacity and skill of these diverse groups is as dangerous as underestimating their value.

Case-study of an NGO: Australian Committee of Investigation into War Crimes

This section will focus upon a practical case-study of a small NGO involved in gathering evidence for the ICTY. Many such organizations have assisted the ad hoc tribunals over the past few years and thus this case-study is by no means unique. It does, however, provide a useful insight into the general range of issues needing to be addressed if civil society is seriously to offer its skills and expertise.

The Australian Committee of Investigation into War Crimes (ACIWC) was established in 1994 in Melbourne, Australia. The committee was formed in response to a specific request from a women's centre in Zagreb called Tresnjevka. An Australian woman was sent to Tresnjevka by Austcare[31] to assist female survivors of the conflict in the former Yugo-slavia. While she was working in Zagreb, a women's group in Melbourne, Women's Interlink (WIL), wrote to her, wanting to know what could be done back in Australia to assist those in Tresnjevka. After discussing the matter with the women in the Zagreb centre, she responded that the women wished rape to be deemed a war crime and for it to be prosecuted at the ICTY.

With limited resources and no access to the tribunal, WIL decided to investigate what procedures were available for refugees within Australia from the region of the former Yugoslavia to give evidence to the ICTY. It was deemed that the best way to ensure the prosecution of the crime of sexual assault, and thus to create a clear legal precedent, would be to encourage women who were survivors to give evidence. After a number of phone calls it became apparent that, despite Australia advocating its strong support for the ICTY, there was no governmental department responsible for, or willing to assist in, the gathering of evidence in Aus-tralia. Nor was there any NGO or international legal academic group working on the issue. These conclusions led a number of members of WIL and a few other interested individuals to create ACIWC.

The first task ACIWC undertook was to contact Graham Blewitt, Deputy Prosecutor at the ICTY, to enquire whether there was any role for a small and non-funded Australian NGO to assist in the goal of international justice for female victims of sexual violence. Blewitt advised that it would be extremely useful if potential witnesses could be identified and screened so that the tribunal would be able to know the quality and quantity of evidence available within the relevant refugee population in Australia. He also sent information papers to ACIWC, including "Coop-eration between Non-Governmental Organizations and the International Criminal Tribunal for the former Yugoslavia", and stressed that limited screening would be more beneficial to the ICTY than the taking of de-tailed statements, which could create difficulties.

ACIWC then created an Advisory Committee in order to obtain legal guidance and legitimacy.[32] The next task was to gain the acceptance and confidence of the Serbian, Croatian and Bosnian-Muslim communities in Melbourne. This was difficult because some of the communities were suspicious and were attempting to cope with a large influx of traumatized refugees who required their community services.[33]

Numerous informal meetings were arranged with community leaders, and personal relationships were established between members of ACIWC and representatives from the relevant ethnic groups. After discussing the proposed screening of witnesses with community members from the former Yugoslavia, it was decided that ACIWC's mandate should be broadened to include any individual (both sexes and all ethnic groups involved in the conflict) who wished to give evidence on any crime within the ICTY's jurisdiction.

A screening kit was drafted and sent to the ICTY Prosecutor's Office for review. The kit identified the aims of ACIWC, the background to the committee and a standard sheet on which individuals could answer limited questions. These questions included the geographical region in which they lived between 1991[34] and 1995; whether they were victims of or witnesses to a crime; the type of crime; whether they knew the identity or details of the perpetrators; and whether they would be prepared to provide further details to the Prosecutor's Office. The kit also asked whether the individual wished to be provided with confidential counselling services. The ICTY suggested a few amendments to the kit and ACIWC also consulted the relevant ethnic communities in relation to the process and the documentation. Once the kit was finalized it was translated into the three relevant languages.

ACIWC contacted the Federal Attorney General's Department and the State Department of Immigration and Multicultural Affairs to inform them of the preparations and to request financial assistance for tasks such as translation of the screening kit. Unfortunately, the governmental departments were unable to provide any funds. ACIWC decided to finance all activities itself and to submit applications for grants to various philanthropic organizations. Eventually, the Myer Foundation[35] provided ACIWC with A$6,000 to cover the cost of a fax machine, mobile phone, translators, interpreters and transport for those giving evidence.

Because of the nature of the work to be undertaken, security (both for those giving evidence and for those gathering evidence) was deemed important. After discussing the process of screening with a member of the Federal police who had experience within the relevant ethnic communities, a number of suggestions were implemented. These included screenings to be undertaken in a neutral and professional environment and that there would always be at least two members of ACIWC involved at any one time. Previously, ACIWC had planned to screen witnesses at committee members' homes, which was advised against owing to potential security risks. It was then necessary to identify a suitable location. The screening kit was also amended to indicate clearly that ACIWC was interested solely in victims of war crimes and not in hunting or investigating war criminals. The latter task had to be left to the Prosecutor.

In relation to the protection of those being screened, it was understood that developing adequate systems of confidentiality was essential. In previous international war crimes tribunals, such as Nuremberg and Tokyo, prosecutions were held at the end of the armed conflict and there was no fear among those giving evidence that immediate retribution would occur to loved ones still caught up in the conflict. With the ICTY this was not the case. Slavia Ilic, a community worker for the Slavic community in Melbourne, highlighted this point to ACIWC. Ilic advised the committee that one of her clients, a female refugee from the former Yugoslavia who was a survivor of multiple rapes while in the region, wished to give evidence to the tribunal. Ilic stated:

X would very much like to become involved in the process as she wants to see justice done. However, her parents are currently being hidden in a supportive neighbour's place in the territory of the former Yugoslavia. X is terrified that if she gives evidence she will be identified, putting at risk not only the lives of her parents but their protectors as well. X's dilemma is not unusual for refugees from the region.[36]

To overcome these fears, ACIWC implemented a code system to ensure that those taking part in the screening process could not be identified. Statements of intent to keep all information obtained during the screening interview confidential were drafted, to be signed by all parties to the interview including the interpreters. Indeed, ACIWC discovered that identifying the right interpreter was an important task. The wrong interpreter, especially if he or she were of the ethnic group that perpetrated the initial crime, could create fear and discomfort for an individual giving evidence. In countries of resettlement, such as Australia, communities from the region involved in the armed conflict are small and relatively insular. To those considering giving evidence, the possibility that an interpreter might "gossip" about the content of interviews was a grave concern, particularly when dealing with sensitive matters such as sexual assault within the context of different cultural and religious views on sexuality:

People in Australia are very afraid that news about what has happened to them may spread in the community. This would bring great shame upon not only the victim, but also their family. A wrong choice of interpreter could be very dangerous.[37]

In April 1995, Blewitt faxed ACIWC requesting that screening commence, with a focus, if possible, upon individuals from the Prijedor region because of the pending *Tadic* case citing alleged crimes in that area. Good contact had already been established with "Mohammed", the Bosnian-Muslim community group in Melbourne. A number of individuals from the area were identified and approximately 10 wished to be involved in the process. Over the next 15 months, ACIWC screened some 20 individuals from both the Bosnian-Muslim and Croatian communities and assisted in identifying over 15 individuals in New South Wales. Although approaches had been made to the Serbian community, with some positive communication, no one came forward from that ethnic group to undertake screening with ACIWC.

The process consisted of a face-to-face interview. A standard introduction explained the process and the fact that at this stage only very limited details were required. It was stressed to the interviewee that there would not be any expectation of a need to testify, because, despite the quality of the evidence, the ICTY might not require the specific information he or she had to offer. The screening kit was then filled out in English by the interviewee, often with the assistance of an interpreter. All members of ACIWC had completed a short workshop with counsellors from the Centre for Survivors of Torture and Trauma (Foundation House) so that they were sensitized to some of the issues that might arise in the interview. Following the screening process, each interviewee was offered free follow-up counselling with Foundation House. It was understood that in many cases it would not be possible for individuals to give limited "yes/no" answers to questions about horrific events in their lives without stirring up a range of difficult memories and emotions.

The screening kits were then faxed to the Office of the Prosecutor at the ICTY, with only the ID number on the papers. If a member of the Prosecutor's Office was interested in the initial screening, ACIWC would be contacted and a telephone interview with the individual, identified by their number, requested. On the basis of this work, the Prosecutor sent a Senior Legal Adviser, Grant Niemann, and an Investigator, Thomas Ackim, to Australia in late 1995 to undertake detailed interviews with a number of the identified witnesses.

ACIWC disbanded in late 1996 for several reasons, including reduced responses from the community groups, difficulty with resources and the time-consuming nature of the process. All members were in full-time employment and the intensity of the process of screening was hard to balance in the time available. The lack of assistance from relevant government departments was also a problem that could not be easily overcome. Similarly, before the Myer Foundation funding had been granted, the process had been expensive for individual members of ACIWC to cover. For example, no discounted rate for the interview rooms at the Law Society in Melbourne was offered and thus the cost of A$100 per evening had to be borne by the committee members. It is apparent that a process such as screening would be easier if professional groups such as the Law Society or members of the Bar were able to assist.

As a case-study, the experiences of ACIWC provide some useful lessons for NGOs wishing to undertake similar work. It is essential to communicate with, and take directions from, an international legal body as well as the relevant community groups. The proper use of interpreters, translators, locations and follow-up counselling is a necessary element if the NGO is to be successful in its aims. Treating all those providing information with respect and ensuring that expectations of the outcomes of the process are reasonable are essential if victims and survivors are not to be further damaged. Resources are always going to be required and government bodies should at least listen and respond to requests from such organizations if they appear credible and in a position to implement their proposed activities professionally. Similarly, professional organizations should be included in the dialogue and provide assistance when they are able. ACIWC did assist the ICTY in gathering important evidence. The Office of the Prosecutor expressed its approval of the work undertaken by ACIWC in a letter written by Blewitt:

From the Tribunal's point of view NGOs play a very important part in our work, and I am sure that in the event that a Permanent International Criminal Court is established, NGOs will continue to play a critical role. In particular the work of the ACIWC in Australia has led to the discovery of several important witnesses and I am confident that further witnesses will be identified in the future. The ACIWC is one of the most professional NGOs that the Tribunal is currently dealing with and I applaud the work that it is doing.[38]

Amicus curiae briefs

The capacity for NGOs and a range of non-state actors, including individuals such as academics, to provide *amicus curiae* briefs in international criminal proceedings can add to the quality of judicial considerations. *Amici curiae*, or "friends of the court", are not parties to cases but they still present matters of fact or law within their knowledge during the legal proceedings. Usually, *amici curiae* are involved in cases when matters of public interest in the administration of justice are being considered and deal with long-term and significant matters of public concern. The presentation of *amicus curiae* briefs is usually done with the permission of the court, and in many domestic jurisdictions a variety of criteria must be met before such permission is granted. The ICTY and ICTR allow for such submissions[39] and the Rules of Procedure and Evidence of the ICC also grant the capacity for such input from non-parties to the case.[40]

This is another more formal way in which NGOs can assist in international criminal proceedings, particularly in areas where there is a lack of international legal precedent. Case-studies of the ICTY and ICTR indicate that both tribunals have made use of such briefs in their deliberations and in a number of instances actively requested submissions on certain topics.[41] The tension inherent in balancing the ideal of "correct" judgment with the economies of judicial administration has required the creation of internal guidelines within the ad hoc tribunals for *amicus curiae* submissions.[42] Looking to the future, the ICC should carefully review the successes and difficulties this procedure has created and develop clear and concise guidelines to assist NGOs and other non-state actors to enhance the quality of judicial deliberations at such trials.

International criminal trials are not the only international forums at which such submissions are useful. Other international bodies such as the Inter-American Court of Human Rights and the European Court of Human Rights provide for a range of non-party submissions and initiations.[43] Indeed, the International Court of Justice (ICJ) has numerous articles that allow the presentation of information, through oral or written statements, expert opinions on request, or the initiation of public organizations.[44] These provisions are little used[45] and could potentially provide a powerful method for civil society to assist the development of international jurisprudence. An excellent case-study on the role of NGOs in the workings of the ICJ is that of the "World Court Project", which was involved in the *Advisory Opinion on the Threat or Use of Nuclear Weapons in Armed Conflict*.[46] A better understanding by civil society of the existing provisions within international legal institutions is necessary to harness the knowledge and skills NGOs have and could contribute to a range of important judicial developments.

Suggestions for the ICC and future international criminal proceedings

Although it is difficult to grapple in a strict academic fashion with the nebulous nature of NGOs and their capacities and limitations,[47] lessons must be learnt from the wealth of experience to date in this area. When the ICC and other international criminal forums establish procedures to deal with NGOs, careful reflection on the practical experiences of the ICTY and ICTR is crucial. Civil society is increasingly interested in the prosecution of those accused of atrocities and will not allow itself to be sidelined. As Falk states: "It is no longer satisfactory to conceive of international law on the basis of classical 'sources of law' and 'enforcement'. A global law of peoples is emerging, and it is past time for jurists to provide a suitable framework for its comprehension and assessment."[48]

Responsibility also lies with NGOs and non-state actors to consider the complexity of the issues raised by their involvement in international criminal prosecutions. For NGOs in the field, a serious review must first be undertaken on whether providing evidence fits into their mandate. All potential consequences should be honestly canvassed before embarking upon this process. If gathering information for prosecution is a priority for an organization, skills must be developed and adequate resources committed to this complex task. There must also be further reflection and a transparent debate among humanitarian organizations working in the field on situations already experienced with the ad hoc tribunals.

In relation to all international criminal trials, it is critical that the confidentiality of information provided by NGOs to the Office of the Prosecutor is respected. The safety and dignity of all involved should be a major consideration, and containing expectations and providing ample information about the process should be a high priority. In order for the ICC to make the most of non-state actors' various contributions, the court should create a position for a coordinator or liaison officer to deal professionally with, and to create an open dialogue between, the range of non-state actors.

Unlike the ad hoc tribunals, with their geographical and temporal limitations, the ICC will not be able to build up a detailed database in each area of prosecution. When the ICC is operational, a number of different prosecutions are likely to be being held concurrently in different situations. In this sense, the ICC will not be able to research each event, situation and geographical area in the same detail as the ad hoc tribunals can. It will therefore be important for the ICC to have a strong dialogue with non-state actors in the field and in third countries where large numbers of potential witnesses are sheltering. Supplying NGOs with ample and clear information, similar to the briefing paper provided by the ICTY, will be essential. Providing a standard screening kit to those considering gathering evidence would be of significant assistance both to the ICC and to non-state actors, particularly members of the NGO community.[49]

The creation of a list of NGOs, identifying the sort of work they are undertaking and their location, could be a useful tool for the ICC and the work of the ICTY and ICTR. This "Who's Who" of civil society would provide the Office of the Prosecutor with vital contacts and a place to start approaching those who might have valuable evidence. Those non-state actors not wishing to give evidence, such as the ICRC, would not have to put their details in the list and the ICC would see the range of options it has with other organizations. Providing information to NGOs and encouraging an honest and rigorous dialogue on the topic of what these actors can and cannot do will ensure a profitable relationship between international criminal forums and this vital sector.

Conclusion

The victims of atrocities tend not to be government officials but are most often "ordinary people" – foot-soldiers, female refugees, elderly people, students or children. In attempting to deal with future tragedies, change the current culture of impunity, give victims a voice and build international peace and security, all forms of international criminal law need as much help as they can get. Many members of the general public are interested in international criminal law – interested enough to have pushed for the creation of the ICC, to have raised funds to send NGOs to the negotiations, to have signed letters and to have lobbied their own governments on this topic. Many people have participated in the presenting of evidence to the ad hoc tribunals; young law students have worked alongside professional lawyers gathering resources to enable witnesses to "have their say". Many academics and other concerned individuals have written briefs, in the hope of encouraging judges to consider more broadly the impact of international law on the suffering of individuals.

Unlike states, NGOs do not have the power to make, implement or enforce international law. However, the decentralization of the authority of the state has facilitated the growth of NGOs pursuing goals that transcend national and local identities. As this chapter has demonstrated, NGOs and other non-state actors have developed skills, commitment and unique capacities to assist in international criminal prosecutions. The lofty aim of changing the culture of impunity to a culture of accountability will not be achieved without the carefully considered assistance of NGOs.

Notes

1. "The International Tribunal for the Prosecution of Persons Responsible for Serious Violations of International Humanitarian Law Committed in the Territory of the Former Yugoslavia since 1991", SC Res 827, 48 UN SCOR (3217th mtg), UN Doc. S/RES/827, 1993; 32 ILM 1203.
2. "The International Tribunal for the Prosecution of Persons Responsible for Genocide and Other Serious Violations of International Humanitarian Law Committed in the Territory of Rwanda and Rwandan Citizens Responsible for Genocide and Other Violations Committed in the Territory of Neighbouring States, Between 1 January 1994 and

31 December 1994", SC Res 955, 49 UN SCOR (3453rd mtg), UN Doc. S/RES/955, 1994; 33 ILM 1598.

3. *The Rome Statute of the International Criminal Court*, 17 July 1998, UN Doc. A/CONF.183/9, at www.un.org/icc; entered into force July 2002.

4. For example, see common law legislation such as *Crimes Against Humanity and War Crimes Act 2000*, c.24 (Canada), at www.canlii.org/ca/sta/c-45.9/; *International Criminal Court Act 2001*, c 17 (United Kingdom), at www.hmso.gov.uk/acts/acts2001/20010017.htm; *International Crimes and International Criminal Court Act 2000* (New Zealand), at http://rangi.knowledge-basket.co.nz/gpacts/public/text/2000/an/026.html. The South African approach can be seen at "International Criminal Court Bill 2001 (Draft)", at www.parliament.gov.za/bills/2001/b42-01.pdf.

5. See especially the *Pinochet* case (House of Lords, Judgment – *Regina v Bartle and the Commissioner of Police for the Metropolis and Others Ex Parte Pinochet*).

6. This chapter will focus exclusively on the international criminal responsibility of individuals.

7. Harold Koh, "International Human Rights Law", *Indiana Law Journal*, vol. 74, 1999, p. 1417.

8. See David Weissbrodt, "The Contribution of International Non-Governmental Organizations to the Protection of Human Rights", in T. Meron, ed., *Human Rights in International Law: Legal and Policy Issues*, Oxford: Clarendon Press, 1984, pp. 429–430.

9. Article 71 of the Charter provides: "The Economic and Social Council may make suitable arrangements for consultation with non-governmental organizations which are concerned with matters within its competence."

10. Peter Willetts, "Introduction", in Peter Willetts, ed., *The Conscience of the World: The Influence of Non-Governmental Organizations in the UN System*, London: Hurst, 1996, p. 5. See also Baehr, who writes: "NGOs are defined by what they are not. They emphasise their distance and independence from governments, yet at the same time, it is mostly the actions and activities of national governments that are the very cause and purpose of their existence" (Peter R. Baehr, "Human Rights Organizations and the UN: A Tale of Two Worlds", in Dimitri Bourantonis and Jarrod Wiener, eds., *The United Nations in the New World Order*, London: Macmillan, 1995, p. 171).

11. Currently there are 2,091 NGOs in consultative status with the Economic and Social Council (ECOSOC) and 400 NGOs accredited to the Commission on Sustainable Development, a subsidiary body of ECOSOC: "Consultative Relationships between the ECOSOC and NGOs", at www.un.org/eas/coordination/ngo/, 29 April 2002.

12. Richard A. Falk, *Revitalizing International Law*, Ames, Ia: Iowa State University Press, 1989, p. 6.

13. For discussion on this topic, see Paul Ghils, "International Civil Society: International Non-Governmental Organizations in the International System", *International Social Science Journal*, vol. 44, 1992, p. 417; Lester Salamon, "The Rise of the Nonprofit Sector", *Foreign Affairs*, vol. 73, 1994, p. 109; William Fisher, "Doing Good? The Politics and Antipolitics of NGO Practices", *Annual Review of Anthropology*, vol. 26, 1997, p. 439; John Boli and George Thomas, "World Culture in the World Polity: A Century of International Non-Governmental Organizations", *American Sociological Review*, vol. 62, 1997, p. 171.

14. Di Otto, "Non-Governmental Organizations in the United Nations System: The Emerging Role of International Civil Society", *Human Rights Quarterly*, vol. 18, 1996, p. 107.

15. P. Simmons, "Learning to Live with NGOs", *Foreign Policy*, no. 112, 1998, p. 84.

16. Simmons writes: "Embracing a bewildering array of beliefs, interests, and agendas, they have the potential to do as much harm as good. Hailed as the exemplars of grassroots

democracy in action, many NGOs are, in fact, decidedly undemocratic and unaccountable to the people they claim to represent" (ibid., p. 82).

17. *USA v Weiss*, Trial Transcripts, Roll 3, Target 3, vol. 5, p. 316.

18. Michael Posner, "Transitions in the Midst of Crisis: The Role of the Non-Government Organization", *American University of International Law and Policy*, vol. 5, 1990, p. 989.

19. See Rule 74, *International Tribunal for the Prosecution of Persons Responsible for Serious Violations of International Humanitarian Law Committed in the Territory of the Former Yugoslavia since 1991, Rules of Procedure and Evidence*, as amended, UN Doc. IT/32 Rev 13, 1998.

20. The ICRC is not an NGO, rather an international organization and part of the general elements of civil society. See Yves Beigbeder, *The Role and Status of International Humanitarian Volunteers and Organizations: The Right and Duty to Humanitarian Assistance*, Dordrecht: Nijhoff, 1991.

21. Stroun, Deputy Director of Operations of the ICRC states, "public denunciation, for instance, may sometimes compromise the dialogue with the authorities concerned and jeopardise work for victims in the field" (J. Stroun, "International Criminal Jurisdiction, International Humanitarian Law and Humanitarian Action", *International Review of the Red Cross*, vol. 321, 1997, p. 625).

22. *The Prosecutor v. Blagoje Simic, Milan Simic, Miroslav Tadic, Steven Todorovic and Simi Zaric*, Case No. IT-95-9-PT, 7 June 2000.

23. For more details on this topic, see S. Jeannet, "Testimony of ICRC Delegates before the International Criminal Court", *International Review of the Red Cross*, vol. 840, 2000, p. 993.

24. G. Blewitt, "The Relationship between NGOs and the International Criminal Tribunals", *Final Report of the Conference on Cooperation between Humanitarian Organizations and Human Rights Organizations*, Amsterdam: Médecins Sans Frontières, February 1996, p. 21.

25. P. Alston, "Introductory Speech", *Final Report of the Conference on the Cooperation between Humanitarian Organizations and Human Rights Organizations*, Amsterdam: Médecins Sans Frontières, February 1996, p. 8. Alston states: "[C]ooperation [between humanitarian and human rights organizations] is no longer an optional proposition but a necessity ... The reality is there is no option but to explore the interlinkages between these different concerns and to seek to develop some different forms of cooperation, albeit carefully tailored to the needs of the situation."

26. For a discussion on the different mandates and actions of NGOs, see Paul Bonnard, *Modes of Action Used by Humanitarian Players: Criteria for Operational Complementarity*, Geneva: International Committee of the Red Cross, 1999.

27. Interview with Patricia Sellers, Legal Adviser on Gender Issues, ICTY, The Hague, 7 September 1997.

28. R. Copeland, "Surfacing Gender", *Hastings Women's Law Journal*, vol. 5, no. 2, 1994, p. 248.

29. *Final Report of the Commission of Experts Pursuant to Security Council Resolution 780, 1992*, SC Res 780, 47 UN SCOR (3119th mtg), UN Doc. S/RES/780, 1992; 31 ILM 1476; UN Doc. S/674/1994 Annex, 1994 (Final Report).

30. See R. William Pace and M. Thieroff, "Participation of Non-Governmental Organizations", in Roy S. Lee, ed., *The International Criminal Court: The Making of the Rome Statute: Issues, Negotiations, Results*, New York: Transnational Publications, 1999.

31. Austcare is an Australian NGO that deals with the problems experienced by refugees.

32. The Advisory Committee comprised Professor Philip Alston, Professor Hilary Charlesworth, Professor Timothy McCormack and Ms Pene Mathew. Justice Elizabeth Evatt agreed to be patron of ACIWC.

33. From 1991 until 1995 Australia accepted 14,000 refugees from the former Yugoslavia: M. Einfeld, "Humanitarian Aid Delivery in the Balkans", Report of a Mission, September 1995, p. 11.

34. The ICTY has jurisdiction only over crimes committed after 1991.

35. The Myer Foundation is a philanthropic organization based in Melbourne, Australia.

36. Interview with Slavia Ilic, aid-in-grant worker for the Slavic community, Melbourne, 10 October 1994.

37. Interview with Emeria Bostjak, active member of the Bosnian-Muslim community, Melbourne, 17 October 1998.

38. Letter from Graham Blewitt, Deputy Prosecutor ICTY, The Hague, 26 September 1995.

39. Rule 74 of the Rules of Procedure and Evidence of both tribunals states:
A chamber may, if it considers it desirable for the proper determination of the case, invite or grant leave to a State, organization or person to appear before it and make submission on any issue specified by the chamber.

40. Rule 103 of the Rules of Procedure and Evidence of the ICC states:
1. At any stage of the proceedings, a chamber may, if it considers it desirable for the proper determination of the case, invite or grant leave to a State, organization or person to submit, in writing or orally, any observation on any issue that the chamber deems appropriate.

41. *Prosecutor v Tihomir Blaskic, Order Submitting the Matter to Trial Chamber II and Inviting Amicus Curiae*, Case No. IT-95-14, 14 March 1997.

42. *Information Concerning the Submission of Amicus Curiae Briefs*, UN Doc. IT/122, 1997 ("ICTY Internal Guidelines").

43. For details on this topic see Dinah Shelton, "The Participation of Non-Governmental Organizations in International Judicial Proceedings", *American Journal of International Law*, vol. 88, 1994, p. 611.

44. Articles 34, 50 and 66 of the Statute of the International Court of Justice.

45. For a full discussion on an attempt to use such provisions, see R. Clark, "The International League for Human Rights and South West Africa 1947–1957: The Human Rights NGO as Catalyst in the International Legal Process", *Human Rights Quarterly*, vol. 3, 1981, p. 103.

46. For more details, see K. Mothersson, *From Hiroshima to the Hague: A Guide to the World Court Project*, Zurich: International Peace Bureau, 1992, p. 31; N. Grief, *The World Court Project on Nuclear Weapons and International Law: A Joint Project of the International Association of Lawyers against Nuclear Weapons, the International Peace Bureau and the International Physicians for the Prevention of Nuclear War*, Tucson, Ariz.: Aletheia Press, 1993, pp. 8–14; and Kate Dewes and R. Green, "The World Court Project: How a Citizen Network Can Influence the United Nations", *Pacific Review*, vol. 7, no. 2, 1995, pp. 12–37.

47. Fisher writes that the literature on NGOs "as a whole is based more on faith than fact. There are relatively few detailed studies of what is happening in particular places or relations of power among individuals, communities and the State" (Fisher, "Doing Good? The Politics and Antipolitics of NGO Practices", p. 447).

48. Richard Falk, "The Nuclear Weapons Advisory Opinion and the New Jurisprudence of Global Civil Society", *Transnational Law and Contemporary Problems*, vol. 7, 1997, p. 352.

49. The ICTY has a general screening kit to be used by non-state actors in gathering information.

10

Democracy, global governance and the International Criminal Court

Madeline H. Morris

The International Criminal Court (ICC) is to be a permanent, international judicial institution with jurisdiction over genocide, war crimes and crimes against humanity.[1] The crucial fact motivating the establishment of the ICC is that, when crimes of that character are committed, the state on whose territory the crimes occurred may be unable or unwilling to pursue the prosecution of those responsible. Indeed, governments themselves, not infrequently, are implicated in the commission of crimes of this nature. The ICC is intended to provide a forum to ensure the accountability of perpetrators of these grave international crimes in cases in which they would otherwise escape accountability.

However, this solution presents a dilemma. The jurisdictional structure of the ICC poses a tension between two sorts of accountability: the legal accountability of the perpetrators of international crimes, on the one hand, and the democratic accountability of the ICC itself, on the other. This tension arises in the following way. The relationship between the ICC and national courts is to be governed by the "complementarity regime" laid out in the Rome Statute, which is the constituting document of the court.[2] Under the system of complementarity, the ICC may exercise jurisdiction only if states are unable or unwilling to do so.[3] As Article 17 of the Rome Statute states, a case shall not be admissible before the ICC if the case "is being investigated or prosecuted by a state which has jurisdiction over it, unless the state is unable or unwilling genuinely to carry out the investigation or prosecution".[4] In this way, complementarity gives priority to *states* in the enforcement and development of humanitarian law. Yet it also provides the ICC with the authority to conduct prosecutions when states are unable or unwilling genuinely to do so. If the state where the crime is alleged to have occurred – the "territorial state" – is a party to the ICC Statute, or consents ad hoc to the jurisdiction of the court, then the ICC would have authority to prosecute even if the defendant's state of nationality were not a party to the Statute and did not consent to ICC jurisdiction.[5] ("Consent" will be used in this chapter to include both consent via participation in the ICC Statute and ad hoc consent.) This authority is the ICC's so-called "jurisdiction over non-party nationals".

The clear advantage of affording the ICC this power to prosecute without the consent of the defendant's state of nationality is that this jurisdictional structure circumvents the problem of perpetrator regimes shielding their own nationals from justice. States, not infrequently in cases of genocide, war crimes or crimes against humanity, collude in the crimes and then attempt to shield the perpetrators. If the ICC required the consent of the defendant's state of nationality before it could prosecute, the court's purpose would be largely defeated. An international court is needed most when a government shields the perpetrator. For that reason, the ICC needs and has, by the terms of the Rome Statute, genuinely "supranational" powers, which are to be used in those particular instances where a state is unable or unwilling to render accountability at the state level. In those instances, the defendant is called to account not before the court of any state, but before an international institution. In essence, this is a supranational solution to the problem of national transgressors.

This kind of supranational authority is a new departure. Even while complementarity comports with, and supports, the authority of states in a state-based international system, it also goes beyond state authority; it makes an exception. Where genocide, war crimes or crimes against humanity are alleged, there is now to be an authority higher than the state.

One might ask at this point whether the ICC is really a supranational authority or whether, instead, it is merely the delegate of the territorial state's authority. After all, for the ICC to have jurisdiction over non-party nationals in any given instance, the territorial state must be a treaty party or consent ad hoc to jurisdiction. However, the ICC is *not* merely the delegate of the territorial state's authority; the ICC is indeed a truly supranational authority. Even though the ICC's jurisdiction arises from the delegation of jurisdiction by the states parties, those states parties also delegate to the ICC substantial control over the exercise of that jurisdiction – such that the ICC is empowered to operate as a truly separate and distinct international entity. This is manifested in a variety of ways.

First, under complementarity, the ICC is the ultimate judge of whether the territorial state has genuinely exercised jurisdiction over a case. If the ICC determines that the territorial state's exercise of jurisdiction has not been genuine, then the ICC may exercise jurisdiction, even over the objection of that state. So, in a dispute over jurisdiction between the territorial state and the ICC, the ICC has authority, superior to that of the territorial state, to override the territorial state's claims and seize jurisdiction.

A second manifestation of the truly supranational nature of the ICC's authority is found in its governance structure. The ICC is loosely governed by its Assembly of States Parties (composed of a representative from each state party). The Assembly of States Parties has control over both administrative and substantive matters, including, for example, changes to the Elements of Crimes (that is, the legal definitions of the crimes within ICC jurisdiction). The Assembly of States Parties governs by majority (or super-majority) rule. Therefore, in any particular prosecution, the ICC may be applying rules and law that were decided upon by a majority or super-majority of the ICC's member states over the dissenting vote of the state on whose territory the particular crimes occurred.

Third, the ICC will have influence and law-making authority beyond that of the territorial state or, for that matter, of any state. The ICC, like the International Court of Justice, will have the power to shape and make international law to a degree far exceeding that of any state's domestic courts.

In these respects, and many more, we see that the ICC is not in any simple way the agent or delegate of the territorial state. It is a separate and distinct international institution. The ICC really does present a supranational solution to the problem of national transgressors. And this is a genuine innovation. Nevertheless, there is a feature of this innovation that has gone curiously unexamined. Yet this feature is at the crux of the controversy concerning complementarity and, in particular, jurisdiction over non-party nationals. A supranational judicial authority has been created, but there has been virtually no examination of its democratic legitimacy. In contrast to the case of the World Trade Organization (WTO), for instance, where a so-called "democratic deficit" has been a focus of debate, in the case of the ICC a powerful new international institution has been created with virtually no discussion of the democratic features of this new power.

The ICC will wield governmental authority. As a judicial body, it will prosecute and punish individuals. However, where is the democratic linkage between this institution of governance and the governed? For nationals of states that are parties to the ICC Statute, their representation comes through their own governments' consent to the statute, and continues through their governments' participation in the Assembly of

States Parties.[6] What, then, about non-party states? What is the democratic basis for the ICC's power as applied to populations whose states have *not* consented on their behalf? Here, the ICC's claim to democratic legitimacy breaks down. There is no democratic linkage between the ICC and those non-party nationals over whom it would exercise authority.

Why, then, have we heard no clamour – indeed, no discussion – of democratic legitimacy in relation to the ICC? Why has there been virtually no discussion of democracy relative to the ICC, even though the "democratic deficit" of other international institutions, such as the WTO, has been a *cause célèbre*? The reason is comprehensible. The mandate of the ICC is viewed as being very thin and very important. The unarticulated assumption seems to be that, if ICC jurisdiction over non-party nationals entails any democratic loss at all, it is *de minimus* – because the court's mandate is so narrow. The implicit reasoning is that, first, the ICC's jurisdiction over non-party nationals is an exception that gives the ICC authority to act only when states fail to do so. Second, exception to states' prerogatives is a thin one because, unlike the WTO, the ICC is not intended to make law and policy. Rather, its mandate is to apply clear, uncontroversial – indeed, *jus cogens* – precepts of existing international law.

Genocide, war crimes and crimes against humanity are crimes. Nobody debates that, so there is no democratic or *un*democratic decision-making to discuss. Here, though, the reasoning fails. It is true that the prohibitions of genocide, war crimes and crimes against humanity are unquestionable. Yet, applying that law will turn out to be far more complex, and politically fraught, than are the definitions of the core prohibitions. There will be questions, both large and small, about the content and interpretation of the law, notwithstanding the excellent delineation of the Elements of Crimes produced by the ICC Preparatory Committee.[7] For example, relative to the war crime of excessive incidental death, injury or damage,[8] are countries with the resources to use precision-guided munitions obliged to use those weapons, in order to minimize collateral damage, rather than using the much less expensive ordinary kinetic weapons? Relative to that same war crime of excessive incidental death, injury or damage, are belligerents who have not invested in – or cannot afford – night-vision goggles prohibited from fighting at night, because excessive collateral damage could be avoided with the goggles? Relative to the crime of genocide,[9] what is the *mens rea* required for command responsibility for genocide? Where the commander knows of his subordinate's genocidal intent but does not entertain that *mens rea* himself, does he have the necessary *mens rea* for a conviction for genocide? Relative to the war crime of attacking civilian objects,[10] what is the status of "dual use" targeting – where the target is an object, such as a bridge or television station or electrical grid, that is partially in military use and partially in civilian use?

These are not thin questions. Each involves areas where the law is indeterminate and the politics are weighty. These questions do not require anything like the "mere" "application of the law to the facts". These issues implicate enormous political, and even moral, issues and controversies. The questions concern the size of military budgets, determining how much of a country's domestic revenue must be spent for a given degree of military strength; basic issues of North/South politics; which countries can afford to fight with which allies in coalitions; and what will be the cost of warfare, including humanitarian interventions.

And that describes the situation only as it stands *now*. The ICC's subject matter jurisdiction is going to get broader, not narrower. The ICC Statute stands open to amendment, modification, extension, and the definition and redefinition of existing and future crimes. This is contemplated explicitly in the document itself. For instance, the Rome Statute provides that the crime of aggression will come within the ICC's active jurisdiction in the future, when the Assembly of States Parties has amended the statute to define "aggression".[11] That matter is specified to be among the topics of a review conference to be convened seven years after the statute comes into effect.[12]

Beyond the crime of aggression, the Final Act of the Rome Conference, in Resolution E, states that the Rome Conference "[a]ffirm[s] that the Statute of the ICC provides for a review mechanism, which allows for an expansion in future of the jurisdiction of the Court, [and] [r]ecommends that a Review Conference ... consider the crimes of terrorism and drug crimes with a view to arriving at an acceptable definition and their inclusion in the list of crimes within the jurisdiction of the Court".[13] These foreseen, and other unforeseen, alterations and expansions of the ICC's domain would all occur with no representation of the nationals of non-party states.

The ICC will be a feature and an organ of global governance as it makes and applies international law and policy. If ICC jurisdiction over non-party nationals means that the ICC is, to that extent, undemocratic, the problem is not *de minimus*.

The ICC Statute, insofar as it provides for jurisdiction over non-party nationals, displaces the state as the conduit of democratic representation and provides no alternative mechanism for democratic governance. Advocates of ICC jurisdiction over non-party nationals might be tempted to suggest that the solution to this democratic dilemma is for all states to become parties to the ICC Statute and, consequently, to participate in the Assembly of States Parties. Still, this suggestion would not address the fundamental, underlying problem of consent. Insofar as the states parties govern the court through voting in the Assembly of States Parties, the ICC involves a form of governance by majority rule. The offer to non-party states cannot be: you enter into this new, majority-rule form of decision-making with us – or, if you do not, then we will simply govern you without your consent or representation. A system based on the consent of the governed requires that consent be meaningful, that is, that it be optional, that there be the alternative of not consenting.

The possibility of majority rule in any form at the international level is a notoriously complex issue. The questions concerning global democracy – within or outside the UN system – are enormous: What is the largest scale on which democracy is feasible? Is there a meaningful demos or polity on the global level? These questions go well beyond the scope of this essay. What is clear, however, is that, even if it were possible to have a meaningful international polity on some thin set of issues, the issues within the jurisdiction of the ICC will inevitably not, in practice, be thin. States therefore make a weighty choice – and are entitled to have a *real* choice – in deciding whether to participate in the ICC.

The ICC Statute seeks to make important headway in ensuring the accountability of the perpetrators of genocide, war crimes and crimes against humanity. However, it does so at a cost to the democratic legitimacy of the ICC itself. There is a tension embodied within the Rome Statute between the human right to freedom from violent abuse and the human right to representative government. Neither should be sacrificed: the abuse and suffering of innocent men, women and children should not be countenanced; and neither should the erosion of democratic governance. Indeed, the two are joined – it is typically the erosion of democracy that leads eventually to violent abuse. It would be a mistake to think that this dilemma could be easily negotiated away. We have yet to grapple successfully with the two-fold demands of justice *and* democracy in an emergent international system.

Conclusion

There is a notable reluctance to take a critical view of jurisdictional mechanisms for the prosecution of genocide, war crimes and crimes against humanity. Perhaps because of the heartrending nature of those crimes, proposed enforcement mechanisms too often escape rigorous scrutiny. In constructing international institutions that will wield governmental powers, the utmost care is required to ensure democratic control. As we contemplate the establishment of organs of international governance, we must ask very pointedly whether the structures are sustainable, democratic and constructed in a way that should be approved as a system of governance. We have shown inadequate concern for democratic values in the formulation of the ICC's jurisdiction. Notwithstanding the compelling nature of the problem of grave international crimes, circumspection is required in crafting the solutions. Particularly sober attention is required now, while the law of international jurisdiction is in the process of such rapid and significant development.

Notes

1. See *Rome Statute of the International Criminal Court*, Art. 5, 17 July 1998, UN Doc. A/CONF.183/9. Although the ICC Statute also provides for jurisdiction over the crime of aggression (see Art. 5(1)(d)), the statute further provides that the ICC shall not exercise jurisdiction over that part of its subject matter jurisdiction until such time as the statute is amended to include provisions defining the crime of aggression and setting out the conditions under which the court will exercise jurisdiction over that crime (see Art. 5(2)).
2. See *Rome Statute of the International Criminal Court*.
3. Ibid., Art. 17.
4. Ibid.
5. See ibid., Art. 12.
6. For states parties that are non-democratic, the "governed" are not represented by their governments – either in the ICC or anywhere else. But this is a separate problem, beyond our immediate concern.
7. *Report of the Preparatory Commission for the International Criminal Court, Addendum, Part II, Finalized Draft Text of the Elements of Crimes, Adopted 2 Nov. 2000*, UN Doc. PCNICC/2000/1/ Add.2.
8. Ibid., Art. 8(2)(b)(iv).
9. Ibid., Art. 6.
10. Ibid., Art. 8(2)(b)(ii).
11. See *Rome Statute of the International Criminal Court*.
12. Ibid., Arts. 5 and 123.
13. *Final Act of the United Nations Diplomatic Conference of Plenipotentiaries on the Establishment of an International Criminal Court, Annex I, Resolution E, Adopted 17 July 1998*, UN Doc. A/CONF.183/10.

Part III

Effectiveness and limitations

11

Reconciling fractured societies: An African perspective on the role of judicial prosecutions

Kingsley Chiedu Moghalu

Introduction

In 2001 in Rwanda, an old Rwandan woman visiting the Information and Documentation Center of the International Criminal Tribunal for Rwanda (ICTR) in Kigali requested a copy of the judgment of the tribunal in the case of *Prosecutor v. Jean-Paul Akayesu*, rendered by the international tribunal on 2 September 1998. The old woman did not read it, but she held the judgment solemnly in her hands for several moments before replacing it. In that fleeting moment, when time nevertheless stood still for her, the judgment, which convicted Akayesu, the former mayor of the Rwandan town of Taba, for genocide and crimes against humanity, represented justice for the crimes he had committed. The full weight of what that judgment meant to her life was obvious to the onlookers of this scene.

International criminal justice, or international judicial intervention, is the third and new dimension in international relations, following diplomacy and the use of force as organizing principles of international action by states. It has taken the recognition of individuals as subjects, not just objects, of international law to new heights by establishing as a new reality of our time the accountability of individuals for crimes in which humanity itself is the victim. These crimes are genocide, crimes against humanity, and violations of the Geneva Conventions and the laws and customs of war.

Yet what is the aim of this new instrument? It is not solely individual-istic – the punishment of violations of individual victims of mass crimes. Rather, precisely because international criminal justice addresses *mass* crimes, which inevitably dislocate societies, its ultimate aim is to heal fractured societies and help establish peace and reconciliation by ad-dressing the root cause of such destabilization – impunity.

Impunity may be defined as the absence of accountability and of the rule of law within states or other formal organizational structures; a situation in which coercive power, not rules, regulations or law, is the "organizing" principle. If impunity is the absence of accountability, then it follows that the establishment of a culture of accountability is necessary to eradicate it. Thus, it is necessary to introduce an element of account-ability in order to secure a long-term resolution and reconciliation of the conflicts that are inevitably generated by situations of impunity. Ac-countability in a complete sense is not – or should not be – subject to subjective definitions. It means legal responsibility and punishment for criminal illegal acts or omissions. It does not mean "truth-telling" for mass atrocities without the consequence of responsibility, which is justice. This is so, although other goals, including the establishment of the truth, may be conceived as the end result of that process.

The question is: What is the best way to reach peace and reconcilia-tion? Is it truth commissions aiming at uncovering the past by sometimes promising amnesty to individuals prepared to confess their crimes, or is it courts and tribunals whose task is criminal prosecution and that therefore may dissuade some involved in the subject of the enquiry from cooper-ating to create a complete picture of the events in question?

This chapter will argue that justice for mass atrocities, as dispensed by international criminal tribunals and national courts, is a fundamental, though not the only, component of reconciliation, and will recognize that these choices are not mutually exclusive. The chapter will note the char-acteristics, strengths and weaknesses of truth commissions and of crimi-nal courts and tribunals. In this context it will examine the challenges facing the Rwandan judicial system and the contributions of the ICTR to reconciliation in Rwanda.

Prosecute or pardon: Truth commissions as a middle ground

Should perpetrators of mass atrocities be prosecuted or pardoned, espe-cially when they are also political leaders with whom it may be necessary to make the peace that may end the war? There are, admittedly, no simple answers to these and other related questions. Political exemptions from prosecution for individual criminal responsibility are not new. Following World War II, the International Military Tribunal for the Far East, which prosecuted Japanese war criminals, did not prosecute the Japanese Emperor Hirohito. This deliberate decision not to prosecute Hirohito was largely due to the views advanced by the Senior Allied Military Commander, General Douglas MacArthur of the United States, who believed that Hirohito had an essential role to play in rebuilding post-war Japan. It is important, however, to recall the deep wounds that the acts of Japanese war criminals have left in some countries to this day, particularly in South Korea.

In some other countries in which brutal atrocities were committed, such as Nigeria in 1970 after the Biafran civil war and in Mozambique following the peace settlement in 1992 that ended that country's civil war, complete amnesties were given for acts committed in these conflicts. Looked at from a certain point of view, it is fair to say that amnesty – impunity, in effect – was the price to be paid for peace and reconciliation.[1] However, in the 1990s, a middle ground between political exemptions from prosecution for mass crimes and courtroom trials emerged. This was the phenomenon of truth commissions, most famously exemplified by the truth commissions of Latin America and that of South Africa, which facilitated the transition from apartheid to majority rule. Since the Argentinian example, about 25 countries have utilized a combination of truth commissions and amnesties as a method of facilitating transitions towards stability.

Although truth commissions and criminal trials have broadly similar aims of contributing to reconciliation in strife-torn societies, they approach these goals in fundamentally different ways. In exchange for full confessions to South Africa's Truth and Reconciliation Commission (TRC), individuals responsible for major political crimes in South Africa under apartheid were able to obtain amnesty for those crimes.[2] Although apartheid's ghost had to be laid to rest, trials for crimes against humanity were considered inappropriate in a situation in which the difference between the outcome of a peaceful transition of power to the black majority and a bloody war with a well-armed white minority government lay in the success or failure of negotiations. What resulted was a TRC based on the premise of the cleansing power of revelations of truth, but largely without the accompanying legal culpability for mass crimes against the black majority.

At an international conference in 1998, Professor John Daniel, a member of the TRC, said that, during the life-span of the Commission, South Africa did not see retributive justice as an indispensable prerequisite for reconciliation. "The TRC approach trades justice for truth," he observed. "It is surely for every nation to decide its own approach to these kinds of difficult situations."[3] As will be demonstrated later, although this is an admirably honest rationalization of the TRC, its attempt mutually to exclude truth and justice is fundamentally problematic.

Daniel tried to underscore his position by making an interesting attempt to distinguish between the amnesty granted by the TRC and a blanket amnesty, as if the former ensured some significant level of accountability, which in fact it has not. This is buttressed by his apt acknowledgement of the disappointment of some South Africans at seeing "murderous henchmen of the former regime walking free, with their crimes exposed and recorded but not punished".[4] The distinction he made was as follows:

In fact the TRC was the best solution. It ensured that amnesty did not mean what the word literally means in Greek ("forgetting"), but was accompanied by a full revelation of the truth; a blanket amnesty would have allowed the criminals to hide everything forever.[5]

Truth commissions have important limitations that make them – where unique political circumstances so demand – only a secondary option to trials. First, as a general rule, truth and reconciliation commissions, because they cannot ensure or enforce accountability for mass crimes, ultimately fail to address the yearning of the victims for justice. Experience in several post-conflict societies has shown that, where culprits were not prosecuted for a number of reasons, the banished ghost of the victims' thirst for justice returns years later to haunt these societies, reopening old wounds thought to have been healed. This weakness has been illustrated by the situation in Latin American countries, and most famously by the spate of lawsuits, in Chile and abroad, that have sought to bring former Chilean leader Augusto Pinochet to justice in recent years, as well as the polarization of Chilean public opinion that has accompanied his return to that country. Many now hold the view that his amnesty a decade ago was simply another form of impunity. South Africa's case may appear unique, but not enough time has elapsed since the TRC exercise to evaluate it more definitively.

Regarding societies that choose the collective amnesia of blanket amnesties, the recent experience of countries such as Nigeria is instructive. Thirty years after its civil war ended, Nigeria has moved from a point of blanket amnesty ("no victor, no vanquished" was the phrase used by the then head of state General Yakubu Gowon) to one of a truth commission with a temporal mandate stretching back more than three decades. What this evolutionary process suggests is that judicial accountability in the form of full-blown trials for mass crimes is a future possibility that cannot be precluded. Nevertheless, it may well be that, for some societies, deferring the day of reckoning may put them in a stronger position to handle such truth commissions or trial processes at a later stage.

A second weakness of truth commissions is that they tend to make a false distinction between truth (as represented by TRCs) and justice (as represented by criminal trials). There is no convincing argument that criminal trials, despite the inherent clash of interests of the defendant and the prosecutor, are intrinsically incapable of arriving at the truth or indeed frequently fail to achieve that objective. Further, in some cases before the international criminal tribunals, in particular the ICTR, accused persons have pleaded guilty and confessed the details of the crimes they committed.[6] In none of these cases have these pleas of guilt been in exchange for an amnesty, because courts are bound to impose punishment once the guilt of the defendant is established either by the prosecutor or by admission by the defendant. Further, such confessions, as will be seen later, contribute in no small measure to establishing the truth and to national reconciliation.

Thirdly, although truth and reconciliation commissions are an option (even if a less than perfect one) for dealing with some types of mass crimes – especially crimes against humanity, which are frequently motivated by political considerations – that approach offers little help when the crime committed is genocide. There is now a consensus among lawyers, human rights activists and states that the crime of genocide must be prosecuted.[7]

During the genocide and other serious violations of humanitarian law that occurred in Rwanda in 1994, upwards of 800,000 people, mostly Tutsis and moderate Hutus, were killed within a 90-day period. The scope of the atrocities was so vast, the time-span of their commission so short and their cruelty so shocking that the Rwandans and the international community decided that justice must be done before reconciliation could be possible. The victorious Allies in World War II similarly took the path of justice for the Holocaust, trying war criminals from Germany and Japan at Nuremberg and Tokyo. Today, the former Allied powers and the Axis powers they defeated and prosecuted are political, economic and military partners. Justice cleared the path to reconciliation.

This is not to say that truth commissions do not have significant advantages. First, truth commissions approach reconciliation with a strong – and welcome – focus on victims, i.e. restorative justice. This approach is commendable because, with a perpetrator confessing his crimes, the victim, by exercising forgiveness (or at least having the option to do so), is empowered and thereby restored in a psychological sense. Several commentators have noted that victim-focused approaches to justice (reflected significantly in TRCs if accompanied by reparations or restitution) are more akin to original concepts of justice in many African societies.[8] Further, many criminal trials, especially in common law systems or international tribunals utilizing similar procedures, fail to address the victim as a person and focus exclusively on the perpetrator. A second major benefit of truth commissions is the healing effect they can have on the wider society in some instances, although, as noted earlier, this may ultimately be a passing fancy. However, there is anecdotal evidence that the public airing of crimes accompanied by confessions certainly has a healing effect on national psyches and engenders a greater degree of public participation than criminal trials do. Third, truth commissions, because of the amnesties they sometimes offer, encourage greater willingness to participate in the process and thus generally yield a far more complete narrative of events than trials do.

The distinction between truth commissions and trials, however, may be an artificial one. The two processes are not mutually exclusive, and absolutist positions are often unworkable in the real world. Because states may make sovereign choices that do not extinguish the jurisdiction of international tribunals or other national courts for crimes of universal jurisdiction, it is quite possible that the options of truth commissions and trials could be exercised at different points of a continuum. A state may begin with one and bring closure with the other. Sierra Leone is an example of a post-conflict society that will utilize both truth commissions and criminal trials for violations of international humanitarian law. The United Nations Secretary-General has recommended a similar approach for Cambodia.

Trials in national jurisdictions: The experience of Rwanda

In many post-conflict societies, courts and the judiciary have increasingly become an essential instrument of reconstruction and, directly or indirectly, reconciliation. Nevertheless, this is a difficult task in countries where, even at the best of times, the judiciary is not a strong and independent institution. In many cases it was the very absence of an independent judiciary and a rule of law culture that encouraged the progressive culture of impunity which led to the conflict and crimes that shattered these societies. This is why, from places such as Kosovo to East Timor, the United Nations has instituted judicial activity as a core component of its peacekeeping operations. It is also part of the reason that international criminal tribunals, such as the ICTR, the International Criminal Tribunal for the former Yugoslavia (ICTY), and the mixed international–national Special Court for Sierra Leone and a similar court envisaged for Cambodia, were established.

Nowhere has the role of justice been more central to the process of conflict settlement and reconciliation than in Rwanda. Here the challenge has been so overwhelming on both national and international dimensions in the search for justice that new approaches and policies are constantly being invented. Justice for the Rwandan genocide is being pursued on a parallel track through domestic prosecution and the trials at the ICTR, the international tribunal created at the request of the government of Rwanda in 1994.

The genocide clearly overwhelmed the Rwandan judiciary, which, even at the best of times, was not well developed. The early and continuing challenges that domestic trials have faced, and continue to face, in Rwanda, despite having to bear the responsibility for the vast majority of prosecutions for the genocide, illustrate why international tribunals are essential components of the search for peace and reconciliation. An estimated 120,000 individuals are awaiting trial in Rwanda in crowded prisons. At the rate of disposition of the cases, it is estimated that it will take 200 years to complete these trials. This is clearly an impossible situation.

At the end of the conflict, only 16 practising attorneys remained in Rwanda, there was no law against genocide (Rwanda had ratified the Genocide Convention, but its parliament first had to adopt national legislation to make genocide a crime[9]) and only 26 judicial police inspectors, the officials with responsibility for criminal investigations, were in service.[10] Because Rwandan law or policy does not permit foreign lawyers to judge cases in Rwandan courts (they were allowed to act as advisers), large numbers of new Rwandan lawyers, magistrates and investigators had to be trained by various non-governmental organizations from Belgium, Canada and other countries.[11] Although significant improvements in the functioning of the judicial system have been recorded, serious problems remain. In five years of domestic genocide trials in Rwanda, the established courts had tried only 6,000 people, less than 5 per cent of the current prison population.[12]

There are no easy solutions in the search for peace through justice in Rwanda. It is tempting to be glibly dismissive of the process on the basis of well-known and documented concerns over the standards of fairness of the trials, but this temptation should be resisted. What is the alternative? Rwanda is faced with a crisis and is meeting the challenge to the best of its ability. As will be shown later, the ad hoc international tribunal at Arusha has a different and unique, though related, aspect of the task of rendering justice, but is not in a position to take on the burden of thousands of prosecutions. Contrary to the expectations and assertions of some commentators, an ad hoc international tribunal such as the ICTR, though performing a critical function, does not bear the "burden" of hearing all war crimes cases.[13] The ICTR has held seminars on law, procedure and judicial policy for a limited number of Rwandan judges and magistrates through its outreach programme to Rwanda and intends to hold similar seminars in the future. The best perspective – one that has so far been borne out by experience – is the hope that, in post-conflict situations, the influence and functioning of the judiciary will increase and improve over time.[14] Hasty judgments by domestic courts or international tribunals are often faulty and, with the passage of time, have been proved wrong in recent years.

An innovative approach to the challenges that have attended domestic prosecutions in Rwanda is the establishment of 11,000 new *gacaca* courts (people's courts) to try genocide cases. This development is the application of an adaptation of age-old, traditional justice, utilized for settling minor disputes, to the crime of genocide. It is a bold gamble. Under the system, which became operational in 2002, individuals of high moral integrity elected in open, public elections will judge thousands of accused genocide perpetrators, charged with all but the highest category of crimes,[15] at three levels: a General Assembly of the adult population, the Seat (19 judges) and its coordinating committee. In an interesting construction of checks and balances, the General Assembly may remove judges who do not perform properly. *Gacaca* courts at the provincial level will serve as appeal courts for appeals from the district levels.

A number of concerns have been raised about the *gacaca* system. The first is not only the lack of formal training in law of these "people's judges" but the fact that many of the elected judges are illiterate, although the Rwandan government has announced plans to train the elected judges for several months prior to their taking office. There are also doubts about their potential independence and impartiality and the possibility of reprisals against persons who, as provided for in the law establishing these courts, may confess their crimes and receive reduced penalties.[16] The *gacaca* process lays heavy emphasis on truth-telling, melding the main feature of truth commissions with the accountability of a judicial process.

Despite these concerns, it would appear that this bold attempt, if handled with a sense of the judgement of history on it, might give Rwandan society the chance it desperately needs to purge itself of the demons inflicted by a mass crime that has fractured it in a seemingly irreparable manner. As noted earlier, superficial assessments, which take no cognizance of context, offer little help to a society that faces such a huge challenge and yet is so constrained by a dearth of human and material resources. This analysis appears to be borne out by the preponderance of public opinion inside Rwanda.[17]

International justice: The international tribunal

In its Resolution 955 (1994), the Security Council decided to establish the International Criminal Tribunal for Rwanda for the purpose of prosecuting persons responsible for genocide and other serious violations of international humanitarian law committed in the territory of Rwanda and Rwandan citizens responsible for genocide and other such violations committed in the territory of neighbouring states between 1 January 1994 and 31 December 1994. The preamble to Resolution 955 also stated the *raison d'être* of the international tribunal as follows:

The Security Council,

... Expressing once again its grave concern at the reports indicating that genocide and other systematic, widespread and flagrant violations of international humanitarian law have been committed in Rwanda,
Determined to put an end to such crimes and to take effective measures to bring to justice the persons responsible for them,
Convinced that in the particular circumstances of Rwanda, the prosecution of persons responsible for genocide and the above-mentioned violations of international humanitarian law would enable this aim to be achieved and would contribute to the process of national reconciliation and to the restoration and maintenance of peace,
Believing that the establishment of an international tribunal for the prosecution of persons responsible for the above-mentioned violations of international humanitarian law will contribute to ensuring that such violations are halted and effectively redressed.

The main objectives of the ICTR thus appear to be those of accountability, deterrence and contribution to national reconciliation and the maintenance of peace. It is against these objectives that the jurisprudence of the international tribunal should be assessed.

Genocide

On 2 September 1998, the ICTR in *Prosecutor v. Jean-Paul Akayesu* delivered the first ever judgment for the crime of genocide by an international court. The tribunal's Trial Chamber I had to address the question of whether the widespread and horrendous massacres that took place in Rwanda in 1994 constituted genocide. In a contemporary and legal sense, this is important because the word "genocide" is emotive and is a label frequently and loosely attached to widespread killings.

Article 2 of the ICTR Statute provides a definition of genocide that replicates exactly that of the Genocide Convention. According to Article 2(2) of the ICTR Statute,

Genocide means any of the following acts committed with intent to destroy, in whole or in part, a national, ethnical, racial or religious group as such:

Killing members of the group;
Causing serious bodily or mental harm to members of the group;
Deliberately inflicting on the group conditions of life calculated to bring about its physical destruction in whole or in part;
Imposing measures intended to prevent births within the group;
Forcibly transferring children of the group to another group.

Trial Chamber I found that, contrary to popular belief, the crime of genocide does not require the actual extermination of a group in its entirety but occurs once any of the acts mentioned above are committed with the intent to destroy the group in whole or in part.[18] It also found that genocide is unique among crimes because of its embodiment of a special intent or *dolus specialis*, which lies in the intent wholly or partially to destroy a national, ethnic, racial or religious group as such.[19]

The *Akayesu* judgment established a far-reaching precedent by interpreting for the first time the application of the definition of the crime of genocide in the Genocide Convention, albeit based on the definition in the ICTR Statute, to a practical situation. The chamber found Akayesu, former mayor of the Rwandan town of Taba, guilty on nine counts of genocide and crimes against humanity. He was found not guilty on six counts of violations of Article 3 common to the Geneva Conventions. Akayesu was subsequently sentenced to life imprisonment on 2 October 2000, and the ICTR Appeals Chamber dismissed his appeal against conviction and sentence on 1 June 2001.

Trial Chamber I adopted the reasoning that, since the special intent to commit genocide was to be found in the intent wholly or partially to destroy a national, ethnic, racial or religious group, the precise meaning of these social categories needed to be defined. Relying on the *travaux préparatoires* of the Genocide Convention, the ICTR judges found that a common criterion in these four groups protected by the Convention was that membership in such a group would not be normally challenged by its members, who belong to it automatically, by birth, in a continuous and often irremediable manner.[20]

Based on the *Nottebohm* decision rendered by the International Court of Justice, the ICTR held that a national group is defined as a collection of people who are perceived to share a legal bond based on common citizenship, coupled with reciprocity of rights and duties; an ethnic group is generally defined as a group whose members share a common language or culture; the conventional definition of a racial group is based on the hereditary physical traits often identified with geographical region, irrespective of linguistic, cultural, national or religious factors; and the religious group is one whose members share the same religion, denomination or mode of worship.[21]

The application of these legal definitions to the situation in Rwanda was complicated by the fact that the Tutsi population did not fit neatly into any of the above definitions, because they do not have a language or culture of their own different from the rest of the Rwandan population. Generations of intermarriage had wiped out any hereditary physical traits that formerly distinguished Tutsis from Hutus. Thus, the absurd conclusion that could have been drawn from this situation is that the Tutsis are not a protected group under the Genocide Convention, and so genocide, as legally defined by the Convention and the ICTR Statute, had not occurred in Rwanda.[22]

Deploying innovative legal reasoning, the ICTR's Trial Chamber I asked itself "whether it would be impossible to punish the physical destruction of a group as such under the Genocide Convention, if the said group, although stable and membership is by birth, does not meet the definition of any one of the four groups expressly protected by the Genocide Convention". The judges answered in the negative. In their view, it was important to respect the intention of the drafters of the Genocide Convention, which, according to the *travaux préparatoires*, was patently to ensure the protection of any stable and permanent group.[23] The chamber held that the Tutsis were a stable and permanent group for the purpose of the Genocide Convention, basing this conclusion on the clear identification of the Tutsis as an "ethnic" group in official classifications of Rwandan society, perpetuated by, among other ways, ethnic classifications of all Rwandans in their national identity cards before 1994. This addition to the rubric of the four protected groups in the Geneva Conventions of stable and permanent groups whose membership is largely determined by birth will influence future cases involving the crime of genocide.[24]

The judgment of Trial Chamber I of the ICTR in *Akayesu* has provided a universal precedent to other jurisdictions such as the International Criminal Tribunal for the former Yugoslavia and the International Criminal Court. It is pertinent to note in this context that the ICTY handed down its very first conviction for the crime of genocide on 2 August 2001 in the case of Radislav Krstic. Hitherto, that tribunal had handled mostly cases of war crimes (grave breaches of the Geneva Conventions of 1949 and violations of the laws or customs of war) and crimes against humanity, and there had been considerable debate over whether the events in the former Yugoslavia or parts thereof constituted genocide or were simply extreme cases of ethnic cleansing. Applying the relevant tests to determine the occurrence or otherwise of genocide, as had been done in several cases by the Rwanda tribunal, the Yugoslavia tribunal in its judgment in this case concluded that, "by deciding to kill all men of fighting age, a decision was taken to make it impossible for the Muslim people of Srebrenica to survive. Stated otherwise, what was ethnic cleansing became genocide."[25]

Rape and sexual violence

The ICTR has similarly blazed a trail in international humanitarian law in the area of sexual crimes against women. The *Akayesu* case was again the setting for this development. As in most armed conflicts, civil or international, the Rwandan conflict had as a significant characteristic the systematic rapes of women, in this case mostly women of Tutsi origin. In addressing the acts of rape, the judges of the ICTR have sought to show the circumstances in which this sordid act of sexual violence is a component of the crimes within the competence of the tribunal. Rape, which in and of itself is a crime in most, if not all, national jurisdictions, comes alive in the jurisprudence of the ICTR as an intrinsic aspect of genocide and crimes against humanity.[26]

In *Akayesu*, the Prosecutor's original indictment of the accused, confirmed on 16 February 1997, did not contain specific charges of sexual crimes. However, the testimony of two witnesses in the course of the trial contained graphic references to sexual violence against Tutsi women during the genocide – often accompanied by degrading language against the victims – and some of it, in the *Akayesu* case, allegedly occurred in Akayesu's office at the *bureau communal*. As a result of these testimonies, the Prosecutor conducted further investigations and amended the indictment during the trial on 17 June 1997, specifically charging Akayesu, *inter alia*, with rape as a crime against humanity in Count 13 of the indictment and rape as a violation of Article 3 common to the Geneva Conventions in Count 15. Various non-governmental organizations had also been pressing for greater attention to sexual crimes in prosecutions at the ICTR, including by way of an *amicus curiae* brief.[27]

In its judgment, Trial Chamber I explained its acceptance of the amendment as follows:

On June 17, the indictment was amended to include allegations of sexual violence and additional charges against the accused under Article 3(g), Article 3(I) and Article 4(2)(e) of the ICTR Statute. In introducing the amendment, the Prosecution stated that the testimony of Witness H motivated them to renew their investigations of sexual violence in connection with events that took place at the Bureau Communal. The Prosecution stated that the evidence previously available was not sufficient to link the Accused with acts of sexual violence and acknowledged that factors to explain this lack of evidence might include the shame that accompanies acts of sexual violence as well as insensitivity in the investigation of sexual violence. The Chamber understands that the amendment of the indictment resulted from the spontaneous testimony of sexual violence of witness J and H during the course of this trial and the subsequent investigation of the prosecution, rather than from public pressure. Nevertheless the Chamber takes note of the interest shown in this issue by non-governmental organizations, which it considers indicative of public concern over the historical exclusion of rape and other forms of sexual violence from the investigation and prosecution of war crimes. The investigation and presentation of evidence relating to sexual violence is in the interest of justice.[28]

In its judgment, the Trial Chamber found Akayesu guilty of crimes against humanity (rape) as charged in Count 13 of the indictment. This verdict revolutionized the jurisprudence on sexual violence crimes in international humanitarian law in three ways. First, the *Akayesu* judgment was the first time an individual had been convicted of rape as a specific crime under the rubric of crimes against humanity by an international tribunal. The importance of this advance is brought into sharper perspective by the fact that there was no mention of rape in the Nuremberg Charter. Although there was reference to rape in the judgment of the International Military Tribunal for the Far East – evidence was presented of sexual atrocities committed upon women in Nanking, the Philippines and other locations – rape and sexual violence were not charged as specific crimes but were lumped together as crimes against humanity/inhumane treatment. As one commentator and practitioner of international law so aptly put it:

This situation resulted in a blur. Rape was lost in the barbarous mass of the overall crimes. It became a passing reference in a tale of horror. In the end, no one knew whether rape in time of conflict could be prosecuted as a separate, substantive crime standing on its own merits in international law ... but today, we find ourselves in an enormously stronger position to investigate, document and prosecute rape and other forms of sexual violence ... And it all started quietly within the International Criminal Tribunal for Rwanda.[29]

Second, the *Akayesu* judgment of the ICTR provided for the first time in legal history a definition of rape as a crime under international law. In paragraphs 596–598 of the judgment, the chamber stated:

The Chamber must define rape, as there is no commonly accepted definition of this term in international law. While rape has been defined in certain national jurisdictions as non-consensual intercourse, variations on the act of rape may include acts, which involve the insertion of objects, and/or the use of bodily orifices not considered to be intrinsically sexual. The Chamber considers that rape is a form of aggression and that the central elements of the crime of rape cannot be captured in a mechanical description of objects or body parts ... The Chamber defines rape as a physical invasion of a sexual nature, committed on a person under circumstances that are coercive. Sexual violence, which includes rape, is considered to be any act of a sexual nature which is committed on a person under circumstances which are coercive.

This groundbreaking definition of rape has been cited in subsequent cases in the ICTR and in the ICTY at The Hague in its judgments in the *Furundzija*,[30] *Celebici*[31] and *Kunarac*[32] judgments. But is the definition so revolutionary as to be ahead of its time? It is not, although some experts in international criminal law are inclined to that view and expressed opinions in this vein in informal discussions during meetings of the Preparatory Committee for the Establishment of an International Court in New York. Had there been any problem with this definition, the ICTR's Appeals Chamber might have addressed the matter in its judgment on appeal in *Akayesu*. To the extent it did not, this brilliant postulation of international humanitarian law must stand for what it is: a revolution in legal thinking. Note should be taken in this context of the arguably more conservative approach of ICTY jurisprudence, which has so far examined rape mostly from a national jurisdiction perspective that is anchored in body parts.[33] However, a close reading of the jurisprudence of the Yugoslavia tribunal reveals an elasticity in adopting national definitions of rape that encompass parts of the Rwanda tribunal's definition in *Akayesu*.[34] This would appear to give credence to the holding of the ICTR's Trial Chamber I that its definition of rape is more helpful in international law. At any event, it is correct to say that the two types of definition simply reflect two different approaches to rape in international criminal law.

The third and perhaps most important manner in which the sexual violence aspect of the *Akayesu* judgment advanced international humanitarian law was by ruling that rape was an act of genocide and thus a genocidal crime. As noted earlier, Trial Chamber I found that rape was systematically used as a weapon in the campaign to destroy the Tutsis by violating Tutsi women precisely because they were of Tutsi ethnicity. Many were killed in the process of these rapes, whose clear intent was to kill or inflict mental or bodily harm as part of the process of destroying an ethnic group in whole or in part.

Concluding that the special intent unique to genocide accompanied and motivated these rapes, the chamber ruled:

In light of all the evidence before it, the Chamber is satisfied that the acts of rape and sexual violence described above were committed solely against Tutsi women, many of whom were subjected to the most public humiliation, mutilated and raped several times, often in public, in the Bureau Communal premises or in other public places, and often by more than one assailant. These rapes resulted in physical and psychological destruction of Tutsi women, their families and their communities. Sexual violence was an integral part of the process of destruction, specifically targeting Tutsi women and specifically contributing to their destruction and the destruction of the Tutsi group as a whole.[35]

It is noteworthy that, in the indictment against *Akayesu*, rape was not specifically charged as an act of genocide. Yet, based on the overwhelming evidence in that case, the bench of Chamber I followed the proof of facts to their logical, ultimate conclusion in their decision: rape as a means of genocide. As another expert has (correctly) described the judgment, "the Akayesu decision is overwhelming in its holdings and dicta concerning sexual violence".[36]

However, women were not only the victims in the Rwandan genocide. Some were alleged perpetrators too. The ICTR has also made history by becoming not only the first international criminal tribunal to indict a woman, but also the first to charge a woman with rape. In *Prosecutor v. Pauline Nyiramasuhuko and Arsene Shalom Ntahobali*,[37] the first accused, Rwanda's minister of women and family affairs in 1994, who was arrested in Kenya in 1997, was originally indicted jointly with her son, Arsene Shalom, on charges of genocide, crimes against humanity and serious violations of Article 3 common to the Geneva Conventions. Her indictment was amended in 1999 to include charges of rape as a crime against humanity under the principle of superior responsibility. The indictment had earlier been amended to include rape as a crime against humanity against Mr. Ntahobali.[38]

These developments in the trials before the ICTR demonstrate the tribunal's achievement of providing a road map for the prosecution and adjudication of sexual crimes in international humanitarian law. In so doing, the tribunal has lifted sexual crimes against women from the status of mere offences against honour[39] and a spoil of war to their rightful place in the code of conduct in conflict situations. The tribunal's jurisprudence on rape has also contributed in a significant manner to the reconciliation process. It should not be forgotten that, in the aftermath of the genocide, widows and orphans are a dominant component of the society and so women are increasingly becoming a potent force in the shaping of that society. Addressing crimes unique to women, as the ICTR is doing, is thus an important part of the healing process for female victims and, by extension, for Rwandan society as whole.

Shattering the concept of "sovereign impunity"

All through contemporary history, the international law doctrine of sovereign immunity, by which a sovereign is immune from legal process for official acts committed in his or her capacity as head of state, has been mixed with the practice of "sovereign impunity". As a result, leaders who have directed and participated in the most heinous crimes, usually for political reasons or "reasons of state", have been beyond the reach of the law.

As indicated by the preambular paragraphs of Security Council Resolution 955 of 1994, one of the main objectives of the International Criminal Tribunal for Rwanda is to deter the culture of impunity by confronting it with accountability. Indeed, part of the explanation for how more than 500,000 people could have been killed in a period of three months in Rwanda in 1994 lies in the fact that, for the past 40 years, there have been cyclical waves of mass killings orchestrated by political leaders in the Great Lakes region of Africa, in particular in Rwanda and Burundi, with no one held to account in a judicial process.[40] It is no surprise, then, that occasional mass killing along ethnic lines had become something of a favoured solution in the internal political power struggles in the region. Ensuring accountability has also been the objective behind the establishment of other international criminal tribunals such as the International Criminal Tribunal for the former Yugoslavia, the Special Court for Sierra Leone,[41] the proposed tribunal for Cambodia and the permanent International Criminal Court.[42]

It is commonly agreed, both as a matter of policy of governments and by practitioners of international law, that one of the most effective ways to ensure the promotion and observance of international humanitarian law is by bringing to justice in properly constituted courts of justice the political and military leaders who, in virtually every case of mass atrocities in war and peace, have been the planners, instigators and commanders of such crimes as genocide, crimes against humanity and war crimes. The violations of international humanitarian law in Rwanda were no exception: they were known to have been inspired and directed by high-ranking individuals. As a matter of policy, the Office of the Prosecutor of the ICTR has, since the tribunal commenced operations in 1995, focused its investigative and prosecution energies mostly on such high-ranking accused persons and suspects – the "big fish".

In this pantheon of senior figures so far apprehended and brought to trial by the ICTR, the most senior individual has been Jean Kambanda, prime minister of Rwanda and head of the interim government from 8 April 1994 until he left the country on or about 17 July 1994, the three months during which the genocide occurred. The Kenyan authorities arrested Kambanda in July 1997 based on a formal request submitted by the tribunal's Prosecutor on 9 July 1997 in accordance with the provisions of Rule 40 of the Rules of Procedure and Evidence of the ICTR.[43] On 16

July 1997, Judge Laity Kama, ruling on the Prosecutor's motion of 9 July 1997, ordered the transfer and provisional detention of the suspect at the detention facility of the tribunal under Rule 40 *bis*. The indictment against Jean Kambanda was confirmed on 16 October 1997 by Judge Yakov Ostrovsky, who issued a warrant of arrest and ordered the continued detention of the accused.

The indictment against Kambanda charged the former prime minister with genocide, conspiracy to commit genocide, direct and public incitement to commit genocide, complicity in genocide, and crimes against humanity. In the concise statement of facts in the indictment, the Prosecutor averred, *inter alia*, that Kambanda as prime minister exercised *de jure* and *de facto* authority and control over the members of his government, senior civil servants including *prefets* (regional governors), and senior officers in the military; and that he presided over meetings of the Council of Ministers, attended by Pauline Nyiramasuhuko, Eliezer Niyitegeka and Andre Ntagerura,[44] among others, where the massacres of the civilian population were discussed. He was also accused of inciting massacres of Tutsis and moderate Hutus at public meetings and through the media.

In a landmark event in the annals of international humanitarian law and the work of the ICTR, Jean Kambanda, at his initial appearance before the tribunal on 1 May 1998, pleaded guilty to the six counts in his indictment. Kambanda had signed a plea agreement with the Prosecutor in which he agreed that he was pleading guilty because he was in fact guilty and acknowledged full responsibility for the crimes alleged in the indictment.[45] In the document, Kambanda explained the motivation for his guilty plea: "the profound desire to tell the truth ... his desire to contribute to the process of national reconciliation in Rwanda", and his consideration that his confession would contribute to the restoration and maintenance of peace in Rwanda.[46] Trial Chamber I verified the validity of Kambanda's guilty plea[47] before formally entering a plea of guilty and setting a date for the pre-sentencing hearing.

On 4 September 1998, Trial Chamber I convicted Kambanda on all counts in the indictment against him and sentenced the former prime minister to life imprisonment for his crimes. The International Criminal Tribunal for Rwanda thus became the first international tribunal in history to punish a head of government for genocide, dealing the first practical blow to the concept of sovereign immunity, which had been expressly negated in the statute of the tribunal.[48] Indeed, the chamber made clear in its judgment and sentence that, despite the ordinarily mitigating factor of a guilty plea, it considered the combination of the gravity of the offence and Kambanda's high position of authority to be overridingly aggravating factors. The chamber stated:

The heinous nature of the crime of genocide and its absolute prohibition makes its commission inherently aggravating ... The crimes were committed during the time when Jean Kambanda was Prime Minister and he and his government were responsible for the maintenance of peace and security. Jean Kambanda abused his authority and the trust of the civilian population. He personally participated in the genocide by distributing arms, making incendiary speeches and presiding over cabinet and other meetings where the massacres were planned and discussed. He failed to take necessary and reasonable measures to prevent his subordinates from committing crimes against the population.[49]

Jean Kambanda's subsequent appeal against his judgment and sentence, in which he requested a trial or, in the alternative, a reduction of his sentence, was unanimously rejected and his sentence confirmed by the tribunal's Appeals Chamber on 19 October 2000.[50]

The *Kambanda* case was another milestone in international humanitarian law, with overwhelming political and other significance.[51] It was the first confession by an individual for the crime of genocide 50 years after the Genocide Convention. It confirmed that the criminal enterprise that was Rwanda's genocide was a state-sponsored plan aimed at wiping out the country's ethnic minority.[52] Kambanda's confession destroyed the credibility, such as it was, of a small number of revisionist historians and lawyers in certain quarters, who claimed that there was no genocide in Rwanda. It also had a discernible impact on the more than 100,000 genocide suspects imprisoned in Rwandan jails, triggering a significant number of confessions from some of these suspects shortly afterwards.

In a contemporary, global sense, the *Kambanda* judgment pre-dated – and was cited by human rights groups in – the 1998 case in which the United Kingdom's House of Lords, overruling a lower court, ruled that General Augusto Pinochet, former head of state of Chile, was not immune from prosecution for international crimes such as crimes against humanity, torture and hostage-taking.[53] Even more directly, the *Kambanda* judgment served as a precedent for the 1999 indictment of Slobodan Milosevic, former president of the Federal Republic of Yugoslavia, and his transfer to The Hague to face trial before the ICTY.

The limitations of justice via criminal trials

There are few perfect options for confronting impunity and effecting reconciliation. The process of criminal trials, national or international, is no different. Utilizing justice as an element of conflict resolution is not as straightforward a process as might be assumed. International tribunals are less than perfect mechanisms for dealing with mass atrocities for a number of reasons: only a relatively small number of people can be tried, though even trying modest numbers of persons may contribute significantly to the reconciliation process if those tried are the planners and leading perpetrators of mass crimes as opposed to minor culprits; and trials are unavoidably lengthy because of the intricacies of judicial proceedings conducted in several languages. These trials also tend to be perfectionist in aspiration because of the need to respect due process and the accused's right to a fair trial. All of this can tax the patience of victims and observers and raise questions about the true deterrent effect of trials.

The two international criminal tribunals for Rwanda and the former Yugoslavia have faced these challenges. Yet what is the alternative? Do nothing and raise the spectre of self-help vigilante justice? That would not be acceptable. It should be recalled that international tribunals are established largely to meet situations, as in Rwanda and the former Yugoslavia, where national judicial systems could not or would not assume responsibility for bringing the leading perpetrators of mass crimes to justice.

There are yet other limitations to the contribution of trials to conflict resolution and reconciliation. One is that some observers believe that international criminal tribunals are no substitute for early global intervention. At its most cynical, this viewpoint believes that these institutions came "too late", were created "after the fact" and have not had much impact for the victims of violations of international humanitarian law, even if they have brought some justice to them. The hope of this viewpoint is that the permanent International Criminal Court will have a more preventive contribution to conflict resolution when it becomes fully operational.

Trials in courts of law for crimes that are usually committed in a political context are also no substitute for political and other processes of reconciliation. They provide a necessary foundation for such alternative processes but, on the other hand, may be seen as vengeance by parties to the conflict who consider themselves the weaker party at the time of such trials. The point here is that, especially in the case of civil wars, post-conflict reconciliation processes should include political dialogue involving groups, even where trials determining individual criminal responsibility and ensuring accountability are major components.

Other critiques of the validity of international criminal tribunals as agents of conflict resolution include the perception of arbitrariness – why are some people prosecuted and others not?[54] – and arguments against the assignment of individual responsibility for acts described by law professor Mark Osiel as "administrative massacre". According to Osiel, incidents of administrative massacre characteristically involve many people in coordinated ways over space and time and therefore impede adherence to the necessity of proving wilful acts by particular defendants.[55]

The case for criminal trials

Nevertheless, there are a number of arguments that may make trials a superior route, or, at the very least, a necessary component of long-term conflict resolution and reconciliation in fractured societies. The first is that justice and accountability have a deep psychological impact on individuals and, by extension, societies. When justice is done, and seen to be done, it provides a catharsis for those physically or psychologically scarred by violations of international humanitarian law. Deep-seated resentments – key obstacles to reconciliation – are removed and people on different sides of the divide can feel that a clean slate has been provided for coexistence. Obviously, this objective is better met if the justice that is handed down is a complete one, involving not only retribution but, where necessary, restitutive or restorative justice. Whereas the rules of the ICTR have only very limited provisions for restitution of property in certain circumstances,[56] the International Criminal Court, by providing in its statute for restorative justice for victims of crimes under the court's jurisdiction in addition to retribution against perpetrators,[57] has a good chance of fully meeting the aspirations of victims.

A second fundamental benefit of trials is that they establish individual responsibility for the crimes adjudicated, thus negating the notion of collective guilt, which can be a significant obstacle to genuine reconciliation. Other members of the group to which a defendant or group of defendants may belong are thus spared the weight of guilt for crimes they did not commit and are free to participate in national life on equal terms with others. In this context, one may disagree with Osiel's concept of administrative massacre as a possible vitiation of individual responsibility on both legal and policy grounds. The act of participation in a conspiracy to commit genocide, for example, is an *individual* decision, regardless of the prevailing pressures of the existing circumstance. Only a valid defence of mental incapacity, as established in a court of law, should exempt individuals from personal responsibility for their acts or omissions. Even the well-known concept of following superior orders offers no relief from individual criminal responsibility under the statutes of the ICTR and the ICTY, but may be considered only in mitigation of punishment.[58] From a policy viewpoint, accepting the concept of administrative massacre would militate against the policy goal of law as an effective instrument of conflict resolution.

Yet a third fundamental point in favour of trials and tribunals in conflict resolution is that impartial trials conducted by independent international tribunals establish an indisputable historical record of events with legally binding consequences where guilt is established, thus banishing extremists from the political space and giving room for the growth of a democratic culture. This has been one of the most important contributions of the ICTR to the rebuilding of Rwandan society.[59]

Finally, in addition to their deterrent function, the ICTR and the ICTY have made important, long-term contributions to conflict resolution through the precedents they have established for the ICC and the Special Court for Sierra Leone.[60] Repudiating cynics' expectations of their failure, these courts have demonstrated that international criminal justice is workable, even if imperfect. Without their examples, the establishment of the ICC, which entered into force in 2002, would still have been out of reach.

Requirements for international tribunals' more effective contributions to conflict resolution

A number of factors hamper international tribunals from attaining their full potential as vectors of conflict resolution. Many of these factors have to do with perception and reality. The first is the relatively slow pace of their trials. Although there are understandable reasons for this, insofar as built-in delay factors attend their work, it is important that the tribunals for Rwanda and the former Yugoslavia explore every avenue to expedite the pace of their judicial proceedings. This process is already far advanced in both tribunals. Rule changes and greater control of proceedings have reduced delays significantly. More judicial personnel, in the form of *ad litem* judges, have been granted to the ICTY at its request by the United Nations Security Council and General Assembly.

A second problem that needs to be overcome if the two existing tribunals are to maximize their potential is the perception that they have limited contextual relevance to the societies whose wounds they seek to address. In other words, the two tribunals suffer from the absence of a sense of ownership by these societies.[61] Both tribunals have for the past few years operated outreach programmes in Rwanda and the former Yugoslavia. These programmes have made a discernible impact, especially in Rwanda where there is a somewhat more receptive milieu. Yet there is much more to be done, and the effectiveness and reach of these activities need to be improved to the fullest extent possible. In this context, it remains to be seen if there is more to be said for a mixed international–national tribunal like the Special Court for Sierra Leone. In this genre of international justice, significant roles will be played by citizens of countries at which the work of such courts is primarily targeted. The international courts will have their seat in these countries, as opposed to tribunals that are purely international and are located outside their geographical jurisdiction.[62]

Thirdly, the issue of global publicity for the work of the international tribunals is crucial. This problem is more applicable to the ICTR than to the ICTY. Comparatively speaking, the global media have not focused on the work and achievements of the ICTR as they have on the ICTY. Much of the publicity, especially in the past, has accentuated problems rather than giving a balanced portrayal of the tribunal's arguably leading contribution to the development of international criminal justice in terms of its groundbreaking jurisprudence. The question is: why? There are no satisfactory answers, especially considering the international community's acknowledged inaction in the face of the Rwandan genocide. Considering the nature of international tribunals, depending as they do on political and public support for their efficacy in reversing the culture of impunity with one of accountability, the world needs to be fully aware of the ICTR if it is to maximize its potential to accomplish this task. The paucity of global media coverage of the tribunal does this purpose a disservice.

Finally, as noted by several observers, in addition to the first core principle of individual criminal responsibility as a facilitator of reconciliation, a second core dimension is impeccable impartiality. Not only must international criminal tribunals be impartial, they must be *seen* to be impartial.[63] Guilt for violations of international humanitarian law in times of conflict is rarely equal, and so indictments need not be equally distributed to various sides of the conflict. Nevertheless, it is important to manage the perception of the work of the tribunals in this context, provided the actions of the tribunals are supported by *prima facie* evidence rather than a perceived need to undertake political balancing acts.

It is important that the international criminal tribunals established by the United Nations for Rwanda and the former Yugoslavia avoid a future judgement of history that they are victors' or partial tribunals – as several critics of the Nuremberg trial have done. Such criticisms, should they be well founded, would damage the tribunals' historical legitimacy and might reduce their actual contribution to resolving the conflicts in both geographical areas. This is already a challenge for these tribunals. In the case of the former Yugoslavia, the ICTY is fighting a perception in some quarters that its work is biased against Serbs. And in Rwanda, the question has been raised as to whether or when alleged violations of international humanitarian law by the Rwandan Patriotic Front (which had predominantly Tutsi leadership) during the armed conflict in that country will be the subject of indictments or trials by the ICTR.

The truth, however, is that, in fractured societies, which have come to that state as a result of the demagoguery of leading political figures, attempts will be made to deflect efforts to exact individual accountability with propaganda that seeks to undermine the perception of the impartiality of justice. As noted above, it is sometimes the fact that crimes falling under the mandate of an international tribunal may have been committed preponderantly, even if not exclusively, by individuals from specific groups against those of another. In Rwanda, for example, the genocide, by definition, sought to exterminate the Tutsi group, the main victims. However, the ICTR's mandate also includes crimes against humanity and violations of Article 3 common to the Geneva Conventions. The Prosecutor of the tribunal has publicly stated that there will be indictments in the future for crimes allegedly committed by individuals who were members of the RPF. It is a matter for future observation how this aspect of the work of the tribunal will unfold, and, if it does, how it will affect the reconciliation process.

Conclusion

It is true that, seen from a viewpoint that has a high degree of faith in human character, truth and reconciliation mechanisms may appear to have advantages over courtroom trials and prosecutions, which do not necessarily bring out the best in human nature. Yet it should not be forgotten that justice is an irreducible principle of morality and is indeed a theological underpinning of several major religions, just as forgiveness and reconciliation are. This chapter has attempted to make the case that, far from discouraging reconciliation, justice indeed serves that end in a more effective manner than most. It is not, as some viewpoints hold, vengeance, to the extent that it has higher functions beyond retribution.

As a former policy maker in the United States government has put it, "It is a very simple lesson, but one that peacemakers seem to learn with great difficulty, and that is that peace – real peace – is not possible without justice, real justice, particularly when it was genocide and crimes against humanity that shattered the peace in the first instance."[64]

Notes

1. Jonathan Derrick, "Reconciliation and Impunity: Incompatible or Inseparable?", *African Topics* (London), August–September 1999, pp. 10–12.
2. Ibid.
3. Statement at the 17th General Conference of the International Peace Research Association held in Durban, South Africa, June 1998, quoted in Kingsley Moghalu, "Justice Will Help Reconciliation in Rwanda", *Conflict Trends*, no. 1, 1998, pp. 18–19.
4. Ibid.
5. Ibid.

6. Other accused persons who have pleaded guilty before the ICTR to genocide and crimes against humanity are Jean Kambanda, former prime minister of Rwanda (sentenced to life imprisonment), Omar Serushago, a leader of the Interahamwe militia (sentenced to 15 years in prison), and Georges Ruggio, a former journalist (sentenced to 12 years in prison).

7. Convention on the Prevention and Punishment of the Crime of Genocide, adopted by the United Nations General Assembly in 1948 (hereafter Genocide Convention).

8. Martha Minow, *Between Vengeance and Forgiveness*, Boston, Mass.: Beacon Press, 1998, p. 81, who quotes Archbishop Desmond Tutu of South Africa: "Retributive justice is largely Western. The African understanding is far more restorative – not so much to punish as to redress or restore a balance that has been knocked askew. The justice we hope for is restorative of the dignity of the people."

9. Organic Law on the Organization of Prosecutions for Offenses Constituting the Crime or Crimes against Humanity, J.O., 1996, Year 35, No. 14 (Rwanda). For an excellent discussion on post-genocide challenges, responses and prospects of the Rwandan judicial system, see William A. Schabas, "Justice, Democracy and Impunity in Post-Genocide Rwanda: Searching for Solutions to Impossible Problems", *Criminal Law Forum*, vol. 7, no. 3, 1996.

10. Jennifer Widner, "Courts and Democracy in Postconflict Transitions: A Social Scientist's Perspective on the African Case", *American Journal of International Law*, vol. 95, no. 1, 2001, p. 97.

11. Julia Crawford, *Hopes and Fears as Rwanda Launches Participative Justice*, 11 October 2001, at www.hirondelle.org.

12. Widner, "Courts and Democracy in Postconflict Transitions", p. 98.

13. Ibid., p. 99.

14. Ibid.

15. This category, one of four under Rwandan law, consists of the planners, rapists and persons who committed the crimes with "zeal" or "excessive wickedness", who will be tried by the ordinary courts.

16. Crawford, *Hopes and Fears as Rwanda Launches Participative Justice*.

17. IBUKA, the influential association of victim-survivors of the genocide, has formally and publicly accepted the new *gacaca* system: "We have accepted gacaca because there is simply no alternative to tackle the current judicial crisis in Rwanda," the association's president, Antoine Mugesera, has said. See Crawford, *Hopes and Fears as Rwanda Launches Participative Justice*.

18. *Prosecutor v. Jean-Paul Akayesu, Judgment by Trial Chamber I*, Case No. ICTR-96-4-T, 2 September 1998, para. 497 (hereafter *Akayesu Judgment*).

19. Ibid., para. 498.

20. Ibid., para. 511.

21. Ibid., paras. 512–515.

22. Paul J. Magnarella, *Justice in Africa: Rwanda's Genocide, Its Courts, and the UN Criminal Tribunal*, Brookfield, Vt.: Ashgate Publishing, 2000, p. 98.

23. *Akayesu Judgment*, para. 516.

24. Magnarella, *Justice in Africa*, p. 99.

25. Summary of the judgment of the ICTY in the *Krstic* case, quoted in Marlise Simons, "General Guilty in Srebrenica Genocide", *New York Times*, 3 August 2001, p. 1.

26. No accused person in the ICTR has yet been convicted of rape as a violation of Article 3 common to the Geneva Conventions, or even of any other aspect of that crime itself, although some accused persons and convicts have been charged with rape under this rubric.

27. Amicus Curiae Brief submitted under Rule 74 of the Rules of Procedure and Evidence

of the ICTR in May 1997 by the Coalition for Women's Human Rights in Conflict Situations.

28. *Akayesu Judgment*, para. 417.
29. David Scheffer (former United States ambassador at large for war crimes issues), "Rape as a War Crime", Remarks at Fordham University, New York, 29 October 1999, at www.converge.org.nz.11z/pma.rape.htm.
30. *Prosecutor v. Anto Furundzija, Judgment*, Case No. IT-95-17/I-T, 10 December 1998 (hereafter *Furundzija Judgment*).
31. *Prosecutor v. Delalic et al., Judgment*, Case No. IT-96-21-T, 16 November 1998.
32. *Prosecutor v. Kunarac et al., Judgment*, Case No. IT-96-23/2, 22 February 2001.
33. See *Furundzija Judgment*, where the ICTY's Trial Chamber II reviewed national laws on rape to arrive at an accurate definition of rape based on the criminal law principle of specificity (para. 177).
34. In *Furundzija*, the ICTY judges concluded that most legal systems consider rape as the forcible sexual penetration of the human body by the penis or the forcible insertion of any other object into either the vagina or the anus (para. 181). However, *Furundzija* acknowledged a significant discrepancy between various national definitions of rape when it held that "the forced penetration of the mouth by the male sexual organ constitutes a most humiliating and degrading attack upon human dignity" and thus ought to be included in the definition of rape (para. 183).
35. *Akayesu Judgment*, 1998, para. 121.
36. Betty Murungi, "Prosecuting Gender Crimes at the International Criminal Tribunal for Rwanda", *Africa Legal Aid Quarterly Journal*, April–June 2001, pp. 14–17.
37. Ibid.
38. See also Joe Lauria, "Rape Added to Rwandan Woman's UN Charges", *Boston Globe*, 13 August 1999.
39. Murungi, "Prosecuting Gender Crimes at the International Criminal Tribunal for Rwanda".
40. Between 1959 and 1964, hundreds of thousands of Rwandan Tutsis were killed in Rwanda following the "social revolution" of 1959, which toppled and abolished the Tutsi monarchy. The "revolution" was led by Gregoire Kayibanda, a Hutu extremist who became president of Rwanda when the country became independent in 1962. In neighbouring Burundi, where the Tutsis held political power after independence, Hutus were the victims of mass killings on nearly similar scales to those of the Tutsis in Rwanda. In 1972, about 100,000 Hutus were massacred in Burundi. These killings in both countries led to massive refugee outflows of the victims of the massacres into both countries and other countries in East and Central Africa.
41. See *Report of the Secretary-General on the Establishment of a Special Court for Sierra Leone*, UN Doc. S/2000/915, 4 October 2000.
42. *Rome Statute of the International Criminal Court, Adopted on 17 July 1998*, UN Doc. PCNICC/1999/INF/3, 17 August 1999.
43. Rule 40(A)(I) provides that, in case of urgency, the Prosecutor may request any state to arrest a suspect and place him in custody. Although it is more normal for the tribunal to issue a warrant of arrest for an accused person against whom an indictment prepared by the Prosecutor has been confirmed by a judge of the tribunal – which indictment is transmitted to the relevant state by the Registrar of the tribunal – the Prosecutor resorts to Rule 40 when operational considerations make it imperative, usually to prevent the escape of a suspect whose location has been identified but who has not yet been formally indicted by the tribunal.
44. These former officials are among 11 cabinet ministers in Kambanda's government who are currently on trial or detained by the International Criminal Tribunal for Rwanda.

45. *Prosecutor v. Jean Kambanda, Plea Agreement Between Jean Kambanda and the Office of the Prosecutor, Annexure A to the Joint Motion for Consideration of Plea Agreement Between Jean Kambanda and the Office of the Prosecutor*, 29 April 1998.
46. Ibid.
47. *Prosecutor v. Jean Kambanda, Judgment and Sentence*, Case No. ICTR 97-23-S, 4 September 1998. Kambanda affirmed that (a) his guilty plea was voluntary, (b) he clearly understood the charges against him and the consequences of his guilty plea, and (c) his guilty plea was unequivocal, in other words, the said plea could not be refuted by any line of defence.
48. Article 6, which provides for individual criminal responsibility for crimes within the tribunal's competence, states in sub-para. (2): "The official position of any accused person, whether as Head of State or government or as a responsible government official, shall not relieve such person of criminal responsibility nor mitigate punishment." An identical provision is contained in the ICTY Statute, and the Nuremberg Charter contained a similar provision. However, the ICTR judgment in *Kambanda* was the first ever application of the provision in practice to an individual of such senior rank in a government.
49. *Kambanda Judgment and Sentence*, paras. 42 and 44.
50. *Jean Kambanda v. Prosecutor, Judgment of the Appeals Chamber*, Case No. ICTR-97-23-A, 19 October 2000.
51. Magnarella, *Justice in Africa*, pp. 85 and 93.
52. Kingsley Chiedu Moghalu, "Rwanda Panel's Legacy: They Can Run But Not Hide", *International Herald Tribune*, 31 October–1 November 1998, p. 6.
53. *Regina v. Bartle and the Commissioner of Police and Others (Appellants) Ex Parte Pinochet (Respondent); Evans and Another and the Commissioner of Police and Others (Appellants) Ex Parte Pinochet (Respondent)*, Decision of the House of Lords on appeal from a Divisional Court of the Queen's Bench Division, 25 November 1998.
54. Minow, *Between Vengeance and Forgiveness*, p. 40.
55. Mark Osiel, "Ever Again: Legal Remembrance of Administrative Massacre", *University of Pennsylvania Law Review*, 1995 (cited in Minow, ibid.).
56. Rule 106 of the Rules of Procedure and Evidence of the ICTR provides that, where there has been a verdict of guilt against an accused for a crime that has caused injury to a victim, a victim or persons claiming through him or her may on the basis of such a judgment bring an action in a national court or other competent body to obtain compensation. To the best of my knowledge, this provision has not been utilized.
57. Article 75 of the *Rome Statute of the International Criminal Court* provides for reparations for victims through restitution, compensation and rehabilitation. Article 79 provides for the establishment of a Trust Fund for victims for these purposes. In his statement to the meeting of the Preparatory Committee for the Establishment of an International Court in New York in May 1998, the ICTR Registrar had called for the inclusion of these provisions in the ICC Statute.
58. Article 6(4) of the *Statute of the ICTR*, UN Doc. S/RES/955(1994), Annex.
59. "Neither Hutu nor Tutsi, Just Rwandan", *The Economist*, 3 April 1999. This article, set in Taba, discussed the local elections in Rwanda – the first since the genocide – and noted the convictions of Akayesu, the former mayor of Taba, for genocide and crimes against humanity by the ICTR.
60. The Rules of Procedure and Evidence of the ICTR will apply *mutatis mutandis* to the Special Court for Sierra Leone. See *Report of the Secretary-General on the Establishment of a Special Court for Sierra Leone*, UN Doc. S/2000/915.
61. The ICTY was established by the United Nations Security Council without an invitation from any of the erstwhile component states of the former Yugoslavia, although – and perhaps partly because – the conflict was still raging in May 1993 when the tribunal was

established. In contrast, the ICTR was established at the request of the newly installed government of Rwanda in 1994, which defeated the previous government that was responsible for the genocide. See *Letter from the Permanent Representative of Rwanda Addressed to the President of the Security Council (Sept. 28, 1994)*, UN Doc. S/1994/115. Subsequently, however, the new Rwandan government, which held a non-permanent seat in the Security Council at the time, was the only member of the Council that voted against Resolution 955 of 8 November 1994, which established the ICTR (China abstained). The reason for this dramatic reversal, though largely symbolic and calculated to express the government's initial displeasure with the legal framework of the tribunal, was the non-inclusion of the death penalty, applicable in Rwandan domestic law, in the statute of the international tribunal.

62. There are, of course, good policy reasons why the ICTR and the ICTY were not located in Rwanda and the former Yugoslavia, respectively, at the time of their creation. In Rwanda, these included the emotional issue of the death penalty and the perception that impartial justice might not be facilitated by the prevailing climate in Rwanda at the time. In the former Yugoslavia, the fact that the conflict was ongoing and the evident lack of desire on the part of the protagonists for a legal accountability mechanism were almost certainly influential factors in addition to a prevailing international policy viewpoint that some degree of distance from the events in question strengthened the perception of impartiality in the work of international tribunals.

63. Aleksandar Fatic, *Reconciliation via the War Crimes Tribunal?*, Aldershot: Ashgate Books, 2000, p. 81.

64. John Shattuck (former US Assistant Secretary of State for Democracy, Human Rights and Labor), "Preventing Genocide: Justice and Conflict Resolution in the Post-Cold War World", *Hofstra Law and Policy Symposium*, vol. 3, 1999, p. 15.

12

Demystifying Osama bin Laden: Fair trials for international terrorists

Geoffrey Robertson

Introduction

The immediate and rightful response of the United States to the atrocity of 11 September 2001 was to demand "justice", although that word sounded, in many powerful mouths, like the cry of the lynch mob for summary execution, assassination squads and Osama bin Laden's "head on a plate".[1] He was soon presidentially fingered as the "prime suspect", who was wanted "dead or alive", his mug-shot dropped in leaflets over Afghanistan promising a US$25 million reward for his capture.

The confusion over the meaning of the word "justice" became acute when the Pentagon chose "Operation Infinite Justice" as its first brand name for the bombing of Afghanistan. This made no philosophical sense, because human justice is both finite and fallible. More importantly, it begged the question, which Western leaders so notably failed to address, of exactly what forensic procedure they proposed to adopt to persuade the rest of the world that their cause was right. Milosevic in the Hague dock was an early aim of NATO's war over Kosovo, which had recently come to pass. The Lockerbie tribunal had resulted from the long economic war against Libya for blowing up an American aircraft, and led to an imposed life sentence on one of the perpetrators. Yet what court, if any, awaited bin Laden and his lieutenants, or indeed Mullah Omar and his ministers?

The last thing Western leaders wanted was for Osama bin Laden to come out with his hands up. Bill Clinton claimed to have secretly authorized a CIA assassination after the embassy bombings in Nairobi and Dar es Salaam in 1998, and President Bush and his advisers made it clear that they preferred him dead rather than alive. Ironically, this was the consummation bin Laden himself devoutly wished: in his belief system, the prospect of paradise required him to die mid-jihad, and not of old age on a prison farm in upstate New York. (His 12-year-old son had been instructed and equipped to perform an instant act of euthanasia should his wounded father be on the verge of capture.) It did not occur to the presidential policy makers who produced the plans for a "military commission" to convict and speedily execute the al-Qaida leader in the unfortunate event that he were taken alive that this would ensure his earthly martyrdom and (if only in his own mind) his fast-track to paradise. Yet, suppose he were to be captured and interrogated, and later sit like Milosevic for some months in a criminal court dock and then, after a reasoned judgment, be locked for the rest of his life in a cell in Finland? Surely this would greatly assist the work of demystifying the man, debunking his cause and de-brainwashing his many thousands of followers. A fair trial before an independent court might serve this practical purpose, and it is also what international law requires.

There can be no warrant for the cold-blooded execution of a surrendered terrorist. Although at one point in history it was common instantly to hang captured pirates – terrorists of the high seas – from the yard-arm, the better practice (at least of the British navy) was to return them for trial at the Old Bailey. Summary execution of terrorists is tempting to law enforcement agencies because it avoids the danger of exposing informers or secret intelligence at a trial, and it pre-empts further terrorist hostage-taking by their comrades in efforts to free them. However, the right to life, or at least the right not to have life extinguished by the state without due process, is fundamental even in war. From the moment that America and its allies intervened on the side of the Northern Alliance in its civil war with the Taliban, the Geneva Conventions of 1949 applied, requiring humane treatment for all combatants who surrender and no punishment without some form of fair process. This much was accepted in principle, if not in practice, by the Afghan Northern Alliance, even in respect of al-Qaida's hated Arab and Chechen fighters. It was idle to postulate a local trial for the leadership of al-Qaida and the Taliban, however, given the chaotic absence of any court system or a local law that could sensibly deal with a crime against humanity committed pursuant to (or in lieu of) foreign policy. There were realistic trial options in America, but not in courts where justice could be seen to be done.

Jury trial, New York

In New York, bin Laden was already under indictment for the embassy bombings. He had been charged by the grand jury with conspiracy to murder, bomb and maim and to kill US nationals (four co-defendants had been convicted in May 2001). There would be no jurisdictional problem with adding counts relating to September 11th to the existing indictment, or with charging the Taliban leaders with aiding and abetting. However,

1. A New York jury, quite literally "twelve angry men", would be too emotionally involved in the events of September 11th to consider the evidence dispassionately. Even if the trial was moved upstate or to another city (Timothy McVeigh's trial for the Oklahoma bombing had for this reason been moved to Denver), the event was so traumatic for all Americans that an unbiased jury would be difficult to empanel in any state of the Union.

2. Any verdict of "guilty" would need to persuade doubters and cynics throughout a world that regards trial by jury as something of an Anglo-American eccentricity. One word from the jury foreman is not calculated to convince in the mosques of Pakistan or the universities of Europe; what is needed for this purpose is a closely and carefully reasoned judgment, joined by Muslim jurists, setting out an incontrovertible, "beyond reasonable doubt" case for guilt. Just as the judgment at Nuremberg confounded holocaust-deniers over the next half-century, so any trial of al-Qaida or the Taliban had to end with an impeachable historical record.

3. Upon conviction, the jury would hear evidence to decide the punishment and, given the casualties of September 11th, the death penalty would probably be a foregone conclusion. The spectacle of bin Laden spot-lit in some hospital theatre large enough to accommodate relatives of his victims (in some states they have a right to be present) would be too grotesque to contemplate.

In its favour, however, is the fact that a jury trial is at least a full-blooded, adversarial affair in which the defendants can, if they choose, be aggressively defended and the government evidence will be tested for all to see its truth or its falsity. The issues at a criminal trial concern what the defendants did, and what knowledge they had of what their accomplices were doing; their political and religious beliefs are irrelevant. In bin Laden's case, for example, any evidence he gave would be confined to denying his alleged role, and there would be no forensic basis for permitting speeches or evidence to justify the crime. Since the crime against humanity committed on September 11th is legally indefensible (other than by a plea of insanity), the court can admit no evidence other than facts that prove or undermine the prosecution's case for complicity. Yet the assumed danger of giving al-Qaida its day in court weighed heavily on the Bush administration, and on 13 November 2001 the President signed an Executive Order to provide an alternative method of trial and execution.

Trial by military commission

The perpetrators of September 11th "don't deserve to be treated as prisoners of war", declared Vice President Cheney, announcing the Executive Order. "They don't deserve the same guarantees and safeguards that would be used for an American citizen going through the normal judicial process."[2] Instead, they deserved to be "executed in relatively rapid order", like German saboteurs tried in secret during World War II by a special military commission – a presidentially ordained tribunal last used to convict General Yamashita, one of the few Japanese generals whom historians now believe was innocent. The United States proposed such a court to Scottish law officers as a model for Lockerbie, but they emphatically rejected it because of its palpable unfairness. It is important to understand that a "military commission" is not the same as a court martial – a genuine court in the Anglo-American adversarial tradition used to try members of the armed forces. A "special military commission" comprises a group of officers ordered by the President, their Commander in Chief, to sit in judgment on certain defendants according to rules set out in the presidential order.

These military commissions are, as the *New York Times* editorialized, "a breathtaking departure from due process".[3] They fail abjectly to conform with the fair trial guarantees under the European Convention, a matter that should prevent the extradition to the United States of terrorist suspects captured in Europe.[4] They do not comport with fair trial guarantees in the Universal Declaration of Human Rights or any other human rights convention, and they breach the minimum due process safeguards in the 1949 Geneva Convention III Relative to the Treatment of Prisoners of War. A trial of al-Qaida members or Taliban leaders before such a military commission, especially if followed by executions "in relatively rapid order", would provoke derision and anger throughout the world, much of it from US allies and supporters. The principal objections would be:
1. Such a commission is not independent or impartial, as required by Articles 84 and 85 of the 1949 Geneva Convention on the Treatment of Prisoners of War, which the United States (and 187 other countries) have ratified. The army officers who act as "judges" are paid and promoted by the Defense Department, an arm of the government that has

alleged the defendants' guilt and that acts in any event as their detaining power. These officers are commissioned to sit as "judges" by the President, their Commander in Chief, who has "determined in writing" that the defendants should be prosecuted and who thus has a vested interest in their conviction.

2. There is no appeal, except to the President, who cannot be impartial, because the decision appealed against is that of his own tribunal.

3. There are no normal evidentiary rules or safeguards – evidence is admissible if the Presiding Officer thinks it should be admitted. A distinguished US judge who made a recent study of the records of military commissions in Japan after World War II concludes that they "provide a stark example of the potential for abuse when rules of evidence are so flexible as to be non-existent".[5]

4. According to reports of draft rules prepared by the US Defense Department, the hearing would be in secret and transcripts would not be made available.

5. There is no provision for the burden of proof to be placed on the prosecution or for it to meet a standard of "beyond reasonable doubt". Guilt is simply to be established by evidence "of probative value to a reasonable person". The officers who form the "jury" need not be unanimous – a vote of two-thirds (i.e. two out of three – the likely number of officers forming the commission panel) will secure a conviction. They do not give a reasoned written judgment.

6. The death sentence is traditionally carried out by an army firing squad. The Defense Department, presumably, would decide whether relatives would be permitted to attend an event that would not be different in essence from the Taliban's football-pitch executions.

The military commission has been widely criticized as a "kangaroo court", but in truth it is not a court at all. It is an extension of the power of the President, who personally, or through the officers he commands, acts as prosecutor, judge and jury, and court of appeal judge. The military commission is really a government device for execution, which is as summary as it thinks it can get away with, at a time when the American public has ceased to protest about the denial of constitutional rights to aliens. Should the Bush administration insist upon this option, it would mark an historic *volte-face* from the position of President Truman, who rejected the military commission model when it was suggested for Nuremberg. The need to impress upon the rest of the world the true evil of al-Qaida's philosophy, to expose bin Laden and his lieutenants to the light of day before they acquire mythic or martyr status, and to expound the irresponsible misuse of sovereign power by the Taliban would be lost in special military commissions, sacrificed to a fear that "justice", properly so called, will not be up to the job.

The Lockerbie alternative

The United Nations brokered an agreement between the United States, the United Kingdom and Libya to establish a special court to try the two Libyan intelligence officers accused of placing a bomb on board Pan Am flight 103, which exploded over Lockerbie, Scotland, on 21 December 1988, killing 259 passengers and crew. The court, which on 31 January 2001 convicted the senior officer, Abdul Basset Ali Al-Megrahi, reflected territorial jurisdiction (the offence having been committed in Scotland) by comprising three Scottish judges, applying Scots law and giving audience only to Scottish advocates, but it sat at Camp Zeist – a disused American airbase in the Netherlands, which had been placed under UK sovereignty for the purpose of the trial. The charge was conspiracy to murder, rather than to commit a crime against humanity, but the international justice principle that such crimes required a reasoned verdict was adopted, removing the jury and allowing the judges to determine facts as well as law. An international flavour also came from the fact that the prosecution was a joint operation, the evidence having been gathered for over 12 years by US as well as Scottish law enforcement agencies.

The Lockerbie model, although the outcome of many years of US pressure and UN sanctions, offers an alternative mode for the trial of those suspected of complicity in September 11th. The court could take the form of three independent professional American federal judges, sitting in a neutral location but operating under and applying the law of the State of New York, delivering a reasoned written decision in lieu of a jury verdict, with sentencing options to exclude the death penalty.

An ad hoc tribunal

September 11th caught the international justice movement on the hop. The Rome Statute of the International Criminal Court (ICC) had attained 42 ratifications, and the creation of the International Criminal Court was on course for 2002, 60 days after the sixtieth state party pledged support. So there was as yet no Prosecutor in place to open the investigation into the responsibility for this crime against humanity (which could have been requested, under the Rome Statute, by the Security Council). It was too much to expect the United States, given its hostility to the ICC, to take the imaginative leap of arranging speedy ratifications so that the court could be brought into being immediately, with a new and retrospective mandate to try the perpetrators of September 11th. However, President Bush did have the option of requesting the Security Council to use its Chapter VII power to establish an ad hoc tribunal, as it had in The Hague for the former Yugoslavia and for Rwanda.

The Council would readily have acceded to such a request, given its unanimous support for the United States after the atrocity, which it had characterized in two September resolutions as a threat to international peace (the precondition for exercise of Chapter VII power). There would have been no difficulty obtaining a high-profile American prosecutor, and judges, including Muslim jurists, could have been appointed from coalition countries. The ICTY Rules of Procedure and Evidence afford basic rights to defendants while permitting the reception of all relevant and reliable evidence, with protocols for evaluating the kind of hearsay evidence that may be necessary to prove terrorist conspiracies, and protecting from public disclosure on national security grounds the identity of informers or evidence from electronic intercepts and other means of secret intelligence-gathering. A trial of bin Laden and other al-Qaida leaders, together with Mullah Omar and his top ministers and generals, would be most appropriately held in The Hague, away from local pressures and prejudices in America or Afghanistan and less obviously a target for terrorist reprisals, although doubtless an isolated island might be used if such reprisals were on the cards.

American constitutional law apologists for the Bush administration's hostility to this course have argued that the Pentagon has accepted restraints on bombing targets advised by its own lawyers, and would be inhibited and embarrassed if "second guessed" by an international tribunal: "the US government won't support a new tribunal that has authority over US forces."[6] That's for sure – but the objection is irrelevant, because there would be no need to give a new tribunal any such authority. Its mandate would be to prosecute, judge and punish those who bear criminal responsibility in international law for the crime against humanity committed on 11 September 2001. It would not have any broader jurisdiction over the entirely different issue of war crimes committed during the fighting in Afghanistan; in the case of American soldiers, any allegations would be investigated and tried by US courts martial. Although the ICTY was accorded jurisdiction over all such crimes in the former Yugoslavia (at a time when no one believed NATO would fight a war there), and the United States was irritated that Prosecutor Carla del Ponte should even look at evidence that it had breached the laws of war (she found no case to answer), this is not an issue that a tribunal trying al-Qaida and Taliban leaders would ever need to address.

Concluding remarks

Although an international court was first proposed by the League of Nations (in 1937) to deal with terrorist crimes, and the idea was revived in

1987 by President Gorbachev for the same purpose, there is no precedent – and, in the absence of any paradigm, cynical diplomats and nervous politicians raise spectres of terrorists who will be permitted to justify their crimes from the witness box, and of guilty men who will walk free on legal technicalities or by retaining clever defence counsel. Yet this has not been the experience of the United Kingdom in bringing Irish Republican Army bombers to justice (the gravest danger has been of prejudiced juries and wrongful convictions) or of the United States in trials of violent radicals of the 1960s and 1970s. At Lockerbie, the one finding of guilt was inferred from demonstrable facts about the defendant and his movements, linked with forensic traces from painstaking scientific analysis of timers, circuit boards and clothing. There is no reason why an international court cannot perform as well as a local court in this respect (with the added presentational advantage over a jury of producing a written judgment). In judging political and military leaders, the international court has the advantage of impartiality and can apply command responsibility principles. "Heroic" terrorist leaders such as bin Laden would be subject to a demystifying process, which would confront them with evidence of the moral and physical squalor in which they have operated, of their hypocrisies and cruelties and of the barbaric results of their rhetoric and theology. Any cult status they have acquired must dissipate with evidence that their savage God has failed. His promise of triumph, or of a martyr's glorious death, is refuted by the simple fact that they are now neither in power nor in paradise, but in the dock.

This is one reason, of course, why al-Qaida members never came out with their hands up. Their choice of suicide rather than surrender derives from the superstition that by dying mid-jihad they will be transported into paradise, but there is also a recognition among the leadership that capture, followed by trial, would fatally damage the cause. That is because a criminal trial would strip bare al-Qaida's philosophical basis and reduce it to one essential element: the *mens rea* for commission of a crime against humanity. The hateful and hate-filled mind thus displayed – through prosecution evidence and the optional addition of defendants' testimony (confined to the issue of whether they really did intend to kill innocent civilians) – will not inspire love or respect or emulation. The trial of bin Laden is hypothetical, because he is likely to die by his own hand if not by that of others. Nevertheless, it is worth envisaging, if only to realize the cathartic impact it might have on his own followers. In the dock he would no longer appear the tall, wistful, Christ-like figure on the mountain, or leave the world with pictures of his martyr's body, strung from a lamppost by the Northern Alliance or stretched, Che Guevara-like, on a mortuary table. On trial he is reduced to human stature – sub-human, if he goes into the witness box and admits (as he must) to engineering the killing of women and children. His disciples have shown through their kamikaze acts on September 11th and on the Afghan battle-field an obsession with sacrificing their own lives in a holy war for Islamic domination. Logic has its limits in persuading people bent on glory through death: committed minds cannot be pried open by rational argu-ment, and terrorism of this nature self-evidently will not be deterred by the death penalty. Still, since their belief is essentially mystical, a process of demystifying its apostles is necessary – a fair trial of al-Qaida leaders might serve to start the de-programming process.

Notes

1. "Some Lawmakers Prefer bin Laden Dead", *New York Times*, 16 November 2001.
2. "Senior Administration Officials Defend Military Tribunal for Terrorist Suspects", *New York Times*, 15 November 2001.
3. Editorial, "A Travesty of Justice", *New York Times*, 16 November 2001.
4. *New York Times*, 24 November 2001, p. 1.
5. Evan J. Walloch, "The Procedural and Evidentiary Rules of the Post World War II War Crimes Trials", *Columbia Journal of International Law*, vol. 27, 1990, p. 851.
6. Jeremy Rabkin, "Terrorists Must Face US Justice", *The Australian*, 23 November 2001, p. 11.

13

The complexity of international criminal law: Looking beyond individual responsibility to the responsibility of organizations, corporations and states

Andrew Clapham

It has also been suggested that International Law is a vague and complicated thing and that private industrialists should be given the benefit of the plea of ignorance of the law.[1]

Introduction

This chapter addresses the international criminal law obligations of non-natural persons. Most of the focus in international criminal law has been on the natural person – the individual. In contrast, this chapter looks at the international obligations placed on legal persons, and it concentrates in particular on one type of legal person – the corporation. Other types of legal persons such as political parties and the state will be touched on. A more comprehensive account would include international organizations, not-for-profit non-governmental organizations and organized criminal gangs.

In considering the obligations of corporations under international criminal law it is worth returning to the Nuremberg trials and looking a little more closely at how those trials were conducted. We could draw four lessons from those trials. First, the prosecutors for the International Military Tribunal (IMT) in Nuremberg deliberately selected the defendants in order to highlight the role that organizations had played during the war and their contributions to the crimes on trial. Second, industrialists were deliberately targeted as critical to the perpetration of the crimes of aggression and war crimes. Third, the International Military Tribunal and the work of the subsequent US military tribunals established in Germany under Control Council Law No. 10 actually set the scene for the conclusion that corporations/legal persons or *personnes morales* (perhaps the better label is juridical persons) can commit international crimes under international law. Fourth, the use of the concepts of conspiracy and complicity at that time is fundamental to the developing understanding of these notions in contemporary international law. The clues to understanding how wide we can cast the net around an individual actor in order to catch those who assisted, abetted or facilitated the crime depend on our understanding of the notion of complicity as developed in a series of cases based on the approach taken in Nuremberg.

Lessons from Nuremberg

Selecting individual defendants by virtue of their role in the organization and the issue of collective punishment

Turning to the first issue, at the Nuremberg trial before the International Military Tribunal, the major war criminals were in part selected according to the organizations/parties that the Allies wanted to put on trial.[2] The representational aspect did not stop with the individuals connected to the official parties. As Richard Overy explains:

The idea of representation was without question legally dubious, but it resolved many of the disputes between the Allies over how large the eventual trial should be. Streicher stood for anti-Semitism; Hitler's military *chef de cabinet*, Wilhelm Keitel, and his deputy for operations, Alfred Jodl, stood for German militarism; the unfortunate Schacht and his successor as economic minister, Walther Funk, were made to represent German capitalism.[3]

The IMT Charter provided that organizations could be declared criminal and the organizations themselves in fact had lawyers to represent them, even though the tribunal did not have criminal jurisdiction over the organizations as such. In the end the tribunal declared the leadership corps of the Nazi Party, the Gestapo, the Sicherheitsdienst des Reichführer SS (SD) and the Schutzstaffeln der Nationalsocialistischen Deutschen Arbeiterpartei (SS) to be criminal.

However, there was considerable unease amongst many of the lawyers involved that these findings at the international level would pave the way for guilt by association or collective punishment at the national level in the trials that would follow the judgment of the International Military Tribunal. The idea of the international criminality of organizations got off to a shaky start. The *Goering et al.* judgment was careful to state in this context:

Since the declaration with respect to the organizations and groups will, as has been pointed out, fix the criminality of its members, that definition should exclude persons who had no knowledge of the criminal purposes or acts of the organization and those who were drafted by the State for membership, unless they were personally implicated in the commission of acts declared criminal by Article 6 of the Charter as members of the organization. Membership alone is not enough to come within the scope of these declarations.[4]

In particular, the American judge had been concerned that using the IMT Charter to brand organizations as criminal could give the Soviets (and others) authority to shoot people on proof of membership.[5] This legitimate concern about collective punishment has its legacy today in the discussion of the criminal liability of organizations or legal persons under international law. The fear of collective punishment goes a long way to explain why some lawyers, in particular from human rights organizations, were unenthusiastic about the possible inclusion of legal persons or corporations within the jurisdiction of the new International Criminal Court, and why they have remained opposed to the inclusion of legal persons in the context of subsequent criminal law treaties in contexts such as the fight against terrorism.[6]

The importance of the firms and their industrialists to the Nuremberg trials

Returning to the International Military Tribunal in Nuremberg, as we have seen it was not only the political organizations that concerned the prosecutors and judges. There was also a determination to ensure that the German industries and businessmen who had supported the German war effort were exposed and punished.

This brings me to my second insight. One of the original indictees at the IMT was Gustav Krupp von Bohlen und Halbach. When the trial was due to start, he was said by his lawyers to be unfit for trial owing to senile dementia. The court ordered medical examinations and, even though he could not respond to simple commands such as turn your head from left to right, they refused to drop him from the indictment. The reasons given by the different international prosecutors are interesting. The US prosecutor was prepared to substitute Krupp von Bohlen's son Alfried on the indictment. This is an odd idea at first sight, but the documents reveal the extent to which justice was to be served by prosecuting the firm, rather than the individual, even in a situation in which the court had jurisdiction only over individuals. The US answer drafted by Robert Jackson stated:

Public interests, which transcend all private considerations, require that Krupp von Bohlen shall not be dismissed unless some other representative of the Krupp armament and munitions industry be substituted. These public interests are as follows: Four generations of the Krupp family have owned and operated the great armament and munitions plants which have been the chief source of Germany's war supplies. For over 130 years this family has been the focus, the symbol, and the beneficiary of the most sinister forces engaged in menacing the peace of Europe. During the period between the two World Wars, the management of these enterprises was chiefly in Defendant Krupp von Bohlen. It was at all times however a Krupp family enterprise. Only a nominal owner himself, Von Bohlen's wife, Bertha Krupp, owned the bulk of the stock. About 1937 their son, Alfried Krupp, became plant manager and was actively associated in the policymaking and executive management thereafter.... To drop Krupp von Bohlen from this case without substitution of Alfried, drops from the case the entire Krupp family, and defeats any effective judgment against the German armament makers.[7]

The British prosecutor objected to any substitution or delay. For him, special considerations made it essential for Gustav Krupp to be tried in his absence. He argued that, because this was a conspiracy charge, the evidence directly concerned with the actions and speeches of Gustav Krupp and the Krupp company would be evidence against all the remaining defendants. The British argued that, if Gustav Krupp were to be dropped from the list of defendants, "there will be no advocate so well qualified to deal with those allegations on behalf of the other defendants against whom they will still be preferred".[8]

In the end the tribunal decided that Gustav Krupp could not be tried because of his condition but that he should be "retained for trial thereafter, if the physical and mental condition of the defendant should permit".[9] However, his son Alfried was later tried with 11 others by one of the United States' military tribunals set up in Nuremberg to try further war crimes after the IMT had finished its work. He received a 12-year sentence.

In Alfried Krupp's case, the defence suggested that international law did not attach to private industrialists who did not act on behalf of the state. They sought to distinguish the IMT's judgment in *Goering et al.*, concerning the responsibility of the individual, by claiming that these individuals had been state agents:

One must consider, however, that in the case of the International Military Tribunal, the persons involved were not private individuals such as those appearing in this case, but responsible officials of the State, that is such persons and only such persons as, by virtue of their office, acted on behalf of the State. It may be a much healthier point of view not to adhere in all circumstances to the text of the provisions of International Law, which is, in itself abundantly clear, but rather to follow the spirit of that law, and to state that anyone who acted on behalf of the State is liable to punishment under the terms of penal law, because as an anonymous subject, the State itself can not be held responsible for the compensation of damage. In no circumstances is it permissible, however, to hold criminally responsible a private individual, an industrialist in this case, who has not acted on behalf of the State, who was not an official or an organ of the State, and of whom, furthermore, in the face of the theory of law as it has been understood up to this time, and as it is outlined above, it is impossible to ascertain that he had any idea, and who, in fact had no idea that he, together with his State, was under an obligation to ensure adherence to the provisions of International Law.[10]

The prosecution dealt with this:

It has also been suggested that International Law is a vague and complicated thing and that private industrialists should be given the benefit of the plea of ignorance of the law. Whatever weight, if any, such a defense might have in other circumstances and with other defendants, we think it would be quite preposterous to give it any weight in this case. We are not dealing here with small businessmen, unsophisticated in the ways of the world or lacking in capable legal counsel. Krupp was one of the great international industrial institutions with numerous connections in many countries, and constantly engaged in international commercial intercourse. As was said in the judgment in the *Flick* case: "... responsibility of an individual for infractions of International Law is not open to question. In dealing with property located outside his own State, he must be expected to ascertain and keep within the applicable law."[11]

The conspiracy charges with regard to waging an aggressive war failed, but the counts regarding plunder, spoliation and employing prisoners of war (POWs) and foreign civilians under inhuman conditions connected to the war succeeded. With regard to plunder, we might mention that the allegations essentially centred on the Krupp firm as such. By giving one example from the charges related to the removal of machines from the Netherlands, we can see how the tribunal reasoned:

The evidence showed that the Krupp firm had through the Commissioner for the Netherlands of the Reich Ministry for Armaments and War Production secured the sponsorship for these factories which gave the firm the strict supervision over orders and deliveries. It was further shown by the evidence that practically all the machinery, goods and equipment from these factories had been confiscated and shipped to Germany on government orders by which the Krupp firm had availed itself, and with the participation of the Krupp firm. Practically all the machines, goods and equipment had been sent to the Krupp factories in the Ruhr. A comment reported to have been made by two representatives of the Field Economic Office had referred to the Krupp men concerned as the "Robbers". Energetic protests by the managers of these Dutch firms had been of no avail. Active resistance was impossible and out of the question. Obstruction on the part of the Dutch owners was met with the threat of calling in the Wehrmacht. The evidence showed that all the various Dutch industries referred to above had been exploited and plundered for the benefit of the German war effort and for the Krupp firm itself in the most ruthless way.[12]

The tribunal then concluded that the evidence disclosed "active participation" in the acquisition of the machines by Alfried Krupp and four others. In a further paragraph, the tribunal drew further conclusions with regard to the Krupp firm:

It was further shown by the evidence that the initiative for the acquisition of properties, machines and materials in the occupied countries referred to above, was that of the Krupp firm and that it had utilized the Reich government and Reich agencies whenever necessary to accomplish its purposes.[13]

We might draw the interim conclusion that it was the Krupp firm that was essentially at the heart of this set of convictions. In fact, the tribunal took time to identify the intention and purposes of the firm, as well as ensuring that the directors were held accountable, even if the firm itself could not be prosecuted before this particular tribunal.

The way in which the Nuremberg trials dealt with the firms as such

Third, we can examine the extent to which the corporation itself can be the bearer of international law duties. We find here another important legacy from the Nuremberg trials. Of course the tribunals did not have jurisdiction over the corporations; the tribunals had jurisdiction only over individuals. Although they had the power to declare certain political organizations criminal, they had no power to try and convict any organizations.

However, a careful examination of the judgments reveals an acceptance of the notion that in some cases the corporation itself committed the war crime and its directors were being convicted for belonging to the organization that had committed the criminal act. In the *Farben* case, the relevant international jurisdiction stemmed from the Allied legislation Control Council Law No. 10 and not the IMT Charter. Control Council Law No. 10 included Article II(2), which criminalized membership of a group or organization connected with the commission of crimes covered by the legislation. The US military tribunal in fact considered Farben, as a corporation, to have violated the laws and customs of war. The tribunal judgment stated:

> The result was the enrichment of Farben and the building of its greater chemical empire through the medium of occupancy at the expense of the former owners. Such action on the part of Farben constituted a violation of the Hague Regulations. It was in violation of the rights of private property, protected by the Laws and Customs of War.[14]

The tribunal indicted and brought to trial 21 officials of the Farben corporation, 13 of whom were convicted and sentenced to terms of imprisonment ranging from one and a half years to seven years for charges including plunder, spoliation, employment of prisoners of war, forced labour and employment of concentration camp inmates under inhuman conditions.

Three interim conclusions seem appropriate here in relation to the International Criminal Court (ICC). First, the United States military tribunal considered that a corporation was capable – that is to say, had the requisite legal capacity – to violate the laws and customs of war, even if the tribunal had no jurisdiction over the company as such. National jurisdictions that are developing national competence over international crimes may find that claims could be brought alleging that a company has committed a crime even though the ICC has no jurisdiction over the crime in question. This is most likely to occur where national legislation assumes that the term "person" in national legislation is to be interpreted as including both natural and legal persons.[15]

Second, some of the counts accused the defendants of having acted through the *instrumentality of Farben*. In the ICC Statute, Article 25(3)(a), criminal responsibility is foreseen where individuals commit a crime "through another person, regardless of whether that other person is criminally responsible". One could imagine that in the future, even in the absence of ICC jurisdiction over legal persons, individuals might be indicted for having acted through a corporation. In this way, the corporation would be indirectly implicated in the ICC process and there would be a public discussion of the instrumentality of the company. In extreme circumstances one might imagine that it would be necessary to have lawyers representing the company itself. It should be recalled that, in the *Farben* case, the defendants, as a group, had specialists and expert accountants working to explain the behaviour of the entity.[16]

Third, where a corporation has clearly been involved in the commission of international crimes one might see claims for reparations from victims of these crimes. We should recall the recent settlements with regard to the Swiss banks and the German industries accused of having facilitated or benefited from war crimes committed during World War II. These settlements took place in the absence of an international jurisdiction to hear the complaint, and some are directly linked to the Farben trial just discussed.[17] It is quite possible that, in the context of future trials of individuals before the International Criminal Court, one might see similar expectations that reparations be paid to the victims.

In a recent paper by Thordis Ingadottir, a careful examination of the possibilities for reparations has revealed a number of possible future developments regarding the relevance of state and corporate violations of international law in the context of reparations through the ICC.[18] First, the definition of "victim" for the purposes of reparations to victims paid from the ICC Trust Fund is likely to encompass organizations and institutions. The Rules of Procedure and Evidence adopted by the Assembly of States Parties include Rule 85(b): "Victims may include organizations or institutions that have sustained direct harm to any of their property which is dedicated to religion, education, art or science or charitable purposes, and to their historic monuments, hospitals and other places and objects for humanitarian purposes."[19] Second, Ingadottir points out that, "as the experience of the United Nations Compensation Commission demonstrates, it is unlikely that sufficient funds could be exacted from convicted persons to pay all claims".[20] The report suggests that fines and forfeiture be transferred to the Trust Fund to supplement the reparations obtained from the convicted person. The report then points out: "The Rome Statute provides that upon warrant of arrest or summons, the Court might ask states parties to identify, trace and freeze proceeds, property and assets and instrumentalities of crimes for the purpose of eventual forfeiture, should the indictee be found guilty."[21] Third, the report speculates on what states and corporations might do even in the absence of ICC jurisdiction over them: "States might nonetheless feel the moral obligation to contribute to the reparation of certain crimes e.g. when the convicted person is a national of theirs, or when crimes have been committed under a previous government which has been overthrown."[22] Ingadottir cites the final report of Cherif Bassiouni, Special Rapporteur of the UN Human Rights Commission, with regard to the right to restitution, compensation and rehabilitation for victims of gross violations of human rights and fundamental freedoms, which includes Principle 18:

In the event that the party responsible for the violation is unable to or unwilling to meet these obligations, the State should endeavor to provide reparation to victims who have sustained bodily injury or impairment of physical or mental health as a result of these violations and to the families, in particular dependants of persons who have died or become physically or mentally incapacitated as a result of the violation. To that end, states should endeavor to establish national funds for reparation to victims and seek other sources of funds wherever necessary to supplement these.[23]

Ingadottir continues: "Similarly, corporations might have an interest in victims' redress and the Trust Fund might benefit from their contributions."[24]

Questions of conspiracy and complicity in Nuremberg

The fourth and last lesson from the Nuremberg trials that I wish to tackle here is related to the issues of conspiracy and complicity. These concepts were central to problems associated with the Nuremberg and Tokyo trials.[25] The Tokyo trial has been heavily criticized for the conviction of defendants on the charge of complicity in the conspiracy to secure the military, political and economic dominance of East Asia and the Pacific and Indian Oceans and wage a war of aggression against any country in opposition. The Japanese defence lawyer quoted an article from the *Harvard Law Review* on conspiracy:

It is a doctrine as anomalous and provincial as it is unhappy in its results. It is utterly unknown to the Roman law; it is not found in modern Continental codes; few continental lawyers ever heard of it.... Under such a principle everyone who acts in cooperation with another may some day find his liberty dependent upon the innate prejudices or social bias of an unknown judge. It is the very antithesis of justice according to law.[26]

Further controversy surrounded the fact that none of the members of the powerful Japanese businesses, the *zaibatsu*, were included in the indictment, even if their activities with regard to the narcotics trade in opium were raised at the Tokyo trial.[27] Brackman tells how, at the time, *Pravda* and the Soviets scored ideological points by highlighting the failure of the tribunal to deal with the businessmen, with the Soviet associate prosecutor stating in the Moscow newspaper *New Times*: "The big capitalist concerns exercised a very great influence on the entire political life of Japan. It was they that were the mainsprings of piratical aggression. Wherever the Japanese armies appeared, the giant monopoly octopuses stretched their tentacles."[28]

The conspiracy legacy of the international trials has had repercussions with regard to the very latest attempts to hold corporations accountable for violations of international criminal law, even in the absence of jurisdiction in the International Criminal Court. In the US District Court for the Central District of California, the case against the Unocal corporation, which was accused of being involved in forced labour practices in Myanmar, at first hinged on an interpretation of the scope of conspiracy under international law. The District Court judgment of 31 August 2000 relied in part on a joint action test being proven through evidence of conspiracy. The court held that there was no evidence of conspiracy; there was evidence of a goal of a profitable project, but not of participation in the unlawful conduct or conspiracy. For the forced labour claim against Unocal, the District Court reviewed the Nuremberg US military tribunal cases and stated that the plaintiffs' suit failed. According to the judgment, the plaintiffs had not shown that the defendant corporation met the Nuremberg test of seeking to employ slave labour, rather than simply benefiting from the practice. The court interpreted the Nuremberg US military tribunal judgments as demanding that the defendant actively participates in the unlawful conduct.[29]

However, the Nuremberg tribunals did in fact condemn the companies for benefiting from the war, and some individual directors were convicted on the basis of participating in that plunder. The US District Court focused on the necessity defence successfully invoked by some of the defendants before the US military tribunals in Nuremberg to rule that the suit had to be dismissed. But this reliance on the necessity defence was rejected as inappropriate by the US Court of Appeals in the same case. In fact the judgment of the appeal court, which overturned the District Court's ruling, shifted the focus from conspiracy to complicity.

The District Court incorrectly borrowed the "active participation" standard for liability from war crimes cases before Nuremberg military tribunals involving the role of German industrialists in the Nazi forced labour programme during World War II. The military tribunals applied the "active participation" standard in these cases only to overcome the defendants' "necessity defence". In the present case, Unocal did not invoke – and could not have invoked – the necessity defence. The District Court therefore erred when it applied the "active participation" standard here. I, however, agree with the District Court that, in the present case, one should apply international law as developed in the decisions by international criminal tribunals such as the Nuremberg military tribunals for the applicable substantive law.

I shall now very briefly consider the question of complicity in this context.[30] As we have seen, the trials after World War II also gave rise to convictions for membership in criminal organizations and the trials of the German industrialists. Criminal organizations were held to be analogous to criminal conspiracies. But, as we saw above, the International Military Tribunal was careful to ensure that individual members could not be prosecuted on the grounds of membership alone; knowledge of the criminal acts of the organization was necessary. Alternatively, the individual had to be personally implicated in the commission of the international crimes. Although membership alone was not enough, membership of the governing board (*Vorstand*[31]) of the large corporations was relevant, and we should look again at what the US military tribunal said in the *Farben* case about the actual requisite participation:

It is appropriate here to mention that the corporate defendant, Farben, is not before the bar of this Tribunal and cannot be subjected to criminal penalties in these proceedings. We have used the term Farben as descriptive of the instrumentality of cohesion in the name of which the enumerated acts of spoliation were committed. But corporations act through individuals and, under the conception of personal individual guilt to which previous reference has been made, the prosecution, to discharge the burden imposed upon it in this case, must establish by competent proof beyond a reasonable doubt that an individual defendant was either a participant in the illegal act or that, being aware thereof, he authorized or approved it. Responsibility does not automatically attach to an act proved to be criminal merely by virtue of a defendant's membership in the Vorstand. Conversely, one may not utilize the corporate structure to achieve an immunity from criminal responsibility for illegal acts which he directs, counsels, aids, orders or abets. But the evidence must establish action of the character we have indicated, with knowledge of the essential elements of the crime.[32]

Aiding or abetting an international corporate crime can give rise to international criminal liability for the individual where there is knowing participation.[33] This sort of complicity can give rise to a finding of liability even in the absence of international jurisdiction with regard to the corporation itself. This is what may happen with regard to those complaints, such as the Unocal case already mentioned, that have been brought under the Alien Torts Claims Act (ATCA) in the United States.[34]

As mentioned above, the US Court of Appeals actually re-examined the sort of support that Unocal is alleged to have given the Myanmar authorities in the context of the forced labour claims. The appeal court's ruling gives an indication of the sort of *practical* assistance that would be evidence of the material element of the crime:

The evidence also supports the conclusion that Unocal gave practical assistance to the Myanmar Military in subjecting Plaintiffs to forced labor. The practical assistance took the form of hiring the Myanmar Military to provide security and build infrastructure along the pipeline route in exchange for money or food. The practical assistance also took the form of using photos, surveys, and maps in daily meetings to show the Myanmar Military where to provide security and build infrastructure.[35]

The court found that this assistance had a *substantial effect* on the perpetration of the forced labour, and that the forced labour would most probably not have occurred in the same way "without someone hiring the Myanmar Military to provide security, and without someone showing them where to do it".[36] The US Court of Appeals examined the evidence and applied a reasonable knowledge test. The requisite mental element for corporate complicity in these circumstances seems to be that the company knew or should have known that its acts assisted in the crime.

The exclusion of legal persons from the jurisdiction of the ICC and the continuing international initiatives that demand that states address corporate behaviour

Having dealt with the lessons from Nuremberg, let us now consider some more recent developments with regard to the responsibility of corporations and states for acts that qualify as international crimes within the ICC Statute.

Two years after the conclusion of the *Farben* trial, the International Law Commission (1950) had already started drafting a statute for an International Criminal Court. Early meetings of the governmental Committee on International Criminal Jurisdiction considered proposals to include jurisdiction over juristic persons, but "in the light of the Nuremberg and Tokyo trials, it was considered undesirable to include so novel a principle as corporate criminal responsibility in the draft statute".[37] The notion seems to have been that collective responsibility for the actions of organizations had cast the conspiracy net too wide and led to injustice.

By the time of the 1998 Rome Conference, a fresh look at the issue was overdue; the legacy of Nuremberg was a hazy memory. The Working Group on General Principles established informal consultations on the question of legal persons. These representatives sought to draft an article that could garner enough support to ensure that legal persons could be included within the jurisdiction of the proposed ICC. Although the initiative started in the context of criminal organizations, the work evolved to cover legal persons in such a way that corporations could be tried by the ICC. The examples used by the proponents of the inclusion of corporate responsibility in the statute related to the Rwanda genocide, bulldozers to cover up graves, radio stations, and even questions of private security companies fighting wars in Africa and the Pacific.

But there was no agreement within the Working Group. The primary problem was that many legal systems simply do not recognize corporate criminal responsibility.[38] Further problems related to the focus of the conference on individual responsibility and the need to marry this with any extension to responsibility for legal persons. A dominant theme became the issue of which individuals would trigger corporate account-ability before the International Criminal Court: the board of directors, the chairperson, the managing director, any employee, or simply the controlling mind? The closest the conference came to an acceptable text suggested that a natural person and the juridical person could both be charged by the Prosecutor where the "natural person charged was in a position of control within the juridical person" and the "crime was com-mitted by the natural person acting on behalf of and with the explicit consent of that juridical person and in the course of its activities".[39] In fact, the concept of the liability of entities controlled by the individual perpetrators of international crimes has survived.

Security Council Resolution 1373 (2001) of 28 September 2001 creates an obligation for all states to prevent and suppress the financing of ter-rorist acts. In addition, states must freeze without delay the funds and assets of "entities owned or controlled directly or indirectly by" persons who commit, or attempt to commit, terrorist acts or participate in or facilitate the commission of terrorist acts. The vicarious liability of cor-porations owned or controlled by those involved in terrorism is assumed even if it is not specifically criminalized by this resolution. Owing to the problems of establishing corporate criminality in national law, most in-ternational initiatives, such as the Convention on Terrorist Financing and the draft Comprehensive Convention on International Terrorism, have left national legal systems a degree of flexibility. The Conventions de-mand that *liability* be established for legal persons where the relevant natural person has committed an international crime.

The UN draft Comprehensive Convention on International Terrorism includes an obligation for states to prohibit the illegal activities of orga-nizations that encourage or knowingly finance the commission of terrorist offences. But the interesting innovation in this draft treaty is that it fore-sees that states parties should hold legal entities liable "when a person responsible for the management or control of that legal entity has, in that capacity, committed an offense referred to in Article 2. Such liability may be criminal, civil or administrative."[40] The continuing focus on terrorism and transnational organized criminal groups means that international criminal law is likely to continue to insist that steps are taken at the na-tional level to suppress this activity. It seems fair to say that we are likely to see increasing use of international criminal law to determine the terms and scope of this suppression.

The complexity of international criminal law

As we saw, the ICC has no jurisdiction over the corporation itself; but there may still be international obligations from customary international law on corporations. Moreover, other jurisdictions may be competent to condemn a corporation as such and even order reparations. Returning to the importance of the complicity concept, I can complicate matters by pointing out that in addition to this basic layer of obligations, whereby corporations themselves can be said to have actually directly committed violations of international criminal law, there is a complex web of possible complicitous conduct by a corporation.[41] First, the corporation could have facilitated or assisted a violation of international criminal law by a state. Secondly, the corporation may have assisted another corporation to commit a crime. And, thirdly, the corporation may have facilitated a crime committed by an individual. In this last situation, the ICC may have jurisdiction over the individual(s) and one could imagine an indirect finding that the corporation was liable at least to the extent that it created an expectation that compensation would be paid into the Trust Fund. In addition, as we saw above, the court itself may actually order that states parties assist the court by freezing or seizing assets. These could be transferred to the Trust Fund and eventually used for victims in the event of an order for forfeiture.

Moreover, we can see here that, even if corporations were excluded from the jurisdiction of the International Criminal Court, they are being targeted in recent treaties for acts that, although classified as terrorist acts, might also qualify as war crimes, acts of genocide or crimes against humanity.[42] In the end, although terrorist acts as such were not included in the Rome Statute, the same crimes may now be reclassified as crimes within the statute. The complexity of international criminal law is such that an act of torture or killing could simultaneously trigger the international jurisdictions foreseen for violations of the laws of armed conflict, genocide or crimes against humanity, as well as universal jurisdiction at the national level for a crime such as torture or a grave breach of the Geneva Conventions. The same act could qualify as several different types of international crime and, in addition, be simultaneously justiciable in several jurisdictions.

There are, then, two layers of complexity in this context. On the one hand, we may have one act falling within the definition of different international crimes: torture, genocide, crimes against humanity, war crimes or even acts of terrorism. On the other hand, the same act can be prosecuted in different jurisdictions: at the national level, at an ad hoc international tribunal or at the International Criminal Court.

The responsibilities of states

In fact, we could add a third layer of complexity. The same act can give rise to separate sets of responsibilities from multiple actors. A single act of genocide could give rise to individual criminal responsibility under customary international law. The individual could be tried at the national level or in a relevant international tribunal. In addition, where the act is also attributable to a state, there may be state responsibility both under customary international law and under the Genocide Convention of 1948. This means not only that other states could invoke such state responsibility and demand cession and reparation for the beneficiaries,[43] but also that another state party to the Genocide Convention could complain to the International Court of Justice under Article IX of the Convention. This was precisely what happened in the suit brought by Bosnia and Herzegovina against the Federal Republic of Yugoslavia.[44]

The layers of responsibility do not end there, however. One could also foresee either an inter-state complaint under a human rights treaty such as the International Covenant on Civil and Political Rights or any of the regional human rights treaties that provide for such complaints, or a complaint by an individual or a group of individuals that there had been a violation of a human rights treaty for this same act. The violation could flow from the fact that the behaviour of a state official is attributable to the state in question, or it could be that the state is accused of failing through omission to protect someone within its jurisdiction or to prosecute the alleged perpetrator.

The absence of states as potential defendants from the criminal jurisdiction of the International Criminal Court does not mean that they do not have international responsibility for the sort of activity prohibited by international criminal law. Failure to fulfil this international responsibility could be invoked by other states under customary international law with regard to nearly all the offences in the Rome Statute. Where an international jurisdiction exists, there could be a suit brought by an individual, an organization, a group of individuals or even another state.[45] Such a claim would be not a criminal case but rather a civil or delictual claim.

We should finally also remember that the categories of non-natural persons are not limited to corporations, criminal organizations and states. The International Law Commission was careful to state in its Articles on State Responsibility that the articles are without prejudice to the question of the responsibility under international law of an international organization or of an individual acting on behalf of a state (see Articles 57 and 58 of the Articles on State Responsibility adopted by the International Law Commission at its 53rd session).[46]

Final remarks

The history of international criminal law is in part a history of states focusing on the political groups and private organizations that have provided the structures that have enabled individuals to commit international crimes. Despite the absence of jurisdiction over corporations and states in the ICC Statute, it can be suggested that, should the facts point to the central contribution of any organization or state, the mechanisms exist at the national and international level to remind the world that the scope of international law extends beyond the role of individuals and to set the stage for claims for reparations. In fact, we may even see judicial processes focusing on the criminal behaviour of states and organizations, with considerable reparations being paid to victims. Despite the absence of accountability for non-natural persons under the ICC Statute, a short historical trip is enough to remind us that no one should assume that international criminal law is concerned solely with the liability of individuals. Organizations, corporations and states continue to have obligations under international criminal law.

Notes

1. The Prosecution in Case No. 58, *Trial of Alfried Felix Alwyn Krupp von Bohlen und Halbach and Eleven Others*, US Military Tribunal, Nuremberg, 17 November 1947 – 30 June 1948, *Law Reports of Trials of War Criminals*, vol. X, London: United Nations War Crimes Commission, 1949, p. 170.
2. See B. F. Smith, *Reaching Judgment at Nuremberg*, London: André Deutsch, 1977, p. 63, for the suggestion that the defendants represented certain organizations. See also R. Overy, "The Nuremberg Trials: International Law in the Making", in P. Sands, ed., *From Nuremberg to the Hague: The Future of International Criminal Justice*, Cambridge: Cambridge University Press, 2003, pp. 1–29, especially p. 12 for the representational aspect of the list of defendants.
3. Ibid., p. 12.
4. International Military Tribunal (Nuremberg) Judgment and Sentence, 1 October 1946, *American Journal of International Law*, vol. 41, 1947, pp. 172–333, at p. 251.
5. Smith, *Reaching Judgment at Nuremberg*, p. 75.
6. For a recent reassertion of Amnesty International's opposition to the inclusion of legal persons in the scope of an international criminal law treaty, see its Statement to the UN General Assembly with regard to the draft Comprehensive Convention on International Terrorism: "Collective punishment and infringement of the right to freedom of association: Article 9 would permit states to prosecute legal entities, such as trade unions, political parties and other non-governmental organizations, based solely on the commission of a 'terrorist' offense by one of its officers. This could result in collective criminal punishment of an organization – and, possibly, its members – for the criminal act of one individual. This article should be deleted" (AI index: IOR 51/009/2001, 24 October 2001).
7. Answer of the United States Prosecution to the Motion on Behalf of Defendant Gustav Krupp von Bohlen, Robert Jackson, 12 November 1945; available at www.yale.edu/lawweb/avalon/imt/proc/v1-11.htm.
8. Memorandum of the British Prosecution on the Motion on Behalf of Defendant Gustav Krupp von Bohlen, 12 November 1945, Sir Hartley Shawcross; available at www.yale.edu/lawweb/avalon/imt/proc/v1-12.htm.

9. International Military Tribunal (Nuremberg) Judgment and Sentence, p. 173.
10. Case No. 58, *Trial of Alfried Felix Alwyn Krupp von Bohlen und Halbach and Eleven Others*, US Military Tribunal, Nuremberg, 17 November 1947 – 30 June 1948, *Law Reports of Trials of War Criminals*, vol. X, p. 170.
11. Ibid.
12. Ibid., p. 92.
13. Ibid.
14. See *I.G. Farben Trial*, US Military Tribunal, Nuremberg, 14 August 1947 – 29 July 1948, *Law Reports of Trials of War Criminals*, vol. X, p. 50. I have dealt with this in some detail in A. Clapham, "The Question of Jurisdiction under International Criminal Law over Legal Persons: Lessons from the Rome Conference on an International Criminal Court", in M. Kamminga and S. Zia-Zarifi, eds., *Liability of Multinational Corporations under International Law*, The Hague: Kluwer, 2000, pp. 139–195, at pp. 166–171.
15. Consider the cases pending before the Belgian courts against TotalFinaElf: "Myanmar Refugees Seek Belgium Trial for TotalFinaElf", AFP World Wide news Agency, 8 May 2002, www.icai-online.org/xp_resources/icai/oil_companies/myanmar_refugees.pdf. Article 6 of Belgium's 1993 universal jurisdiction law, allowing for the prosecution of alleged war crimes no matter where they took place, and amended in 1999 to include crimes against humanity and genocide, provides that "without prejudice to Articles 4 and 8 of the present Act, all the provisions contained in Book I of the Penal Code shall, with the exception of Article 70, be applicable to the breaches provided for in the present Act" (unofficial translation in *International Legal Materials*, vol. 38, 1999, p. 924).
16. Clapham, "The Question of Jurisdiction under International Criminal Law over Legal Persons", p. 167.
17. M. J. Bazyler, "Nuremberg in America: Litigating the Holocaust in United States Courts", *University of Richmond Law Review*, vol. 34, 2000, pp. 1–283; A. Ramasastry, "Secrets and Lies? Swiss Banks and International Human Rights", *Vanderbilt Journal of Transnational Law*, vol. 31, 1998, pp. 325–456; J. Ziegler, *The Swiss, the Gold, and the Dead: How Swiss Bankers Helped Finance the Nazi War Machine*, London: Penguin, 1999. For details on the decision by Farben to set up a compensation fund, see Clapham, "The Question of Jurisdiction under International Criminal Law over Legal Persons", p. 148.
18. T. Ingadottir, "The International Criminal Court, the Trust Fund for Victims (Article 79 of the Rome Statute). A Discussion Paper", Project on International Court and Tribunals, February 2001, ICC Discussion Paper No. 3.
19. Note also Rule 98(4), which states: "Following consultations with interested States and the Trust Fund, the Court may order that an award for reparations be made through the Trust Fund to an intergovernmental, international or national organization approved by the Trust Fund."
20. Ingadottir, "The International Criminal Court, the Trust Fund for Victims", p. 18.
21. Ibid., p. 18; see Articles 57(3)(e), 93(1)(k) and 79(2) of the ICC Statute. Note that, although the statute suggests such an initiative by the pre-trial chamber to seek cooperation from states parties for forfeiture "in particular for the ultimate benefit of victims" (Art. 57(3)(e)), states parties are to comply with such a request for the "identification, tracing and freezing or seizure of proceeds, property and assets and instrumentalities of crimes for the purpose of eventual forfeiture, *without prejudice to the rights of bona fide third parties*" (Art. 93(1)(k), emphasis added).
22. Ibid., pp. 21–22.
23. Ibid., p. 22, fn 50. The report is *The Right to Restitution, Compensation and Rehabilitation for Victims of Gross Violations of Human Rights and Fundamental Freedoms, Final Report of the Special Rapporteur, Mr. M. Cherif Bassiouni*, UN Doc. E/CN.4/2000/62, 18 January 2000.

24. Ibid., p. 22.
25. See Overy, "The Nuremberg Trials".
26. F. B. Sayre, "Criminal Conspiracy", *Harvard Law Review*, vol. 35, 1922, p. 427. See R. H. Minear, *Victor's Justice: The Tokyo War Crimes Trial*, Princeton, N.J.: Princeton University Press, 1971, p. 41. See also A. C. Brackman, *The Other Nuremberg: The Untold Story of the Tokyo War Crimes Trials*, London: Collins, 1989, p. 95. For further discussion, see C. Hosoya, N. Ando, Y. Onuma, R. Minear, eds., *The Tokyo War Crimes Trial: An International Symposium*, Tokyo: Kodansha, 1986, especially pp. 108–109.
27. Brackman, *The Other Nuremberg*, p. 208.
28. Ibid., p. 96.
29. *John Doe et al v. UNOCAL Corp et al*, F. Supp, 2d, vol. 110, 2000, p. 1294, at p. 1310.
30. For a detailed discussion, see W. Schabas, "Enforcing International Humanitarian Law: Catching the Accomplices", *Review of the International Committee of the Red Cross*, vol. 83, 2001, pp. 439–459; A. Clapham and S. Jerbi, "Categories of Corporate Complicity in Human Rights Abuses", *Hastings International and Comparative Law Review*, vol. 24, 2001, pp. 338–349; and A. Clapham, "On Complicity", in R. Roth and M. Henzelin, *Le Droit pénal à l'épreuve de l'internationalisation*, Geneva/Paris: Georg, LGDI, 2002, pp. 241–275.
31. "The *Vorstand*, somewhat like the executive committee of a board of directors, was charged with the actual responsibility for the management of the corporation and represented it in dealings with others. When the Farben merger took place in 1925–1926, its *Vorstand* consisted of 82 members and most of its functions were delegated to a working committee of 26 members. In 1938 the *Vorstand* was reduced to less than 30 members and the working committee was abolished. There was also a central committee within the working committee, which survived the abolition of the latter. The *Vorstand* met, on the average, every 6 weeks and was presided over by a chairman, who, in some respects, was regarded as its executive head and in others merely as *primus inter pares*" (*Law Reports of Trials of War Criminals*, vol. VIII, pp. 1086–1087).
32. *Law Reports of Trials of War Criminals*, vol. X, p. 52.
33. "As the action of Farben in proceedings to acquire permanently property interests in the manner generally outlined is in violation of the Hague Regulations, any individual who knowingly participated in any such act of plunder or spoliation with the degree of connection outlined in Article II, Paragraph 2 of Central Law No. 10, is criminally responsible thereafter" (ibid., p. 50).
34. For a detailed look at these cases, see A. Ramasastry, "Corporate Complicity: From Nuremberg to Rangoon. An Examination of Forced Labor Cases and Their Impact on the Liability of Multinational Corporations", *Berkeley Journal of International Law*, vol. 20, 2002, pp. 91–159.
35. Appeal from the United States District Court for the Central District of California, argued and submitted 3 December 2001, filed 18 September 2002, at para. 11, www.thailawforum.com/database1/unocal.html. Footnote 29, referring to para. 11, adds: "The evidence further supports the conclusion that Unocal gave 'encouragement' to the Myanmar Military in subjecting Plaintiffs to forced labor. The daily meetings with the Myanmar Military to show it where to provide security and build infrastructure, despite Unocal's knowledge that the Myanmar Military would probably use forced labor to provide these services, may have encouraged the Myanmar Military to actually use forced labor for the benefit of the Project. Similarly, the payments to the Myanmar Military for providing these services, despite Unocal's knowledge that the Myanmar Military had actually used forced labor to provide them, may have encouraged the Myanmar Military to continue to use forced labor in connection with the Project."
36. Ibid., para. 12.

37. *Report of the 1953 Committee on International Criminal Jurisdiction 27 July – 20 August 1953*, UN Doc. A/2645, 1954, para. 85. Note that the Tokyo tribunal had no jurisdiction to declare organizations criminal nor did it deal with the Japanese business community (Brackman, *The Other Nuremberg*, p. 96). See also Minear (*Victor's Justice*, p. 37), "one of the prosecution lawyers [Horowitz], writing after the trial, would explain the unwillingness of the prosecution to indict a businessman – should he be acquitted, his acquittal would be taken as a blanket condonation of the actions of the Japanese business community". Some Dutch military courts apparently prosecuted Japanese criminal groups for specific crimes (P. R. Piccigallo, *The Japanese on Trial: Allied War Crimes Operations in the East, 1945–1951*, Austin: University of Texas Press, 1979, pp. 177 and 183). Note also the protests by Markov in the Russian foreign affairs weekly *New Times* and by *Pravda* concerning the exclusion of the leading industrialists (the *zaibatsu*) described by Piccigallo (pp. 146–148 and the discussion at p. 16, fn 31).

38. K. Ambos, "Article 25", in O. Triffterer, ed., *Commentary on the Rome Statute of the International Criminal Court*, Baden-Baden: Nomos, 1999, pp. 475–493, at p. 478.

39. Working Paper on Article 23, Paragraphs 5 and 6 of the Rome Statute, UN Doc. A/Conf.183.C.1/WGGP/L.5/Rev.2, 3 July 1998; discussed in full in Clapham, "The Question of Jurisdiction under International Criminal Law over Legal Persons", pp. 146–158.

40. Draft Comprehensive Convention on International Terrorism, UN Doc. A/C.6/55/1, 28 August 2000, Article 9. According to the latest report of the Working Group, the full draft texts are as follows: "1. Each State Party, in accordance with its domestic legal principles, shall take the necessary measures to enable a legal entity located in its territory or organized under its laws to be held liable when a person responsible for the management or control of that legal entity has, in that capacity, committed an offense referred to in Article 2. Such liability may be criminal, civil or administrative. 2. Such liability is incurred without prejudice to the criminal liability of individuals having committed the offenses. 3. Each State Party shall ensure, in particular, that legal entities liable in accordance with Paragraph 1 above are subject to effective, proportionate and dissuasive criminal, civil or administrative sanctions. Such sanctions may include monetary sanctions" (UN Doc. A/C.6/56/L.9 of 29 October 2001, Article 9).

41. On the complicity of corporations in international crimes and the international law secondary rules that may be referent to determine liability, see Clapham, "The Question of Jurisdiction under International Criminal Law over Legal Persons".

42. Article 2 of the draft Comprehensive Convention on International Terrorism states: "1. Any person commits an offense within the meaning of this Convention if that person, by any means, unlawfully and intentionally, causes: (a) Death or serious bodily injury to any person; or (b) Serious damage to public or private property, including a place of public use, a State or government facility, a public transportation system, an infrastructure facility or the environment; or (c) Damage to property, places, facilities, or systems referred to in Paragraph 1 (b) of this article, resulting or likely to result in major economic loss, when the purpose of the conduct, by its nature or context, is to intimidate a population, or to compel a Government or an international organization to do or abstain from doing any act. 2. Any person also commits an offense if that person makes a credible and serious threat to commit an offense as set forth in Paragraph 1 of this article. 3. Any person also commits an offense if that person attempts to commit an offense as set forth in Paragraph 1 of this article. 4. Any person also commits an offense if that person: (a) Participates as an accomplice in an offense as set forth in Paragraph 1, 2 or 3 of this article; (b) Organizes or directs others to commit an offense as set forth in Paragraph 1, 2 or 3 of this article; or (c) Contributes to the commission of one or more offenses as set forth in Paragraph 1, 2 or 3 of this article by a group of persons acting

with a common purpose. Such contribution shall be intentional and shall either: (i) Be made with the aim of furthering the criminal activity or criminal purpose of the group, where such activity or purpose involves the commission of an offense as set forth in Paragraph 1 of this article; or (ii) Be made in the knowledge of the intention of the group to commit an offense as set forth in Paragraph 1 of this article."

43. See the Articles of the International Law Commission on State Responsibility, adopted at its 53rd session, 2001, UN Doc. GAOR Supplement No. 10 (A/56/10), Arts. 42, 43, 48 and 54.

44. See the recent judgment by the International Court of Justice which expressly rejected the claim by the Federal Republic of Yugoslavia that the Genocide Convention could not give rise to a general complaint with regard to state responsibility as opposed to a complaint relating to the prosecution of individuals accused of genocide. *Case Concerning Application of the Convention on the Prevention and Punishment of the Crime of Genocide (Bosnia-Herzegovina v. Yugoslavia) Preliminary Objections*, 11 July 1996, paras. 27–33. "32. The Court now comes to the second proposition advanced by Yugoslavia, regarding the type of State responsibility envisaged in Article IX of the Convention. According to Yugoslavia, that article would only cover the responsibility flowing from the failure of a State to fulfill its obligations of prevention and punishment as contemplated by Articles V, VI and VII; on the other hand, the responsibility of a State for an act of genocide perpetrated by the State itself would be excluded from the scope of the Convention. The Court would observe that the reference in Article IX to 'the responsibility of a State for genocide or for any of the other acts enumerated in Article III,' does not exclude any form of State responsibility. Nor is the responsibility of a State for acts of its organs excluded by Article IV of the Convention, which contemplates the commission of an act of genocide by 'rulers' or 'public officials.'"

45. See Article 25(4) of the ICC Statute: "No provision in this Statute relating to individual criminal responsibility shall affect the responsibility of States under international law." See Ingadottir, "The International Criminal Court, the Trust Fund for Victims", p. 21, for the proposals in the Rome Statute that would have included the possibility for the court to order a state to make reparations. Note also Principle 11 of the UN Declaration of Basic Principles of Justice for Victims of Crime and Abuse of Power cited by Ingadottir, ibid., p. 21.

46. "Article 57: These articles are without prejudice to any question of the responsibility under international law of an international organization, or of any State for the conduct of an international organization. Article 58: These articles are without prejudice to any question of the individual responsibility under international law of any person acting on behalf of a State." The ILC Commentary suggests that Article 58 was drafted so as not to preclude any development with regard to international "individual civil responsibility" (see J. Crawford, *The International Law Commission's Articles on State Responsibility: Introduction, Text and Commentaries*, Cambridge: Cambridge University Press, 2002, para. 2 to the Commentary on Article 58, at p. 312).

14

The International Criminal Court and the prohibition of the use of children in armed conflict

Julia Maxted

Introduction

International legal instruments and the near universal ratification of the Convention on the Rights of the Child (CRC) have created a framework for the protection and care of children in armed conflicts. However, comprehensive, sustained and effective action is severely constrained by a lack of understanding concerning the root causes that underlie the increasing use of children in armed conflicts. Although it is crucial to recognize that the severity of the child soldier problem results partly from the characteristics of contemporary conflict, I suggest here that it is magnified by the effects of recent macroeconomic policies on the social fabric of society, which have made livelihoods more insecure and weakened norms that protect children. In light of this, I consider the degree to which the International Criminal Court (ICC) can offer an effective means of realizing a prohibition on involving children in hostilities.

Children are experiencing high levels of death, injury and deprivation in current conflict situations, the majority of which are occurring in developing countries where many people already live in abject poverty. Since 1987, 2 million children have been killed and three times that number have been injured or disabled.[1] Millions of children are caught up in conflicts in which they are not merely bystanders but targets. Some fall victim to a general onslaught against civilians; others die as part of a calculated genocide. Still other children suffer the effects of sexual violence or the multiple deprivations of armed conflict that expose them to hunger and disease. Just as shocking, thousands of young people are cynically exploited as combatants.[2]

The principal reasons for this heightened vulnerability include the nature of contemporary conflicts and the declining security and adequacy of livelihoods throughout much of the developing world. Most contemporary conflicts are no longer international in the sense that they involve cross-border attacks by one state against the territory or citizens of another. For reasons owing much to the artificiality of colonial borders and the forces of uneven development, conflicts occur within states. Fighting may not be "political" as understood by civil wars in the past. It can, and does, span a broad spectrum ranging from competition for economic and natural resources to attempted genocide or even unrestrained lawlessness. In such situations and especially in conflicts that are refracted through the prism of ethnicity, the warring parties are often not prepared to acknowledge the distinctions between combatants and civilians. Food is stolen, towns are looted, roads are mined and villages are burned in order to force civilians to flee or seek survival in the bush or refugee camps.

In countries afflicted by protracted struggles for power, social, economic and physical infrastructures are usually weak and governments are unable to maintain even basic public services. Additionally, children have no sources of shelter and protection when family and community structures have disintegrated. Deprived of normal bases of support, children become homeless refugees when displaced or separated from their families. Many children are killed in fighting, but many more succumb to disease and malnutrition.

One of the most basic principles of humanitarian law, the protection of the civilian population against military attacks, is deliberately being ignored to deepen divisions between people in villages who may once have been neighbours. Attack provokes counter-attack and a cycle of vengeance, terror and population displacement is set in motion. To implement the rule of humanitarian law as set out in the Geneva Conventions, armies have to be sufficiently disciplined to observe the distinction between combatants and non-combatants and between military and non-military objectives. In current conflicts, however, the creation of chaos and suffering has become a strategic objective. As war passes out of the hands of the state and rituals of restraint begin to disintegrate, the level of adherence to humanitarian norms in crisis situations starts to deteriorate dramatically.[3] In these circumstances, traditional restrictions on the conduct of hostilities are cast aside; elders are no longer respected, and mothers and daughters are subjected to sexual violence. It is here that the potency and potential of youth are brutally exploited in order to create a state of constant and collective terror that permeates all social relations and destroys social cohesion. Children are forced, often on pain of death, to assist warring factions to kill, torture, loot or destroy the property of family members or neighbours.[4] Forcing children to take part in gruesome acts of violence against their own communities prevents them from returning home for fear of rejection. Removing them from family support networks also increases their dependence upon the armed group, even as the social isolation makes them more malleable. The abduction of children to commit atrocities demoralizes individuals, destabilizes communities and ensures a far more rapid and greater degree of control over populations than would otherwise be militarily possible.

In the context of reduced or redirected funding to regional military proxies since the end of the Cold War, some armed groups have resorted to the employment of children as active combatants in conflicts to counterbalance the reduction in overt foreign military hardware supplies. This has also led to the increased use of smaller, lighter and cheaper weapons such as M16 semi-automatic rifles or the aluminium AK-47. Owing to technological changes in arms that have made it possible to delegate military tasks to individuals who are neither strong nor technically very competent, children have become militarily useful while still young.

Rebel forces that do not have access to propaganda channels of the state media or the coercive power of the state tend to resort to abduction. The Lords Resistance Army in northern Uganda has kidnapped 10,000 children from schools and villages and taken them across the border to Sudan for indoctrination amid abuse and brutality. Armies are able to control the children's movements until they reach their "productive age" when they can be used in armed conflict. In the meantime, the children may help with non-military tasks. A further explanation for the abduction of increasingly younger children has been suggested: if they are not taken today, the enemy might take and use them tomorrow.[5]

In current conflicts, which are longer and have less clear motives, children have become militarily more useful. Certain characteristics of childhood development, including a lack of risk aversion and short horizons, may compensate for their lack of discipline and make them productive combatants. One Congolese rebel officer explaining why *kadogas* (boy fighters) make good soldiers said it was because they "obey orders; they are not concerned about getting back to their wife and family and they don't know fear".[6] Interestingly, not all children are forced to fight. Sometimes patriotism, grievance or desire for revenge induces them to take up arms.[7] Usually the motive is more basic. Becoming attached to an armed force may offer a better chance of surviving a violent situation for a separated child or for a family that can find no other way to protect itself, for example by migrating or sending children away from the conflict zone.

The economic conditions of many children living in conflict zones are frequently so poor that the offer of food and clothing is sufficient to induce participation. Nearly one-third of the countries in sub-Saharan Africa were affected by major conflict in the 1990s and, in these countries, some 40–50 per cent of all children are living below the poverty line.[8] Arguably, the costs of poverty are being disproportionately absorbed by children, who are forced to give up school and take up paid and unpaid labour when livelihoods fail. Livelihood security, social cohesion and capital have come under intense pressure in the past decade from recent macroeconomic policies, conflict and the HIV pandemic. The manifestations of these impacts can be described as causing a decline in the household and community capacities to nurture and protect and a weakening of norms that protect children. This decline results in the commodification of children, increasing child labour and reducing the importance of health and education.[9]

The experience of economic reform under structural adjustment has revealed a damaging effect on the social fabric of society, including a widening of inequities and declining incomes, asset bases and livelihoods. These harmful adjustments are linked to increases in societal violence and conflict:

[C]hildhood is a once-and-for-all window of opportunity for biological and social development. A child may grow into adulthood and never re-coup the developmental losses of childhood. Policies which rely on short term social costs for long term economic gain are simply not calculating the actual inter-generational costs of economic policies.[10]

In the HIV/AIDS pandemic, deaths are occurring disproportionately among age groups who are capable of reproduction. The implications for children are profound. Where parents or older siblings become sick and unable to work or die, there may be additional demands on children to contribute to household incomes and assist in raising younger brothers and sisters. Children may have to drop out of school because they can no longer afford fees or in order to work. A lack of education multiplies the chances of girls being forced to sell their bodies, seeing sex as the only viable economic option.

Case-studies from Sierra Leone, where as many as 9,000 combatants have been children, revealed that most child soldiers were alone. Having lost family and friends, they joined to find security and protection.[11] In the Liberian civil war, which began in 1989 and has left over 1 million people – half the population – homeless, young people were told that "they would be paid in US dollars, that they would get cars and a house in Monrovia".[12] Once inducted into military units, especially those of rebel groups, children face a life of violence and danger. As combatants, they stand to lose their civilian status and the protection they would normally have under humanitarian law. More seriously, they are presented to the enemy as legitimate targets of war. The child soldier, like any other member of an armed force, is exposed to the traditional aims of warfare – the immobilization and death of enemy personnel.

Children are vulnerable not only to attacks by the enemy but also to exploitation by their own commanders. Through beatings and torture, children are forced to perform acts that regular troops consider too dangerous or degrading to do themselves. Some are given support tasks and perform as guards and messengers as well as porters of food, munitions and looted goods. Additionally, girls are subjected to sexual violence, rape, forced prostitution, sexually transmitted diseases and unwanted pregnancy.[13]

The eventual outcomes of these practices are permanent injury, psychological trauma, social dislocation or death. Those who survive, grow up without the benefit of the fundamental rights to food, clothing, shelter, education, healthcare and a secure family background. Of the ones who are rescued or handed over, some may be reunited with their families, which can be problematic on both sides depending on the circumstances of their recruitment.[14] Others may be put into orphanages and refugee camps, which, as reports from across Africa have shown, are not necessarily places of safety. Many boys who learn a few marketable skills roam the streets looking for legal or illegal opportunities to gain an income. In the current upsurge in conflict in Liberia, many former child soldiers have been re-recruited to fight. Only 4,300 of Liberia's estimated 15,000 child soldiers have been demobilized. Scores of young ex-combatants are on the streets of Monrovia trying to eke out a living. Unless education and employment opportunities are provided that would discourage them from reverting to violence, such young ex-combatants remain vulnerable to rejoining the military either voluntarily or through coercion.

Existing tools for the prohibition of recruitment

If children are to be spared this fate they must be excluded from any form of combat participation, and an extensive repertoire of rules is already in place to achieve this aim. The sources for existing rules aimed at prohibiting the involvement of children in hostilities lie in humanitarian and human rights law.

The UN Convention on the Rights of the Child is an almost universally accepted human rights instrument, ratified to date by all but two states – the United States and Somalia. The purpose of the treaty is to secure special care and protection for children. Article 38(2) has a special provision on using children in armed conflict: "States parties shall take all feasible measures to ensure that persons who have not attained the age of fifteen years do not take a direct part in hostilities." The extensive ratification of the CRC means that using children under the age of 15 has become illegal almost everywhere.

The CRC generally defines a "child" as any human being below the age of 18 years. However, in situations of armed conflict the convention sets the lower age of 15 as the minimum age for recruitment and participation in armed conflict. The Optional Protocol to the Convention on the Rights of the Child on the involvement of children in armed conflict adopted unanimously by the UN General Assembly in May 2000 helped to correct this anomaly. Articles 2 and 3 of the Optional Protocol, which entered into force on 12 February 2002, establish that no person under the age of 18 shall be subject to conscription into the regular armed forces of states parties and impose an obligation on states to raise the minimum age for voluntary recruitment to at least 16 years. Moreover, Article 4(1) of the Optional Protocol addresses armed groups and the prohibition on their recruiting child soldiers: "Armed groups that are distinct from the armed forces of a State should not under any circumstances recruit or use in hostilities persons under the age of 18 years."

Article 3 of International Labour Organization (ILO) Convention No. 182 of June 1999 on the Prohibition and Immediate Action for the Elimination of the Worst Forms of Child Labour also forbids the forced or compulsory recruitment of children under 18 for use in armed conflict. The African Charter on the Rights and Welfare of the Child, which entered into force in November 1999, includes a similar provision. After emphasizing in Article 2 that "[f]or title purposes of this Charter a child means every human being below the age of eighteen years", the Charter in Article 22(2) obliges all states parties to "take all necessary measures to ensure that no child shall take a direct part in hostilities and refrain in particular from recruiting any child". The African Charter is the only regional instrument that specifically prohibits the recruitment and use of child combatants under 18 in both international and internal armed conflicts.

These recent developments follow the provisions on the use of children in armed conflict as set in the 1977 Additional Protocols I and II to the Geneva Conventions of 1949. Together they forbid the recruitment and participation of children under 15 in both international and internal conflicts. Both of the additional protocols emphasize the child's special right to care and protection. Additional Protocol II further forbids indirect participation, which encompasses such support activities as getting and transmitting information and performing service tasks such as cooking and cleaning. Recent evidence shows that children who start their military engagement via supporting activities usually end up being active combatants.[15]

The rehabilitation of child soldiers is a paramount concern of international law. Article 6(3) of the Optional Protocol to the CRC requires that:

States parties shall take all feasible measures to ensure that persons within their jurisdictions recruited or used in hostilities contrary to this Protocol are demobilized or otherwise released from service. States parties shall and when necessary accord to these persons all appropriate assistance for the physical and psychological recovery and social reintegration.

One obvious source of tension is that, whereas the use of child soldiers is illegal, countries that do use children as soldiers are required to reintegrate them into society after the conflict. In practice, groups that use child soldiers rarely do this.

The upholding and enforcement of the provisions of the CRC depend on the goodwill of the parties.[16] Compliance with the CRC is supervised by the Committee on the CRC, a body authorized to receive reports on measures that states parties have taken to implement the provisions of the convention. In case of a breach, it may do no more than issue observations and general recommendations. As such, it can offer no improvements to the notoriously weak enforcement procedures contained in the CRC, though there can be no doubt that the publicity surrounding the protocol has done much to heighten consciousness about the plight of child soldiers. Some authors, nevertheless, remain sceptical. Bennett, for example, suggests:

While the expectation seems to be that the protocol can be made to work in the same way as humanitarian treaties, the chance of this happening is remote ... [T]he reason why both governmental and non governmental entities obey the Geneva rules is due to a particular tradition and a unique enforcement machinery – notably the institution of an independent "protecting power," and, of course, the Red Cross.[17]

The difficulties of enforcing international human rights obligations demonstrate a major limitation in the international justice system as a whole: there is an absence of a central authority with the political power and legal authority to force offenders to submit to its jurisdiction. If states are not prepared to protect their nationals or to punish offenders, victims are helpless and wrongdoers escape prosecution.

The International Criminal Court and the recruitment of child soldiers

Geneva Convention IV did not stipulate a crime that would cover the recruitment of child soldiers. Protocol I did regulate the recruitment of children, but it was not mentioned as a grave breach. As a result, recruitment of child soldiers was not a criminal action attracting individual liability. The continuing jealous protection of state sovereignty has been the main stumbling block to punishing serious breaches of human rights and humanitarian law. Only when a permanent international tribunal acquires jurisdiction over offenders, regardless of where they happen to be living, will an international criminal justice system be realized.

The International Criminal Court has been established to bring this goal closer. The 1998 Rome Conference decided that a permanent court should be set up with the authority to exercise legal functions on the territory of any state party. The court's jurisdiction is over the most serious crimes of international concern, namely genocide, crimes against humanity and crimes against the laws and customs of war. People who commit these crimes will be held personally responsible and liable for punishment. Two offences in the statute are of particular significance to the discussion here: the tribunal's jurisdiction over war crimes including rape, sexual slavery and forced prostitution (Article 8(2)(b)(XII)); and conscripting or enlisting children under the age of 15 into the national armed forces or using them to participate actively in hostilities in situations of both international and internal armed conflicts (Article 8(2)(b) (XXVI)). In Article 68(2) the statute provides for the adoption of a special procedure for persons accused of and tried for committing crimes against children. The purpose, which is consonant with the CRC's insistence on a child's particular needs in the criminal justice system, is to protect child complainants from the trauma of being confronted with their assailants in open court.

The age limit has been the single most divisive issue in the many attempts to secure agreements on the substantive law.[18] Certain countries, notably the United Kingdom and the United States, have held out for a lower age in spite of the fact that a survey of more than 100 systems of municipal law indicated that more than two-thirds accepted 18 as the minimum age for compulsory recruitment.[19] Vacillating between the ages of 15 and 18 produces some glaring contradictions. Whereas 18 is in line with the generally accepted definition of childhood and is the age specified for the purposes of controlling child labour, a child may begin working in an army at 15. This type of contradiction is apparent within the ICC Statute itself. It sets a military recruitment age of 15, but in Article 26 bars the trial of persons below the age of 18.

Notwithstanding the strong arguments in favour of raising the age limit to 18, the most common offenders, non-governmental rebel groups, are recruiting children even younger than 15 for reasons outlined above. At another level, it must be appreciated that the conceptions of childhood and youth vary according to economy, polity and culture. Contemporary changes in the global economy on the family, local community and state level are being felt during childhood and youth. We need to move beyond seeing children as dependent consumers and start seeing them as contributors and active citizens whose situation may differ widely depending on age.

Conclusion

The developments described in this chapter have created an important international framework for the protection of children in armed conflict. However, a crucial part of the working of any law lies in its implementation. Prohibiting an activity (e.g. the military exploitation of children), which is a matter of substantive law, and ensuring that the prohibition is actually implemented, which is a matter of enforcement and procedure, pose two quite different problems.

Because of the limited enforcement procedures in human rights law, the best way to give effect to the prohibition is by initiating criminal prosecution against specific offenders. Securing the arrest of offenders is the final step. The purpose of the ICC is to bring present offenders to justice and to deter future offenders. The deterrent effect depends on arrest being a probability and not just a possibility. One has to acknowledge the difficulties inherent in obtaining arrests as well as the tendency of witnesses to melt away under class or ethnic pressures. These problems may be solved indirectly because, once the ICC is operating, the fear that it might supplant municipal procedures could spur states into taking independent action.[20]

Given the current military, demographic, economic and social background against which children are used in armed conflict, it is unlikely that the preventative effects of criminalizing the recruitment of children in armed conflict will be felt for some years. It is more likely that the immediate effect of the ICC will be retributive. The transformation of perceptions, norms and values is an uneven process in time and space. It is only relatively recently that the seriousness of using child combatants has been understood. In the 1977 Protocols to the Geneva Conventions, recruiting children was considered wrong but not a grave breach of humanitarian law attracting criminal liability.

The implications of child soldiers for long-term development are disastrous. In many countries, an entire generation has known nothing but conflict; war has been the single factor conditioning their political, economic, social and cultural lives. As a result, rehabilitation and reinsertion back into their communities, which themselves have been changed and reconfigured under the multiple impacts of conflict, poverty and disease, pose a number of serious difficulties. Next of kin have frequently been slain or have fled. In Sierra Leone, up to half the population are still either internally displaced or living as refugees in neighbouring countries. In some cases, households have refused to take children back because of the abuses they were forced to commit.[21] Children themselves are anxious about the availability of education and employment opportunities.[22]

Compared with the many deficiencies in the existing enforcement provisions within human rights and humanitarian law, the ICC offers a more effective means of realizing a prohibition on involving children in hostilities. Particular offenders can be held personally accountable for infractions of the rules; commanders of rebel groups cannot hide behind the technicality that they are not bound by international law, and criminals will no longer find it as easy to get shelter in sympathetic countries.

The ICC represents a major step towards real international accountability and a great advance in promoting the rule of law. Nevertheless, broader policy intervention tools to address the whole spectrum of factors that perpetuate conflicts must mirror this legal development. Ways have to be found to identify and change the behaviour of those individuals for whom war and plunder have become livelihood strategies, whether they are existing state élites and military establishments, new actors such as warlords, mercenaries, and arms and diamond merchants, or ordinary combatants, including child soldiers. Policy intervention could include creating tighter controls on the diamond and mineral trade, encouraging small arms moratoriums, rebuilding police and law and order systems, resettling former combatants, and, over the long run, providing the education and employment opportunities that would discourage young people from reverting to violence. Although identifying the use of children as active participants in war to be a violation of international legal standards is extremely significant, a deeper understanding of the modalities of contemporary conflict, the processes of impoverishment and the complex ways in which children enter social space is required if we are to eradicate this problem.

Notes

1. "Kalashnikov Kids", *The Economist*, 10 July 1999, pp. 47–49, at p. 47.
2. G. Machel, *The Impact of Armed Conflict on Children*, Document A/51/306, New York: UN Department of Information, 1996, p. ii.

3. M. Ignatieff, *The Warrior's Honor: Ethnic War and the Modern Conscience*, London: Vintage, 1999, p. 128.
4. Human Rights Watch, *Conspicuous Destruction – War, Famine and the Reform Process in Mozambique*, New York: Human Rights Watch, 1992, p. 27.
5. J. C. Andvig, *An Essay on Child Labor in Sub Saharan Africa*, Working Paper No. 613, Norwegian Institute of International Affairs, 2000, p. 42.
6. "Kalashnikov Kids", p. 48.
7. Krijn Peters and Paul Richards, "Fighting with Open Eyes: Youth Combatants Talking about War in Sierra Leone", in Celia Petty and Patrick Bracken, eds., *Rethinking the Trauma of War*, London and New York: Free Association Books and Save the Children, 1998, pp. 76–111, at p. 76ff.
8. World Bank, *Status Report on Poverty in Sub Saharan Africa*, Washington D.C.: World Bank, 1997, p. 25.
9. Carolyn Harper and Rachel Marcus, *Child Poverty in Sub-Saharan Africa*, Save the Children Fund, UK, Background Paper to the 1999 World Bank Africa Poverty Status Report, p. 24.
10. Ibid, p. 15.
11. See International Labour Organization, *The Reintegration of Young Ex-Combatants into Civilian Life*, Expert Meeting on the Design of Guidelines for Training and Employment of Ex-Combatants, Africa Region, Geneva: ILO, 1995.
12. Human Rights Watch, *Easy Prey: Child Soldiers in Liberia*, New York: Human Rights Watch, 1994, p. 27.
13. Amnesty International, *Sierra Leone: Rape and Other Forms of Sexual Violence against Girls and Women*, AI Index: AFR 51/35/00, 2000.
14. Amnesty International, *Sierra Leone: Childhood: A Casualty of Conflict*, AI Index: AFR 51/069/2000, 2000, p. 8.
15. R. Brett and M. McCallin, *Children: The Invisible Soldiers*, Stockholm: Radda Barnen, 1998, pp. 126–127.
16. See Jenny Kuper, *International Law Concerning Child Civilians in Armed Conflict*, Oxford: Clarendon Press, 1997.
17. T. W. Bennett, *Using Children in Armed Conflict: A Legitimate African Tradition? Criminalising the Recruitment of Child Soldiers*, Institute for Security Studies Monograph No. 32, Pretoria: ISS, 1998, p. 9.
18. Ibid., p. 17.
19. G. S. Goodwin-Gill and I. Cohn, *Child Soldiers: The Role of Children in Armed Conflict*, New York: Oxford University Press, 1994, pp. 53–75.
20. Bennett, *Using Children in Armed Conflict*, p. 19.
21. See Susan Litherand, *Children: Doubtful Value of Counseling for Child Victims of War*, Inter Press Service, 25 February 1998; Human Rights Watch, *Easy Prey*.
22. Save the Children, UK, Workshop on Family Reunification, Monrovia, Liberia, 6–8 August 2001.

15

The International Criminal Court: Obstacle or contribution to an effective system of human rights protection?

Cees Flinterman

Introduction

This chapter will address the establishment of the International Criminal Court (ICC) from a human rights perspective. After a general view on the present system of human rights protection, attention will be drawn to the likely role of the ICC as an instrument to seek the punishment of the perpetrators of human rights abuses. There are, however, also some concerns regarding the potential influence of the ICC on the international struggle for human rights protection. The conclusions will reflect the view that the ICC may provide a substantial contribution towards an effective system of human rights protection if it does not have a negative impact on the imperative need further to consolidate, strengthen and expand the existing, still fragile, international mechanisms of protection of human rights.

Historical background

The system of international human rights protection is a post-1945 phenomenon. The promotion and protection of human rights were among the main purposes of the international community after World War II. It was, therefore, not surprising that the UN Charter imposed upon the United Nations and its member states the legal obligation to promote respect for human rights and fundamental freedoms. Over the years, a well-defined normative and supervisory system was developed. This system consists at present of a large number and variety of binding and non-binding regional and international standard-setting instruments; supervision of the implementation of these substantive norms has been entrusted to bodies based on the UN Charter and UN treaties, as well as to a substantial number of regional arrangements.

The efforts of the international community in promoting and protecting human rights have been concentrated in three areas: standard-setting, promotional activities, and monitoring and enforcement. Whereas in the first decades after World War II the international community was mainly engaged in standard-setting, at present most emphasis is given to the implementation and enforcement of normative human rights standards. In this respect, all United Nations treaty bodies provide for a reporting system aiming to assess the progress made by states in implementing their treaty obligations. On the other hand, the United Nations Commission on Human Rights (UNCHR), the most important Charter-based human rights (political) body, is empowered to consider human rights violations around the world; country and thematic special rapporteurs are playing an increasingly important role.

Despite a general willingness of states to promote and protect human rights, governments still fall short in respecting them as much in practice as they do in law. Moreover, on many occasions the international community has been confronted with grave and systematic human rights violations in various parts of the world, such as Tibet, Pakistan, Cambodia, Bosnia, Rwanda and Kosovo. One of the reasons for this is the culture of impunity, which has prevailed for a long time. As stated in different UNCHR resolutions: "the practice of impunity for the perpetrators of violations of human rights in various regions of the world is a fundamental obstacle to the observance of human rights."[1]

The first steps in the development of legal means to combat impunity were undertaken by the victims of human rights abuses themselves. In 1992, the Inter-American Commission was confronted with the question of whether a national law that put an end to the possibility of prosecuting the perpetrators of human rights abuses violated the American Convention on Human Rights. The Commission answered in the affirmative, referring to Article 8(1) of the Convention.[2] In the same year, the Sub-Commission on Prevention of Discrimination and Protection of Minorities decided to request El Hadji Guisse and Louis Joinet to "draft a study on the impunity of perpetrators of violations of human rights" and "to propose measures to combat that practice".[3] The report presented identified the many facets of organized impunity and sought strategies against impunity.[4] Since then, the United Nations, representing the international community, has steadily strengthened its role in the struggle against impunity for gross violations of human rights.

International criminal courts as an effective instrument in promoting international respect for human rights

Substantial progress in the struggle against impunity was achieved by the establishment of the two ad hoc International Criminal Tribunals for the former Yugoslavia and Rwanda in the early 1990s after the unfolding grave human rights tragedies in those countries. Bearing in mind that there is no peace without justice, the tribunals' case law has since demonstrated that justice can be achieved through the application of international law. Moreover, the case law has further elaborated and clarified the relevance of international law on individual accountability for grave human rights abuses.

However, both tribunals have limited jurisdiction. They are authorized to address only crimes committed within certain territories and during specific periods. They will cease to function when the trials and appeals of all those indicted have run their course and those who have been found guilty have been incarcerated.

In this respect, it is important to note that the establishment of the permanent ICC may diminish or altogether do away with the need for the establishment of other ad hoc tribunals, providing therefore, in principle, a more effective system of international justice. Drexel Sprecher, referring to the crime of genocide, stated: "had we a permanent criminal tribunal ready to go with trained people, of high stature, we'd have been a lot further down the road to minimizing genocide as a state policy than we are today."[5]

It is hoped that the existence of the permanent International Criminal Court tribunal will end forever the culture of impunity, thereby deterring the commission of gross human rights violations in the future. By providing justice, the ICC will ease the way to peace in countries that have experienced grave human rights violations. Moreover, a trial before the ICC will bring *in concreto* acknowledgement of the victims, assignment of specific, individual accountability – thereby avoiding collective guilt – and an accurate historical record of the nature of and responsibility for the crimes committed.

In all these aspects, the contribution of the ICC to the protection of human rights will, of course, be most welcome. However, its establishment will not provide a definitive solution to the international struggle against human rights abuses. The ICC may even create problems for and obstacles to the efficiency of the existing system of international human rights protection. I consider a number of these concerns in the next section.

Concerns

First of all, the Rome Statute by which the ICC is created is not based on the concept of universal jurisdiction. Besides cases referred by the Security Council,[6] the ICC may, in general, exercise its jurisdiction only if one or more of the following states are parties to the statute or have accepted the jurisdiction of the court:[7]
a) The State on the territory of which the crime occurred;
b) The State of which the person accused of a crime is a national.
Considering this limited jurisdiction of the court, as well as the fact that a number of countries, including some militarily and otherwise powerful states, are unlikely to ratify the Rome Statute in the foreseeable future, the persecution of perpetrators of gross human rights abuses will remain in most of the cases a matter of national law. Moreover, by not imposing an obligation on states to establish universal jurisdiction for the crimes under the statute, the Rome Statute unfortunately supports the traditional and inefficient "no link theory" that is so often adopted by national states.

It is true that some grave human rights abuses already involve universal jurisdiction as a result of customary or treaty law. However, the situation is not very clear with regard to certain war crimes mentioned in the statute that were not until recently considered to be crimes of individual responsibility. The same problem may in due time arise with regard to the crime of aggression, since some states take the view that this crime has not been defined under customary law for the purpose of individual criminal responsibility.

In these circumstances, by not explicitly recognizing the extension of the principle of universal jurisdiction to the gravest and most serious human rights abuses, the Rome Statute may discourage national states from exercising universal jurisdiction. The role of the ICC in bringing a real end to the culture of impunity is therefore in doubt.

A second concern relates to the scale of protection of individual human rights, although it goes without saying that the Rome Statute in general provides for substantial rights for the victims of the acts committed as well as for those who are investigated and prosecuted. However, the Rome Statute does not provide the defence with adequate authority to investigate the facts of the case in the territory of the state concerned. Nor does it explicitly recognize a right to proper funding of the investigation undertaken by the defence if the defendant cannot afford the costs him- or herself.[8]

With regard to the victims, the statute recognizes the authority of the ICC to award reparations to, or in respect of, the victims, consisting in restitution, compensation and rehabilitation.[9] Nevertheless, the ICC will not be empowered to order states to make reparations to the victims.[10]

Further, a number of issues related to the rights of the accused and of the victims are to be established by the states parties to the ICC. The establishment of the immunities and privileges of the defence counsel[11] and the determination of how the Trust Fund assisting the victims will be managed[12] fall into this category. It remains to be seen how these individual human rights will be further elaborated, in particular in the Rules of Procedure and Evidence of the court. Moreover, rules are much easier to adopt than to implement. In this aspect, the case law of the International Criminal Tribunals for the former Yugoslavia and Rwanda regarding the protection of individual human rights may constitute a model to be followed by the ICC.

A third concern is that, as a new mechanism, the success of the ICC requires the *de facto* cooperation of national states, as well as effective coordination between the ICC and other human rights organs and institutions. In this respect, it is to be regretted that the drafting process of the Rome Statute, which raised different issues related to human rights treaties, took place without relevant input from the UN treaty bodies.[13] Active interaction between the ICC and other human rights institutions is of great importance.

The ICC could learn a lot from the history of the evolution of the jurisprudence of the European Court of Human Rights and the Inter-American Court of Human Rights. Furthermore, the interpretation by UN human rights bodies of different human rights provisions relevant to the work of the ICC ought to be taken note of and respected by the ICC. Reference can be made here to, *inter alia*, the right to life and the prohibition of torture and other cruel, inhuman and degrading treatment or punishment.

Moreover, the reports and recommendations of the several UN human rights bodies on human rights situations may serve as evidence both to initiate the conduct of investigations and to be presented to the court. If the ICC judgments do not seriously take into account the views, observations or judgments adopted by other judicial, quasi-judicial and political human rights organs or do not reflect continuity and consistency in the approach to violations of human rights and fundamental freedoms, the whole idea of an international system of human rights protection will be threatened.

A fourth concern is related to the high economic costs of the ICC. Running an independent and efficient prosecutorial office, engaged in high-profile cases all over the world, is likely to be very expensive. Funds are needed for the registry and also for the maintenance of adequate prison arrangements. Moreover, in order to guarantee judges' immunity from political pressure, substantial salaries ought to be paid. Respect for the rights of victims and for those of the accused is also very likely to require extensive funding.

According to the Rome Statute, the ICC will be funded from assessed contributions made by states parties and funds provided by the United Nations, subject to the approval of the General Assembly, in particular in relation to the expenses incurred as a result of referrals by the Security Council. States parties' contributions will be in accordance with an agreed scale of assessment based on a scale adopted by the United Nations for its regular budget and adjusted in accordance with the principles on which that scale is based. Ultimately, the willingness of the international community will be decisive. If the international community is not willing to pay the high costs, the success of the court will be jeopardized.

On the other hand, the economic resources of the international community should not be focused solely on the ICC. The ICC represents only an additional, albeit highly important, strategy to deal with human rights abuses. The effective functioning of the present human rights system will remain of vital importance. In this respect, it is important to realize that, at present, the most serious problems the human rights system is facing are related to the fact that the system has insufficient financial resources to carry out its functions. As a result, human rights bodies are very often confronted with far-reaching restrictions on interpretation, staff reassignment, delays in the translation of reports, as well as delays in the preparation of summary records and recommendations.[14] The existing human rights instruments are, therefore, in need of significant additional financial support. However, it is clear that the political will to provide this additional financial support will not be readily forthcoming. Against this background there is a clear threat that the establishment of the ICC will further aggravate the financial situation of the present system.

The ICC could also form an obstacle to the further development of institutional arrangements in the field of human rights. One very desirable future development would be to implement the idea of establishing a United Nations Human Rights Court. Two regional human rights courts already exist and a third is in the process of being established in Africa. However, the human rights provisions in the United Nations Charter refer to universal standards. Such universality of human rights would be best supported by a United Nations Human Rights Court entrusted with the interpretation and application of universal human rights law; such a court would increase the effectiveness of the international and regional systems of human rights protection.

Of course, the establishment of such a court would raise a large number of different problems, including problems of an economic nature like those considered above. Even the idea of the establishment of a United Nations Human Rights Court with limited jurisdiction would be strongly opposed by many states, in particular at the beginning. Therefore, as Buergenthal has stated, "the sooner the subject is discussed, the sooner a court will be created".[15] In this respect the experience gained by the establishment of the ICC could help the international community in establishing a United Nations Human Rights Court.

Concluding observations

There is no doubt that the ICC can and should be seen as a major step forwards in establishing an effective international system to protect human rights. The ICC will fulfil a number of functions in preventing and suppressing grave human rights abuses. At the same time, it is clear that the contribution of the ICC to human rights protection will be limited because of its restricted, complementary jurisdiction. The establishment of the ICC should, therefore, not draw the attention of the world community away from the imperative need to consolidate, strengthen and further elaborate the existing mechanisms of regional and international protection of human rights. The old saying, and perhaps truism, that an ounce of prevention (in the field of human rights) is worth more than a pound of cure should always be borne in mind. The ultimate aim of the international community should be to make the ICC superfluous in due course by creating a situation in which human rights violations, if and wherever they take place, are investigated, prosecuted and adjudicated by independent national authorities.

Notes

1. See, *inter alia*, Commission on Human Rights, *The Administration of Justice and the Human Rights of Detainees: Question of Human Rights and States of Emergency. Fifth Annual Report and List of States Which, since 1 January 1985, Have Proclaimed, Extended or Terminated a State of Emergency, Presented by Mr. Leandro Despouy, Special Rapporteur Appointed Pursuant to Economic and Social Council Resolution 1985/37*, UN Doc. E/CN.4/Sub.2/1992/23, 29 June 1993; *Question of the Violation of Human Rights and Fundamental Freedoms, Including Policies of Racial Discrimination and Segregation and of Apartheid, in All Countries, with Particular Reference to Colonial and Other Dependent Countries and Territories: Report of the Sub-Commission under Com-*

mission on Human Rights Resolution 8 (XXIII), letter dated 26 July 1993 addressed to the Centre for Human Rights by the Permanent Representative of Peru to the United Nations office at Geneva, UN Doc. E/CN.4/Sub.2/1993/37, 3 August 1993; *Question of the Violation of Human Rights and Fundamental Freedoms in Any Part of the World, with Particular Reference to Colonial and Other Dependent Countries and Territories. Situation of Human Rights in Albania. Report of the Secretary-General Submitted Pursuant to Commission on Human Rights Resolution 1992/69*, UN Doc. E/CN.4/1993/43, 16 February 1993.

2. See the *Case of Uruguay*, IACHR Rep. No. 29/92, approved on 2 October 1992, and the *Case of Argentina*, IACHR Rep. No. 28/92, approved on 2 October 1992.

3. UN Doc. E/CN.4/Sub.2/1992/23, 29 June 1993.

4. *The Administration of Justice and the Human Rights of Detainees: The Question of Human Rights of Persons Subjected to Any Form of Detention or Imprisonment. Progress Report on the Question of the Impunity of Perpetrators of Human Rights Violations, Prepared by Mr. Guisse and Mr. Joinet, Pursuant to Sub-Commission Resolution 1992/23*, UN Doc. E/CN.4/Sub.2/1993/6, 19 July 1993.

5. Interview with Nuremberg Trial Prosecutor Drexel Sprecher, December 1995; at www.courttv.nuremberg.com.

6. *Statute of the International Criminal Court* (hereafter *Rome Statute*), UN Doc. A/CONF.183/9, 37 *International Legal Materials* 1998, Art. 14.

7. Ibid., Art. 12.

8. Kenneth S. Gallant, "The Role and Powers of Defense Council in the Rome Statute of the International Criminal Court", *International Lawyer*, vol. 34, no. 1, 2000.

9. *Rome Statute*, Art. 75.

10. See the proposal by the United Kingdom and Northern Ireland with regard to Article 66 (45 *bis*) and Compensation to Victims, UN Doc. A/Ac. 249/1998/WG.4 DP.19, 1998.

11. See the final Act of the UN Diplomatic Conference of Plenipotentiaries on the Establishment of an ICC, Annex I, Res F., secs. 5(f)9.

12. *Rome Statute*, Art. 79.

13. See *Effective Functioning of Bodies Established Pursuant to United Nations Human Rights Instruments. Note by the Secretary-General, Annex: Final Report on Enhancing the Long-Term Effectiveness of the UN Human Rights Treaty System*, UN Doc. E/CN.4/1997/74, 27 March 1996.

14. See *Report of the Human Rights Committee, Volume I, General Assembly Official Records – Fifty-Third Session*, Supplement No. 40 (A/53/40), New York: United Nations, 1998; and *Report of the Human Rights Committee, Volume I, General Assembly Official Records – Fifty-Fourth Session*, Supplement No. 40 (A/54/40), New York: United Nations, 1999.

15. Thomas Buergenthal, "A Court and Two Consolidated Treaty Bodies", in Anne F. Bayefsky, ed., *The UN Human Rights Treaty System in the 21st Century*, The Hague: Kluwer, 2000, p. 301.

16

Dealing with guilt beyond crime: The strained quality of universal justice

Ramesh Thakur

In these days of post-Enlightenment Europe, we tend to forget that the phrase "crimes against humanity" was coined by the African-American George Washington Williams to describe Belgian atrocities against the natives of Congo in the last two decades of the nineteenth century. Similarly, "genocide" (the crime of crimes: the destruction of a nation or of an ethnic group) was coined by the Jewish-American Raphael Lemkin in 1944 to describe Nazi German atrocities against the Jews in the first half of the twentieth century. Writing in 1946 to her former professor Karl Jaspers of Heidelberg University, who had remained there throughout World War II, Hannah Arendt questioned how one could comprehend what the Nazis had done within the existing compass of criminal law. "The Nazi crimes ... explode the limits of the law; and that is precisely what constitutes their monstrousness," she wrote. "We are simply not equipped to deal on a human, political level, with a guilt that is beyond crime and an innocence that is beyond goodness or virtue."[1] Objecting that such a moral vocabulary would endow Nazi crimes with "satanic greatness", Jaspers insisted on seeing them instead "in their total banality"[2] – a phrase that Arendt famously used in the subtitle of her book published almost two decades later.[3]

How can we reduce the magnitude of the crimes of genocide and crimes against humanity to accommodate them within the lens of present-day international criminal law? As Kingsley Moghalu notes in Chapter 11 of this volume, international criminal justice follows diplomacy and force as the third organizing principle of international action by states in the contemporary world. This project was conceived in terms of international criminal justice lying at the interface of law and politics. The theme of the project thus was the dynamic interaction between law and politics in the search for universal justice. As Paul Lauren points out in Chapter 1 of this volume, that search is rooted in the growing recognition that perpetrators and victims alike are real and identifiable individuals, not just abstract entities. No one with a commitment to order in and through justice can be happy in the knowledge that scores of murderer-leaders roam free, or are provided with generous hospitality by foreign governments more forgiving than their own people, or are even still in power. The roster of rogue leaders is surely larger than that of rogue states. But justice is not an absolute goal that trumps every other goal. Politics in the broadest sense, and in the good sense of the concept, must sometimes override or at least temper justice, as with the case of pardoning former presidents for minor transgressions in the interests of state.

The way to apprehend and punish the perpetrators of conscience-shocking crimes on a mass scale is through an international legal framework that establishes the notion of "universal jurisdiction", where jurisdiction in respect of such crimes depends not on the place where they are committed but on the nature of the crime itself. If they are truly "crimes against humanity", they can properly be prosecuted before the courts of any country. The Geneva Conventions of 1949 established a new category of war crimes called "grave breaches", which could be prosecuted in the courts of all countries that have ratified the Conventions. The arrest and transfer of former Serbian strongman Slobodan Milosevic to the International Criminal Tribunal for the former Yugoslavia (ICTY) at The Hague were but the latest of several dramatic twists and turns in the past few years in the search for universal justice. Just as the indictment issued against him during the NATO war in Kosovo in 1999 was described as an electrifying moment, so his passage to The Hague in 2001 was hailed as a defining moment in international justice. The "internationalization of the human conscience"[4] has thus been followed by "substantial advances in the internationalization of criminal law in the area of war crimes", as Justice Richard Goldstone puts it in his "Foreword" to this volume.

Part of the Nuremberg legacy, as Andrew Clapham reminds us in Chapter 13, is that the process of internationalizing criminal law was extended to accept the notion that a private corporation can commit war crimes, and its directors can be held criminally liable.[5] Thus international criminal law has gradually eroded corporate as well as state impunity. Moreover, as noted by Christine Chinkin in Chapter 6, "a striking example of the move from impunity to accountability under international criminal law" is the set of developments that have taken place with regard to gender-related crimes. As Moghalu recounts in Chapter 11, the International Criminal Tribunal for Rwanda (ICTR) has been instrumental in defining rape as a crime under international law and in advancing international humanitarian law by ruling that rape can be a genocidal crime if committed with the intent to destroy a group in whole or in part.[6]

Activists assert the primacy of justice without borders; sceptics warn of international anarchy if we depart from realpolitik in a state-based system of world order; opponents fear outcomes of injustice across borders. State sovereignty, any more than the UN Charter, was never meant to be a tyrant's charter of impunity or the constitutional instrument of choice for self-protection. More worrisome than the challenge to national sovereignty posed by international judicial accountability is the unpredictability of the potent new weapon as an instrument of the new international order. Its potential for abuse for mischievous, vexatious and vindictive purposes – selective justice, if not self-destructive injustice – is unlimited, unless codified in permanent and universal institutions, and perhaps even then if US fears about the International Criminal Court (ICC) are justified. After the Iraq war in 2003, British Prime Minister Tony Blair and some of his cabinet colleagues (such as the defence and foreign ministers) were accused of crimes against humanity by Greek lawyers who lodged a case with the ICC on 28 July 2003.[7] The doctrine of universal jurisdiction was employed also to threaten prosecution against President George W. Bush and General Tommy Franks (commander of the US forces in Iraq).[8] Defense Secretary Donald Rumsfeld retaliated by warning that if US officials could no longer travel to Brussels without fear of prosecution, then the NATO headquarters would clearly have to be relocated to another country.[9] In July 2003, Belgium finally amended its controversial law on universal jurisdiction and restricted trials in Belgian courts to crimes committed or suffered by its citizens or residents.

As we move inexorably from the restrictive culture of sovereign impunity of previous centuries to an enlightened culture of international accountability more suited to the modern sensibility,[10] it is worth making five arguments about the relationship between justice being done (the domain of law) and justice being seen to have been done (the realm of politics):[11]

1) Justice can be seen not to have been done.
2) Justice may not be seen to have been done.
3) It will be difficult for justice to be seen to be done with regard to the Milosevic trial at the ICTY at The Hague.
4) Justice most likely will be done in the Milosevic case at The Hague.
5) In some cases justice may not be done despite being seen to have been done.

The five propositions permit us to frame the arguments and themes canvassed by the various distinguished authors in this volume. Of course, the ideal outcome would be for justice to be done and to be seen to have been done. But here again we must recall the caution about the importance of justice being seen to have been done, not just by the élite in the industrial countries but also by the forgotten half of the world's population, namely the people of the world in general, and the women of the world in particular. In addition, as will be discussed in the final substantive section of this chapter, there can be some tension between the goals of peace and reconciliation through restorative justice and of peace and progress through retributive justice.

Justice is seen not to have been done

First, in East Timor *justice was seen not to have been done* when six men convicted of killing three UN aid workers (an American, a Croat and an Ethiopian) were given sentences of 10 to 20 months by a Jakarta court on 4 May 2001. In one of the worst attacks ever against UN staff anywhere in the world, the UN personnel were stabbed and stoned to death and their bodies were set alight by pro-Indonesian militias. The sentences were so manifestly inadequate to the gravity of the crimes that they were tantamount to a very public slap in the face of the international community. The injustice should not have been permitted to stand.

In some respects this recalls the argument between the Americans and the British, to which Andrew Clapham draws our attention in Chapter 13, over which should be privileged – "senile dementia" or "public interest". When the elder member of the Krupp family was deemed to be unfit for trial at Nuremberg owing to senile dementia, the Americans wanted to substitute the son (over British objection). Their argument was that the Krupp family had owned and operated the armaments and munitions plants for four generations over 130 years during which the family was "the focus, the symbol, and the beneficiary" of those operations. Public interest would not be served by dropping the father without substituting the son's name, for then justice would be seen not to have been done. It is ironic, therefore, that justice was also seen not to have been done with respect to the US officers convicted of the My Lai massacre in Viet Nam.[12]

Justice is not seen to have been done

Second, with regard to former Presidents Mohamad Suharto of Indonesia and Augusto Pinochet of Chile, as well as others around the world (Idi

Amin in Uganda, the Khmer Rouge in Cambodia, Saddam Hussein in Iraq), *justice has not been seen to be done*, at least not yet.[13] Tyrants and dictators need to be called to account for their past misdeeds. If the judicial route is taken, they must be subjected to free and fair trials, preferably in their own countries. In the end, the decision on whether to try them or go down the route of truth and reconciliation commissions has to be made by the people and the countries concerned, not by outsiders.

Europeans in particular need to avoid the temptation of launching a fresh wave of judicial colonialism (or what David Forsythe, in a related vein, calls "judicial romanticism"[14]), substituting their courts and morality for the choices made by the affected societies. It is patently absurd for Israeli President Ariel Sharon, or any other former head of government or state (or former secretaries of state such as Henry Kissinger[15]), to have to risk being arrested in a third country for past actions in their own or in a second country, on the orders of an investigating magistrate in a fourth country (such as Belgium or Spain), following the precedent of the Spanish Inquisition against Pinochet while he was visiting Britain. Only the previously traumatized and war-torn societies can make the delicate decisions and painful choices between justice for past misdeeds, political order and stability today, and reconciliation for a common future tomorrow.

Another unsettled question in this respect is how far back in history do we wish to go? Japan's neighbours remain unsatisfied – not dissatisfied, but unsatisfied – with the official policy on the question of comfort women during World War II. Christine Chinkin, having been one of the judges in the mock war crimes trial on the subject in Tokyo recently, knows this only too well in full painful detail.[16] Australia's aboriginal population was subjected to genocidal practices (in terms of the official definition in the Genocide Convention) during living memory, but the present government refuses to apologise or consider paying reparations.[17] Some of the most divisive and heated squabbles at the Durban conference on racism in 2001 occurred over the question of apologies and reparations for colonialism and slavery. And what of the establishment of the state of Israel on a pre-existing Palestinian population – was Palestinian nationhood confiscated and expropriated in order to assuage Christendom's guilt over the Holocaust and, if so, how can it be reversed without creating a permanent cycle of injustice between communities and across generations?

Perceptions of the Milosevic trial as being problematic

Third, it will be *difficult for justice to be seen to be done in the case of Milosevic* at The Hague tribunal. As the first international trial of a former head of state, this would have been challenging enough in any case. Especially after the Dayton Accords of 1995, Hjalmar Schacht's question is pertinent to the Serbs as well: "How were the German people supposed to realize that they were living under a criminal government when foreign countries treated this same government with such marked respect?"[18] If indeed a leader is deemed criminal only with convenient hindsight, what is the element of complicity of foreign governments that engaged in full diplomatic intercourse with that leader? Leaving aside the question of legitimacy divorced from law, NATO's unlawful war against Serbia in 1999 has made the Milosevic trial deeply problematic,[19] for a familiar litany of reasons: the tribunal is sited in a NATO country, it was set up by a Security Council in which NATO countries are disproportionately dominant, its expenses are met mainly from NATO members' contributions, the indictment of Milosevic during the war on the basis of evidence supplied by NATO – even the timing of releasing the evidence was deliberate, not coincidental – infected the process of criminal justice with security-political calculations, and the enforcement of the tribunal's indictment of Milosevic and cronies as war criminals has been totally dependent on the same NATO powers. The problem of perception was compounded by the refusal of the Chief Prosecutor to investigate alleged NATO crimes with equal vigour. Forsythe informs us in Chapter 3 that even some former judges of the ICTY believe that this was a mistake. These elements of structural coercion, based on influence asymmetries and power imbalances, do not entirely negate justice outcomes, but may serve to undermine the perception thereof.

The International Criminal Court (ICC)

President Martti Ahtisaari notes in the Preface to this volume that the ICC will help to attenuate perceptions of one justice for Europe and another for the rest of the world. The ICC received its sixtieth ratification in April 2002 and came into force in July that year in accordance with Article 126 of its statute. The US rejection of the ICC seriously compromises American moral standing with respect to ad hoc international criminal tribunals,[20] even if it is in keeping with the shallow moralism and profound hypocrisy of the United States with respect to dealing with the My Lai massacre in Viet Nam. The ICC's attraction is that its scope is global, giving it the authority to investigate heinous international crimes wherever, whenever and by whomever they are committed. Only universal liability can arrest and reverse the "drift to universalism"[21] from the Nuremberg and Tokyo tribunals to the Yugoslavia and Rwanda tribunals, along with such other way-stations as the detention (albeit temporary) of Pinochet in Britain.

All of these are not merely ad hoc; they also suffer from particularism.

Permanent status and institutionalized identity attenuate perceptions of politically motivated investigations and selective justice. Permanence also helps to cumulate and build on precedents. The ICC will be an efficient and cost-effective alternative to ad hoc tribunals with respect to money, time and energy, and may also provide sensible alternatives to dubious sanctions and unilateral military retaliation. Madeline Morris surely has a valid point in arguing in Chapter 10 that the ICC, "insofar as it provides for jurisdiction over non-party nationals, displaces the state as the conduit of democratic representation and provides no alternative mechanism for democratic governance". The ICC is not embedded in a broader system of democratic policy-making; there is no political check on the ICC; and therefore it should not have the authority to overturn policy established by national democracies. But, however we define it and whatever criterion we use to measure it, the democratic deficit of the ad hoc international criminal tribunals, set up by the UN Security Council with enthusiastic US support, is just as surely greater than that of the ICC.

Subjecting prosecutorial investigations and indictments to UN Security Council authorization, one of the key US demands, would have politicized the process and tainted its impartial credibility from the very start: it would have been born in sin. The five permanent members (P5) would be able to veto any action against themselves while pressing charges against all others. The international community has been concerned for some time to limit the scope of the P5 privileges, not to extend the veto's application still more. The notion that US personnel should enjoy blanket exemption from any possible investigation is such an egregious example of double standards, of exceptionalism rooted in the self-definition of the United States as the virtuous power that cannot be held to account to standards that must nevertheless apply to everyone else, that it was never taken seriously even as a negotiating ploy.[22] There are real safeguards for all countries against whimsical and idiosyncratic abuse of the ICC procedures. The ICC is being set up as a court of last resort, complementary to national courts that are unable or unwilling to dispense justice. The Prosecutor will be accountable to a panel of judges exercising due oversight. The World Court's experience with respect to the election of international judges is essentially a positive story.

Given these advantages, was the US rejection of the ICC rooted in anything more substantial than a spasmodic fit of chauvinism or petulance? There are in fact two other respects in which the US fears may be well founded: the rule-of-law standards and the integration of criminal justice within an overarching framework of governance.

First, for justice to be done, it is not enough that the accused actually have done the crimes for which they are charged. It is just as important to ensure that the rule-of-law standard is scrupulously observed with regard to the collection and presentation of evidence, the right to cross-examination of witnesses, and all the other procedures that we associate with a fair trial. As Ahtisaari reminds us in the Preface, a necessary condition of a fair trial is the possibility of a verdict of innocence. It cannot be the case that "the person will be hanged, but only after a fair trial", for that is the standard of show trials. For the trial to be authentic, the possibility of acquittal must be as much an inbuilt requirement as the possibility of conviction.

The US criminal justice system goes about the farthest in the world in protecting the rights of the arrested and accused. International criminal law, by contrast, has shifted the focus from the defence to the prosecution, for example with respect to the right of the accused to confront the accuser versus the anonymity of witnesses in order to protect them from harm and to reduce their sense of humiliation when confronting perpetrators of sexual violence crimes. As William Schabas notes in Chapter 8: "Establishing an appropriate balance in both the procedural and substantive rules of criminal law that recognizes the rights of the defence and yet does not impose insurmountable obstacles to the prosecution is a considerable challenge." In the past, and in the US legal–constitutional culture in particular, human rights law gave primacy to protecting the rights of the accused, without real regard to guilt or innocence. Impelled by the momentum of international accountability, the balance has shifted in favour of the victim and in favour of conviction. Certainly the conviction rates of the international criminal tribunals have been notably higher than for criminal prosecutions in the established Western democracies. Washington has itself been complicit in this transformation from protecting the rights of the accused to privileging the case for the prosecution, for example in insisting that Milosevic be handed over to the ICTY in The Hague, regardless of Serbian legal niceties, or else.

The ICC came into effect in July 2002,[23] and on 22 April 2003 Luis Moreno Ocampo of Argentina, who helped to put his country's former military rulers on trial, was elected as its first Prosecutor. Washington heaped insult on injury when it vetoed a routine extension of the United Nations' peacekeeping mission in Bosnia in the same month because of the failure to get a blanket and permanent immunity from prosecution of its peacekeepers by the ICC. Stung by the fierce criticism from even its diehard European friends and allies, the United States softened its position slightly, and won a renewable 12-month exemption for the peacekeepers of all countries that had not ratified the ICC Statute. Remarkably, the vote in the Security Council on this was unanimous in 2002 (although not in 2003, when even Kofi Annan warned that, if exemption became an annual routine, the Security Council would undermine its own authority as well as that of the ICC[24]) – when the rest of the world seemed to be as appalled as they were strongly opposed. The Canadians in particular argued that the outcome was a sad day for the United Nations: damage was done not just to the integrity of the court, but also to the integrity of treaty negotiations and the credibility of the Security Council itself. Lloyd Axworthy, who as Canada's foreign minister had been a powerful voice in the campaign to establish the ICC, cautioned that "the compromise acquiesces to the Security Council's questionable right to amend by interpretation a treaty arrived at in open discussion by representatives of more than 100 nation states in a founding convention".[25]

Could it be that fears of politically motivated prosecution of Americans – a stated reason for staying outside the ICC – are derived from experience of selective (and highly expensive) prosecutions of demonized adversaries and enemies through political organs such as the Security Council? International economic blackmail – financially on its knees, Yugoslavia was promised almost US$1.3 billion in aid immediately after Milosevic was turned over to The Hague – and domestic power struggles have been greater determinants of the fate of Milosevic than concerns about criminal justice.

The failure to prosecute with matching zeal mass crimes committed against Serbs by their historical Balkan enemies, including acts of reverse ethnic cleansing by Kosovars since the 1999 war under the protective noses of NATO troops, feeds the sense of victimhood among Serbs: if Milosevic, why not Franjo Tudjman? What was most needed instead was an open trial within Serbia that brought home to the Serbs, beyond any reasonable doubt, the crimes that were committed in their name. They are the ones who need to confront the recent ugly past, punish the guilty in their midst and move on with their lives. Only an open trial conducted inside Serbia will hold up a mirror in which the collective past can be seen in all its ugliness. It is difficult to see how overriding the constitutional court by domestic political rivals will help to embed and strengthen democratic structures of governance that are robust and resilient and a system of power based on and mediated through the rule of law.

Ad hoc international criminal tribunals are important but episodic advances in the evolution of individual criminal accountability. They leave the process of international law more vulnerable to the pursuit of power politics than would be possible in the ICC. It is also arguable that, at least in origins, The Hague and Arusha ad hoc tribunals were set up as *substitutes* for effective action to halt the atrocities in the two regions: they were alibis for no action, not indicators of toughening new standards of international judicial accountability. Legal principles should be used to advance the cause of universal justice, not to settle political scores and advance victors' justice or to camouflage the lack of courage for mustering the political will to tackle pressing humanitarian problems.

The ICC thus marks a major milestone on the road to being rescued from the tyranny of the episodic in international criminal justice. Washington seems to have been tripped in the end by its own "curious mixture of American idealism and Stalinist opportunism", as Geoffrey Robertson has argued,[26] that led it to support the establishment of ad hoc tribunals. In a fitting symmetry, the driving force behind the US rejection of the ICC is an equally curious mixture of exceptionalism and power politics, as David Forsythe argues in Chapter 3. Washington may preach universalism, but it practises national particularism and cultural relativism. As in the case of arrears to the UN budget, where the amounts involved are inconsequential to the United States, the principle at stake is far more significant than the rhetoric of rejection. And the principle is the same in both cases, namely the audacity of the "international community" to constrain or direct US international behaviour. Just as any law constrains capricious behaviour and puts limits on the arbitrary exercise of power, so international law would constrain US international power and behaviour: there lies the rub. As Edward Luck notes, "[f]rom a U.S. perspective, the purpose of the UN is to augment national policy options, not to limit them".[27] The effort to establish an effective rule of law is precisely the problem, not the solution that one might mistakenly construe from the rhetoric. Building on this, the real difficulty could come not with *rogue* prosecutors but with *responsible* ones. From the World Court's pronouncements against the United States with regard to Nicaragua in the 1980s, to NATO's choice of targets and armaments in the Balkans and the actions of the US military in Afghanistan, it is possible to imagine circumstances in which the domestic political atmosphere is too hostile within the United States to permit national investigations and prosecutions, and a conscientious ICC Prosecutor decides to take up the case (see Chapter 3 in this volume). Similarly, the problem may lie not so much with junior and middle-ranking military personnel as with generals and defence secretaries and even presidents – those with command responsibility making policy and issuing the orders, not the foot-soldiers merely carrying out orders.

Second, a judicial system comes at the end of the civilizational evolution of any given political system, not the beginning. Even in the great single European project, the continent-wide judicial institutions have followed politics and economics, not preceded them. The strong affirmation of the ICC by the Europeans and most of the international community has collided with the equally determined rejection of the new court by the Americans. If the European stance is more evolutionary and progressive, Washington's is more consistent over time. The United States has always acted in the belief that, when it comes to international criminal justice, politics trumps law. It is the Europeans who wish to advance to elevating law above politics. Whereas the US tradition is to rely on military power for national security, Europe, reflecting its own troubled history of assertive sovereignties causing catastrophic wars, has succeeded in establishing peace on the continent through embedding cooperation in inclusive economic, political and military institutions.

In the context of the present state of evolution of the institutions of world order, however, Washington does have a point. In stable polities, constitutional order has advanced to the point where the justice system is separated from the legislative and executive branches in order to enhance the credibility of all three. But this is possible only because the constitution articulates the agreed political vision for the community as a whole. Such first-order questions are yet to be settled for the "international community", and therefore the interplay of law and politics is far more intimate.

With the ICC, Washington may have been tripped up by its own cleverness in setting up the ad hoc criminal tribunals for Yugoslavia and Rwanda. But both were odd mixtures of idealism, opportunism and guilt. They were alibis for inaction, not indicators of toughening new standards of international criminal accountability. And, by keeping them under the jurisdiction of the UN Security Council, the United States made sure that it controlled their destiny. Unfortunately for Washington, they seem to have generated an unstoppable momentum for a permanent ICC with genuinely universal jurisdiction.

Just desserts for Milosevic

Fourth, although justice may not be seen to be done at The Hague (because of the above doubts), it is highly probable that *justice will be done with regard to Milosevic*. After all, the ICTY was established before winners and losers had emerged from the various conflicts sparked across former Yugoslavia. Its judges, like their counterparts in Arusha, have come from many countries, some not involved in the conflicts at any stage. According to Bert Swart in Chapter 7, their proceedings demonstrate high standards of fairness in evidential matters, and their verdicts have represented exciting developments in the extension, deepening and broadening of international humanitarian law and international criminal justice, including convictions for genocide and of a head of government and indictments of a head of state. Crucially, unlike the Tokyo tribunal after World War II, the new ad hoc tribunals have eschewed the death penalty – which may perhaps have influenced the decision calculus of some indictees from countries where capital punishment is still an option for national criminal prosecutors.

There is no question but that Milosevic was at the centre of the most murderous decade in Europe since World War II. That others may have escaped justice is regrettable. This may detract from but cannot negate the importance of bringing the first former head of state to international criminal judgment. At the end of the day, most of us will go to bed with the sense of quiet satisfaction that the wheels of justice caught up with him, and that he will get his just desserts. Moreover, regardless of whether Milosevic is acquitted or convicted, the Rwanda ICT has already made history by convicting and sentencing a head of government, former Prime Minister Jean Kambanda, for genocide.

Justice is seen to be done but is not done

Fifth, and finally, it is possible of course that *justice can be seen to have been done when in fact it has miscarried.* The risks of such an outcome are at their highest in crimes arousing strong emotions, such as domestic or international terrorism, or in conditions of mass hysteria when prosecutors and kangaroo courts operating under intolerably lax standards of judicial rigour succumb to public and political pressure to show results. The public thirst for instant justice may well be satisfied under McCarthyist witch hunts. To that extent, and in that sense, justice will be seen to have been done by a particular community. But the very phenomenon of McCarthyism is today symbolic of the fact that justice was not done; instead, injustice was perpetrated.

Let us consider the implications of this tension between doing justice and being seen to be doing justice swiftly, in the emotional hothouse after 11 September 2001. The point is alluded to by Ahtisaari (in the Preface) and by Biddiss (in Chapter 2) and argued forcefully by Geoffrey Robertson (in Chapter 12). The whole series of measures put in place by the US administration after that date called into question the commitment to fair trials and justice: the arbitrary determination by the administration of the status of captured people in order to have them tried by US military commissions, their detention offshore in Guantanamo Bay, Cuba, in order to escape US judicial processes, the lengthy detention without trial of suspects, doubts about whether it will be possible for any accused prisoners to receive a fair trial in the United States, and so on. The UN High Commissioner for Human Rights, Mary Robinson, claimed that the Bush administration had blocked her from remaining at her post because she had had the temerity to criticize these policies.[28] Even the task force of the American Bar Association, the country's largest lawyer association, criticized the administration's treatment of "enemy combatants". It objected to the indefinite detention of US citizens without charges, without judicial review and without right to attorney: "It cannot be sufficient for a president to claim that the [government] can detain whomever it wants, whenever it wants, for as long as it wants, as long as the detention bears some relationship to a terrorist act once committed by somebody against the United States."[29]

Let us reflect on the dissonance between what is known – the facts about the terrorists having lived, trained and studied in Germany, the United States and perhaps the United Kingdom, and about the majority of them being Saudi Arabian – and what is asserted – that they were al-Qaida, backed by the Taliban in Afghanistan, etc. Consider the Taliban government's response to the ultimatum of handing over the named alleged plotters: "first show us the evidence." Was that so unreasonable? Moreover, as Andrew Clapham reminds us in Chapter 13, "The history of international criminal law is in part a history of states focusing on *the political groups and private organizations that have provided the structures* that have enabled individuals to commit international crimes" (emphasis added). By this standard of complicity, the circle of groups and actors, including state actors, to be implicated in the financing, arming and establishment of the al-Qaida network in Afghanistan would be wider than just the Taliban government of Afghanistan. For some, perhaps even most, of the principal creators and patrons of the Taliban resided outside Afghanistan.

Retributive versus restorative justice

What Washington has not argued in its case against the ICC – it would be on firmer ground in asserting it, but cannot argue it because of its own role in establishing the ad hoc tribunals – is that international criminal justice, including the ICC, may do more damage and solidify the very social cleavages that led to the crimes of genocide, ethnic cleansing and crimes against humanity.[30] The legal clarity of judicial verdicts sits uncomfortably with the nuanced morality of confronting *and overcoming*, through a principled mix of justice and high politics, a jointly troubled past. The choice is not restricted to international criminal prosecution, vigilante justice or the repression of mass horror into collective amnesia. An international criminal justice system does not just assert the primacy of the "international community" over domestic jurisdiction. In addition, and more importantly, it privileges the process of criminal prosecution over all other considerations, including politics in the broadest and best sense of the term. In Chapter 2, Michael Biddiss quotes the British Lord Chancellor Simon's warning from 1945 that the question of determining the fate of the government leaders of defeated Germany "is a political, not a judicial, question".

As part of the foreclosing of political choices, the international criminal justice system takes away from domestic authorities the options of alternative modes of healing and restitution with a view to reconciliation that puts the traumas of the past firmly in the past.[31] In South Africa, this was successfully done by means of the Truth and Reconciliation Commission (TRC).[32] The South African case is especially interesting and instructive because the criminal apartheid state was such an international *cause célèbre* for such a long time, and also because the TRC became such a celebrated case of the genre. The so-called South African "miracle" – the essentially peaceful transition from a racist apartheid regime to a multiracial democracy – came at a cost. The price paid for peace was to rule out retribution in favour of reconciliation. If the leaders of the African National Congress (ANC) had insisted on exacting revenge through the full powers of the law for acts of crime under the apartheid regime, the transition, *in the best professional judgement of the ANC leaders themselves*, would have been more painful, violent and protracted. As a corollary, the new South Africa would have been a correspondingly less stable and vibrant democracy if the politicians, police and military of the *ancien régime* feared a Nuremberg-style trial. Grasping the significance of this, arguing the case with his own people and acting on that basis marked the difference between Nelson Mandela being merely a politician and being a visionary statesman.

In Mozambique it was equally successfully done through communal healing techniques. In a country of 16 million people, between 600,000 and 1 million lost their lives in the bitter 17-year civil war leading to independence. In the peace agreement signed in 1992, all participants in the war were given complete amnesty for acts committed during the war. As warriors, victims, exiles and the displaced came home, communities reverted to traditional healing rituals designed to take the violence out of the individual person and facilitate reintegration into the community.[33] Their belief is that all those affected by the violence – perpetrators and victims alike – need to be purified from its baleful effects.

In Rwanda the ICT route took away from the Rwandan people and government the right to decide *whether, how* and *who* to prosecute for alleged mass crimes, and *what* punishment to inflict on those found guilty. Ironically, the international community was strongly motivated to go down the ICT route by guilt over its failure to halt, or significantly mitigate the consequences of, the terrible genocide of 1994. Moreover, the sense of guilt is stronger precisely because this was a failure of will, of civic courage at the highest levels of political responsibility and moral consequence, not a failure of capacity to act. In yet another twist of irony,

Rwanda was a member of the UN Security Council when the ad hoc ICT for Rwanda was established in November 1994; it cast the sole negative vote against the ICTR.[34] Richard Sezibera, Rwanda's ambassador to the United States, gave a good explanation for his country's preferred approach when he said that their policy rested not just on the one pillar of retribution but on four pillars: deconstruction of myths, punishment of perpetrators of crimes, rehabilitation of victims, and the construction of a new *Rwandan* national identity.[35] Rwanda has attempted to do this through the local *gacaca* system of people's courts, whose overriding goal is not to determine guilt or apply state law but to restore harmony and social order. An essential element of that is to re-include the person who caused or was the source of the social disorder. The *gacaca* system has arguably been more productive and efficient, whereas the international criminal tribunal track has been slow, hesitant, time consuming and money intensive, and has had very little to show for it all at the end of the day. Seven years after its establishment, its "lamentable" performance was to have handed down verdicts on nine defendants, despite more than 800 employees, three Trial Chambers, nine judges (one verdict per judge in seven years!) and an annual budget of US$90 million.[36]

Reflecting the frustrations with the slow pace and expense of the International Criminal Tribunals in former Yugoslavia and Rwanda, which are entirely UN bodies, the Special Court set up for Sierra Leone in April 2003 was a UN–Sierra Leone hybrid with a limited budget and time-frame. It was established by treaty between the United Nations and Sierra Leone and it was given the mandate to try the people who organized and oversaw the atrocities rather than those who carried them out.[37]

The South African, Mozambican and Rwandan cases were all deliberate efforts through social and political channels to *escape* cycles of retributive violence coming out of decades of tumultuous political conflicts congealed around communal identity; the purely juridical approach to "transitional justice"[38] traps and suspends communities in the prism of past hatreds. Their record of bringing closure to legacies of systematic savagery in deeply conflicted societies is superior to that of institutions of international criminal justice, whose closure is more authoritative but also more partial and premature. These cases fall within the tradition of "restorative justice"[39] systems rather than retributive justice systems. There are many such examples around the world in widely different societies. What they have in common is an essentially communitarian vision of the proper relationship between the individual and society. To the extent that human beings are social animals, each person's individual identity is the product of a complex social construction of communal identity, and cannot be isolated from that. But, if society is privileged over the individual, then restoring social harmony is more important than punishing individual wrongdoers. As President Ahtisaari reminds us in the Preface, "[c]riminal law, however effective, cannot replace the social policies needed to combat deprivation and social injustice"; nor is a criminal trial always "the best instrument for memory and healing".

As almost all these examples show, the logics of peace and justice can be contradictory.[40] Peace is forward looking, problem solving and integrative, requiring reconciliation between past enemies within an all-inclusive community. Justice is backward looking, finger pointing and retributive, requiring trial and punishment of the perpetrators of past crimes. Technical criminal proceedings can miss the big picture and fail to provide the cathartic relief that may be more easily obtained under truth commissions, formal state apologies and reparations. The pursuit of human rights violators can delay and impede the effort to establish conditions of security so that displaced people can return home and live in relative peace once again.

However, although mercy has a role to play in reconstituting society after trauma, justice has many more, and perhaps more fundamental, roles to play beyond simply bringing wrongdoers to account:[41] acknowledging the suffering of victims; educating the public; deterring future criminal atrocities elsewhere as well as in the conflicted countries of immediate concern; establishing universal justice; easing the Kantian transition from barbarism to culture. In this volume, the case for international criminal justice as a *solution* to the problem of peace and reconciliation after mass crimes in fractured societies is made most passionately in Chapter 11 by Moghalu. He notes that the Allied and Axis powers from World War II are at peace not just *despite* the Nuremberg and Tokyo tribunals but also *because* justice cleared the path to reconciliation. Criminal trials establish individual responsibility for the crimes adjudicated, and thereby negate the notion of collective guilt that can otherwise impede inter-communal reconciliation. By contrast, because the victims' thirst for justice was not satisfied in the case of Pinochet, old wounds were reopened in Chile. Hence Moghalu's scepticism about "the collective amnesia of blanket amnesties".

For the same reason, we may need to reserve judgement on the lasting success of the South African TRC. Many victims, and their relatives, of the crimes of apartheid feel strongly that justice was not done and harbour bitter resentment against the TRC in consequence. Chaired by Archbishop Desmond Tutu, the Commission granted amnesty to more than 1,000 people – and the 21,000 victims of apartheid, as identified by the Commission itself, have received nothing. The public hearings of the Commission (which made the whole exercise more of a "truth-memorializing" undertaking than a "truth-revealing" one[42]), giving victims a voice while establishing the truth, proved a cathartic experience for many victims – but not all. In South Africa, Khulumani, a victims' support group, has brought a lawsuit claiming reparations for victims, arguing that the wounds of apartheid will get deeper without reparations. In the United States, a class action suit has been brought against the American and Swiss banks that financed the apartheid regime. The two cases risk undermining South Africa's determination to look forward to a common bright future rather than dwell on the past pain of bitter divisions.[43]

Thus the tension between peace and justice is not simple to resolve. Criminal indictments of factional or state leaders can hamper efforts to negotiate with the very same people to bring violence to an end. Why should a leader agree to relinquish power and/or go into exile if faced with the threat of criminal prosecution? Conversely, it can be argued that a public indictment serves notice on the diplomats that appeasement of an indicted war criminal is not an option, erodes the morale of his followers and stiffens the resolve of those fighting him. Certainly the indictment of Milosevic was electrifying in its effect of rallying those whose resolve in the war had begun to waver. But would an earlier indictment of Milosevic have shortened the Balkans tragedy in the 1990s or obstructed the Dayton peace accords? Did the indictment of Liberian President Charles Taylor for crimes against humanity by the Sierra Leone war crimes court, issued on 4 June 2003, hasten or slow his departure from the country in August? The conventional wisdom today is that the Lomé agreement on Sierra Leone, in pushing aside justice by accommodating Foday Sankoh (later indicted as a war criminal) into the government, prolonged the war by several years. Where is the correct balance between politicizing international justice and derailing delicate peace negotiations?

The point is not to deny that the choice may be a painful one, that the government and the people may be divided on the issue, and that the public policy that results may turn out to be flawed and wrong. Rather, the point is that these are *profoundly political* choices that may involve complex trade-offs, not primarily and simply legal decisions. For that very reason, the choice is one that only the country concerned can make, not the least because it is that country that paid the price in the past and will have to live with the immediate and long-term consequences of the decisions made. In a similar vein, three years after Indonesian-backed militias had laid waste to his country, East Timor's President-elect, Xanana Gusmao, declared that justice for the victims by trying the perpetrators of the violence would be subordinated to the need for development and social justice. "We fought, we suffered, we died for what," he asked. "To try other people or to receive benefits from independence?"[44] The tension, between peace or justice or peace through justice, must be reconciled on a case-by-case basis rather than according to a rigid formula. And it is best resolved by the countries concerned, whether in Chile, South Africa, East Timor or Northern Ireland. Moreover, the choice may not be as dichotomous as posited: a society may choose to begin with one but move to bringing closure with the other, as is starting to happen in some Latin American countries with respect to their legacies of "dirty wars".

Conclusion

For justice to be done, and to be seen to be done, it is imperative that we do indeed make the transition from the culture of sovereign impunity to the culture of international accountability. But what might this mean in practical terms? Christine Chinkin quotes in Chapter 6 from one of the international criminal cases, referring to the Bosnian-Muslim women victims of war-related sexual violence, that consent could not be freely given when the women had nowhere to go and no place to hide. We will perhaps have made our transition from barbarism to culture when the burden of that haunting phrase is transferred from the victim to the perpetrators and would-be perpetrators: "know that henceforth, you will have nowhere to go, no place left to hide." Then, and only then, instead of being footnotes to history, international criminal accountability will bear daily witness to history.

Notes

1. Hannah Arendt, letter to Karl Jaspers, 17 August 1946, in Hannah Arendt and Karl Jaspers, *Hannah Arendt Karl Jaspers: Correspondence, 1926–1969*, ed. Lotte Kohler and Hans Saner, translated from German by Robert and Rita Kember, New York: Harcourt Brace Jovanovich, 1992, p. 54.
2. Jaspers, letter to Arendt, 19 October 1946, ibid., p. 62.
3. Hannah Arendt, *Eichmann in Jerusalem: A Report on the Banality of Evil*, Harmondsworth: Penguin, 1963.
4. *The Responsibility to Protect: Report of the International Commission on Intervention and State Sovereignty*, Ottawa: International Development Research Centre for the International Commission on Intervention and State Sovereignty (ICISS), 2001, p. vii. The report is also available at www.iciss.gc.ca. I was one of the ICISS Commissioners.
5. In 2002, 11 residents of Aceh province of Indonesia filed a lawsuit in a federal court in Washington against Exxon Mobil, alleging complicity in human rights atrocities (torture, rape, kidnapping) by Indonesian troops. The State Department submitted a non-binding opinion saying that the suit should be dismissed because it would damage US national interests. See Kenneth Roth, "Human Rights: U.S. Hypocrisy in Indonesia", *International Herald Tribune*, 14 August 2002.
6. Chapter 11 in this volume, section on "Rape and sexual violence". ICISS accepted this argument and included rape as a calculated instrument of ethnic cleansing – "the sys-

tematic rape for political purposes of women of a particular group (either as another form of terrorism, or as a means of changing the ethnic composition of that group)" – that can trigger international intervention (*The Responsibility to Protect*, pp. 32–33, paras. 4.19 and 4.20).

7. Helena Smith, "Greeks Accuse Blair of War Crimes in Iraq", *Guardian* (London), 29 July 2003.

8. See George Monbiot, "Let's Hear It for Belgium", *Guardian* (London), 20 May 2003.

9. Noell Knox, "Rumsfeld Warns Belgium about War-Crimes Law", *USA Today*, 13 June 2003, p. 8A. Not for the first time, and probably not for the last, US officials ignore the directly equivalent practice of US courts in subjecting foreign officials and officers to the jurisdiction of American courts. See Robert H. Bork, "Judicial Imperialism", *Wall Street Journal Europe*, 18 June 2003.

10. For an application of this to children specifically, see *International Criminal Justice and Children*, No Peace without Justice and UNICEF Innocenti Research Centre, September 2002.

11. I am grateful for the helpful and insightful comments by John Fousek and Ted Newman on an earlier draft of this paper.

12. See Telford Taylor, *Nuremberg and Vietnam: An American Tragedy*, Chicago: Quadrangle, 1970; Jay W. Baird, ed., *From Nuremberg to My Lai*, Lexington, Mass.: Heath, 1972; Joseph Goldstein et al., *The My Lai Massacre and Its Cover-up: Beyond the Reach of Law?* New York: Free Press, 1976.

13. Former Ugandan dictator Idi Amin, responsible for killing 200,000–300,000 of his people, died in comfortable retirement in Saudi Arabia in mid-2003.

14. David Forsythe, "Justice after Injustice: What Response after Atrocities", E. N. Thompson Forum on World Issues, University of Nebraska–Lincoln, 28 November 2000, p. 6.

15. For his own views, see Henry A. Kissinger, "The Pitfalls of Universal Jurisdiction", *Foreign Affairs*, vol. 80, no. 4, 2001, pp. 86–96. For a contrary view in response, see Kenneth Roth, "The Case for Universal Jurisdiction", *Foreign Affairs*, vol. 80, no. 5, 2001, pp. 150–154.

16. See Christine Chinkin, "Women's International Tribunal on Japanese Military Sexual Slavery", *American Journal of International Law*, vol. 95, no. 2, 2001, pp. 335–340.

17. See *Bringing Them Home: Report of the National Inquiry into the Separation of Aboriginal and Torres Strait Islander Children from Their Families*, Sydney: Human Rights and Equal Opportunity Commission, 1997.

18. Quoted in Chapter 2 in this volume.

19. For discussions of the lawfulness and legitimacy of the war, see Christine M. Chinkin, "Kosovo: A 'Good' or 'Bad' War?", *American Journal of International Law*, vol. 93, no. 4, 1999, pp. 841–847; Richard Falk, "Reflections on the Kosovo War", *Global Dialogue*, vol. 1, no. 2, 1999, p. 93; Michael J. Glennon, *Limits of Law, Prerogatives of Power: Interventionism after Kosovo*, New York: Palgrave, 2001; Louis Henkin, "Kosovo and the Law of 'Humanitarian Intervention'", *American Journal of International Law*, vol. 93, no. 4, 1999, pp. 824–828; *Kosovo Report: Conflict, International Response, Lessons Learned*, Oxford: Oxford University Press for the Independent International Commission on Kosovo, 2000; Hideaki Shinoda, "The Politics of Legitimacy in International Relations: A Critical Examination of NATO's Intervention in Kosovo", *Alternatives*, vol. 25, no. 4, 2000, pp. 515–536; and Ruth Wedgwood, "NATO's Campaign in Yugoslavia", *American Journal of International Law*, vol. 93, no. 4, 1999, pp. 828–834.

20. See Yves Beigbeder and Theo Van Boven, *Judging War Criminals: The Politics of International Justice*, New York: St. Martin's Press, 1999; Steven R. Ratner and Jason S. Abrams, *Accountability for Human Rights Atrocities in International Law: Beyond the Nuremberg Legacy*, 2nd edn., Oxford: Clarendon Press, 2001; David Scheffer, "The

United States and the International Criminal Court", *American Journal of International Law*, vol. 93, no. 1, 1999, pp. 12–22; and Sarah B. Sewall and Carl Keysen, eds., *The United States and the International Criminal Court: National Security and International Law*, Lanham, Md.: Rowman & Littlefield, for the American Academy of Arts and Sciences, 2000.

21. Gary Jonathan Bass, *Stay the Hand of Vengeance: The Politics of War Crimes Tribunals*, Princeton, N.J.: Princeton University Press, 2000, p. 283.

22. On the importance of exceptionalism in US foreign policy, see Samuel P. Huntington, "American Ideals versus American Institutions", in John G. Ikenberry, ed., *American Foreign Policy: Theoretical Essays*, 3rd edn., New York: Longman, 1999, pp. 221–253.

23. For background to the ICC, see William A. Schabas, *An Introduction to the International Criminal Court*, Cambridge: Cambridge University Press, 2001.

24. "Annan Warning over US Immunity", BBC News, at http://news.bbc.co.uk/go/pr/fr/-/2/hi/americas/2985362.stm, 12 July 2003, 16.04.08 GMT.

25. Lloyd Axworthy, "Stop the U.S. Foul Play", *Globe and Mail* (Toronto), 17 July 2002.

26. Geoffrey Robertson, *Crimes against Humanity: The Struggle for Global Justice*, London: Penguin, 1999, p. 211; quoted by Biddiss in Chapter 2 of this volume.

27. Edward C. Luck, *Mixed Messages: American Politics and International Organization 1919–1999*, Washington D.C.: Brookings, 1999, p. 294.

28. Brian Knowlton, "UN Rights Chief Cites U.S. Role in Departure", *International Herald Tribune*, 1 August 2002.

29. As reported in the *Financial Times* (Tokyo), 10–11 August 2002.

30. For an excellent exploration of this theme in the context of Rwanda, see Helena Cobban, "The Legacies of Collective Violence: The Rwandan Genocide and the Limits of Law", *Boston Review*, vol. 27, no. 2, 2002, pp. 4–15.

31. The growing literature on the subject includes Bass, *Stay the Hand of Vengeance*; Richard J. Goldstone, *For Humanity: Reflections of a War Crimes Investigator*, New Haven, Conn.: Yale University Press, 2001; Martha Minow, *Between Vengeance and Forgiveness: Facing History after Genocide and Mass Violence*, Boston: Beacon Press, 1998; Robert I. Rotberg and Dennis Thompson, eds., *Truth v. Justice*, Princeton, N.J.: Princeton University Press, 2000; and Ruti G. Teitel, *Transitional Justice*, Oxford: Oxford University Press, 2000.

32. A good general account is Priscilla Hayner, *Unspeakable Truths: Confronting State Terror and Atrocity*, London: Routledge, 2001. Hayner was a participant in this project's workshop held in Utrecht in November 2001. In a remarkably prescient letter that anticipated the truth and reconciliation commissions, Jaspers wrote in 1960 that, for mass crimes, "a process of examination and clarification" was preferable to a criminal trial. "The goal would be the best possible objectification of the historical facts" (letter to Arendt, 16 December 1960, in Arendt and Jaspers, *Correspondence*, p. 413).

33. See Carolyn Nordstrom, *A Different Kind of War Story*, Philadelphia: University of Pennsylvania Press, 1997.

34. Cobban, "The Legacies of Collective Violence", p. 6.

35. Interview with Helena Cobban, quoted in Cobban, "The Legacies of Collective Violence", p. 8.

36. International Crisis Group, *International Criminal Tribunal for Rwanda: Justice Delayed*, Brussels: ICG, 2001, p. ii.

37. See Douglas Farah, "War Crimes Tribunal Offers New Model", *Japan Times* (reprinted from the *Washington Post*), 22 April 2003.

38. See A. James McAdams, ed., *Transitional Justice and the Rule of Law in New Democracies*, Notre Dame, Ind.: University of Notre Dame Press, 1997.

39. See Wesley Cragg, *The Practice of Punishment: Towards a Theory of Restorative Justice*, London: Routledge, 1992.

40. For an elegant discussion of the challenge of marrying peace with justice out of the morass of war's injustices, see Rama Mani, *Beyond Retribution: Seeking Justice in the Shadows of War*, Cambridge: Polity, 2002.

41. Some of these are discussed in Helen Durham, "Mercy and Justice in the Transition Period", in William Maley, Charles Sampford and Ramesh Thakur, eds., *From Civil Strife to Civil Society: Civil and Military Responsibilities in Disrupted States*, Tokyo: United Nations University Press, 2003, pp. 145–160.

42. James P. Sewell, "Justice and Truth in Transition", *Global Governance*, vol. 8, no. 1, 2002, pp. 119–134 at p. 121.

43. For an account of the two cases, see Nicol Degli Innocenti, "Reconciliation or Justice – South Africa's Bitter Dilemma", *Financial Times*, 29–30 June 2002.

44. Quoted in Don Greenlees, "East Timor Puts Justice to One Side", *Weekend Australian*, 4–5 May 2002.

Contributors

Martti Ahtisaari was President of the Republic of Finland during the period 1994–2000. In June 2003, he was appointed as the UN Secretary-General's Special Envoy for the Humanitarian Crisis in the Horn of Africa.

George J. Andreopoulos is Professor of Government at the John Jay College of Criminal Justice and at the Graduate School and University Center of the City University of New York, United States.

Michael D. Biddiss is Professor of History at the University of Reading, United Kingdom.

Christine Chinkin is Professor of International Law at the London School of Economics and Political Science, United Kingdom.

Andrew Clapham is Professor of Public International Law at the Graduate Institute of International Studies, Geneva, Switzerland.

Helen Durham is Legal Adviser to the International Committee of the Red Cross (ICRC) for the Pacific Regional Delegation.

Cees Flinterman is Professor of Human Rights and Director of the Netherlands Institute of Human Rights and the Netherlands School of Human Rights Research. Since August 2002 he has been a member of the UN Committee on the Elimination of Discrimination against Women (CEDAW).

David P. Forsythe is the Charles J. Mach Distinguished Professor of Political Science and University Professor at the University of Nebraska-Lincoln, United States.

Richard J. Goldstone is Justice of the Constitutional Court of South Africa and was Chief Prosecutor of the United Nations International Criminal Tribunals for the former Yugoslavia and Rwanda.

Paul G. Lauren is the Regents Professor at the University of Montana, United States.

Peter Malcontent is a researcher and lecturer at the Netherlands Institute of Human Rights, Utrecht University, the Netherlands.

Julia Maxted teaches geography at the University of Pretoria, South Africa, and is a research associate on the "Children in Armed Conflict Project" at the Institute for Security Studies, Pretoria.

Kingsley Chiedu Moghalu was Special Adviser to the Registrar of the International Criminal Tribunal for Rwanda and is presently associated with the Center for American and International Law, Dallas, United States.

Madeline H. Morris is Professor of Law at Duke University, North Carolina, United States, and Director of the Duke/Geneva Institute in Transnational Law.

Geoffrey Robertson QC is Head of Doughty Street Chambers and an Appeal Judge of the UN Special Court for Sierra Leone. He is also a Visiting Professor of Human Rights at Birkbeck College, United Kingdom.

William A. Schabas is Professor of Human Rights Law at the National University of Ireland, Galway, and Director of the Irish Centre for Human Rights.

Bert Swart is Van Hamel Professor of International Criminal Law at the University of Amsterdam, the Netherlands, and *ad litem* judge in the International Criminal Tribunal for the former Yugoslavia.

Ramesh Thakur is the Senior Vice Rector of the United Nations University (UNU) and Assistant Secretary-General of the United Nations. He is a member of the UNU's senior academic staff and heads its Peace and Governance Programme.

Michail Wladimiroff is a leading partner in the Dutch law firm Wladimiroff, Walings, Schreuders. During 2001–2002 he was Advocate *Amicus Curiae* in the Milosevic case at the International Criminal Tribunal for the former Yugoslavia.

Index

Catalogue Request

Name: _____

Address: _____

_____

Tel: _____

Fax: _____

E-mail: _____

To receive a catalogue of UNU Press publications kindly photocopy this form and send or fax it back to us with your details. You can also e-mail us this information. Please put "Mailing List" in the subject line.

 **United Nations University Press**

53-70, Jingumae 5-chome
Shibuya-ku, Tokyo 150-8925, Japan
Tel: +81-3-3499-2811 Fax: +81-3-3406-7345
E-mail: sales@hq.unu.edu http://www.unu.edu